ADVANCES IN
EXPERIMENTAL
SOCIAL PSYCHOLOGY

VOLUME 5

CONTRIBUTORS TO VOLUME 5

ROBERT S. BARON

KENNETH L. DION

RICHARD E. GORANSON

EDWIN P. HOLLANDER

JAMES W. JULIAN

IRWIN KATZ

HOWARD LEVENTHAL

NORMAN MILLER

ELLIOT G. MISHLER

IVAN D. STEINER

NANCY E. WAXLER

ADVANCES IN

Experimental
Social Psychology

EDITED BY

Leonard Berkowitz
DEPARTMENT OF PSYCHOLOGY
UNIVERSITY OF WISCONSIN
MADISON, WISCONSIN

VOLUME 5

ACADEMIC PRESS   New York and London   1970

ACADEMIC PRESS, INC.
111 Fifth Avenue, New York, New York 10003

United Kingdom Edition published by
ACADEMIC PRESS, INC. (LONDON) LTD.
Berkeley Square House, London W1X 6BA

LIBRARY OF CONGRESS CATALOG CARD NUMBER: 64-23452

PRINTED IN THE UNITED STATES OF AMERICA

CONTENTS

Media Violence and Aggressive Behavior: A Review of Experimental Research

Richard E. Goranson

Studies in Leader Legitimacy, Influence, and Innovation

Edwin P. Hollander and James W. Julian

Experimental Studies of Negro-White Relationships

Irwin Katz

Findings and Theory in the Study of Fear Communications

Howard Leventhal

Perceived Freedom

Ivan D. Steiner

Experimental Studies of Families

Nancy E. Waxler and Elliot G. Mishler

Why Do Groups Make Riskier Decisions than Individuals?

Kenneth L. Dion, Robert S. Baron, and Norman Miller

CONTRIBUTORS

Numbers in parentheses indicate the pages on which the authors' contributions begin.

ROBERT S. BARON,[1] *University of Minnesota, Minneapolis, Minnesota* (305)

KENNETH L. DION,[2] *University of Minnesota, Minneapolis, Minnesota* (305)

RICHARD E. GORANSON, *York University, Toronto, Ontario, Canada* (1)

EDWIN P. HOLLANDER, *State University of New York at Buffalo, Buffalo, New York* (33)

JAMES W. JULIAN, *State University of New York at Buffalo, Buffalo, New York* (33)

IRWIN KATZ, *Graduate Center of the City University of New York, New York* (71)

HOWARD LEVENTHAL, *Department of Psychology, University of Wisconsin, Madison, Wisconsin* (119)

NORMAN MILLER,[3] *University of Minnesota, Minneapolis, Minnesota* (305)

[1]Present address: University of Toronto, Ontario, Canada.
[2]Present address: University of Iowa, Iowa City, Iowa.
[3]Present address: University of Southern California, Los Angeles, California.

ix

ELLIOT G. MISHLER, *The Massachusetts Mental Health Center, Cambridge, Massachusetts* (249)

IVAN D. STEINER,[4] *University of Illinois, Urbana, Illinois* (187)

NANCY E. WAXLER, *Harvard Medical School, Cambridge, Massachusetts* (249)

[4]Present address: University of Massachusetts, Amherst, Massachusetts.

CONTENTS OF OTHER VOLUMES

xi

ADVANCES IN
EXPERIMENTAL
SOCIAL PSYCHOLOGY

VOLUME 5

MEDIA VIOLENCE AND AGGRESSIVE BEHAVIOR: A REVIEW OF EXPERIMENTAL RESEARCH

Richard E. Goranson
YORK UNIVERSITY
TORONTO, ONTARIO

1

I. Introduction

While great concern is periodically expressed over the possible harmful effects of the kind of violence depicted in the mass media, only recently has any real volume of experimental research been directed toward the problem. Reviews of commentary and research findings on this topic have been written by Bandura and Walters (1963), Berkowitz (1962), Klapper (1963), and Maccoby (1964). Going beyond these reviews, the last few years have seen the development of several new lines of research which have defined some of the complex issues involved and provided partial answers to several questions that have been raised.

THE ISSUES

Much of the recent work on the psychological effects of media violence has been devoted to a limited number of central issues. Discussion of this research will be organized around the following basic issues and questions:

1. *Effects on learning*: Are children likely to learn and remember new forms of aggressive behavior by watching the kind of violence presented in the mass media? What are the conditions, if any, that encourage the actual performance of aggressive acts learned through observation?

2. *Emotional effects*: Does the repetition of violence in the mass media result in decreased emotional sensitivity to media violence? Is a decreased emotional sensitivity likely to have any implications for the probability of actual aggressive behavior in real-life situations?

3. *The question of catharsis*: Does watching the kind of aggression shown in the media result in "aggression catharsis" — a "draining off of aggressive energy"? Does the observation of pain, horror, and suffering result in catharsis?

4. *Effects on aggressive behavior*: Are there any conditions of observed violence that can serve either to inhibit or to facilitate aggression?

II. The Relevance of Psychological Research

Before going into the recent research on these questions, it is first necessary to look at some of the issues regarding the relevance of psychological research on media violence effects.

A. The Definition of Aggression

It is apparent that various investigators have employed quite different measures and operational definitions of aggression. To avoid confusion, some distinctions between these different usages should be made clear at the outset. While some researchers have used paper and pencil, or "verbal" measures of aggression (perhaps better called hostility), most have concentrated on behavioral measures. A major distinction can be made between two types of behavioral definitions: the *harm intent* definition, and the *response form* definition.

1. Harm Intent Measures

A *harm intent* definition is based on the measurement of the *intentional inflicting of pain or injury on another person*. Much of the research using this type of definition has measured the number, intensity, or duration of electric shocks that subjects have been willing to give to another person. Verbal responses or ratings that are potentially capable of causing harm to the target person have also been used as measures of aggression. The *harm intent* type of definition corresponds to one common use of the word aggression, and some writers have expressed a preference for this kind of measure (Hartley, 1964; Weiss, 1970).

2. Response Form Measures

The *response form* type of definition, on the other hand, is based on the *physical characteristics of aggressive actions*: hitting, kicking, striking with a hammer, etc. These responses have a *form* which is commonly called "aggressive" even when the responses are directed toward nonhuman targets. Bandura and Walters (1963) have argued for this type of definition, particularly in research on the learning of aggressive acts by children. They point out that aggressiveness is not a directly measurable quality of an act but is, rather, a label applied as a social judgment. Furthermore, when "harmless" responses having an aggressive form are learned and later transferred to interpersonal situations, they can be very *harmful* indeed (Walters & Brown, 1963).

We should not however, automatically assume that all measures of aggression and aggressiveness are actually measuring the same thing. For example, there is evidence that some personality measures of aggressiveness correlate poorly with behavioral measures of aggression (Liebowitz, 1968). Similarly, verbal measures and self-ratings of anger may be largely independent of actual aggressive behavior (Geen, Rakowsky, & O'Neal, 1968; Liebowitz, 1968).

On the other hand, there is a good deal of consistency among various *behavioral* measures of aggression. There is, in fact, some justification for thinking of a given behavioral measure as representative of a whole *class* of aggressive responses. The results of a number of empirical studies have indicated the essential comparability of a variety of different behavioral measures of aggression. Studies by Berkowitz (1965a, 1965b), Walters and Brown (1963), and Williams, Meyerson, Eron, and Semler (1967) found that different behavioral aggression measures were affected in roughly the same way by different experimental treatments. Also, Williams *et al.* (1967) found that aggressive behavior in everyday situations, as rated by peers, was closely related to subjects' aggression on a laboratory "aggression machine" apparatus.

The important implication of these studies is that the results obtained with laboratory measures of aggression can have implications for other, more serious kinds of aggression occurring outside the laboratory.

B. INDIVIDUAL DIFFERENCES

There is no question that the same kind of experience can have quite different effects on different people. This is surely the case for the effects of violence witnessed in the mass media. The primary purpose of psychological research on media violence effects, however, is *not* to analyze completely the reactions of specific individuals. Rather, the main interest of research in this area is focused on the *likelihood that a substantial proportion of the audience will be influenced*, regardless of the identity of the particular persons making up that proportion. For this reason, little attention will be given to individual differences in reactions to observed violence.

C. THE GENERALITY OF RESEARCH FINDINGS

The problem of the *generality* of research findings refers to the degree to which the results of an experiment can be directly applied to situations occurring in everyday life. For present purposes, the question of generality centers on two main points: (1) the representativeness of the sample of subjects studied and (2) the representativeness of the research setting.

1. The Representativeness of Subjects

Typically, the subjects studied in a given experiment have been drawn from a relatively narrow group—few psychology experiments are conducted with a completely representative sample of subjects drawn from all areas of the general population. It is dangerous, then, to generalize too freely on the basis of results from a single study. However, our confidence in a particular research result is greatly increased when a number of experiments using different subject samples produce similar patterns of results. When the same kind of findings are obtained from different experiments using children, teenagers, and male or female adults, there is good reason to assume a high degree of generality for the results.

2. The Representativeness of the Research Setting

Much the same kind of argument holds true for the problem of the generality of results obtained from a particular research setting. The results from a *single* laboratory study might well depend on some peculiar feature of the experimental procedure. However, when the same kind of findings are obtained in a number of different studies, using quite different research techniques and measures, our confidence in the general validity of the conclusions is strengthened.

Furthermore, while the laboratory situation may not represent in detail the ordinary movie theater or living room, certain important aspects of the real-life setting may be represented in the laboratory — the television set or film screen, the audience, etc. Other features of the living room, such as table lamps or drapes on the wall, for example, may be quite unimportant in determining whether the findings obtained in the laboratory will hold for the American home. In other words, it is not really necessary to duplicate the home or theater in complete detail in order to have *some* degree of generalization from the laboratory to the real world.

Frequently, however, there will be real limitations on the generality of specific research findings. These limitations should be clearly recognized, especially when a result has been obtained only once or twice. In the present case, we should realize that no amount of experimental research can ever provide complete certainty about the exact effects of media violence; the conclusions drawn from research findings must always be taken as probability statements about the likelihood of these effects, rather than as statements of absolute truth.

III. Learning Aggression through Observation

An issue of concern to both parents and social theorists stems from the possibility that young people may learn new techniques and strategies of aggressive behavior through their exposure to media violence.

The teaching potential of the media, particularly the visual media, has led some critics to speak of television as a "school for violence" (Wertham, 1954) and as a "preparatory school for delinquency" (Banay, 1955). In contrast to this kind of alarm, psychologists and learning theorists have not, until quite recently, focused much attention on learning via the mass media. Learning researchers have traditionally been preoccupied with the role of material rewards and punishments *during the active practice of overt responses.* The absence of these factors in the passive viewing situation has, no doubt, served to divert their attention from the media.

Recently, however, a dramatic series of experiments by Albert Bandura and his co-workers has demonstrated how complex and novel behavior sequences can be learned directly through observing the actions of others. Since much of this work has dealt with the learning of aggressive behaviors, it is particularly relevant here. Discussion of this research can be conveniently divided into (1) factors affecting the learning and retention of aggressive acts and (2) postobservational factors determining the actual performance of these acts.

A. Conditions Affecting the Learning of Aggressive Behavior through Observation

1. Acquisition

Since a similar set of basic procedures has been employed in a number of the experiments to follow, it will be worthwhile to look at the methods of one representative study in some detail. An experiment by Bandura, Ross, and Ross (1963b) provides a good example.

Nursery school children, both boys and girls, were individually given the opportunity to observe an adult perform a series of novel aggressive actions. In this particular study, the adult model's behavior was presented in one of several alternative forms; some children saw a live model perform the aggressive acts, others saw a film of the same sequence, and still others saw the model costumed as a cartoon character with the sequence presented on a television set. In each case, the model punched a large inflated doll in the face, kicked the doll, and struck it in the face with a hammer. In addition to these physical acts, the model made a variety of aggressive verbal comments such as "pow . . . kick him . . . socko." A fourth set of subjects who saw no model at all served as a control group.

Following exposure to one of these conditions, the children were subjected to a mild frustration—they were first given some attractive toys to play with, and then the toys were arbitrarily taken away. Each child was then allowed to play for twenty minutes in a room containing, among other things, the inflated doll previously attacked by the model. During this period, an observer kept a record of the child's responses, noting the acts of *imitative* aggressions (including kicking or punching the figure, or striking it in the face with a hammer), as well as *partially imitative* aggression, and *nonimitative* aggressive responses. Results from this study showed that aggressive behavior was sharply higher in each of the model conditions in comparison with the control, and further, that most of this difference was due to the direct imitation of the model's aggressive behaviors. Differences between the various viewing conditions — live, film, and television — were negligible.

Before looking at a number of additional studies that have supported and clarified these findings, we should consider how far such findings can be applied to the mass media. The results of this study, of course, were obtained under a highly specific set of circumstances: (1) the children were frustrated just prior to testing, (2) they were tested in a situation that was highly similar to the one in which they had seen the model perform, and (3) they were tested right after they had observed the model. The results must be considered with these qualifications in mind. The study does demonstrate clearly, however, that under the specified circumstances children *can* perform new sequences of aggressive behaviors after watching someone else carry out similar actions, even when the model is seen only in a single short session. Observation alone can be sufficient to add novel aggressive response patterns to the viewer's behavioral repertoire. It seems reasonable to infer that novel techniques of aggression (such as karate chops or knife throwing, for example) may be acquired by young children merely by observing these actions on television or in the movies.

2. Retention

The effect of the lapse of time between the observational learning and the performance of novel responses is an important issue, and one which has not been completely answered by research done to date. Two studies by David Hicks have been directed toward this matter. One experiment (Hicks, 1965) used films of aggressive models presented in a simulated television program. All children were observed and rated in a procedure similar to that described above. Again, those subjects who observed the aggressive model showed much more imitative aggression than the no-model control subjects. Subjects in this experiment, however, were tested a second time without further exposure to the model after an interval of six months. Again, the experimental subjects were much more aggressive than the controls, although the level of spontaneous imitation was a good deal lower than on first testing.

A second study (Hicks, 1968) also dealt with the long-term retention of aggressive behaviors learned through observation. Children saw a filmed model perform a number of novel acts, some of which were clearly aggressive. After an interval of two months, the behaviors were shown again and subjects were given an opportunity to perform the responses. The tests for immediate retention given at this point showed that better than 60% of the aggressive responses were recalled. A final test for retention was conducted after an interval of eight months. By this time, about 40% of the behaviors were still recalled.

The interpretation of the results of these two studies in terms of the long-term retention of observation-learned aggression must be tempered, however, by the recognition that the second testing in each of these studies was, in fact, a *retest* rather than a delayed test—that is, the experimental subjects had each been given what amounted to a practice trial immediately after having observed the model. Thus, recall and reproduction of these responses may not have been based on the initial *observation* alone, but also on the subjects' recall of their previous *performance* of the acts. This distinction is important for the assessment of the social effects of media aggression, since violent actions in films and television programs are not likely to be "practiced" immediately after they have been seen. Research comparing the retention of practiced versus unpracticed responses is needed in order to determine the relative permanence or transience of aggression learning by observation in the media.

The research findings on observational learning of aggressive behavior discussed up to this point can be briefly summarized as follows: Novel, aggressive behavior sequences are learned by children through exposure to aggressive actions shown on television or in films, and a large proportion of the aggressive behaviors learned by observation are retained over long periods of time if the responses have been practiced at least once, although the length of retention for unpracticed aggressive responses is not known.

B. POSTOBSERVATIONAL CONDITIONS AFFECTING THE
    PERFORMANCE OF AGGRESSIVE BEHAVIOR

1. *The Similarity Factor*

When children observe aggressive models, in a modeling experiment or in the mass media, the aggression is always seen in a particular setting containing a variety of cues. In the research situation, the child is usually given an opportunity to imitate the aggression in a highly *similar* test setting, one containing practically all of these cues. Following exposure to media aggression, however, the child may or may not later encounter a situation similar to the media setting. The level of similarity, then, between the initial viewing situation and the later behavioral setting should be considered in evaluating the likely effects of media violence.

The importance of this variable is suggested by the results of several experiments in which the similarity factor was quite low. Studies by Lovaas (1961) and Siegel (1956) employed animated *cartoon* films depicting a large number of highly aggressive behaviors. After seeing the films, children were observed in settings which contained few, if any, of the cues present in the cartoons. In only one of the four studies reported by these investigators was there any reliable indication of heightened aggressiveness induced by the film. These borderline results contrast sharply with Bandura's findings, and the factor of intersituation cue similarity may well account for the difference. An experiment reported by Meyerson (1966) was conducted specifically to examine this possibility. Children in this study were exposed to the filmed aggressive performance of a model. They were then observed in a test situation having either high, medium, or low similarity to the observed setting. The results showed that the level of imitative aggression increased with increasing similarity between the film and the postfilm settings.

To summarize then, we can say that the likelihood of imitation is determined, in part, by the level of cue similarity between the observed material and the real-life situations that the observer later encounters. Imitation of aggression appears to be quite "cue-specific"; imitative aggression is most likely when the child encounters cues in real life that are very similar to the cues in the observed scene of violence. The fantasy figures and settings in cartoons, for example, are not likely to be encountered in real life. Imitation of more realistic aggression portrayed in everyday settings is much more likely.

The implications of the similarity factor, however, are bound closely together with the question of the permanence of unpracticed, observational learning. If acts learned through observation tend to "fade" rather quickly, then the aggressive responses may be lost before the appropriate stimulus situation arises. If, on the other hand, observational learning is more permanent than this, the likelihood of encountering an appropriate cue situation while the aggressive responses are still available will be greatly increased.

2. The Effects of Observed Rewards or Punishments to the Aggressor

Research discussed so far has dealt mainly with the *acquisition* and retention of aggressive responses through observation. However, the fact that the potential for making a response has been learned does not imply that the response must necessarily be performed. Failure to distinguish between the *acquisition* and the *performance* of aggressive behaviors has been a frequent source of confusion in discussions of learned aggression. The importance of this distinction can be seen in several recent studies of aggression learning by observation.

Bandura (1965a), for example, conducted an aggression modeling experiment essentially similar to those already described. In this study, however, following the initial test for spontaneous imitation, children were offered positive incentives (food and trinkets) for performing the behaviors that they had observed. With this explicit promise of reward, the children produced roughly twice as many imitative aggressive responses than they had shown before. Clearly, the subjects had learned far more than they had demonstrated spontaneously at the first testing. Hicks (1965), in the study of retention of observational learning cited above, also gave positive incentives for imitative aggression following the delayed retest for spontaneous imitation. Again there was a highly significant effect due to introduction of the incentives, showing that even after an interval of six months there were still far more aggressive, imitative responses available to the subject than were spontaneously performed.

Keeping in mind the distinction between acquisition and performance, we can ask, "What are the features of the film or television presentation that will inhibit or facilitate the later performance of aggressive responses learned through observation?" One likely feature of this sort is the observed *consequences* for the aggressive model. An experiment by Bandura, Ross, and Ross (1963c) approached this question directly by showing a televised model either being lavishly rewarded or harshly punished for his aggression. Subjects in two control groups saw either a nonaggressive model or no model at all. The subjects who had seen the aggression rewarded subsequently showed reliably more imitative aggression than did the children in the other groups.

Another study by Bandura (1965a) also looked at the effects of observed reinforcement. Models in this study were again either rewarded or punished for their aggressive behavior. In comparison with a control group that saw the model neither rewarded nor punished, the model-punished group later showed much less aggression. The no-consequences control group was almost as aggressive as the model rewarded group, however, suggesting that children may be just as likely to imitate an aggressive character who "gets away with it" as they are a model who is explicitly rewarded for his aggression.

Putting these studies into some kind of perspective, the imitation of observed aggression may be seen as part of the child's strategy in reaching his goals — the obtaining of rewards and the avoiding of punishments. It is the observed sequence of events that teaches him a "lesson" about the use of aggression as an effective means of achieving his goals.

What, then, is the relation between the use of violent methods and successful goal achievement as typically portrayed in the mass media? A detailed thematic analysis of the content of popular television programs conducted by Larsen (1968) showed that (1) violent methods are the single most popular means employed by characters to reach desired goals and (2) that socially disapproved methods are more frequently portrayed as being successful than are approved methods. These relations were found to be particularly strong for programming directed specifically toward children. If we are justified in putting these two lines of research together, we might then conclude that young viewers are constantly being given the message that *aggression* "*works*"; they are taught that aggression is a highly effective means of achieving one's goals even though it may be socially disapproved. The perceived effectiveness of aggressive actions may thus serve to encourage young viewers actually to use some of the techniques of aggression that they have learned from the media.

3. *Effects of the Social Context*

Subjects in most of the studies cited so far have been left by themselves while they watched the model's televised or filmed performance. Children's everyday exposure to violence in the media, however, frequently occurs when the child is with others — often older children, adults, or other important socializing agents. The attitudes expressed by these other people in the audience may be an important factor determining the child's view of the appropriateness of the observed aggression.

Hicks (1968) investigated this possibility by having children watch a televised, aggressive model while in the presence of an adult "co-observer." The co-observer appeared to be involved in the program and spontaneously made a variety of positive evaluative comments ("Boy look at him go" . . . "He sure is a tough guy") for one set of subjects, and a number of negative comments ("He shouldn't do that" . . . "That's awful") for another group. In a control group, the co-observer remained silent. The effect of these evaluative comments appeared when the subjects were put into the test situation along with the co-observer; under the watchful eye of the co-observer, those children who had heard the positive comments showed a high level of imitative aggression, while those who heard the negative comments showed a reduced level of aggression in comparison with the controls. Three additional groups in this experiment were given the same three treatments except that the co-observer was absent in the testing situation. Interestingly, this variation caused the condition differences to be washed out. Thus the co-observer's comments proved effective only when children were under the surveillance of this same co-observer. In a similar experiment reported by De Rath (1963) the model provided more explicit verbal prohibitions against specific aggressive acts shown in the film. These prohibitions later served to inhibit aggressive behavior both in the presence of the adult who had invoked the prohibitions, and in the presence of another "neutral" adult.

Extrapolating from these results to the media viewing situation, the implication is that parental evaluation or instruction regarding the permissibility of aggression seen in the media can be effective in controlling aggression imitation, but this communication may be irrelevant when adults are not later present to monitor the child's behavior.

4. Other Factors

There are other features of the observed material that also operate to elicit or inhibit imitation. Liking for the model, established by the prior experience of warm nurturant interaction, has been shown to facilitate the imitation of nonaggressive behaviors, although *aggressive* behaviors are likely to be imitated regardless of the quality of the model-child relationship (Bandura, Ross, & Ross, 1961). In the case in which more than one model is presented, there is some evidence that children will be most likely to imitate the model who is perceived to have the greatest social power (Bandura, Ross, & Ross, 1963a).

IV. Emotional Effects

THE BLUNTING OF EMOTIONAL RESPONSES

A number of writers have expressed concern that *the abundance of violence and brutality in the mass media has the effect of blunting viewer's emotional sensitivity.* In attempting to assess the validity of this contention, it is necessary first to establish that people do, in fact, initially show some special emotional reactions to observed violence; available research suggest that this is the case. A sizable proportion of the children in a well known survey study of media effects (Himmilweit, Oppenheim, & Vince, 1958) reported that they were upset by watching the killings on television. In the study by Siegel (1956) mentioned earlier, an aggressive film did not increase aggressive behavior, but it did produce a highly significant increase in the level of rated anxiety. With adult subjects, several studies by Berger (1962) have demonstrated physiologically that intense emotional reactions are produced in persons watching someone else receiving an electric shock. Taken together, these experiments leave little doubt that people do show a special emotional responsivity to observed violence.

1. The Habituation of Emotional Responses to Observed Violence

What happens, though, when these emotional responses are evoked again and again? A general principle, long accepted by psychologists and physiologists, is that the repeated elicitation of an emotional response results in a progressive decrease in the strength of this response. The phenomenon has been given various names: habituation, adaptation, satiation, and accommodation. There is evidence that this kind of emotional habituation takes place with the repeated observation of violence. Adult subjects in several of Berger's (1962) experiments saw a victim receiving an extended series of electric shocks. The strength of the observer's galvanic skin response (the measure of emotional arousal) decreased progressively through the series. This habituation occurred even when the victim was observed to jerk convulsively on each shock trial. Several studies by Lazarus and his colleagues (Lazarus, 1966; Lazarus & Alfert, 1964; Speisman, Lazarus, Mordkoff, & Davidson, 1964) have measured the physiological responses of adult observers watching a film dealing with a primitive tribal ritual called subincision. A series of different victims were shown with each one being subjected to bloody and painful genital mutilation. Again the process of habituation was apparent as the emotional reactions showed a marked progressive diminution throughout the series. Although none of these studies was designed specifically to investigate emotional habituation to observed violence, it seems safe to conclude that this process also occurs during the repeated presentation of violence in the mass media; the viewer becomes progressively less emotionally responsive to repeated observation of scenes of violence.

2. Some Possible Implications of Emotional Habituation

While the viewer may become habituated to media violence, it is quite another thing to assert that he will lose his aversion to actual violence when it occurs in real-life, face-to-face situations. There is some indirect evidence, however, that just such a process could occur.

Desensitization, one of the techniques of modern behavior therapy, involves the progressive introduction of anxiety provoking stimuli, again and again, to patients who are relaxed in otherwise nonthreatening surroundings (Wolpe, 1958). For example, a patient with a phobic fear of snakes may be placed in a relaxed situation and then exposed to stimuli associated with snakes — the word "snake," pictures of snakes, rubber snakes, then small, live snakes. As long as the patient remains relaxed, the intensity of the stimuli is increased. Finally, sometimes after hundreds of repeated presentations, the patient may be "cured" of his phobia; he can remain in close proximity to large snakes without anxiety, and may even be able to touch or handle large snakes.

In more general terms, the effect of such a procedure is that phobic patients gradually become less and less anxious with repeated presentations of the anxiety evoking stimuli; they are eventually able to tolerate direct confrontation without the aversion they previously experienced. Transfer of this tolerance from the therapy situation to real-life, face-to-face behavior is often quite complete. "Cured" patients are frequently able to engage freely in behaviors that were previously difficult or impossible because of intense anxiety (Krassner and Ullman, 1968).

Sears, Maccoby, and Levin (1957) argue that members of our culture " . . . do not tolerate aggression comfortably, neither their own nor that displayed by others. It evokes too much anxiety. . . ." The parallel between the above-mentioned behavior therapy procedures and the situation of the media viewer who is repeatedly exposed to violence while relaxing at home or in the theater suggests the possibility that viewers can be *"cured"* of this kind of aggression anxiety. If this sort of process is going on, viewers may increasingly be willing to accept real-life acts of extreme violence without attempting to interfere, and may themselves be less reluctant to engage directly in aggression when provoking circumstances arise.

The research which is most relevant to this possibility comes again from Bandura's laboratory at Stanford University. Several studies by Bandura and his co-workers have dealt with the extinction of phobic behavior with observational treatment techniques. Children, in one of these studies (Bandura, Grussec, & Menlove, 1967), were selected because they showed consistent fearful avoidance behaviors toward dogs. In the course of a number of brief sessions, the experimental groups saw a peer engaged in a variety of interactions with a brown cocker spaniel. Control groups were either shown the dog alone or were given no special treatment at all. When subsequently tested, the subjects in the experimental groups showed a sharp reduction in avoidance behavior.

Many were now able to engage in intimate and potentially fearful interactions not only with the dog they had seen before but also with an unfa-
miliar dog. Statistically, the avoidance in the experimental groups was
significantly lower than in the control groups, and these differences were
maintained in a follow-up test a month later.

A second study along these same lines (Bandura & Menlove, 1968)
employed motion picture films. Over a period of time, groups of children
who were initially fearful of dogs were shown a number of different films
depicting a peer playing with a single dog, or alternatively, "numerous
dogs varying in size and fearsomeness." A control group of dog-phobic
children was shown a parallel series of nonthreatening films containing
no dogs at all. Again, there was a striking reduction of fearful avoidance
behavior in the experimental groups. The untreated subjects in the control group, however, continued to be fearful and maintained their avoidance at a high level.

Repeated observation of the anxiety provoking activity, then, in
both of these studies, served to eliminate the subjects' initial anxiety-
based avoidance responses. If results from these studies can be generalized to the effects of aggressive episodes repeatedly presented in the
mass media, the repetition of media violence may have the effect not
only of reducing emotional reactivity to fictional violence but also it may
make viewers more willing to actually involve themselves in aggressive
actions when provoking circumstances arise. It must be emphasized
again, however, that none of these experiments was directed specifically
toward the investigation of media-violence effects per se. Experiments
using media-type violence materials along with direct measures of aggression are needed before these conclusions can be drawn with confidence.

V. The Question of Symbolic Aggression Catharsis

The concept of *catharsis* has been with us for literally thousands of
years; Aristotle wrote of the "purging" of audiences' feelings of sorrow
and grief through watching these emotions portrayed on the stage. Some
more contemporary theorists, arguing by analogy, have speculated that
the impulse to *aggression* might likewise be "purged" through the observation of aggression in the mass media. Only recently, however, have
there been any serious attempts to validate this notion of "symbolic catharsis" empirically. Despite some early supporting evidence, the more
recent findings have not supported the idea that aggressive behavior is
reduced by observing the kind of violence seen in the mass media. In

fact, most experimental studies on this issue have found aggression *stimulating* effects rather than "aggression catharsis." The main points of the research on this important issue are covered in the following section.

A.   RESEARCH ON THE CATHARSIS HYPOTHESIS

In a study which has produced a good deal of subsequent research, Feshbach (1961) had college men assigned to one of several experimental conditions. Some men were initially insulted with "a number of unwarranted and extremely critical remarks." Subjects then saw either an extremely aggressive film sequence taken from a brutal prize fight, or a neutral control film on the spread of rumors. Following the film, subjects were given a questionnaire on which they could evaluate the insulting experimenter (their ratings were supposedly to be used by the department chairman to judge the experimenter's competence). Comparison of ratings from the insulted groups showed a lower level of punitiveness in the group that had seen the fight film. Two parallel groups of noninsulted subjects showed no difference on this measure. The difference between the two groups of insulted subjects was interpreted as a result of catharsis in the group shown the aggressive film. According to this interpretation, both groups of insulted subjects had been made angry, but the group shown the aggressive film had their anger "drained off" by the cathartic effect of their vicarious participation in the filmed aggression. Supposedly, the subjects seeing the neutral film did not experience this cathartic "draining off" of anger, and for this reason, they were subsequently more punitive in their judgments.

Catharsis, however, is not the only explanation for this result. An alternative interpretation (Berkowitz & Rawlings, 1963) stresses the idea that the extremely brutal film aroused aggression anxiety and guilt feelings in the angered subjects. The aggressive actions in the film (and perhaps the subjects' own emotional reactions to them) may have served as inhibiting cues, reminding the subjects of their own socially disapproved hostile reactions. As a result of their awareness of these internal responses, subjects were then careful not to display much overt hostility or punitiveness on the questionnaire. While the hypothesis may appear relatively complicated, the catharsis explanation is actually a good deal more complex than it may seem, making as it does, assumptions about the "building up" and "draining off" of aggressive energy and the process of "vicarious participation" in symbolic events. Later studies designed to test this matter more directly have consistently supported interpretations other than the original symbolic catharsis explanation (see

Bandura, 1965b), and have thus cast considerable doubt on the validity of the symbolic catharsis hypothesis.

A substantial number of studies have, in fact, shown that under a variety of conditions, the observation of violence *increases* rather than decreases the viewer's subsequent aggressiveness. Walters, Thomas, and Acker (1962) found that subjects increased their willingness to inflict physical pain as a result of exposure to filmed aggression. Some of the details of their experimental procedure can be given since their method has served as a prototype for other more recent studies. The subjects (adult men) were led to believe that they were participating in a study of the effects of punishment on association learning, and were asked to administer punishing electric shocks to a learner every time the learner made an association error. The errors were signaled on a display board in front of the subject, and the signals were secretly preprogrammed so that 15 out of the 30 trials were registered as errors. After each "error," the subject was to select one of the eleven intensity levels of the electric shock used as punishment. Following an initial series of 30 trials, subjects saw a film clip from a commercial movie showing two teenage boys engaged in a vicious knife fight. The remaining subjects saw a control film dealing with art work. Everyone was then given a second series of 30 trials in which they again punished the learner's errors with electric shocks. Analysis of the prefilm to postfilm changes in the average intensity of shocks showed that the group that had seen the aggressive film shifted to a higher punishment level in comparison with the control group. Aggression scores based on shock duration showed a similar outcome. Walters and Thomas (1963) have used this same experimental paradigm with a number of different subject populations, and have consistently found the same pattern of results across groups of teenage males, male adults, and female adults.

The results obtained by Walters *et al.* (1962; Walters & Brown, 1963; Walters & Thomas, 1963) were obtained under conditions where the subjects were not deliberately frustrated, insulted or otherwise angered before seeing the film. However, a number of studies have also found aggression-inducing effects of observed violence in angered subjects under conditions designed to minimize aggression anxiety. One aspect of observed aggression that might be expected to influence the arousal of aggression anxiety is whether or not the witnessed attack is perceived as being warranted within the fictional context in which it occurs. Berkowitz and Rawlings (1963) investigated this factor in an experiment with college students by using two alternative introductory contexts to a highly aggressive boxing film. In one version, the boxer was represented as being a villainous character well deserving of the beating he received (justified version). Alternatively, he was represented as the victim of unfortunate circumstances, an admirable, generally sympathetic character (unjustified version). The authors found that angered subjects expressed significantly less hostility toward their previous antagonist after they witnessed the scene of "unjustified" rather than "justified" aggression. The interpretation offered for this outcome is that the subjects seeing the justified aggression were temporarily convinced of the righteousness of expressing their anger toward their tormentors. In the less justified condition, however, the sight of the ethically unwarranted aggression aroused aggression anxiety which inhibited the expression of overt hostility.

Another study in this same vein employed measures which can more clearly be interpreted as measures of overt hostility. Berkowitz, Corwin, and Heironimous (1963) extended the above design to include a control group shown a film on canal boats. Subjects were either insulted or not insulted by one experimenter and then were shown, by a second experimenter, the aggressive film. Subjects then responded to a number of questions, some of which were evaluations of the experimenters and their procedures. (Again, the evaluations were to be delivered to the psychology department chairman.) For the subjects who had not been angered, no reliable differences between conditions were obtained. Among those previously insulted, however, the group exposed to the justified version expressed significantly more hostility toward the insulting experimenter than the control group. The unjustified aggression group did not differ from the controls.

In a third study, Berkowitz (1965a) used electric shocks as a measure of aggression toward a confederate posing as a fellow subject. Subjects were again either angered or not angered, and were shown a prize fight sequence preceded by the justified or unjustified introduction. The greatest aggression once more came from those subjects who, according to the aggression-anxiety line of reasoning, should have been least inhibited. Both in terms of the number and the duration of shocks, the highest level of aggression was obtained from angered subjects who had been given the justified film version.

A recent study by Hoyt (1967) was designed to examine more closely some of the factors defining the justified-nonjustified dimension. College students serving in the context of a learning experiment were provoked by receiving an unfairly large number of electric shocks from a confederate posing as a naive subject. Following the presentation of the fight film, subjects were given an opportunity to give shocks to the confederate as punishment for the confederate's errors on a learning task.

The experimental variations in this study centered on the type of introduction provided for the film sequence. Four conditions were formed by the combination of the presence or absence of two different types of aggression justification in the film introduction. In one condition, the justification was based on the *vengeance* motive — the eventual victor was seen as avenging an unfair beating that he had previously received. Justification in a second condition was based on the *self-defense* motive with the victor portrayed as defending himself in a "kill or be killed" situation. A third condition was formed by a combination of these two motives, and a fourth condition served as a control group with no mention of any justifying circumstances.

The results, in terms of the number and duration of shocks given, showed the lowest level of postfilm aggression in the condition where no justification was provided. Subjects in the *vengeance* justification condition gave the confederate more shocks than did subjects given either the neutral introduction or the *self-defense* justification. Hoyt's interpretation of these results stresses the degree of similarity between the situation of the subject and the context of the observed aggression. In the two conditions which included the *vengeance* justification, the subject, who had himself been unfairly abused by the confederate, may have been influenced by motives similar to those portrayed in the film. This correspondence, of course, would be absent in the other two conditions. Thus, the aggression inhibiting or facilitating effects of filmed aggression may depend, in part, on the similarity of the context of the film and the viewer's perception of his own situation.

The findings of these studies, then, are generally consistent with the idea that inhibition of aggression results when an angered viewer watches aggressive action in a context where the aggression is not justified.

Taken together, the results of all of the studies of "emotional catharsis" through observed aggression provide little support for any simple conception of the aggression catharsis hypothesis. The few studies showing a reduction in aggressiveness can easily be explained without assuming that any cathartic "draining off" of aggressiveness has occurred (Berkowitz, 1964). Results have, in fact, given a good deal of support to the opposite view; the bulk of these studies have found aggression-stimulating effects rather than catharsis.

The aggression-stimulating effects have been most evident when the witnessed aggression was seen in a justified context. This last point is particularly ironic in light of current media programming policies. In showing that "crime does not pay" by depicting the hero's successful and justified use of violence against the "bad guys," the media may be creating those very conditions most conducive to the instigation of aggression.

B. Research on a Revised Catharsis Formulation

While a simple conception of vicarious hostility catharsis may no longer be tenable, several recent attempts have been made to test a revised catharsis hypothesis. This reformulation contends that it is not the observation of aggressive *attacks* that results in catharsis. Rather, it is the perception of the tragic *results* of aggression that produces catharsis. According to this hypothesis, the aggressiveness of angered persons should be reduced when they witness the horrific stimuli associated with the *aftermath* of violence — injury, pain, blood, and suffering.

An intriguing study by Bramel, Taub, and Blum (1968), employed such a revised catharsis concept in studying "an observer's reaction to the suffering of his enemy." Male college students were initially either insulted or not insulted by an experimenter. A second experimenter then took over and played a tape that purported to be a recording of the reactions of the first experimenter while he was serving as a subject in a drug experiment. Three versions of the tape were prepared, each based on a different reaction to the drug: a euphoria reaction version, a neutral version, and a misery reaction version. The results of the experiment were somewhat complex and open to alternative interpretations, but in summary it can be said that subjects' punitiveness was reduced by observing the insulting experimenter suffer. Subjects were unaffected, relative to the controls, by observing him experiencing euphoria. The authors explain this outcome in terms of their revised catharsis hypothesis; the subject's desire to punish the antagonist was reduced by the perception of him undergoing an experience of extreme suffering.

The relevance of this study for the understanding of media effects is obviously limited by the fact that the viewer rarely if ever sees the suffering, in the media, of anyone who has just attacked or insulted him personally.

An experiment by Hartmann (1965), on the other hand, looked at a somewhat more general case. In this study, three versions of an experimental film were prepared. A control version showed a group of boys engaged in a vigorous, but nonviolent basketball game. In the two other versions, the game was interrupted by an argument between two of the boys that quickly developed into a one-sided fist fight. In one version, the film focused on the attacker's responses, his punching fists, kicks, angry facial expressions, and aggressive verbalizations. In another case (the pain-cues version), the camera focused on the plight of the victim including close-ups of his face as he was knocked down, his groans, cries, and other expressions of distress.

The effects of prior anger arousal were also tested in this study. The subjects were teenage juvenile delinquents. At the outset, some of them were angered by overhearing their partner (actually a paid confederate) make a number of highly insulting remarks about them. Other subjects were not angered, hearing only neutral comments. Following this, subjects were shown one of the three film versions, and then given a sanctioned opportunity, in the context of a learning task, to administer electric shocks to the confederate.

The results, in terms of the intensity and duration of shocks given, showed that, for the *angered subjects*, the effect of the aggressive film versions was to increase the subjects' aggressiveness. These subjects were, in fact, most aggressive following the pain-cues film. For the nonangered subjects, however, the results were different. Here, the pain-cues film tended to *reduce* the level of aggression. The results from these nonangered subjects, as well as the outcome of the preceding study, might be interpreted in terms of the revised catharsis hypothesis. Alternatively, however, the results can be seen as the result of a more active inhibitory process. Exposure to cues of the witnessed suffering may have *sensitized* subjects to the possible serious consequences of their own punitive responses. The salience of this possible danger may have functioned to inhibit their aggressive reactions. Note that this explanation is quite different from the idea of a "cathartic drainage" of anger and aggressive tension.

A recent, unpublished study by Tannenbaum and Goranson sheds some light on the relative validity of these alternatives. All subjects in this study were college men, and all were initially angered. Angering was achieved by having a confederate give them an unfairly large number of shocks as a judgment of their task performance as "learners" in a procedure disguised as an experiment in education. Each subject then saw a film of a highly aggressive boxing match with a taped ending given in one of three alternative versions. The first version stressed a *positive outcome* with the protagonist leaving the ring in good physical condition, and later going on to a life of success and fame. An alternate version depicted a highly *negative outcome* with stress on the defeated boxer's injuries, a cerebral hemorrhage, extreme agony, and painful death. A *control* version merely recapitulated the events of the fight. When subjects were subsequently put in the position of giving shocks to a "learner," the intensity of shocks they chose to administer was significantly reduced by exposure to the *negative outcome* version. In a follow-up study (Goranson, 1969) using similar procedures, this inhibitory effect was obtained even when the horrible and bloody suffering of the protagonist was not directly attributable to the fight. Comparison of mood ratings, however, indicated that this reduced aggressiveness was not due to any pleasurable, cathartic reduction of anger or tension due to the perception of suffering. Changes in anger and tension ratings were roughly the same in the different outcome conditions, and the *negative outcome* group actually reported feeling significantly *less* happy following the film.

The most reasonable explanation again seems to be that the perception of the horrible effects of the violence served to *sensitize* the subjects to the potential harm that they themselves might inflict. If this rather plausible explanation for the four preceding studies can be accepted, then this conclusion again runs directly counter to the current media programming policy. Production codes for radio, television, comic books, and motion pictures all include prohibitions against the portrayal of physical agony and suffering. A leading radio and television trade magazine (*Broadcasting*, August 19, 1968, p. 23) quotes one television producer as saying "Anything that shows too much agony, too much punishment, or is too bloody, anything that could be too startling, whether it's in context or whether it was done for good and valid reasons, is being taken out or reduced, wherever possible." When this kind of *de facto* self-censorship serves to sanitize violence by "prettying up" or entirely omitting the real consequence of aggression, the result again is the unwitting creation of the very conditions found most conducive to the instigation to aggression.

C. The Status of the Symbolic Aggression Catharsis Hypothesis

In reviewing the evidence on symbolic aggression catharsis, we have found only a single study giving support to this doctrine; a study using paper and pencil measures of hostility obtained after the presentation, without any justifying context, of a highly aggressive fight scene. Evaluation of the implications of this one experiment provides a good example of the dangers inherent in generalizing too freely from the results of a single piece of research. Additional experiments have indicated that the results of this study were very likely due to the arousal of aggression anxiety and the subsequent inhibition of overt hostility, rather than the result of symbolic catharsis. More recent experiments that have minimized the factor of aggression anxiety have almost uniformly found that observed violence results in the stimulation of aggression. These results, along with the earlier mentioned findings of modeling experiments with children, all argue against the idea that observed violence results in a cathartic discharge of aggressive energies.

A revised formulation has been proposed, based on the idea that aggression catharsis may result from the observation of pain, horror, and suffering. Although this formulation has not been as thoroughly tested as the original, the catharsis concept has, again, not been supported; while the observation of intense suffering may temporarily inhibit aggressive responses, this is probably not due to a cathartic process.

In light of the persistent belief in symbolic aggression catharsis, and the volume of research evidence against it, perhaps the time has come to recognize the extremely limited validity of the symbolic catharsis doctrine. This conclusion should not be too surprising. Bandura (1965b) has pointed out that we would scarcely advocate that adolescents be shown libidinous films as a means of reducing sexual behavior, nor would we advise that a starving man observe the eating of a delicious meal in order to diminish his hunger pangs. Similarly, we should not expect that the outpourings of violence in the mass media will have the effect of reducing aggressive behavior.

Perhaps much of the persistence of belief in the aggression catharsis notion stems from a misapplication of Aristotle's original concept of catharsis. Goodman (1964) has noted that Aristotle's use of the word *catharsis* applies only to "tragic" feelings such as sadness, grief, and sorrow. When a "tear jerker" arouses these feelings, they may be given immediate, active expression. The audience may feel better after "having a good cry." In the case of aggression however, the situation is very different; when aggressive impulses are aroused in the theater, they cannot be given immediate release. Overt aggression must be inhibited, bottled up, at least until the end of the performance. It is likely that, in the case of aggression, Aristotle would have predicted the very effects of observed violence that have so consistently been found—a facilitation, rather than a reduction of subsequent aggressive behavior.

VI. The Inhibition and Facilitation of Impulsive Aggression

In looking previously at the results of modeling studies done with children, we found that the observed consequences for the aggressor could serve either to inhibit or to facilitate the expression of aggressive behavior. The likelihood of postfilm aggression was determined by the perceived effectiveness of aggressive behavior as a means of goal attainment. No doubt human behavior is very often guided by such utilitarian strategies, but we should recognize that sometimes aggressive behavior is determined by far less rational motives. Under some circumstances, an angered person may respond with *impulsive* aggression, never considering the long-range implications of his actions. A complete analysis of media violence effects must take into account some of the conditions affecting the expression of this impulsive aggression.

A. THE INHIBITION OF IMPULSIVE AGGRESSION

In the earlier discussion of research on the question of catharsis, some of the features of observed violence that serve to inhibit aggression were covered, so a few brief comments can be made without going into the details of the work on this topic.

The inhibitory effects found to result from the perception of *unjustified* aggression presumably arose because subjects were reminded that aggression was morally wrong. Thus, we should not assume, just because impulsive aggression is irrational, that it cannot be modified or inhibited by an awareness of one's ethical principles. Again, we should note that aggressive action in the media is often performed by the "good guy" under provoking circumstances that minimize the likelihood that the viewer will be reminded of his own principles regarding the immorality of violence.

Research on the revised catharsis hypothesis has identified another feature of observed violence that serves to inhibit the aggressive impulses of the viewer. Recall that when subjects were made aware of the bloody, painful aftermath of aggression, they were then inhibited in their willingness to inflict harm on others. In the typical media presentation, however, the action is rarely designed to remind the viewer of aggression's horrible consequences. Critic Robert Warshaw (1962), in discussing "Western" movies, has noted that ". . . our eyes are not focused on the sufferings of the defeated, but on the deportment of the hero." It is just these painful sufferings of the defeated victim, however, that may allow the provoked viewer to "think twice" about acting out his own aggressive impulses.

B. THE FACILITATION OF IMPULSIVE AGGRESSION

1. The Cue Properties of Available Targets

Berkowitz (1965b) has argued that when aggressive responses have been aroused within the individual, his hostility may remain in "low gear" unless the appropriate aggression-evoking cues are present in the environment. Only when these cues are introduced do the person's aggressive impulses become translated into actual aggressive behavior.

Appropriate cues of this sort may be based on the stimuli in the postobservation situation that have some association with previously observed violence. "Thus, a person who sees a brutal fight may not himself display any detectable aggression immediately afterwards, even if his inhibitions are relatively weak, unless he encounters stimuli having some association with the fight" (Berkowitz, 1965b, p. 360).

The impact of the association between the victim of the observed violence and the target of the viewer's aggression has been investigated in a series of experiments by Berkowitz and his co-workers at the University of Wisconsin psychology laboratories.

An experiment reported by Berkowitz (1965b) used college students who were initially either insulted or not insulted by a confederate posing as another subject. The confederate was introduced either as a speech major or as a college boxer. Subjects then watched a film clip of a violent boxing match or of a neutral control film. After the film, all subjects were given an opportunity to give electric shocks to the confederate within the context of a learning experiment. For the insulted subjects, the largest number of shocks were given in the condition where the boxing film had been shown and the confederate had been represented as a boxer. The association between the target and the characters in the observed violence could be seen as "drawing out" the aggressive responses from the angered subjects.

A follow-up study by Berkowitz and Geen (1966) sought to clarify this relationship by establishing the association on the basis of the target's name. The design of the study was similar to the previous one except that half of the subjects seeing the boxing film were introduced to a confederate having the same *name* as one of the boxers. In this study the control film was based on a track race and was thus a highly exciting, although nonviolent, control. When subjects were given an opportunity to administer electric shocks to the confederate, they were most aggressive in the condition where they had been angered by someone having the same name as the character in the aggressive film. Here again, the victim's association with aggression-related stimuli apparently served to produce more intense attacks.

A further extension of this line of experimentation (Geen & Berkowitz, 1966) found that the highest level of aggression was obtained when the person to be shocked was associated by name with the filmed *victim* rather than the filmed *victor*. An additional study (Berkowitz & Geen, 1967) found similar results even when the name-mediated association was formed *after* the film.

Generalization from these results to real-life social problems necessarily requires a certain amount of speculation. One possible, though speculative, implication that might be drawn from this area of research is that when members of minority groups having distinctive cue characteristics are repeatedly portrayed in the media as targets for aggression, there may be an increased likelihood that some member may, because of this association, become the victim of violence. Although, again, caution must be exercised in extrapolating from the results of laboratory experiments, this possibility lends credence to the outcry of some Italian-American interest groups against a once-popular television series featuring a weekly "war" against Italian Mafia villains.

2. The General State of Arousal of the Aggressor

A variety of studies have shown that when subjects have been attacked and then exposed to film violence, they later aggress against a victim more forcefully than subjects who have not been attacked (e.g., see Berkowitz, 1965b; Berkowitz & Geen, 1966). Other studies have shown similar effects following emotional arousal due to *frustration* (Geen, 1968; Geen & Berkowitz, 1967). These results are consistent with the idea that attack or frustration produces a general state of physiological arousal which, in turn, increases the probability of aggression resulting from observed violence (Berkowitz, 1968).

A recent study by Geen and O'Neal (1969) sought to examine the role of arousal more directly. Male college students, in his experiment, were shown either an aggressive boxing film or a film depicting nonaggressive sporting activities. All subjects were then put in the position of giving electric shocks to another student under an appropriate pretext. While they gave the shocks, half of the men in each film group were put in a state of somewhat stressful arousal by having to listen to a loud continuous noise over a pair of earphones.

The highest level of aggression, in number and intensity of shocks given, was shown by the students who received both the aggressive film and the stress-producing noise. One interpretation of this result is that the stress-produced arousal may have served to activate or "energize" latent aggressive responses produced by aggressive cues in the film.

Physiological arousal may arise from a variety of causes such as drugs, personal crises, or even extreme temperature conditions. In light of this, a possible implication of Geen's study is that the aggression-triggering effects of media violence may be particularly severe during periods of continuing stress. Fear of nuclear war, long uncomfortable "hot spells" of weather, and the threat of the military draft are some contemporary sources of stress that come to mind. Under such conditions, violence observed in the media might serve to trigger off acts of impulsive aggression that would otherwise have remained latent.

Generalizations from these laboratory studies of impulsive aggression should probably be taken as *hypotheses*, or possible explanations, rather than as "proven facts." One limitation on this research stems from the fact that the influence of the passage of time has not been investigated. As in the studies of behavior modeling discussed earlier, the implications of the present experiments are much more serious if the aggression-arousing effects are more than just transitory.

Even if such heightened aggressiveness is only short-lived however, it has been pointed out (Larsen, 1968, p. 288) that when there are as many as 20,000,000 people viewing a televised scene of brutal violence, there can be a very real increase in the likelihood of someone's being hurt because of it.

VII. Summary

In summarizing the results of the studies reviewed here, it should be pointed out again that the conclusions drawn from research findings must always be, to some degree, tentative. A truly complete understanding of the exact effects of violence portrayed in the mass media is a goal for researchers to aim for, but, realistically, it is a goal that will probably never be reached. With this *caveat* in mind, the following conclusions seem to be warranted on the basis of available research evidence.

A. LEARNING EFFECTS

Novel, aggressive behavior sequences are learned by children through exposure to realistic portrayals of aggression on television or in films. A large proportion of these behaviors are retained over long periods of time if they are practiced at least once. The likelihood that such aggressive behaviors will be performed is determined, in part, by the similarity of the setting of the observed violence and the cues present in later situations. The actual performance of aggressive behaviors learned from the media is largely contingent on the child's belief in the effectiveness of aggression in attaining his goals while avoiding punishment. The mass media typically present aggression as a highly effective form of behavior.

B. EMOTIONAL EFFECTS

Frequent exposure produces an emotional habituation to media violence. There is indirect evidence that this, in turn, could result in an increased likelihood of actually engaging in aggression.

C. CATHARSIS

The symbolic aggression catharsis hypothesis has not proved tenable. Observed violence serves to facilitate the expression of aggression, rather than to reduce aggression by "draining off aggressive energy." The aggression anxiety aroused by witnessing nonjustified violence may serve to inhibit aggression. The observation of intense pain and suffering results in the inhibition of aggression, but probably not because of catharsis.

D. IMPULSIVE AGGRESSION

Aggressive impulses may be held in check if the viewer has been made especially aware of the "wrongness" of aggression or of the suffering that may result from violence. The target person's prior association with media violence serves to heighten the intensity of aggressive attacks on him.

When we look beyond the work that has been done to date, we can see that a number of specific research questions remain to be answered.

The permanence of media violence effects is a central issue. When novel, aggressive behaviors and techniques are learned by observation, are they quickly forgotten or is this learning more permanent? Does the permanence of this learning depend on the "practice" of aggressive responses immediately after they are observed? When media violence arouses aggressive impulses, are these impulses very short-lived or not?

The effects of different observed outcomes of violent episodes should be studied in greater detail. When the hero guns down the villain, do children really learn that "crime does not pay" or do they learn that it is *good* to kill "bad people"? When media violence is "cleaned up" by removal of the bloody and horrible aftermath of violence, does this make real-life aggression seem more acceptable?

The possibility that emotional habituation may make people less reluctant to commit violence needs further investigation.

Apart from these specific research questions, it is important to know, more generally, just how far the results of these experimental studies can be applied to everyday media effects. We need additional research methods and experimental controls in natural, everyday media viewing situations.

REFERENCES

Banay, R. Testimony before the Subcommittee to Investigate Juvenile Delinquency, of the Committee on the Judiciary, United States Senate, Eighty-fourth Congress. *Senate Research*, April 1955, **62**. USGPO, Washington, D. C.

Bandura, A. Influence of models' reinforcement contingencies on the acquisition of imitative responses. *Journal of Personality and Social Psychology*, 1965, **1**, 589-595. (a)

Bandura, A. Vicarious processes: A case of no-trial learning. In L. Berkowitz (Ed.), *Advances in experimental social psychology*. Vol. 2. New York: Academic Press, 1965. (b)

Bandura, A., Grusec, J. E., & Menlove, F. L. Vicarious extinction of avoidance behavior. *Journal of Personality and Social Psychology*, 1967, **5**, 16-23.

Bandura, A., & Huston, A. C. Identification as a process of incidental learning. *Journal of Abnormal and Social Psychology*, 1961, **63**, 311-318.

Bandura, A., & Menlove, F. L. Factors determining vicarious extinction of avoidance behavior through symbolic modeling. *Journal of Personality and Social Psychology*, 1968, 8, 99-108.

Bandura, A., Ross, D., & Ross, S. A. Transmission of aggression through imitation of aggressive models. *Journal of Abnormal and Social Psychology*, 1961, **63**, 575-582.

Bandura, A., Ross, D., & Ross, S. A. A comparative test of the status envy, social power, and secondary reinforcement theories of indentificatory learning. *Journal of Abnormal and Social Psychology*, 1963, **67**, 527-534. (a)

Bandura, A., Ross, D., & Ross, S. A. Imitation of film-mediated aggressive models. *Journal of Abnormal and Social Psychology*, 1963, **66**, 3-11. (b)

Bandura, A., Ross, D., & Ross, S. A. Vicarious reinforcement and imitative learning. *Journal of Abnormal and Social Psychology*, 1963, **67**, 601-607. (c)

Bandura, A., & Walters, R. H. *Social learning and personality development*. New York: Holt, Rinehart & Winston, 1963.

Berger, S. Conditioning through vicarious instigation. *Psychological Review*, 1962, **69**, 405-456.

Berkowitz, L. *Agression: A social psychological analysis*. New York: McGraw-Hill, 1962.

Berkowitz, L. Aggressive cues in aggressive behavior and hostility catharsis. *Psychological Review*, 1964, **71**, 104-122.

Berkowitz, L. The concept of aggressive drive: Some additional considerations. In L. Berkowitz (Ed.), *Advances in experimental social psychology*. Vol. 2. New York: Academic Press, 1965. (a)

Berkowitz, L. Some aspects of observed aggression. *Journal of Personality and Social Psychology*, 1965, **2**, 359-369. (b)

Berkowitz, L. The frustration-aggression hypothesis revisited. In L. Berkowitz (Ed.), *Roots of aggression: A re-examination of the frustration-aggression hypothesis*. New York: Atherton Press, 1968.

Berkowitz, L., Corwin, R., & Heironimous, M. Film violence and subsequent aggressive tendencies. *Public Opinion Quarterly*, 1963, **27**, 217-229.

Berkowitz, L., & Geen, R. Film violence and the cue properties of available targets. *Journal of Personality and Social Psychology*, 1966, **3**, 525-530.

Berkowitz, L., & Geen, R. The stimulus qualities of the target of aggression. A further study. *Journal of Personality and Social Psychology*, 1967, **5**, 364-368.

Berkowitz, L., & Rawlings, E. Effects of film violence on inhibitions against subsequent aggression. *Journal of Abnormal and Social Psychology*, 1963, **66**, 405-412.

Bramel, D., Taub, B., & Blum, B. An observer's reaction to the suffering of his enemy. *Journal of Personality and Social Psychology*, 1968, 8, 384-392.

De Rath, G. The effects of verbal instructions on imitative aggression. Unpublished doctoral dissertation, Michigan State University, 1963.

Feshbach, S. The stimulating versus cathartic effects of a vicarious aggressive activity. *Journal of Abnormal and Social Psychology*, 1961, **63**, 381-385.

Geen, R. Effects of frustration, attack, and prior training in aggressiveness on aggressive behavior. *Journal of Personality and Social Psychology*, 1968, **9**, 316-321.

Geen, R., & Berkowitz, L. Name-mediated aggressive cue properties. *Journal of Personality*, 1966, **34**, 456-465.

Geen, R., & Berkowitz, L. Some conditions facilitating the occurrence of aggression after the observation of violence. *Journal of Personality*, 1967, **35**, 666-667.

Geen, R., & O'Neal, E. Activation of cue-elicited aggression by general arousal. *Journal of Personality and Social Psychology*, 1969, **11**, 289-292.

Geen, R., Rokosky, J., & O'Neal, E. Methodological study of measurement of aggression. *Psychological Reports*, 1968, **23**, 59-62.

Goodman, P. Letter to the editor. *Scientific American,* 1964, **210**(6), 8.

Goranson, R. Observed violence and aggressive behavior: The effects of negative outcomes to the observed violence. Unpublished doctoral dissertation, University of Wisconsin, 1969.

Hartley, R. The impact of viewing aggression. Office of Social Research, CBS, Multilithed, 1964.

Hartmann, D. The influence of symbolically modeled instrumental aggression and pain cues on the disinhibition of aggressive behavior. Unpublished doctoral dissertation, Stanford University, 1965.

Hicks, D. Imitation and retention of film-mediated aggressive peer and adult models. *Journal of Personality and Social Psychology*, 1965, **2**, 97-100.

Hicks, D. Short and long-term retention of affectively varied modeled behavior. *Psychonomic Science*, 1968, **11**, 369-370.

Himmilweit, H., Oppenheim, A., & Vince P. *Television and the child: An empirical study of the effect of television on the young.* New York: Oxford University Press, 1958.

Hoyt, J. Vengeance and self-defence as justification for filmed aggression. Unpublished master's thesis, University of Wisconsin, 1967.

Klapper, J. The social effects of mass communication. In W. Schramm (Ed.), *The science of human communication.* New York: Basic Books, 1963.

Krassner, L., & Ullman, L. *Research in behavior modification.* New York: Holt, Rinehart & Winston, 1968.

Larsen, O. *Violence in the mass media.* New York: Harper & Row, 1968.

Larsen, O., Gray, L., & Fortas, J. Achieving goals through violence on television. In O. J. Larsen (Ed.), *Violence in the mass media.* New York: Harper & Row, 1968. Pp. 97-111.

Lazarus, R. *Psychological stress and the coping process.* New York: McGraw-Hill, 1966.

Lazarus, R., & Alfert, E. The short-circuiting of threat. *Journal of Abnormal and Social Psychology*, 1964, **69**, 195-205.

Liebowitz, G. Comparison of self-report and behavioral techniques of assessing aggression. *Journal of Consulting and Clinical Psychology*, 1968, **32**, 21-25.

Lovaas, O. Effect of exposure to symbolic aggression on aggressive behavior. *Child Development*, 1961, **32**, 37-44.

Maccoby, E. E. Effects of mass media. In M. L. Hoffman & L. W. Hoffman (Eds.), *Review of child development research.* New York: Russell Sage Foundation, 1964.

Meyerson, L. The effects of filmed aggression on the aggressive responses of high and low aggressive subjects. Unpublished doctoral dissertation, University of Iowa, 1966.

Sears, R., Maccoby, E., & Levin, H. *Patterns of child rearing.* New York: Harper, 1957.

Siegel, A. Film-mediated fantasy aggression and strength of aggressive drive. *Child Development*, 1956, **27**, 365-378.

Speisman, J., Lazarus, R., Mordkoff, A., & Davidson, L. A. Experimental reduction of stress based on ego-defence theory. *Journal of Abnormal and Social Psychology*, 1964, **68**, 367-380.

Walters, R., & Brown, M. Studies of reinforcement of aggression. III: Transfer of responses to an interpersonal situation. *Child Development*, 1963, **34**, 563-571.

Walters, R., & Thomas, E. Enhancement of punitiveness by visual and audio-visual displays. *Canadian Journal of Psychology*, 1963, **17**, 244-255.

Walters, R., Thomas, E., & Acker, C. Enhancement of punitive behavior by audio-visual displays. *Science*, 1962, **136**, 872-873.

Warshaw, R. *The immediate experience.* New York: Doubleday, 1962.

Weiss, W. Effects of mass media on communication. In G. Lindzey & E. Aronson (Eds.), *Handbook of social psychology.* Vol. 5. Boston: Addison-Wesley Press, 1970. Pp. 77-195.

Wertham, F. *Seduction of the innocent.* New York: Holt, Rinehart & Winston, 1954.

Williams, J., Meyerson, L., Eron, L., & Semler, I. Peer-rated aggression and aggressive responses elicited in an experimental situation. *Child Development*, 1967, **38**, 181-189.

Wolpe, J. *Psychotherapy by reciprocal inhibition.* Stanford: Stanford University Press, 1958.

STUDIES IN LEADER LEGITIMACY, INFLUENCE, AND INNOVATION[1]

**Edwin P. Hollander and
James W. Julian**
STATE UNIVERSITY OF NEW YORK AT
BUFFALO

[1]The studies reported here are part of a program of research supported under ONR Contract 4679 from the Group Psychology Branch, Office of Naval Research. We are indebted to Lanning J. Beckman, Lorraine Heilbrun, John B. Morganti, Franklyn A. Perry, C. Robert Regula, Richard M. Ryckman, Richard M. Sorrentino, and David Wiesenthal for their various kinds of assistance in this research. Experiment one appeared originally as Julian, J. W. & Hollander, E. P. A study of some role dimensions of leader-follower relations. Tech. Report No. 3, ONR Contract 4679, State Univ. of New York, Buffalo, N. Y., 1966; experiment two appeared as Hollander, E. P., Julian, J. W. and Perry, F. A. Leader style, competence, and source of authority as determinants of actual and perceived influ-

I. Introduction to the Contemporary Study of Leadership

Leadership affords a rich field for the study of a wide range of sociopsychological phenomena. Among these are role behavior, interpersonal influence, attitude change, conformity, socialization, and intergroup relations. However, even with the broad range of interests inherent in its study, leadership continues to be approached in relatively limited ways with essentially static conceptions. An especially major limitation is the continuing emphasis on leaders as managers, without reference to the wider ramifications of the leadership enterprise. Side by side with this narrow emphasis is the still prevailing view of leaders as occupiers of a fixed position, rather than, in more dynamic terms, as attainers or maintainers of their standing with followers. Together, these emphases have tended to slight the influence process which is basic to leadership phenomena.

While the field of leadership research has made a number of forward strides, it has been encumbered by the lingering effects of earlier fads. The dominant approach for some time was to focus on the leader and his attributes; in this view, the leader was taken to be someone with qualities which would make him achieve leadership in any situation. This approach not only lacked a conception of leadership as a process, but suffered as well from the implicit assumption of a certain homogeneity in the leader's role. Reviews of the leadership literature by Stogdill (1948), Hemphill (1949), and Mann (1959), amply revealed these failings, and led the way for the more recent situational approach to leadership. Among the distinctions which came with this approach was the recognition that some leaders are appointed as leaders, and have their authority vested in them from above, while others are chosen by followers through a literal election or through some less formal, emergent process.

Within the situational framework, leaders were seen to fulfill various role expectancies depending upon the way the group tasks and group structures emphasized particular requirements for leadership. A variety of experiments essentially supported the consideration that who became a leader depended upon the nature of the task and its setting (e.g., Carter, Haythorn, Meirowitz, & Lanzetta, 1951; Carter & Nixon, 1949; Gibb, 1947).

In the 1950's, when it had its greatest impact, the situational ap-

ence. Tech. Report No. 5, ONR Contract 4679, State Univ. of New York, Buffalo, N. Y., 1966; experiment three appeared as Julian, J. W., Hollander, E. P., and Regula, C. R. Endorsement of the group spokesman as a function of his source of authority, competence, and success. *Journal of Personality and Social Psychology*, 1969, **11**, 42–49; and experiment four appeared as Hollander, E. P., Julian, J. W., and Sorrentino, R. M. The leader's sense of legitimacy as a source of his constructive deviation. Tech. Report No. 12, ONR Contract 4679, State Univ. of New York, Buffalo, N. Y., 1969.

proach went a long way toward rectifying the balance which had been overweighted for so long toward leader traits. The research generated by this approach indicated that different situations demanded different capabilities from the person called a "leader." Yet this situational focus, by itself, failed to give sufficient attention to the process of leadership. For the most part, the group's task was regarded as the key element differentiating situations, and the leader was considered to be someone who occupied his position almost in a fixed sense as a consequence of his competency with respect to that task. Less attention was given to followers, their perceptions of the leader, and reactions to his assertions of influence over time. Furthermore, the situational approach encouraged a separation of the leader from the group's situation when, in fact, the leader is an important element in the situation from the followers' vantage point.

All in all, it suffices to say, as we have recently stated elsewhere, that ". . . the two research emphases represented by the trait and situational approaches afforded a far too glib view of reality. Indeed, in a true sense, neither approach ever represented its own philosophical underpinning very well, and each resulted in a caricature" [Hollander & Julian, 1969, p. 388].

A. The Transactional Approach

Given the limitations of these earlier emphases, some new formulations of leadership phenomena were required. Leadership is now coming to be seen as a transaction between leaders and followers which implies a reciprocal influence process. To be influential, as Homans (1961) has observed, the leader must be willing to be influenced by others and, in effect, to exchange rewards with them. Thus, Katz and Kahn (1966) view leadership functions in system terms as an interchange of inputs for outputs. Accordingly, the leader provides a resource for the group by facilitating leadership functions, among which is the direction of the enterprise. Although the leader's contributions and their consequences vary with system demands, the leader is perceived by the other group members as providing the more valued resources needed for the attainment of their common goal (Hollander & Julian, 1968, p. 891).

Put in transactional terms, the leader who fulfills expectations and helps to achieve group goals provides a rewarding resource for others which is exchanged for status, esteem, and greater influence. Thus, he gives something and gets something. And what he gets contributes to his legitimacy insofar as he is "validated" in his role by followers. It is the leader's sense of this legitimacy which then serves as the base on which he may operate to exert influence.

B. IDIOSYNCRASY CREDIT AND LEGITIMACY

Before elaborating further the nature and function of legitimacy, it is useful to observe that the functional effectiveness of an individual's status intimately depends upon other persons' perceptions. The "idio-syncrasy credit" model (Hollander, 1958, 1964) deals in particular with the processes affecting acceptance as a feature of status. Briefly, the essential point of this model is that the leader's influence depends upon how competent others in the group believe he is in helping the group achieve its goals, and his conformity to the group's normative expectations as a sign of his motivation to belong to the group. If seen favorably in these respects, the leader's subsequent assertions of influence are then more readily accepted, even though they may represent deviations from group patterns. Thus, a person gains credits, in terms of the positive impressions held by relevant others, which he may then draw on in exerting influence, particularly regarding deviations from normative expectancies.

The process orientation of this model has produced research with a distinctive sequential feature. An early exemplification of this is revealed in an experiment by Hollander (1960) which showed that a group member with high competence on the task could be highly influential, both with regard to the task and the norms of the group, if he conformed earlier to those norms, but not if he failed to do so. Under those conditions, where such a group member manifested early non-conformity, his influence was markedly curtailed later. A reversal of this sequence, however, produced high influence. Other research by Berkowitz and Macaulay (1961), Harvey and Consalvi (1960), Hollander (1961b), Julian and Steiner (1961), Sabath (1964), and Wiggins, Dill, and Schwartz (1965), support the essential proposition that higher status members could deviate from the group norms with greater impunity. A recent experiment by Alvarez (1968) on deviance in simulated work organizations, provides an interesting confirmation of this. He found that for the same acts of deviance, the higher status person lost esteem at a slower rate, but only in "successful" organizations; where the organizations were "unsuccessful," the higher status person lost esteem at a faster rate than his lower status counterpart.

II. The Study of Legitimacy

Prominent among the several elements making up a leader's role are the manner by which the leader achieves his position, what he is perceived to be doing, and how his actions and motivations are seen to contribute to the group's task. Depending upon the expectations and perceptions held by the others involved, these elements may be interrelated in various ways, thereby determining the leader's ability to influence the others in working effectively toward common goals. This is the essence of the leader's legitimacy. In Goffman's (1959) terms, the impressions he "gives off" will alter the balance of favorability for the leader's success. Indeed, Fiedler (1967) attached particular significance in his "contingency model" to the favorability factor in predicting outcomes of the leadership process.

As we have suggested, one way to approach legitimacy is to understand it as a process involving an exchange of rewards which provides the leader with greater sway for asserting influence. Thus, the person in the role of leader who is able to achieve what is expected of him comes to have greater credits at his disposal. In broadest terms, his legitimacy grows out of the authority vested in his role, the source of that authority, and a set of impressions which followers hold regarding his competence and his motivations. In signaling the acceptance of a leader's legitimacy, two steps appear to be involved: first, the acceptance of the leader in his role as an authority; and, second, the willingness to respond affirmatively to his assertions of influence over time. Ultimately, the latter responses are the more crucial in establishing leader-follower relationships of a sustained sort.

A. Variables Affecting Legitimacy

In framing the program of research to be reported here, three leader characteristics were chosen as determinants of legitimacy which could be experimentally manipulated. These are: (a) the source of the leader's authority, whether the origins are internal or external to the group; (b) the leader's competence on a task which facilitates the attainment of group goals; and (c) his motivations with respect to the task itself and the needs of his followers. How these factors are perceived by followers may be hypothesized to determine the favorability with which they respond to the leader, as an indication of his legitimacy.

Apart from the perceived competence of the leader, few investigations have explored the impact of these variables in eliciting favorable follower reactions. A number of studies (e.g., Croner & Willis, 1961; Hollander, 1960; Mausner, 1954) have demonstrated that individuals seen to be more highly competent exert greater influence on others' task behavior. By contrast, the effects of perceived leader motivations have remained relatively unexplored, although the early study by Fouriezos, Hutt, and Guetzkow (1950) presented some suggestive leads in this vein. Similarly, the effects of the source of the leader's authority have mainly gone unattended, with several exceptions. Cohen and Bennis (1961) found that the continuity of leadership was maintained more by allowing groups the option of electing their own leaders. Goldman and Fraas (1965) have demonstrated differences in the productivity of groups established under four procedures of leader selection, including appointment and election. Also noteworthy are the findings of Raven and French (1958) which indicated that the election of a supervisor produced private as well as public compliance in groups while its absence only produced conformity when it was observable by the supervisor. Taken together, the results of these studies point to the potentialities of further research on the effects of the leader's source of authority.

B.   APPROACH TO THE PROBLEM

In the present set of experiments, we employed a factorial design within which were manipulated several variables. At the outset, we considered the effects on followers of the leader's perceived source of authority, task competence, and relevant motivations. We selected as major dependent variables the followers' acceptance of the leader in his position, and his influence, in terms of their responses and perceptions. In the first experiment, we explored all three of these variables as inputs; in the second, we were concerned with their influence effects, both in behavioral and perceptual terms; for the third experiment, we returned to a focus on the acceptance of the leader where success and failure were introduced subsequent to the followers' initial perceptions of the leader's capability to serve as the group's spokesman; finally, the fourth experiment looked at the phenomenon from a different perspective, that of the leader's sense of his own legitimacy as a determinant of his assertions of influence.

Across conditions, we predicted in general that the leader's perceived competence should be positively related to his acceptability and influence. We also expected that his perceived motivations toward the task and toward others in the group should be positively related to these measures. We recognized, however, that perceived competence and motivation might interact statistically to determine the outcome produced by each. With reference to the "idiosyncrasy credit" concept, it might be predicted for instance that a more competent, task-oriented leader would be reacted to more positively than one of less competence who is group-oriented, even though a simple reward model might favor the latter.

In addition to this possibility of statistical interaction, there were also effects predictable from interactions with source of authority. For the present studies, two sources of leader authority were explored: appointment and election. While clearly not representative of all sources of authority, they are two characteristic and readily understandable ways by which individuals are legitimized in the status of group leader. And they can readily be seen to shape other relationships in a differential way.

III. Experiment One: An Exploration into the Phenomenology of Leadership

The first experiment sought to explore the phenomenology of leadership from the vantage point of followers. Following a procedure employed by Hollander (1961b), information was presented about a leader through a simple description technique. Subjects could then rate the acceptability of this stimulus person and thereby provide a view of the way in which the three kinds of leader characteristics already noted, alone and in various combinations, differentially affected these ratings. This approach was considered to be preparatory to the later experiments presented in sections IV, V, and VI.

A. Method

1. Subjects and Procedure

Six hundred thirty-three undergraduate men and women at the State University of New York at Buffalo participated as subjects. All were students enrolled in introductory psychology and took part during a special one-hour session of the course. The problem was presented as a study of the personal attitudes of people in groups. Salient attributes of a hypothetical leader were described and subjects were then asked to indicate their responses to him. A brief questionnaire booklet included instructions to "Think of a group to which you belong or did belong and imagine an elected leader of your own sex who is described as follows: good performer in the group activity, interested in the group activity, and interested in the members of the group." This exemplifies the several characteristics of the leader which were manipulated by systematically varying the content of the information in this description. Subjects then completed a number of ratings of the hypothetical leader.

2. Leader Characteristics

Source of leader authority was varied in three ways, by describing the leader as "elected," "appointed," or by not mentioning the source of his authority. Leader competence was also varied in three ways by describing him as a "good performer in the group activity," a "poor performer in the group activity," or by not mentioning his competence. The two aspects of leader motivation were each varied in two ways, either by describing the leader as "interested in the members of the group" or not mentioning his motivation, and by describing him as "interested in the group activity" or not mentioning his activity motivation.

3. Design

Combining all levels of these four leader characteristics, 36 hypothetical leaders were described to yield a $3 \times 3 \times 2 \times 2$ factorial design. An analysis of variance was then conducted to discern significant differences in the ratings of these leaders by cell. To compensate for inequalities of N within cells, 36 cases were deleted at random from particular cells and 15 artificial mean cases were added to other cells thus yielding 17 subjects per cell. Given the substantial size of our sample, this procedure provided computational ease without introducing between-cell variability. Degrees of freedom for the estimate of within-cell variability were, of course, appropriately reduced. Each cell of the design represented both men and women in a ratio of approximately one to two.

4. Ratings of the Leader

Reactions of subjects to the group leaders were obtained by ratings along four basic role dimensions: 1. "How willing would you be to have this person continue as the leader of the group?" (leader); 2. "How willing would you be to have this person serve as a spokesman for the group in dealing with other group leaders where important issues are at stake?" (spokesman); 3. "How willing would you be to have this person as a member of the group if you were leader?" (follower); 4. "How willing would you be to have this person as a close friend?" (friend). Each rating response was obtained on a graphic scale with six points ranging from "extremely willing" to "definitely not willing."

B. RESULTS AND DISCUSSION

Table I presents average ratings of the leader as a function of each level of the leader characteristics, collapsed across the four ratings. An overall analysis of variance of these ratings yielded significance beyond the .01 level for the factors of leader competence, interest in group members, and interest in group activity, but not for source of authority. Thus, we have confirmation of the major prediction that the leader's acceptance varies as a function of these perceived attributes.

TABLE I
MEAN RATING OF LEADER FOR EACH INDEPENDENT VARIABLE
ACROSS THE FOUR RATING SCALES
IN EXPERIMENT ONE

	Source of authority	Leader competence[a]	Member motivation[a]	Activity motivation[a]
Elected	4.53			
Appointed	4.45			
Good performer		5.28		
Poor performer		3.19		
Interested in group members			4.65	
Interested in group activities				4.69
Variable not mentioned	4.51	5.02	4.35	4.30

[a]Mean ratings in these columns were significantly different beyond the .01 level.

An additional result from this analysis, in line with prediction, is the significant interaction between the competence of the leader and his interest in the focal activity of the group ($p < .01$). Table II presents the mean ratings displaying this interaction. The contrast between ratings of leaders who were seen to perform well or poorly at the task was most striking. We note that where level of competence was not indicated, favorable endorsement of the leader was quite similar to that for "good performer." It is apparent in Table II that although the leader's interest in group activities had a significant positive impact on member reactions, its major contribution was to the status of the "poor performing" leader. A poor performer could apparently retain considerable status by evidencing a sincere interest in "playing the game." A similar trend was observed for the contribution of "interest in group members," although this failed to reach significance.

TABLE II
INTERACTION BETWEEN COMPETENCE OF LEADER AND HIS INTEREST
IN GROUP ACTIVITY ACROSS THE FOUR RATING SCALES
IN EXPERIMENT ONE[a]

	Competence of leader		
	Good	Poor	Not mentioned
Leader interested in group activity	5.34	3.58	5.15
Not mentioned	5.22	2.80	4.88

[a]The interaction between leader competence and his interest in the group activity was significant beyond the .01 level.

Before we examine the relative importance of these leader characteristics for each of the four role ratings, it is worthwhile to consider the
overall average rating for each role. These means are averages taken
across all cells of the design, and may therefore be viewed as indicating
the relative level of acceptance of a group leader in each of the four
roles. They are shown in the bottom row of Table III. In general, subjects were relatively more willing to accept these "leaders" as followers
or friends than to accept them as leaders or spokesmen. These results
support the obvious contention that group members will tend to be wary
in endorsing someone for a position of authority over them.

The overall analysis of variance also indicated significant interactions between levels of leader competence, member motivation, and activity motivation with the four types of roles. The mean ratings showing
these interactions are given in Table III. All three interactions took similar form, with levels of independent leader characteristics having a
greater effect on the two more relevant roles, i.e., leader and spokesman.
Thus, being a "poor performer on the task" resulted in a dramatic loss of
status in terms of endorsement *as a leader or spokesman*, but had less
effect on endorsement as a follower or friend.

For the most part, the findings of this first experiment confirmed our
expectations. The perceived competence of the leader and his motivations relevant to the group setting had a significant and strong impact on

TABLE III

MEAN RATING OF LEADER IN EACH ROLE FOR ALL LEVELS OF COMPETENCE,
MEMBER MOTIVATION, AND ACTIVITY MOTIVATION
IN EXPERIMENT ONE[a]

Condition		Role			
		Leader	Spokesman	Follower	Friend
Competence:	Good	5.20	5.22	5.49	5.20
	Poor	2.41	2.20	3.84	4.32
	Not mentioned	4.93	4.92	5.27	4.95
Interested in	Yes	4.38	4.35	4.90	4.95
group members:	Not mentioned	3.98	3.88	4.84	4.69
Interested in	Yes	4.39	4.39	5.05	4.95
group activity:	Not mentioned	3.97	3.83	4.70	4.70
Overall average rating[b]		4.18	4.11	4.87	4.82

[a]The interaction of each leader characteristic and the four roles was significant beyond the .01 level.

[b]All pair comparisons here were significant beyond the .01 level (by Duncan Range
Test) except between "follower" and "friend." Degrees of freedom for error equalled
1658.

group members' willingness to accept and endorse him in four distinct role relationships. The inference that these characteristics are salient features in the phenomenology of leader-follower relations is therefore well sustained.

The major variable which failed to produce significant effects, either overall or in interaction with other characteristics, was source of authority. As shown in Table I, levels of response for election and appointment were nearly identical, and certainly not different from the "blank" source of authority condition. Although the null hypothesis remains unassailable from these data, a possible methodological parameter might have rendered the source of authority unimportant in our experimental procedure. As noted above, subjects were instructed to "think of a group to which you belong or did belong and imagine an elected (appointed or not mentioned) leader of your own sex who is described as follows:." There followed a schematic box in which were presented the leader characteristics which comprised the manipulations of the competence and motivational variables. Hence, the information as to source of leader authority was less prominently displayed and may not have been "received" by our subjects.

This interpretation suggested the desirability of an early replication in which all leader characteristics were given equal prominence. Such a replication was conducted, although on a more limited scale than in the original study. The procedure was precisely the same, except that all the independent leader characteristics, including source of authority, were presented within a schematic box. The specific characteristics replicated were: 1. source of authority, *elected, appointed,* and *not mentioned*; 2. competence, *good performer* and *poor performer*; and 3. member motivation, *interested in other group members* and *not mentioned*. Combinations of levels of these three variables yielded 12 hypothetical leaders in a 3 × 2 × 2 design. Ratings were again obtained for each of the four roles. An overall analysis of variance produced results paralleling those of the main study.

Of particular interest again was the failure of source of leader authority to influence the endorsement of the leader, even though care had been taken to give this factor equal weight in the leader descriptions. In view of the size of our samples, the homogeneity of response within the studies, and the replication of results, it could be concluded that for these subjects election or appointment of the group leader was not a salient aspect of the leader-follower relationship. However, due to the artificial nature of the leadership situation with which they were confronted, it seemed best to reserve judgment and pursue the effects of this distinction under more concrete conditions in the second experiment.

IV. Experiment Two: Leader Style, Competence, and Source of Authority

In the next experiment, we extended our investigation to a laboratory situation in which these leader characteristics could be varied under conditions permitting greater control and immediacy. Once again we were interested in the source of the leader's authority, his task competence, and his motivations. In examining the last variable, we employed a manipulation that more closely approximated leader "style." We distinguished between a leader who appeared to be group-oriented as against one who appeared to be self-oriented. The former is a direct parallel to the description of the leader in the first experiment as someone "interested in group members," while the latter is its obverse. This time our major dependent variables were the leader's actual and perceived influence. A multifactor design was again employed, with two sources of leader authority, i.e., election vs. appointment, two levels of leader competence, i. e., high vs. low, and two kinds of leader style, group-oriented vs. self-oriented, thus yielding eight experimental treatments.

A. METHOD

1. Subjects and Procedure

Eighty male undergraduates enrolled in introductory psychology at the State University of New York at Buffalo participated as subjects in the experiment. They were organized into 20 groups, each composed of four true subjects plus a mock subject who in each case became the leader and accordingly served as the stimulus person for the experiment. Each of the 20 groups followed an identical procedure but for one major difference regarding either election or appointment of the leader.

In each group, subjects were seated at a table with partitions that did not allow them to see one another once they had taken their seats. The task was explained as one requiring judgments of which one of three stimulus lights on the wall went off first. It was presented as a matter requiring the recognition and communication of a sequential pattern of information to achieve a common group judgment. The actual sequence with which the stimulus lights extinguished was randomly scheduled using intervals of about .05 seconds. This differential was previously found to be unambiguous.

Following this presentation of the task, subjects filled out forms giving information about themselves and indicating their preference for appointment or election of a group leader. The leader was described as having the following functions: He would report his judgment first on any trial to the group via a signal panel; he would then take account of the other members' judgments communicated to him and would report to the experimenter what he took to be the "group judgment"; and finally, he would decide the distribution of winnings within the group. The personal information sheets were then collected by the experimenter and fictitious carbon copies of each group member's sheet were distributed to the other group members, with the explanation that they could be "read over in order to get better acquainted." Each group member actually received the same set of information about his fellows.

There were 50 trials in all. The first ten trials were described as individual test trials. For these, all members responded to the lights at the same time and there was no "communication" among group members. Performance on these trials was used to manipulate the perceived competence of the group members. For the second set of ten trials, the procedure was as described above with the leader communicating his judgment first to the other group members, and then the members presumably communicating back to the leader. At the end of this first set of *group* trials, group performance was scored and points based on the performance were ostensibly allocated to the members by the group leader. His distribution of the points was varied to manipulate the leader style variable. Then a final set of thirty group trials was conducted following the procedure described. The matching by members of the leader's initial erroneous judgments was the basis for the primary influence measure. It should be noted that the leader always made 20 incorrect judgments distributed across the last 30 trials.

At the end of the session, all members rated the leader in terms of his competence, fairness, and perceived influence, and in addition, reacted to the experiment generally in terms of their satisfaction and enjoyment. Ratings of the leaders were also obtained on ten bipolar scales of the semantic differential sort. The scales were chosen because of their previous loadings on the evaluative, potency, and activity dimensions of connotative meaning (see Osgood, Suci, & Tannenbaum, 1957).

2. *Experimental Inductions*

To manipulate the source of leader authority, the experimenter first ostensibly studied the forms on which group members indicated their preference for election or appointment of the group leader. In ten groups, taken on an alternate basis, the experimenter then announced that a majority favored election, and a contrived election was held. In the other ten groups, the experimenter appointed the leader on what appeared to be an arbitrary basis, after informing the group that there was no clear preference for either election or appointment.

Leader competence was manipulated within each group by early feedback to members regarding their ability at the task relative to the leader and the other group members. This information was communicated following the individual test trials so that two subjects in *each group* perceived the leader to be relatively more competent than they were at the task, while two perceived him to be less competent than they were. This was done with a single feedback score sheet which always showed two members distinctly superior to the others and two members inferior, with the leader always approximately in the middle.

Style of the leader was manipulated across levels of competence after the first ten group trials by having the leader appear either to divide the money earned by the group heavily in his favor (60% to himself and 10% to each of the others) or to divide it on an equal basis (20% to each). One of the two subjects in each of the pairs, who saw themselves as either more competent or less competent than the others, believed the leader to be relatively "self-oriented," while the other members of these pairs saw the leader as "group-oriented."

In any group, therefore, each subject represented one of four treatments in a two-by-two design. Depending on the cell, the leader was variously perceived to be: relatively more competent and self-oriented, more competent and group-oriented, less competent and self-oriented, or less competent and group-oriented. As previously noted, then, the design was a $2 \times 2 \times 2$ factorial, including the variables source of leader authority (election or appointment), leader style, and relative competence of the leader.

B. RESULTS AND DISCUSSION

Data reflecting the extent to which group members were influenced by the leader are displayed in Fig. 1. An analysis of variance testing these means revealed a significant main effect for leader competence only. Replicating the first experiment and previous findings, leaders seen as relatively more competent at the task were significantly more influential than were leaders seen as less competent ($F = 4.08$; $p < .05$ for 1 and 72 degrees of freedom). Effects of other leader characteristics, although not significant, are shown in trends toward greater influence exerted by the elected leader as compared with the appointed leader (8.3 *vs.* 7.1), and the greater apparent influence of the self-oriented leader as compared with the group-oriented leader (8.2 *vs.* 7.1).

In addition to the primary measure of acceptance of influence, the postsession reactions to the leader in terms of his manipulated characteristics lend further insight into the operation of these variables. Although

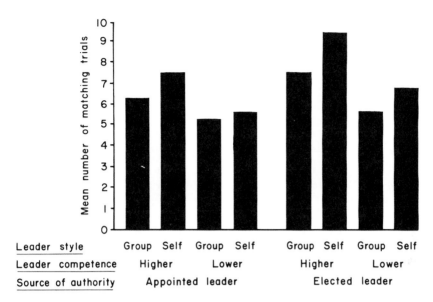

Fig. 1.   Mean number of twenty trials in Experiment Two on which subjects gave leader's erroneous judgments as their own for each treatment. $N = 10$ for each treatment.

we did not find strong effects of the two leader styles on influence, the mean postsession ratings of the fairness of the leader testified to the successful induction of the leader-style variable. Table IV shows the average ratings of leader "fairness" for each experimental condition. Leaders who were group-oriented in distributing points were rated as significantly "fairer" than those who were self-oriented ($F = 160.3$; $p <$

TABLE IV

MEAN POSTSESSION RATINGS OF LEADER FAIRNESS AND COMPETENCE
ON FIVE-POINT GRAPHIC SCALES
IN EXPERIMENT TWO[a]

	Leader style			
	Group-oriented		Self-oriented	
Competence of leader:	High	Low	High	Low
Fairness of leader	4.3	4.6	2.3	2.0
Competence of leader[b]	3.3	3.2	3.3	2.8

[a]No average differences were found as a function of source of authority. Therefore, this breakdown has been omitted.

[b]No comparisons were significant for the rated competence of the leader.

.01). As previously indicated, leaders presented as more competent exerted significantly greater influence during the group judgment task. However, they were not rated more competent following the task. This unexpected result suggested a shift in the evaluation of the leader's competence during the course of the group judgments. Postsession ratings bear the effects of the subjects having seen the group leader make a number of "questionable" judgments.

Ratings of task difficulty and of the leader's perceived influence are presented in Table V and are also pertinent to the issue of the relative competence of the leader. For the rating of task difficulty, group members who saw the leader as of low competence rated the task as significantly less difficult (3.4 *vs.* 4.1; $F = 7.9$; $p < .05$) and reported the leader as exerting less influence on their task judgments (1.5 *vs.* 2.3; $F = 15.0$; $p < .01$). These latter perceptions were, of course, quite veridical, supporting the efficacy of the induction of relative competence on the task, and the validity of the task measure of influence.

Table V also presents the subjects' postsession reactions to the experiment generally. In terms of "enjoyment of the task," no differences were found; however, significant differences emerged on the measure of "satisfaction with one's performance," as a function of both relative competence and an interaction between competence and the style of the leader. Group members who saw the leader as relatively low on competence were significantly better satisfied with their performance (3.1 *vs.* 2.1; $F = 17$; $p < .01$), and further, the orientation of the leader appeared to have a subtle influence on the degree of member satisfaction. For the group members presented with leaders of low competence, leader style had no effect, but for the opposite treatment, leader style was important. Also, group members with leaders of high competence were significantly less satisfied with their *own* performance when the

TABLE V
MEAN POSTSESSION REACTIONS TO EXPERIMENT TWO[a]

	Leader style			
	Group-oriented		Self-oriented	
Competence of leader:	High	Low	High	Low
1. Difficulty of task	4.1	3.3	4.0	3.5
2. Influence of leader	2.3	1.5	2.2	1.4
3. Enjoyment of task	3.5	3.3	3.1	3.4
4. Satisfaction with performance	1.8	3.2	2.5	3.0

[a]No average differences were found as a function of source of authority. Therefore, this breakdown has been omitted.

TABLE VI

MEAN RATINGS OF THE LEADER BY CONDITION IN EXPERIMENT TWO FOR THE
EVALUATIVE, ACTIVITY, AND POTENCY DIMENSIONS[a]

	Leader style			
	Group-oriented		Self-oriented	
Competence of leader:	High	Low	High	Low
1. Evaluative	4.3	4.5	3.7	4.0
2. Activity	2.9	2.6	2.5	2.8
3. Potency	4.1	4.0	4.3	4.1

[a]No average differences were found as a function of source of authority. Therefore, this breakdown has been omitted.

leader had acted in a group-oriented, unselfish way than when he had acted in a self-oriented way.

While source of leader authority was not by itself significant in producing leader influence, it did affect the relationship between actual and perceived influence significantly. The correlation between actual and perceived influence was .57 for the elected leader condition but only .21 for the appointed condition. This difference is significant at the .05 level and raises the interesting point that with elected leadership there exists a greater willingness to acknowledge having been influenced by the leader in one's task performance.

Supplemental information characterizing group member reactions to the leader was available from postsession semantic differential descriptions of the leader. These ratings were scored in terms of the previously identified dimensions of connotation (see Osgood et al., 1957). The mean levels of these ratings by condition are shown in Table VI. The group-oriented leaders were rated more positively on the evaluative dimension ($F = 27.7$; $p < .01$), but in terms of "activity," leader style and competence interacted, with the self-oriented, low-competence leader being seen as distinctly more active than his group-oriented counterpart ($F = 4.02$; $p < .05$). In addition, the "potency" of the leader also varied as a function of his relative competence, with the high-competence leader being described as more potent ($F = 4.44$; $p < .05$). From these descriptions it can be readily inferred that the leader's style had greater impact on the affective relation between the leader and member, but that under the short-term conditions of the group task these differences in style did not affect his ability to exert an influence on the group. Power or potency was tied exclusively to the relative competence of the leader.

In sum, we find again that the single most important variable in determining the leader's successful influence on the group was his perceived competence. Source of the leader's authority, while not a significant factor in itself, did however qualify the relationship between the group members' actual and perceived acceptance of influence. Also, leader style or orientation showed its effect in the more positive evaluations given to group-oriented than to self-oriented leaders following the completion of the task.

V. Experiment Three: Support for the Leader as Group Spokesman

We had indications in the last experiment that source of the leader's authority had relevance in an intriguing, second-order fashion to the subjects' willingness to acknowledge being influenced by the leader. But since our group task was constrained by the absence of face-to-face interaction, we believed there had been only a limited prospect for generating much feeling about the leadership process and the leader. Accordingly, we carried out a third experiment, making a distinction once again between election and appointment as bases for legitimizing leadership. This time we created a task with face-to-face contact under more naturalistic conditions, and also introduced the variable of group "success" or "failure."

Essentially, the effects of three factors were studied: (*a*) the leader's source of authority in either election or appointment; (*b*) his competence in the sense of his perceived capability on the task; and (*c*) his subsequent task success. The main dependent variable was acceptance by group members of the leader in his role as spokesman for the group. Broadly speaking, it was hypothesized that competence, along with success, would be significant determiners of the group's endorsement and that the elected spokesman would be more strongly endorsed than the appointed one, recognizing the distinct prospect of certain statistical interactions that would shape these relationships differentially.

A. METHOD

1. Subjects and Procedure

One hundred thirty-six undergraduate men at the State University of New York at Buffalo volunteered to participate as members of four-man discussion groups. At their appointed hour, an average of 20 men reported to a central screening point where they were assigned to individual rooms, four men to a room. Group discussions began with a review of a fictitious case of cheating on an exam by a hypothetical friend of the group members. Groups were told that as part of the experiment, "Roger's case" was to be presented before a board of inquiry and that their immediate task was to develop arguments for his defense. After a 20-minute discussion, an experimenter indicated that it was time to choose a spokesman to represent the group before the board in Roger's behalf. The experimenter then arranged the procedure so as to manipulate the source of authority (either election or appointment) and the perceived competence of the spokesman (either high or low).

After the spokesman was chosen, he was asked to report to another room where the inquiry would take place. The spokesman was allowed to take any notes or information from the group's discussion which he thought would be helpful. When the spokesman had left, the experimenter distributed a brief questionnaire asking for evaluations of the spokesman and the group's discussion. After a 10- to 15-minute delay the spokesman returned to his group with a sealed envelope containing the board's verdict. After opening the envelope and reading the verdict aloud, the experimenter asked the spokesman again to step outside the room while the group evaluated the verdict. Group members then filled out a second questionnaire responding to the verdict and evaluating the spokesman's performance. It was at this point that the group members indicated the strength of their endorsement of the spokesman.

2. Experimental Inductions

To manipulate the perceived competence of the spokesman, the experimenter for each group made tallies during the discussion of the frequency of participation of each member. The most frequent contributor to the discussion was chosen as the spokesman in the "high perceived competence" condition, while in the "low perceived competence" condition the member who ranked next to lowest in participation was chosen. The purpose was to identify individual group members who were perceived by their peers as more or less able to perform well as the spokesman for the group.

To manipulate his source of authority, the spokesman was either chosen by mock election or by the experimenter's appointing him. For election conditions, ballots were secret, and members rank-ordered their choices, with the winner announced after an ostensible calculation of the highest average rank. Appointment of the spokesman was made arbitrarily by the experimenter after an obvious inspection of the notations he had made during the discussion.

The manipulation of the spokesman's success or failure was distributed randomly across groups. Verdicts of "acquitted" or of "guilty," were simply handed to the spokesman before they returned to their groups. This constituted the sole basis for the group's knowledge of his success or failure.

3. Variables and Measures

The independent variables of source of authority and perceived competence formed a 2 × 2 factorial design for the first questionnaire, and then, with the addition of the success variable, they formed a 2 × 2 × 2 design for the analysis of the second questionnaire. Since there were slight discrepancies in the number of groups per cell, an unweighted means analysis was used. All scores were group averages of individual member ratings.

The major dependent measures were the ratings completed by the discussants immediately following the discussion and then following the announcement of the verdict. These questionnaires were comprised of 6-point graphic rating items. Endorsement of the group spokesman was assessed in the second questionnaire by asking: "How willing would you be to have the spokesman represent the group again?" (Table VII, item 4).

B. RESULTS AND DISCUSSION

The main findings of this experiment concern group members' reactions to and perceptions of the spokesman. In general, these indicate that the perception of the spokesman's task competence or his subsequent success led to greater endorsement by group members. While there were no average differences in the endorsement of elected versus

TABLE VII

MEAN RATINGS OF GROUP SPOKESMAN IN EXPERIMENT THREE

Variable	Competence:	Appointed		Elected	
		High (N = 8)	Low (N = 8)	High (N = 9)	Low (N = 9)
1. How much did spokesman contribute to discussion?		4.7	3.1	5.1	3.7
2. How well qualified is spokesman?		4.0	3.3	4.4	3.7
3. How satisfied with choice of spokesman?		4.4	3.7	4.6	3.8
4. How willing would you be to have spokesman represent group again?		5.1	4.4	4.9	4.2

appointed spokesmen, the impact of this source of authority became apparent in the complex and significant interaction between this variable and perceived competence and success. The nature of the interaction between success and perceived competence took quite a different form for spokesmen who had been elected than for those appointed.

1. Effects of Competence

Reactions to the spokesman gave strong testimony to the important influence of his perceived competence. Variable *1* was most similar to the criterion of competence used for the selection of the spokesman: "How much did the spokesman contribute to the discussion?" Here, differences as a function of competence were highly significant, with the more talkative spokesman rated as having contributed more to the discussion (14.7 and 10.5 for high and low competence conditions, respectively; $F = 40.1, p < .01$).

Confirming our prediction, group members were also better satisfied with the more competent spokesman (Variable *3*; $F = 4.13, p < .05$) and more willing to have him represent the group again (Variable *4*; $F = 11.2, p < .01$). These judgments were consistent with the perceived qualifications of the spokesman (Variable *2*; $F = 8.18, p < .01$). Hence, we find that the criterion of competence fits the group members' perceptions well, and that they evaluated the spokesman on this basis, with stronger endorsement given to the spokesman under those conditions in which a more competent man was chosen.

2. Effects of Source of Authority

As anticipated, there were no overall differences in reactions to the spokesman as a function of his source of authority; however, there was a tendency to evaluate the elected spokesman more positively. He was judged as having contributed more (Variable *1*; $F = 2.88, p < .10$) and as being better qualified (Variable *2*; $F = 3.99, p < .10$).

Although, as seen in Table VII, endorsement of the incompetent spokesman (Variable *4*) was low regardless of whether he was elected or appointed, the significance of source of authority did become apparent in its qualification of the effects of the spokesman's success.

3. Effects of Success

Success was defined as a verdict of acquittal, while failure was a verdict of guilty. The appropriateness of these definitions is seen in a final questionnaire item which asked: "How satisfied were you with the outcome?" Satisfaction with the acquittal verdict was rated 15.7, with the guilty verdict receiving a mean satisfaction rating of 6.2 ($F = 123.1, p <$

.01). The spokesman's success in representing the group also influenced member endorsement. Endorsement of the successful spokesman was 14.8 while the unsuccessful spokesman was rated 13.0 ($F = 7.04$, $p < .05$).

In addition to these findings, Fig. 2 displays the interactive effects of the spokesman's success with his perceived competence and source of authority. Although the level of endorsement did not differ overall for the elected or appointed spokesman, the nature of the interaction between success and perceived competence took quite a different form for the elected and appointed conditions. For the elected spokesman, an incompetent man was rejected regardless of his success at the task, whereas success increased the endorsement of a competent man. For the appointed spokesman, however, it was the competent man who was relatively immune to the effects of success or failure, while his incompetent counterpart suffered a dramatically lowered endorsement if he failed.

Returning to our original conception, we had proposed that endorsement of the group spokesman would vary significantly as a function of his perceived competence and the source of his authority. In addition, we hypothesized that the spokesman's success in representing the group

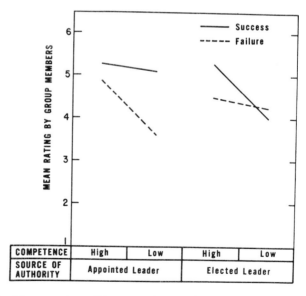

Fig. 2. Mean member willingness to have spokesman represent group again, presented for each condition, in Experiment Three.

would influence member support. These hypotheses received substantial confirmation, although there is clearly a need for clarification of the effects of election and appointment. The more competent and successful spokesmen were endorsed more strongly than less competent and unsuccessful spokesmen, respectively.

The major question remains of how election and appointment qualify endorsement of the spokesman. As noted in the results, there was a tendency to perceive the elected spokesman more positively immediately following the group discussion, although this "halo" did not carry over to the final assessments of member endorsement. In addition, the complex interaction which emerged among competence, source of authority, and the spokesman's success appeared to indicate that there were important differences in member expectations as a function of election or appointment. For the appointed spokesman, endorsement depended merely on some indication that the "system worked," i.e., that it resulted in *either* a competent choice or a successful outcome. For the elected spokesman, however, endorsement depended upon *both* a competent choice and a successful outcome. This result may be interpreted as supporting the general position that *election builds higher expectations for success or higher demands by group members on the leadership role.* When the spokesman was appointed, members were more readily satisfied and responded positively to any sign of a positive result. When he was elected, members failed to support him if he was incompetent or unsuccessful.

If anything, this interaction indicates that election, rather than making the spokesman more secure and immune from task effects, creates a situation in which the spokesman is more vulnerable. This vulnerability may result from the greater involvement and responsibility which group members feel under election conditions, producing a stronger sense of control over the authority structure of the group. Hence, they show a greater willingness to consider alternatives. If their first choice of spokesman did not work out, they could try someone else next time around. Under appointment conditions, however, there was no assurance that members would be involved in any subsequent choice of the spokesman.

VI. Experiment Four: Leader Legitimacy and Attempted Innovation

From the earlier work presented here, it is clear that the source of the leader's authority does have an effect on followers, even in subtle ways. To review briefly, we found in Experiment Two that for elected leaders, in comparison to appointed leaders, there was a significantly stronger relationship between the followers' actual acceptance of the leader's influence attempts and their reports of having been influenced by him. In Experiment Three we saw evidence that the "success" or "failure" of an elected or appointed leader was differentially reacted to by followers, especially in regard to their continued endorsement of him in his role as leader. Thus, depending upon the followers' perception of the leader's initial competence, elected leaders were more vulnerable to a withdrawal of endorsement when they had been unsuccessful in representing the group. This finding lends support to the proposition that election, at least in this context, builds higher demands by group members on the leader's role.

As we have suggested, the group is likely to feel a greater investment in elected leaders, especially when such leadership is both desired and possible to attain. Along with this investment, the elected leader may also be someone to whom the group gives greater latitude to act in behalf of group goals. This interpretation is in line with the "idiosyncrasy credit" concept that a person gains credits which he may then draw on in exerting influence, particularly through innovations from normative expectancies. An experiment by Hollander (1960) revealed that such assertions were likely to have an effect on both the procedures for guiding the group's activity and the actual content of the group's task. For this process to work, however, the person who is a leader must be aware that these credits are at his disposal; he must, in short, sense his legitimacy. Accordingly, our emphasis in this next experiment turned to how the leader's perception of his own legitimacy determines his expressions of deviation. The term "deviation" refers here to an attempt to redirect the group's effort at a task solution. Using the idiosyncrasy credit concept of nonconformity as a feature of higher status, we may consider a willingness to deviate from the group as an indicator of attempted influence. It may also be that deviation reveals resistance to conformity pressures from the group. Thus, the leader may manifest his sense of legitimacy and higher status by assertions of influence or by his resistance to pressures from the others in the group.

It follows from the concept of gaining credits that the elected leader, in light of his supposed choice by the group, will already sense support from the others; for the appointed leader, such support may still need to be gained. The latter may indeed have to overcome the prevailing disposition that a leader should be elected. Therefore, when team members come together as a new group, election should provide a greater sense of credit than does appointment. This ought to be so in many circumstances in which groups, such as committees, are newly organizing for mutual activity. On the other hand, where appointed leadership is characteristic, as in many institutional structures, the legitimacy which goes with the role normally vests the incumbent with the expectancy of having influence. Even with such backing, however, the need exists for him to gain credits through appropriate actions as a leader.

With these considerations in mind, we predicted that where group members expect that leaders may be elected as well as appointed, elected leaders should display greater constructive deviation, as acts of influence assertion, than appointed leaders. We also predicted that a sense of strong endorsement should heighten this deviation. Thus, both source of authority and strength of endorsement as bases for legitimacy should contribute to the leader's willingness to attempt influence or counter-influence. In addition, we expected that, when they are deviating, elected and appointed leaders should differ in the amount and kind of communication they direct to their followers. With a greater sense of legitimacy, the leader's need to justify and conciliate should be lessened. Thus, his messages to the group should be less elaborate in these respects.

A. METHOD

1. Task and Setting

The task was specifically selected to engage interest and to permit the free flow of discussion among subjects in the first phase of an essentially quasinaturalistic experiment. Subsequently, it was to serve as a reasonable vehicle for the clash of ideas so as to assess the willingness of subjects placed in the position of "team leader" to overturn proposals from their team members.

For the first phase of the experiment, 52 male students from introductory psychology classes at the State University of New York at Buffalo took part in one of four discussion sessions. Each of these sessions drew at least 12 subjects, and all four were treated in as comparable a way as possible. Students had volunteered for this study of "group decision making in urban planning" from among other alternative studies available to them. Participation in research was part of their course requirement.

Once assembled for the discussion session, the subjects were provided with name tags and seated in a circle with an identifying number before them. A faculty member was introduced to them as an "expert in urban problems" who would serve as the discussion leader. Orientation materials were then distributed in which they were told: "As we all know, our cities are faced now with a multitude of problems ranging from financial shortages to major social ills. You are here today to help decide which of the problems a city faces appear to be most critical, and what actions can be taken to help alleviate these problems. Our procedure today also will help in looking at the decision-making processes involved in coping with these problems." They were then asked to read a description of about 700 words which had been developed by the Western Behavioral Sciences Institute to cover the problems of an imaginary city dubbed "Colossus." Subjects were then asked to write down the problems they individually considered to be most important, after which each would have a chance to voice his views on these.

The discussion period lasted approximately 40 minutes. Subjects were told that this was a time for them to shape their ideas and to get to know the opinions of others. The level of evident involvement was high. At the close of the discussion, the group was told that the discussion group members would now be separated and reconstituted into three teams, each consisting of a task leader and his staff. Subjects were further informed that the leaders would be separated from the others in their group, although they could pass messages to each other, largely to determine how communication processes affect decisions about ways to deal with big city problems.

2. Design and Induction of Treatments

From each discussion session, ten subjects were isolated in rooms for the second phase of the experiment, the induction of the experimental conditions. Two raters observing the group discussions in the first phase had been tallying interactions to ascertain which subjects among the 12 or more participated least; these subjects remained behind in the discussion room while the other 10 went to their assigned rooms. On arriving there, half of the subjects found an election ballot on which to nominate three people for team leader, by name or number, whichever they recalled; these subjects were in an election condition.

After a few minutes, each subject in the election condition was informed by an experimenter that he had been elected to lead a team, while each person in the appointed condition learned that the expert who had served as discussion leader had chosen him as a team leader. Cutting across these treatments, half of the subjects were told that they were the "top choice" for the leader position and would lead "Team A," and the other half were told they were the "third choice" and would lead "Team C." The result was a 2×2 factorial design with two sources of authority, and two levels of strength of endorsement. Given the five subjects each in the election and appointment conditions, following each discussion session, a counterbalanced number of subjects (2-3, 3-2) was assigned to the strong and not strong endorsement conditions. Furthermore, with four sessions it was possible to have each subject assigned to a particular room following each discussion session to be representative of a different cell in the design. Thus, each room was used only once for each of the treatments, thereby reducing any possible position effects.

3. Dependent Measures

Once isolated, all of the subjects were provided with a sheet listing various urban problems and four action programs for each problem area. In order, the ten problem areas were: Education, Welfare, Culture and Recreation, Housing, Urban Renewal and Beautification, Fiscal Affairs, Race Relations, Police and Riot Control, Industrial and Economic Development, and Transportation.

When each subject had been told he was to be a team leader, he was also provided with a sheet entitled "Task-Group Procedure." This gave him full instructions for the third phase of the experiment. It indicated that the team would be discussing each of the ten problem areas and would consider the four action programs proposed to alleviate each. On a "communication form" the team would then be ranking all four action programs within a problem area by placing a "1" in front of the program they favored most, a "2" before the one they favored next, and so on through "3" to "4," the one they favored least of all.

Each communication form was delivered to the team leader by an experimenter; the leader's task was to decide which of the four action programs should be put into effect. He did this by sending his own rankings back to the team on the same form with any comments he wished to make as a message to the team. In actuality, all of these communication forms had been prepared in advance with the alleged team rankings. The first and third, dealing respectively with the problem areas of Education, and Culture and Recreation, were presented with the actual preference rankings obtained from a pilot study with 17 male subjects drawn from the same population of introductory psychology students. The forms for the other eight problem areas were contrived to present the "team leaders" with precisely the reverse ranking from the true preference order obtained from the subjects in the pilot study. The last seven presentations of these erroneous rankings, beginning with the fourth problem area, "Housing," constituted the seven "critical trials" in sequence. The format for this form is shown below as an illustration of the general pattern employed.

The major dependent variable was the number of critical trials on

COMMUNICATION FORM—4

Indicate your ranking of these action programs in the column marked "Leader's Ranking." Your first choice should be marked "1," your second "2," and so on. Whatever you choose as "1" will be recorded as your team's recommendation.

HOUSING

Team Ranking	Leader's Ranking	
————	————	Construct a "satellite city" offering housing for families at every income level.
————	————	Convert public-housing projects into cooperatives — owned and run by the residents.
————	————	Create a city-housing authority to own and rent housing in the city.
————	————	Sponsor low-cost private housing for poor families, with no down payments and long-term mortgages.

Any Comment:

Fig. 3.   Example of the form used for communicating the team's decisions to their leader.

which the subjects reversed the team's first choice. A reversal would mean assigning a "4" to the action program the team had supposedly marked "1," and a "1" to the action program marked "4." Other dependent measures were obtained through a postdecision questionnaire, which contained five scales, and an analysis of the volume and content of the "comments" the subjects sent back to their teams on the communication forms.

Following consideration of the last of the ten problem areas, subjects were asked to fill out the postdecision questionnaire and were then brought together for a briefing about the nature of the experiment and the inductions employed. The responses to two open-ended items on that questionnaire ("Why were you chosen the leader of one of the three urban planning teams?" and "Would you please take a moment and comment on the nature of your experience as leader of a decision team and your ideas about the hypotheses under investigation?") revealed relatively few signs of suspiciousness about the procedure employed. Indeed, the bulk of subjects found no difficulty whatever in giving a response to the first question in line with either their election or appointment, and with evident satisfaction at having been selected for the role.

B. Results and Discussion

1. Constructive Deviation

Figure 4 shows the major finding regarding the differential deviation of appointed and elected leaders under the two conditions of endorsement, strong or not strong. The index used in this figure is the mean number of trials, out of the seven critical trials, when the leader totally reversed the team's first-rank choice. Recall that four options are provided to be rank-ordered, and that these are presented in a preference order precisely opposite to the actual preference ranking of similar subjects. As will be seen in this figure, elected leaders deviated from their teams considerably more than appointed leaders, and in each case the presence of strong endorsement tended to increase this deviation. The highest reading is for elected leaders under conditions of strong endorsement, a value of 3.4, which indicates that on approximately half of the

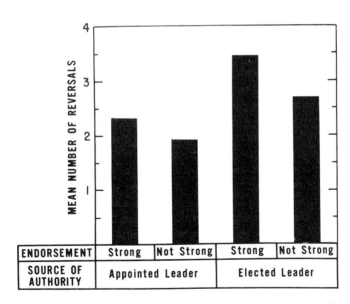

Fig. 4. Mean number of seven critical trials on which leaders reversed team's first rank choice in Experiment Four. $N = 10$ Ss for each treatment.

seven critical trials these leaders totally overturned the team's judgment. An analysis of variance of these data yielded a significant effect for source of authority ($F = 5.11$, $df = 1/36$, $p < .05$).

This finding represents a highly specific confirmation of our main hypothesis. More generally, however, we find that the sum of all deviations from the group rankings on seven trials is significantly higher for elected than appointed leaders. A chi-square analysis shows elected leaders to be significantly inclined toward higher deviation and appointed leaders toward lower deviation ($X^2 = 5.18$, $df = 1$, $p < .05$).

2. Postdecision Ratings

With regard to the success of the inductions, Table VIII provides a number of relevant findings. In response to the first item, as expected, elected leaders reported themselves as having more support. Here again, a chi-square analysis yielded a significant difference between the elected and appointed leaders ($X^2 = 3.8$, $df = 1$, $p < .05$).

TABLE VIII

MEAN RATINGS ON QUESTIONNAIRE ITEMS FOR EXPERIMENT FOUR[a]

	Source of authority and strength of endorsement			
	Appointed leader		Elected leader	
Items	Strong ($N = 8$)	Not strong ($N = 10$)	Strong ($N = 10$)	Not strong ($N = 10$)
1. To what extent team members supported you as their choice for task leader.	3.1	2.7	3.7	3.3
2. To what extent you agreed with planning judgments recommended by your team.	2.8	2.5	2.8	2.5
3. How competent you think you are to recommend policy on urban problems.	3.9	3.8	4.0	4.6
4. How much you enjoyed participating in this study.	4.9	4.9	4.5	4.8
5. How much restrictions on communication affected your final decisions.	4.0	3.6	3.7	4.7

[a]Ratings were on six-point scales, positively oriented.

In connection with the report of agreement with the judgments recommended by the members of the team, the second item of Table VIII reveals no significant difference by treatment. Accordingly, a further analysis was done, employing tetrachoric correlation, to test the association between the deviation reported and the actual sum of a subject's deviations on the seven critical items. The coefficient obtained was .78, with $p < .01$.

Regarding perceived competence in the handling of urban problems, the third item in Table VIII reveals differences which produced significant main effects for both source of authority and strength of endorsement, as well as a significant interaction term. The highest F obtained was for source of authority ($F = 14.70$, $df = 1/36$, $p < .001$), with elected leaders significantly more inclined to see themselves as competent. The main effect for endorsement was less pronounced ($F = 4.41$, $df = 1/36$, $p < .05$). The interaction term, as already noted, was also significant ($F = 9.55$, $df = 1/36$, $p < .01$), and is attributable to the high mean of 4.6 for elected leaders without strong endorsement. This finding is anomalous and will be discussed subsequently.

For the fourth item in Table VIII, enjoyment in participating in the study, no significant difference was found between the treatments, in line with expectation. In general, however, it is noteworthy that all of the means for this item approximate a value of 5 on the 6-point scales, thus revealing a uniformly high degree of enjoyment. For the fifth item, regarding the effect of the restrictions on communication in reaching decisions, a significant interaction was obtained by analysis of variance ($F = 4.50$, $df = 1/36$, $p < .05$). Here again, elected leaders with less strong endorsement showed the high value.

3. Leader Communications

Figure 5 summarizes the results dealing with the number of words used in communications to the team when the leader totally reverses the team's first choice. An analysis of variance revealed a nearly significant main effect for strength of endorsement ($F = 3.01$, $df = 1/36$, $p < .10 > .05$). The strongly endorsed leaders used fewer words when reversing their team's rankings.

Pursuing a related consideration regarding the nature of communications, a content analysis was undertaken of the messages directed to the teams by each of the subjects as leaders. The messages from each were rated independently by the three investigators without knowledge of condition on a scale that ranged from 0 to 3. The quality which proved to have the greatest reliability of ratings, and the greatest relevance to the issues under study here, was referred to as "group orienta-

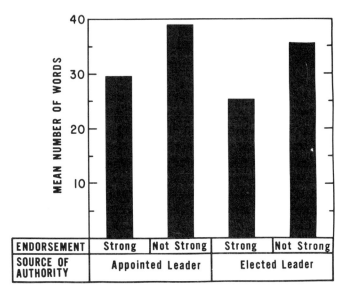

Fig. 5.   Mean number of words contained in written messages from leaders to teams on trials where team's first rank choice is reversed in Experiment Four. $N = 10$ Ss for each treatment.

tion." This is taken to be a willingness to show a recognition of the viewpoint of the team and to conciliate differences. The corrected reliability of this measure, for three raters, was .89. Figure 6 reports the average ratings obtained, on the rating scale of 0 to 3, for leaders in the four treatment conditions. As can be seen, those *least* likely to reveal such an orientation in their messages to members were the elected leaders with strong endorsement. The interaction term, in an analysis of variance, was significant ($F = 6.95$, $df = 1/36$, $p < .01$).

Overall, these findings provide substantial additional evidence of the effects of election or appointment on leader behavior. The leader's sense of legitimacy does appear to be a compelling factor in determining his willingness to assert influence through constructive deviation. Evidently, the leader acts with an awareness of his source of authority, and this has consequences in his responses to the team.

Specific aspects of the results are also in accord with our expectations. Thus, the strongly endorsed elected leader not only deviates significantly more, but he also uses fewer words in his messages to the team when deviating. Furthermore, his messages in general reveal less conciliation and, presumably, less need to justify his position. Alternatively, the appointed leader without strong endorsement appears by comparison to be far weaker as a source of influence, in terms of these measures. Both aspects of legitimacy are therefore found to be effective in producing the leader's response to followers.

Among the results from the postdecision questionnaire are two unexpectedly high means for elected leaders without strong endorsement (see Table VIII, items 3 and 5). The first of these is not in accord with prediction. One may conjecture that some kind of compensatory reaction is being expressed to reveal a greater sense of competence in the absence of strong endorsement. In the case of the effect of restriction of communication, shown in item 5, again the elected leaders without strong endorsement appear to be affected most. All in all, these results suggest that the elected leader expects strong endorsement, as a function of the very process by which he was cast in the leader's role, and that its absence may prove disquieting.

VII. Conclusions and Implications

The findings from these experiments point to several conclusions, both general and specific. On the most general level, it seems eminently clear that the study of leadership can be fruitfully pursued in terms of

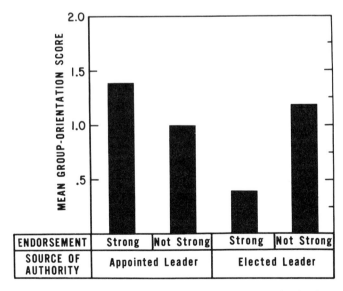

Fig. 6.   Mean Group-Orientation Score from content analysis of written messages from leaders to teams in Experiment Four. $N = 10$ Ss for each treatment.

interpersonal processes, notably the perceptions and expectations of followers. The observed attributes and actions of the leader have a discernible role in creating the impressions which contribute to his legitimacy. Furthermore, as the last experiment indicated, the leader's sense of his legitimacy has a direct impact on his willingness to assert influence.

There is also substantial support in these findings for the efficacy of multifactor designs in the study of leadership phenomena. Several variables may be looked at in combination to reveal their interactions. Indeed, among the more repetitive findings is the extent to which these interactions govern outcomes. Thus, while we had consistent confirmation of the leader's perceived competence as a significant determinant of his acceptability and influence, we also found that this relationship was affected by the followers' perceptions of the leader's motivation. In the first experiment, for example, there was a significant interaction between the leader's perceived competence and his perceived interest in the group's activity. The consequence of this interaction effect was most evident for the allegedly "poor performing" leader who apparently could retain his status when seen as having a sincere interest in that activity.

These relationships are further qualified by the contextual effects of the leader's source of authority. Whether he is elected or appointed also matters, especially under conditions of strain. In the third experiment, for example, the members' support for the elected leader depended both on his initially perceived competence for the role of spokesman and a successful outcome of his activity in behalf of the group; on the other hand, support for the appointed leader appeared to depend on either the perception of his competence or a successful outcome. This suggests, as we mentioned earlier, that election builds higher demands on the leadership role, at least by group members in this situation. It is by no means clear, however, whether this finding will hold where different kinds of group tasks and settings are involved. It is no great surmise to suggest that such differences should shape expectations regarding the leader's source of authority and what its payoffs ought to be. For instance, the relatively stronger position of the appointed leader in the third experiment does not jibe with at least one other relevant finding from the research of Carter, Haythorn, Shriver, and Lanzetta (1951): Their data indicated that the emergent leader was in a more favorable position. It is noteworthy that the dependent measures used in that study were somewhat different from those employed in our work. Yet the point is worth making that characteristics of the setting itself may shade the factor of favorability for the leader, an influence on which Fiedler (1967) has laid particular stress.

In this same vein, the results of the last experiment indicated broadly that the elected leader felt more confident and was more willing to exert influence through constructive deviation from the group's judgments than was the appointed leader. Unlike the third experiment, we did not introduce the variable of success or failure, nor did we examine the reactions of followers to the leader, since neither was a primary focus. Further research can deal with these relationships more fully. In any event, we have confirmation in this last experiment that, given a situation in which it is appropriate to have an elected leader, the incumbent of that role senses the idiosyncrasy credits at his disposal and can expend them through deviation from the group. Within a situation laden with formal organizational constraints, the expectation that there even could be an elected leader would be severely limited and this finding would be unlikely.

Another point that requires attention is the confinement imposed by research over a limited time span in the laboratory. As we moved toward increasingly naturalistic settings in the third and fourth experiments, we found it increasingly possible to study the dynamics of leadership attainment and maintenance. Though difficult to manage at times, the introduction of more reality in the task heightened the involvement of the participants and the scope of our findings. In addition to the often heard injunction to extend research into the field, which seems reasonable enough, it may also prove helpful to create "quasinaturalistic" experiments along the lines of our later studies.

Since leadership implicates various leader roles, beyond the traditional function summed up by Hemphill (1961) as "initiating structure," there is considerable room for studying these functions. In the third experiment we considered the spokesman as an occupant of a leader role, and in the fourth experiment we ventured into decision-making and innovating functions. These distinctions deserve more attention in research on leadership than they have thus far received. Also, additional study might be turned to the sequence implied by attaining a leader role and then maintaining it successfully. Those starting mechanisms which operate in emergent leadership (cf. Hollander, 1961a) may be quite critical in determining the leader's subsequent acceptance and influence, but this process needs to be more fully detailed through research.

We embarked upon this set of experiments within a process-oriented, transactional framework. It has afforded the basis for looking into interpersonal processes of perception and exchange in leadership. On balance, that framework appears to be well sustained as an avenue by which we can understand the workings of these phenomena better.

REFERENCES

Alvarez, R. Informal reactions to deviance in simulated work organizations: A laboratory experiment. *American Sociological Review*, 1968, **33**, 895-912.

Berkowitz, L., & Macaulay, J. R. Some effects of differences in status level and status stability. *Human Relations*, 1961, **14**, 135-148.

Carter, L. F., Haythorn, W., Meirowitz, B., & Lanzetta, J. The relation of categorizations and ratings in the observation of group behavior. *Human Relations*, 1951, 4, 239-254.

Carter, L. F., Haythorn, W., Shriver, E., & Lanzetta, J. The behavior of leaders and other group members. *Journal of Abnormal and Social Psychology*, 1951, **46**, 589-595.

Carter, L. F., & Nixon, M. An investigation of the relationship between four criteria of leadership ability for three different tasks. *Journal of Psychology*, 1949, **27**, 245-261.

Cohen, A. M., & Bennis, W. G. Continuity of leadership in communication networks. *Human Relations*, 1961, **14**, 351-367.

Croner, M. D., & Willis, R. H. Perceived differences in task competence and asymmetry of dyadic influence. *Journal of Abnormal and Social Psychology*, 1961, **62**, 705-708.

Fiedler, F. E. *A theory of leadership effectiveness.* New York: McGraw-Hill, 1967.

Fouriezos, N. T., Hutt, M. L., and Guetzkow, H. Measurement of self-oriented needs in discussion groups. *Journal of Abnormal and Social Psychology*, 1950, **45**, 682-690.

Gibb, C. A. The principles and traits of leadership. *Journal of Abnormal and Social Psychology*, 1947, **42**, 267-284.

Goffman, E. *The presentation of self in everyday life.* Garden City, N. Y.: Doubleday Anchor, 1959.

Goldman, M., & Fraas, L. A. The effects of leader selection on group performance. *Sociometry*, 1965, **28**, 82-88.

Harvey, O. J., & Consalvi, C. Status and conformity to pressures in informal groups. *Journal of Abnormal and Social Psychology*, 1960, **60**, 182-187.

Hemphill, J. K. The leader and his group. *Education Research Bulletin*, 1949, **28**, 225-229, 245-246.

Hemphill, J. K. Why people attempt to lead. In L. Petrullo & B. M. Bass (Eds.), *Leadership and interpersonal behavior.* New York: Holt, Rinehart & Winston, 1961. Pp. 201-215.

Hollander, E. P. Conformity, status, and idiosyncrasy credit. *Psychological Review*, 1958, **65**, 117-127.

Hollander, E. P. Competence and conformity in the acceptance of influence. *Journal of Abnormal and Social Psychology*, 1960, **61**, 365-369.

Hollander, E. P. Emergent leadership and social influence. In L. Petrullo & B. M. Bass (Eds.), *Leadership and interpersonal behavior.* New York: Holt, Rinehart & Winston, 1961. Pp. 30-47. (a)

Hollander, E. P. Some effects of perceived status on responses to innovative behavior. *Journal of Abnormal and Social Psychology*, 1961, **63**, 247-250. (b)

Hollander, E. P. *Leaders, groups, and influence.* New York: Oxford University Press, 1964.

Hollander, E. P., & Julian, J. W. Leadership. In E. Borgatta & W. W. Lambert (Eds.), *Handbook of personality theory and research.* Chicago: Rand McNally, 1968. Pp. 890-899.

Hollander, E. P., & Julian, J. W. Contemporary trends in the analysis of leadership processes. *Psychological Bulletin*, 1969, **71**, 387-397.

Homans, G. C. *Social behavior: its elementary forms.* New York: Harcourt, Brace & World, 1961.

Julian, J. W., & Steiner, I. D. Perceived acceptance as a determinant of conformity behavior. *Journal of Social Psychology*, 1961, 55, 191-198.

Katz, D., & Kahn, R. *The social psychology of organizations.* New York: Wiley, 1966.

Mann, R. D. A review of the relationships between personality and performance in small groups. *Psychological Bulletin*, 1959, 56, 241-270.

Mausner, B. The effect of one partner's success in a relevant task on the interaction of observer pairs. *Journal of Abnormal and Social Psychology*, 1954, 49, 557-560.

Osgood, C. E., Suci, G. J., & Tannenbaum, P. H. *The measurement of meaning.* Urbana, Ill.: University of Illinois Press, 1957.

Raven, B. H., & French, J. R. P. Legitimate power, coercive power, and observability in social influence. *Sociometry*, 1958, 21, 89-97.

Sabath, G. The effect of disruption and individual status on person perception and group attraction. *Journal of Social Psychology*, 1964, 64, 119-130.

Stogdill, R. M. Personal factors associated with leadership: A survey of the literature. *Journal of Psychology*, 1948, 25, 35-71.

Wiggins, J. A., Dill, F., & Schwartz, R. D. On "status-liability." *Sociometry*, 1965, 28, 197-209.

EXPERIMENTAL STUDIES OF NEGRO-WHITE RELATIONSHIPS

Irwin Katz[1]

UNIVERSITY OF NEW YORK
GRADUATE CENTER OF THE CITY

I. Introduction

A. CURRENT STATUS OF RACE RESEARCH

The experimental study of Negro-white relationships is a relatively unexplored field offering unique research opportunities. Until now, most social psychological research on race has been narrowly concerned with the study of verbal prejudice. The marked extent to which social action has been neglected is revealed in a recent review of the literature on race and ethnic relations by Harding, Proshansky, Kutner, and Chein (1969). Approximately eight times as much space is allotted to work on attitudes as to overt behavioral studies. Within the attitudinal domain the chief

[1]Most of this paper was written while the author was at the Educational Testing Service as a Visiting Scholar.

topics are the description of prejudice by means of verbal scales, and the search for individual and demographic correlates. Moreover, only a few methodologically adequate experiments on attitude *change* are mentioned. The sad fact is that over 40 years of fairly active investigation of race and racism in America have had only minimal impact upon the development of social psychological theory, perhaps the only contribution of broad theoretical interest being the work of Adorno, Frenkel-Brunswik, Levinson, and Sanford (1950) and others on the authoritarian personality.

To some extent the limitations of past research on race relations reflected the realities of an earlier era when rigid, caste-like constraints on Negro-white interactions largely precluded studies of social behavior across the color line. Furthermore, because many investigators regarded the attitudes of the dominant majority as the main barrier to change in the *status quo*, they deemed it appropriate to concentrate their attention on those attitudes. But it is now recognized (e.g., Clark, 1965; Hyman, 1969; Rossi, 1963; Williams, 1965) that the more open contemporary situation calls for new directions in research, with greater emphasis upon studies of social action.

There remains the question of whether the relative sterility of race research should be blamed mainly on its descriptive and applied emphases or on its intrinsic nature. In support of the latter view, it can be argued that the phenomena associated with Negro-white relationships are reducible to the same components that are to be found in a broad range of other social phenomena involving status differences. But even if there are no psychological processes unique to race relations, the field still merits considerable attention. As van den Berghe (1967) has noted, the fact that race in the United States is a special, identifiable, and extreme instance of invidious status differentiation makes it an especially strategic vantage point for analysis of social behavior. It affords a stronger and more lasting variation of a number of factors related to social stratification than could ever be created by laboratory manipulations. On the negative side, one must of course deal with the methodological difficulties that inevitably arise when complex, real-life phenomena are investigated directly. What is presently needed in the race area is a synthesis, within one general framework, of the experimental and quasi-experimental data that already exist, so that critical issues can be identified. This paper represents an effort in that direction.

B. SOME GENERAL ASSUMPTIONS ABOUT AMERICAN NEGRO-WHITE RELATIONSHIPS

Present Negro-white relationships in this country are rooted in conflict: a long subordinated minority group is pressing to improve its status in the face of strong resistance from a superordinate majority. The resistance, however, is somewhat mitigated by the majority's increased awareness of racial injustices. Some recent writers (e.g., Blalock, 1967; Matthews, 1969) have proposed analyzing the conflict in terms of the power resources available to each party and the readiness of each to employ its resources.

Whites, as the dominant group, generally have more resources at hand to defend their favored position than Negroes have to improve theirs. But change presumably can occur when whites do not fully mobilize their resources for resistance, or when Negroes are able to convert their present limited resources into new and more effective ones. For example, in their analysis of race politics, Matthews and Prothro (1966) observe that southern Negroes have one major resource – numbers, which can be converted into an important political resource – votes. However, whether the vote can be translated into power to mold public policy will depend upon the reaction of southern whites, most of whom still oppose the Negro's political objectives. Matthews and Prothro point out that although southern whites tend to have overwhelmingly superior resources for political ends, there has been a great deal of "slack" in their utilization of these resources in the past; but the more threatened they feel by evidence of rising Negro political power in the future, the more their disproportionate resources will be invested in politics and the less "slack" there will be. Similarly, whether Negroes can improve their outcomes in such areas as jobs, housing, and education seemingly depends on their ability to make the most of relatively meager resources without increasing the majority group's motivation to resist.

All this suggests that in the study of Negro-white relationships, a crucial aspect of the behavior of whites is the causal determination of reactions to the minority group's efforts to attain racial equality. When are negative reactions – such as interference with personal achievement efforts, exclusion from situations of opportunity, and avoidance of social contacts – likely to occur? Under what circumstances can one expect positive reactions of helping, including, accepting, and the like? Three types of psychological factors seem to be important determinants of white behavior towards Negroes: self-interest, cognitive-emotional predispositions, and social conformity pressure. Each will be discussed briefly.

In the race relations literature, threat of value loss is the aspect of self-interest in the dominant group that has received the most attention. Blalock (1967) distinguishes three basic types of racial threat that whites can experience: status, power, and economic competition. He believes that each type may have its own unique consequences for white behavior. Rokeach's research (e.g., Rokeach & Mezei, 1966) suggests that perceived disparity in beliefs may be another important source of racial threat. Regarding the positive aspect of self-interest, a few investigations (e.g., Allport, 1954; Deutsch & Collins, 1951; Sherif, 1958) have dealt with the tendency toward reduced hostility between groups engaged in cooperative pursuit of common goals.

The strength of various types of positive and negative white self-interest factors (i.e., threat of loss and promise of gain) in a given situation will probably depend on some or all of the following: (a) the behavior of Negro stimulus persons, (b) objective features of the situation, (c) the perceiver's racial attitudes and beliefs, (d) the perceiver's personality, and (e) the perceiver's status, power, and economic position within the white group. In analyzing whites' perceptual reactions, a promising lead is provided by Jones and Davis' (1965) discussion of the influence of the hedonic relevance of an action on interpretations of the actor's intention.

As mentioned earlier, whites' cognitive-emotional predispositions toward nonwhite minorities have probably been studied more often than any other race topic. The great bulk of this research has been concerned exclusively with prejudice, and has been mostly nonexperimental. But a small number of investigations have dealt more or less systematically with effects of prejudice on observed behavior toward racial stimuli, and effects of interracial contact experiences on amount of prejudice. The findings from these studies are amenable to analysis in terms of cognitive consistency principles such as those proposed by Insko and Schopler (1967) and Fishbein (1966).

Racial attitudes other than prejudice have been neglected. Yet one suspects that interactions between (a) prejudice and (b) predispositions, such as sympathy for the underdog and guilt over racial injustice, are much more important than prejudice alone in the determination of white behavior toward Negroes. The wide swings in popular willingness to accommodate the Negro's civil rights demands during the past two decades suggest a phenomenon of *ambivalence* rather than simple attitudes of hostility or friendliness.

Finally, social conformity pressures are probably an important determinant of behavior toward outgroups, operating in the directions of both greater acceptance and greater rejection. Since there has been virtually no systematic research on conformity processes in the field of race relations, it will be mentioned only tangentially in this paper.

Turning to the Negro side of the equation, it was stated earlier that minority group members must acquire and utilize resources they do not now possess if they are to gain a larger share of society's benefits. Of particular importance are the personal resources requisite for economic success, such as intellectual-academic skills. Increasingly, cognitive skills must be learned and applied in integrated classrooms and job settings where cross-racial social interactions and social comparisons can strongly influence performance. Even in segregated situations, white achievement standards may be explicitly employed by authorities for evaluative purposes. The study of cross-racial influences on Negro achievement behavior provides interesting opportunities to apply reference group and social comparison concepts (cf. Pettigrew, 1967), achievement motivation concepts (cf. Atkinson, 1964), and other types of social psychological theory.

A large Negro autobiographical literature attests that face-to-face contacts with white persons are often stressful because the minority person is exposed to the possibility of being derogated and/or rejected. Elsewhere, this author (Katz, 1964) has discussed the likely impact of biracial social stress factors on the cognitive functioning of nonwhite individuals. It was assumed that degree of stress would be directly related to the amount of white hostility displayed, the amount of power possessed by whites in the contact situation, and the extent to which minority members felt intellectually inferior. A further assumption can be made: the Negro's fear of reprisals by white peers will be strong when it appears that his successful achievement may be highly threatening to their interests. In addition to social threat factors, Negro behavior could be adversely affected by low expectancy of success when competing against a white standard of excellence.

However, when these negative motivational factors are at a minimum, it is conceivable that the incentive value of success in biracial situations could be greater than in all-Negro situations, due to the potentially greater value of cross-racial comparisons for self appraisals of ability, and the greater satisfaction associated with receiving approval from members of the dominant, high-status group.

This paper will present evidence bearing upon many of the foregoing assumptions. Clearly, the depiction of the basic features of American race relations is far from complete, but the intention has been to limit the assumptions made here to those that are necessary for interpreting the existing empirical data. On the whole, the review that follows will present only studies involving (a) social behavior or social perception variables, and (b) at least a modicum of experimental control. Most of the investigations tend to fall readily into two categories, according to whether the main focus was on white or Negro subjects. For this reason, and also for convenience in analysis, each racial group will be considered separately.

II. Studies of White Subjects

Research on the majority group's reactions to members of nonwhite minorities can be divided into five categories. There are studies of (a) the effect of interracial contact on racial attitudes, (b) the effect of racial attitudes on behavior toward Negroes, (c) the social reinforcer effectiveness of Negro experimenters, (d) intimate biracial contacts, and (e) social interactions in biracial work groups. These will be discussed below.

A. INTERRACIAL CONTACT AND ATTITUDE CHANGE

Many attitude surveys, dating back to World War II, show a positive relationship between reported personal contact with nonwhites and racial tolerance. Also, white adults and children in racially integrated school, job, and residential situations have usually scored lower on measures of prejudice than whites in segregated environments. To cite a recent example of such findings, Williams (1964), reporting on surveys of representative adult samples in six cities throughout the country, stated that ". . . in all the surveys and in all the communities and for all groups, majority and minorities, the greater the frequency of interaction, the lower the prevalence of ethnic prejudice" [p. 167]. On the whole, the entire literature (recently reviewed by Amir, 1969; Pettigrew, 1969) is consistent with Allport's (1954) well-known hypothesis that intergroup contacts involving shared interests or goals, equal status of participants, and normative support tend to reduce prejudice.

However, in all but a few instances it is not clear from the data whether the favorable attitude or the contact came first. Ambiguity arises most commonly from the *ex post facto* nature of the studies, involving attitude measures taken at only one point in time, so that in addition to possible subject selection biases there was reliance on retrospective reports of contact experiences (Cook, 1963). The studies that are discussed below come closest to providing acceptable evidence on the causal direction of contact-attitude relationships, although they do not entirely transcend the difficulties just mentioned.

One of the best known investigations was done in the U.S. Army during World War II, when racial segregation was still the official Army policy (Stouffer, Suchman, DeVinney, Star, & Williams, 1949). During the last months of European fighting an acute shortage of American combat troops led to the attachment of all-Negro rifle platoons, made up of volunteers from segregated service units, to white companies. Two months later, white officers and noncoms in the receiving companies were interviewed. Whereas 64% of the respondents of each rank reported having been initially opposed to the project, 77% of each group stated that their feelings were now favorable.

Substantial majorities gave favorable evaluations of Negro combat performance and of relations between Negro and white troops. Moreover, 86% of the officers and 92% of the noncoms asserted that with the same army training and experience, Negro troops would perform as well as, or better than, white infantry soldiers. But respondents' support for a general policy of integration in the army was limited to continuation of the practice they had experienced: segregated platoons in biracial companies. Only 7% of officers and 1% of noncoms favored integration of platoons. Consistent with these findings, another survey, done at about the same time on a representative cross section of white field force soldiers in Europe, showed that acceptance of the idea of company-level integration was closely related to degree of exposure to the practice.

Thus, the whites' experience of successful cooperative interaction with Negroes under conditions of shared threat apparently resulted in favorable evaluations not only of the Negroes involved, but also of Negro troops in general. Yet the seeming attitude change did not go beyond acceptance of the limited types of integration they had experienced.

Limited interracial acceptance following equal-status contact was also reported by Harding and Hogrefe (1952) for white, predominantly female, department store workers. Three groups of office workers and sales people were sampled: those who were in departments having (a) Negroes of the same or higher job status, (b) Negroes of lower job status, or (c) no Negroes. Interviews revealed that equal status contact was associated with greater willingness to work with Negroes on an equal basis, but not with greater willingness to engage in other types of association. For example, these respondents were just as unwilling as those in the two other groups to eat at the same table with a Negro in a cafeteria. Additional data suggested that even in the equal-status situation, interracial relationships on the job tended to be casual and superficial.

If the apparent attitudinal effects of equal-status job contacts are limited, do neighborly contacts in interracial housing projects have a stronger influence? Deutsch and Collins (1951) interviewed white housewives in two types of biracial housing project in the North: building integrated and area segregated. The proportion of Negro tenants in the projects ranged from 40 to 70%. Based on respondents' retrospective reports, initial racial attitudes in the two types of project had been similar. Almost half of the women in integrated projects, but virtually none in segregated projects, reported having some type of regular intimate contact with Negro neighbors, and a relatively close friendship with at least one Negro resident. Also, almost half of the integrated sample, but only 4% of the segregated sample, felt that their white friends would favor their interracial social contacts. Integrated respondents had more favorable attitudes toward all Negroes in the project, and toward Negroes in general. Moreover, in both types of project those who said their initial racial attitude had been highly unfavorable were more likely to report a favorable change than those whose recollected initial attitude was less negative.

However, it is interesting to note that there was a marked difference between attitudes about project Negroes and attitudes about other Negroes. When interviewers rated respondents on the overall extent to which they had shown feelings of respect and friendliness toward Negro people in general, majorities in both samples were judged to be prejudiced.

A replication of the Deutsch and Collins study was done by Wilner, Walkley, and Cook (1955) in northern biracial housing projects that were similarly integrated or segregated, except that the proportion of Negro tenants in any project was only about 10%. Hence, proximity to Negro tenants turned out to be a better predictor of behavior and attitude than official occupancy policy. Within each type of project, nearness to Negro residents was related to amount of neighborly contact and favorable evaluation of in-project Negroes. Yet in all projects, the majority of respondents was opposed to a policy of integration within buildings, even if they were presently in or near a building with Negro occupants. Thus, this study is consistent with the previous one in suggesting that only limited change in interracial acceptance resulted from interracial contact.

In the next two studies, subjects were placed in small biracial groups, and the effect of social interaction on evaluations of partners was assessed. Mann (1959a) assigned white and Negro graduate students in the North to six-person discussion groups as part of a course in education. The groups met four times a week for three weeks. At the beginning and end of the series of meetings they were given a sociometric test and part of the California Ethnocentrism scale. Both the E scores and the use of race as a friendship criterion showed declines in the total sample. But the meaning of these changes is ambiguous because the content of the course the subjects were taking could have had a major influence on their attitude scores.

How shared threat modified the attitudinal effect of participation in a biracial problem-solving group was investigated by Burnstein and McRae (1962). White male college students in the South worked on common symbol problems in five-man groups. One member of every group was a Negro confederate who had been trained to proficiency at the task. Regardless of performance, half the groups got failure feedback ("shared threat") and half got success feedback ("no threat"). It was found that among subjects who had previously scored high on an anti-Negro questionnaire (Holtzman's D scale), the Negro confederate was evaluated more favorably following the shared threat experience than following interaction without threat. Low-prejudice subjects' reactions to the confederate were less influenced by the experimental variable. This was taken to mean that contact under the shared threat condition tended to reduce anti-Negro hostility in subjects who initially possessed it. However, no measure was taken of attitude change toward Negroes in general.

To summarize, the foregoing studies suggest that cooperative (or relatively noncompetitive), equal-status contact with Negroes may bring about favorable, but restricted, attitude change in whites. Yet even this limited statement needs to be qualified further.[2] Two studies of children at racially integrated summer camps indicate that even in situations governed by strongly equalitarian norms, racial interactions that are emotionally intense can have equivocal attitudinal outcomes. Mussen (1950) measured racial prejudice in northern white working-class boys, aged 8 to 14, at the beginning and end of a four-week camping session. About 50% of the campers were Negro boys. There was no consistent trend toward either favorable or unfavorable changes in attitude, as measured projectively; change occurred in both directions and was related to personality factors. The TAT stories of negative changers, as compared with positive changers, revealed stronger aggressiveness, greater need to defy authority, more fear of punishment, more frequent feelings of victimization, and the like. The two groups also differed in level of satisfaction with the camping experience and liking for fellow campers.

A team led by Yarrow (1958) studied children of both races, from low-income homes, at an integrated summer camp in a border state. Boys and girls, aged 8 to 13, were interviewed about their reactions to cabin mates at the beginning and end of a two-week session. Racial attitudes as such were not ascertained. Initially, white girls rated Negro cabin mates less favorably than white cabin mates on personal traits, and the final interviews showed no consistent change. White boys initially rated Negroes low on several traits, and two weeks later tended to rate them even less favorably than before. However, on friendship choices, slight initial tendencies for white children to prefer white peers disappeared during the two-week period.

[2]In the field of survey research, a pessimistic note has been sounded by Williams (1964), on the basis of panel data gathered in a northern city. Over a two-year period, 25% of a white gentile sample showed either an increase or decrease in amount of social interaction with Jews and Negroes. Of this number, only about one-seventh fit the hypothesis that contact experiences decrease prejudice of the social distance variety; the other respondents showed no change in prejudice, or change in the wrong direction.

Thus it would seem that research on the effects of contact, as Williams (1964) and Cook (1963) have noted, must become much more specific about (a) the kinds of contact experiences that are supposed to be effective in changing racial attitudes and (b) the kinds of racial feelings and cognitions that are most likely to be changed. The Insko and Schopler (1967) extension of consistency theory to relations among attitudes, beliefs, and behavior provides a useful conceptual approach to this area. The most general implication of their triadic consistency model for work on interracial contact and attitudes seems to be as follows: To have its strongest impact on prejudice, personal contact must do more than provide information that is inconsistent with negative feelings and stereotypes; it must also involve the individual in inconsistent social actions—i.e., in friendly, accepting, helping, etc., behaviors toward the object of prejudice. Moreover, the person must be aware of the attitude-behavior inconsistency. Evidence of the effectiveness of new behavior in bringing about affective-cognitive change comes from research on counter-attitudinal role behavior.

Among the contact studies that were reviewed, there is little indication that subjects whose prejudice remained unchanged had engaged in inconsistent actions. For example, Mussen (1950) found that only boys who had had friendly interactions with Negro campers were likely to show favorable attitude change; and Harding and Hogrefe (1952) reported that most of their white respondents in the equal-job-status condition, who showed very limited attitude change, had experienced only superficial relationships with Negro workers.

Insko and Schopler have proposed three factors that should affect the tendency toward cognitive change, presumably by influencing the degree of awareness of attitude-behavior inconsistency: the polarity of the new behavior and the associated attitude, the commitment the person holds with respect to the new behavior, and the intensity or "compellingness" of the cognition relating the behavior and the attitude. It would be interesting to carry out racial attitude experiments in which these factors were systematically varied.

Another reason mentioned by Insko and Schopler why seeming inconsistency between a new behavior and an attitude may not lead to cognitive change is that the object of behavior may not be the same as the attitudinal object. Referring to race, this can mean that a scale used to measure prejudice may describe a minority group, "Negro," that is undifferentiated with respect to socioeconomic characteristics, whereas the Negro individuals encountered in a contact situation may all be college educated. A white subject who behaves positively toward the latter might not associate them with Negroes in general, if he perceives most

Negroes as predominantly lower class. Further, differentiation of the behavioral object from the attitudinal object may take place after the new behavior has been enacted, as an inconsistency reducing mechanism that is an alternative to attitude change. Such postbehavioral differentiation might account for the finding in the housing studies of marked improvement in attitude toward Negro neighbors, but not toward other Negroes or toward integration as a public policy.

B. ATTITUDES AS PREDICTORS OF BEHAVIOR

Much of the research on overt behavior toward minorities has dealt with the question of the predictive power of verbal attitudes. Interest in the issue dates back to an early provocative study by LaPiere (1934). He visited over 250 hotels, motels, and restaurants with a Chinese couple, who were refused service only once. Yet over 90% of the establishments stated in reply to a subsequent mail questionnaire that they would not serve Chinese. Other field studies have documented the same type of discrepancy between verbal expressions of attitude or intention and actual behavior (e.g., Kutner, Wilkins, & Yarrow, 1952; Saenger & Gilbert, 1950).

More recently, a number of more systematic studies have been done (mostly on college students) in which racial attitudes were assessed, and then at a later time (usually a few weeks or more) behavior was observed in a biracial situation. Four experiments dealt with white subjects' physiological arousal in the presence of white and Negro experimenters. The underlying assumption was that because prejudice involves strong emotion it should be tied to those physiological functions associated with the emotions.

Galvanic skin response was tested by Rankin and Campbell (1955). First, racial attitude scales (an information test containing favorable and unfavorable items, and a direct attitude test consisting of statements of feelings) were administered to northern white male undergraduates in classrooms. At a later time, subjects participated individually in what was ostensibly a study of word association and anxiety. For half of the subjects, a Negro experimenter adjusted a dummy apparatus on the arm, and for half of the subjects this was done by a white experimenter. All subjects tended to have higher GSRs with the Negro experimenter, and the tendency was greater among those who were relatively more prejudiced.

Somewhat similar data were obtained in a replication by Porier and Lott (1967) that improved on the Rankin and Campbell procedure by using several experimenters of each race. The subjects were white male students at a border state college, and prejudice was assessed by means of the California E scale and Rokeach's Opinionation scale. When GSR was measured on a later occasion, a tendency to give larger responses to the Negro experimenter was significantly related to amount of prejudice. But unlike the Rankin and Campbell study, racial bias in GSR responses was not apparent in the sample as a whole.

Photographs instead of experimenters were used by Westie and DeFleur (1959) as racial stimuli in an experiment using northern college students of both sexes as subjects. Anti-Negro prejudice was assessed by means of a social distance questionnaire which controlled on the social class of hypothetical persons. At a later time, individual subjects' GSR and other physiological responses were recorded while they were exposed to colored photographs of Negroes and whites. It was found that the more prejudiced subjects, but not the less prejudiced subjects, gave larger GSR responses and smaller finger pulse responses to pictures of single Negroes than to pictures of single whites. However, level of prejudice was not related to responses when the photographs depicted two persons in a social situation, in various race and sex combinations. Complex interaction effects on responses to the two-person pictures indicated that autonomic responses could not be assumed to reflect simple favorability or unfavorability of feeling toward a social stimulus object. Westie and DeFleur pointed out that "conflicting feelings, indecisions, or even positive involvement might result in large autonomic responses" [p. 346].

GSR reactions to photographs were studied also by Vidulich and Krevanick (1966). Subjects were undergraduates at a southern college who had obtained extreme scores on an anti-Negro scale constructed by the authors. High-prejudice subjects gave larger GSR responses than did low-prejudice subjects to photographs of Negroes alone or Negroes and whites in intimate social situations. The two types of subjects did not differ in their reactions to control photographs. For the sample as a whole, GSR scores were higher for the racial photographs than for control photographs.

Taking the four physiological studies together, they show fairly consistently that relatively prejudiced subjects give stronger autonomic reactions to Negro stimulus persons than do relatively unprejudiced subjects. What this means psychologically will remain ambiguous until physiological arousal has been studied in a wider range of biracial situations.

Psychologists have investigated another type of involuntary response, as it is related to racial prejudice: perception of stimuli presented under stereoscopic conditions of binocular rivalry. Presenting two different photographs, a Negro male and a white male, to the right and left eyes of midwestern college students, Reynolds and Toch (1965) found only weak evidence of a relationship between binocular fusion tendency and prejudice. Extremely low scorers on a modified California Ethnocentrism scale showed slightly more fusion-related responses than extremely high scorers. This marginally significant finding was rendered even more ambiguous by the lack of a nonracial control stimuli condition. Iverson and Schwab (1967) found that northern college students who were extremely high scorers on the Ethnocentrism and Dogmatism scales displayed less binocular fusion than low scorers, both on racially different stimuli and on stimuli that were different along a nonracial dimension. Thus the stereoscopic technique may prove to be useful for studying perceptual-style correlates of the prejudiced personality, but not for revealing relationships between racial attitude and race-specific perception.

A verbal conditioning technique was employed by Smith and Dixon (1968). White female undergraduates at a border state college who scored high or low on Ethnocentrism and F-scale items (by median split) were verbally reinforced by either white or Negro male experimenters for emitting first-person pronouns. It was found that subjects who scored high on these items conditioned with white experimenters only, while low scorers did not condition with either type of experimenter.

In addition to the foregoing research on relationships between verbal prejudice and general behavioral mechanisms, there have been several studies of prejudice and social action. In the experiments to be described, subjects were northern male college students unless otherwise stated.

Willingness to pose with a Negro person of the opposite sex for a photograph that would be publicized was investigated by DeFleur and Westie (1958). Male and female subjects were individually shown several colored photographs of Negro and white mixed-sex pairs seated together and talking, ostensibly as part of a research project unrelated to racial attitudes.

After an interview about the photographs, subjects were told that more such slides were needed for further research and asked if they would be willing to pose for one. A "standard photo release agreement" was shown. It contained a graded series of uses to which the picture might be put, ranging from laboratory research where it would be seen only by sociologists to use in a nationwide publicity campaign advocating racial integration. The subject was asked to sign his or her name to each use of the photograph that would be permitted. The main finding was that subjects high on anti-Negro prejudice, as revealed by scores on a social-distance scale that had been administered in classrooms, were less willing than low-prejudice subjects to have the picture widely publicized.

A similar experiment by Linn (1965), on female subjects only, failed to confirm DeFleur and Westie's main finding. However, this may have been due to weaknesses in Linn's procedure. He did not show subjects actual photographs of racially mixed pairs in an innocuous conversational pose. Instead, they were asked to pose with a Negro male in "typical social scenes," and "dancing" was mentioned as one of the examples. Another possibly significant departure from the script used by DeFleur and Westie was that the photographs supposedly were to be used for profit by a private testing company.

Rokeach and Mezei (1966) tested the hypothesis that differences in belief are a more powerful determinant of discrimination than race or ethnic differences. In two experiments, subjects who had previously filled out an unspecified anti-Negro questionnaire, individually engaged in a 15-minute discussion of a controversial topic with four confederates, two white and two Negro. One white and one Negro tended to agree with the subject, while the other two confederates tended to disagree with him. Afterward, the subject had an opportunity to select two confederates to join him in a coffee break. This was the behavioral variable. It was found in both experiments that belief similarity was a more important determinant of preference than race for both high-prejudice and low-prejudice subjects; prejudice scores were not predictive of choices. An evaluation of the latter finding should consider whether the six-item anti-Negro scale was adequate for measuring prejudice. Further, the social situation used to test racial discrimination was casual and brief. Racial discrimination should be more apparent in social interactions of a more sustained and intimate nature. This generalization is supported by the finding of Triandis and Davis (1965) that belief is a more important determinant of nonintimate behavioral intentions, while race is more important in the case of intimate behavioral intentions.

In an earlier-mentioned study by Mann (1959b), each subject's score on racial discrimination in a biracial discussion group consisted of the mean rankings on overt bias assigned to him by other members of that group. Scores on a part of the California E scale showed a significant correlation with rated bias for the total sample, and for Negro subjects only, but not for white subjects only.

Signing a petition advocating equal opportunities for Negroes has been used as a behavioral measure in two studies: Kamenetsky, Burgess, and Rowan (1956) had male and female subjects in introductory psychology classes as a northern college indicate whether or not they were willing to have their names printed on a petition to be sent to congressmen urging passage of a Fair Employment Practices Act. A few weeks later, the subjects were given a questionnaire dealing with attitude toward legislative control of racial discrimination in jobs, along with a modified version of the Rosenzweig Picture-Frustration test. Petition signing was significantly related to scores on both questionnaires.

In another petition study, done by DeFriese and Ford (1968), white urban residents in a border state were asked to sign an open housing appeal. Apparently, three measures were obtained at the same time by an investigator going door-to-door: (a) attitude toward Negroes, determined with an unspecified attitude scale, (b) willingness to sign a petition either for or against open housing, and (c) perception of the stands of certain reference groups. Only data on (a) and (b) are given by DeFriese and Ford, and these show that attitude and behavior were somewhat related, although there was also a great deal of inconsistency. The study seems to have suffered from major procedural weaknesses: less than two-thirds of the 400 persons contacted supplied complete data, and of this group, about two-thirds refused to sign either the pro or con petition, suggesting that presenting respondents with a choice of two opposed petitions on open housing lacked credibility.

Several studies have dealt with the question of whether or not attitudes toward minority groups are related to susceptibility to influence by members of those groups. The results are mixed. Himmelstein and Moore (1963) exposed subjects to a Negro or white male confederate, posing as a fellow subject, who signed or refused to sign a petition to extend the university library's Saturday closing hour. Then the true subject was asked to sign. Prejudice, as indicated by scores on a previously administered attitude scale of unspecified content, was not predictive of subjects' tendencies to follow the behavior of the model. The general tendency was to follow the model, regardless of his race.

The influence of minority group members on judgments of autokinetic movement was studied by Bray (1950) and Berg (1966). In Bray's study, white Gentile subjects announced their judgments after a confederate had announced his judgment. The confederate was either white with a Gentile name, white with a Jewish name, or Negro. The Likert scale of Attitude Toward the Negro and a short version of the Levinson-Sanford scale of Attitude Toward Jews had previously been administered in classrooms. The data revealed no relationship between anti-Negro prejudice and conformity to the Negro confederate's judgments. (But among subjects categorized as anti-Semitic, there was more conformity to the "Jewish" confederate's judgments than to the "Gentile" confederate's judgments.)

Berg (1966) created a more complex situation in which white sub-

jects made autokinetic judgments along with a white confederate and a
Negro confederate, who always responded before the subject and gave
divergent judgments. The tendency to follow the Negro confederate was
not related to any of three attitude scales that had been administered a
few weeks earlier—the California E and F scales, and the Social Distance scale.

Malof and Lott (1962) used Asch's line judging situation to study
naive subjects' acceptance of influence from a Negro or white confederate who gave correct judgments in opposition to an erroneous majority. The subjects, students at a border state college, had previously
taken the California E scale. Greater susceptibility to the Negro confederate's influence on the part of low-prejudice subjects, as compared with
high-prejudice subjects, appeared as a weak trend (at the .10 level of
confidence).

The effect of the race of a communicator on his persuasiveness with
Northern elementary school pupils was studied by Aronson and Golden
(1962). Several weeks after they had been administered a racial stereotype questionnaire, the children listened to a Negro or white adult, who
was introduced as an engineer or dishwasher, deliver a speech about the
value of arithmetic. Highly prejudiced children showed a smaller amount
of favorable change in attitude toward arithmetic after listening to the
Negro than did children low in prejudice. The effect occurred both when
the Negro had high occupational status and when he had low status.
With a white communicator, the amount of opinion change was intermediate between the levels of opinion change in unprejudiced and prejudiced children who were exposed to a Negro communicator.

Only one piece of research has examined the relationship between
racial prejudice and amount of communication toward Negroes. In an
experiment referred to earlier, Burnstein and McRae (1962) placed
southern college students in small problem-solving groups having a
single Negro confederate. Subjects who had previously received high
prejudice scores on Holtzman's D scale sent fewer notes to the Negro
group member than did subjects with low prejudice scores.

The foregoing studies do not consistently demonstrate relationships
between racial attitudes and social action. In trying to interpret these
results, it will be useful to return to Insko and Schopler's (1967) model
of triadic (i.e., affective-conative-cognitive) consistency.

Two studies dealt with willingness to be seen in a photograph with a
Negro: DeFleur and Westie (1958) reported a significant, but not very
close, inverse relationship between prejudice and willingness to allow
various uses of the photograph, while Linn (1965), using a questionable
procedure, found no relationship at all. To understand why the results in

the first study were not stronger, it should be noted that of the seven graded uses of the photograph for which permission was requested, only one – use in a pro-integration publicity campaign – had a clear relation to the interests of Negroes. Hence only this one item involved a choice between engaging or not engaging in an unambiguously pro-Negro action. Moreover, even for this use of the picture, *not granting permission* was probably not seen by subjects as *harmful* to Negroes, since it could be assumed that someone else would probably give permission.

Referring to Insko and Schopler's discussion of behavioral choice confrontation, it would appear that six of the permission requests did not offer a behavior alternative that was clearly pro-Negro, in the sense of promoting the well-being of Negroes, and none offered a clearly anti-Negro alternative. Hence, for subjects whose predominant attitude was either pro-Negro or anti-Negro (as shown by scores on a social distance scale), the permission items only weakly involved either consistent or inconsistent behavior alternatives.

One must also consider whether the subjects' decisions were influenced by competing tendencies toward consistency in other systems. Insko and Schopler point out that positive behavior which balances a given triad will tend not to occur if it simultaneously imbalances a second triad involving a more polarized attitudinal object. Subjects might have seen public use of a picture of themselves with a Negro as entailing a high risk of social disapproval and loss of status. Thus what seems consistent in terms of a closed system involving attitude and behavior toward Negroes may not be consistent when attention is paid to the total matrix of attitude-behavior relationships.

The same factor of fear of social disapproval could have been operative in the two studies of willingness to sign petitions (DeFriese & Ford, 1968; Kamenetsky *et al.*, 1956). Also in these studies, as in the photograph release experiments, there was no strong motive aroused in low-prejudice subjects to *avoid inconsistency* or in high-prejudice subjects to *seek consistency*, since *not* signing the petitions might not necessarily have been seen as *harmful* to the cause of civil rights.

The studies of social influence on simple perceptual judgments (Berg, 1966; Bray, 1950; Malof & Lott, 1962) provide further examples of behavior that did not involve obviously consistent or inconsistent relationships with the racial attitudes that were measured. Subjects had to make simple perceptual judgments, a task that probably was not seen as requiring intelligence or other valued attributes. Hence, the degree of acceptance of a Negro confederate's influence had no necessary relation to their liking for, or evaluation of, Negroes.

In two additional studies of social influence, there seemingly was more basis for expecting behavior to be related to racial attitudes than in the perceptual judgment experiments. Both researches made use of opinion issues on which the status of an influence source might be seen as affecting the credibility of the source. Himmelstein and Moore (1963) found no significant correlation between prejudice scores and responses to a Negro model's willingness or refusal to sign a petition. However, two weaknesses in this study should be noted: first, the content of the petition—extension of Saturday night library hours—might have seemed trivial to subjects, so that the credibility of the model did not matter to them; second, because of the smallness of the sample and the use of a dichotomous response measure, only a very strong behavior-attitude relationship could have become visible. In the experiment by Aronson and Golden (1962), a relationship was demonstrated between children's racial stereotypes and their susceptibility to persuasion on an important topic by a Negro adult. The finding is readily interpretable in terms of triadic consistency processes.

Finally, of two studies on tendencies to communicate with Negro peers, one found these tendencies related to prejudice scores (Burnstein & McRae, 1962), and the other did not (Rokeach & Mezei, 1966). The latter finding seems to go against a prediction from the consistency principle that individuals will tend to avoid social interactions with members of a disliked group. Perhaps the negative outcome was due to the operation of social constraints in the choice situation (i.e., competing tendencies toward triadic consistency), and also to the superficiality of the social interaction situation—sharing of a brief coffee break.

Summarizing this discussion, studies purporting to report inconsistencies between racial attitudes and behavior have involved, aside from various procedural weaknesses, one or more of the following factors: (a) behavior-attitude inconsistency that was more apparent than real, in that the measured attitude and observed behavior had no perceived relevance to one another (i.e., were in a null relationship), (b) available behavior alternatives did not present a choice between engaging in consistent or inconsistent behavior but only between engaging or not engaging in one of these types of behavior, and (c) a force toward consistency with regard to racial attitude was outweighed by tendencies toward consistency in competing triads of greater polarity.

Recently, Katz and Gurin (1969) have described some of the variables that may determine whether racial prejudice leads to discriminatory behavior in a given situation. They mention characteristics of a prejudicial attitude that increase the likelihood of its being expressed overtly toward members of the object group: centrality in the person's total attitudinal structure, intensity, generality, and defensive function. The authors mention two features of situations that influence the tendency for prejudice to show itself in behavior: arousal potential and regulation potential. Arousal potential refers to the potential amount of threat to a person's security that exists in a particular type of interracial contact situation (e.g., intimate, as contrasted with nonintimate). Regulation potential refers to the extent to which behavior in a given situation is capable of being socially controlled by virtue of its visibility and the possibility of applying positive and negative sanctions. The influence of these variables can be dealt with in terms of Insko and Schopler's triadic consistency model, the most relevant features of which have already been mentioned.

C. Social Reinforcer Effectiveness of Negro and White Adults

Children's responsiveness to Negro and white experimenters was examined by Allen, Dubanoski, and Stevenson (1966). Female adults administered a marble dropping task to midwestern Negro and white boys. Age of subjects (first and second graders *versus* fourth through sixth graders) and type of reinforcement (praise, blame, and control) were used as independent variables, in addition to race of examiner.

The results for white boys were complex and suggest the following: First, in a base-rate period older subjects had higher response rates with white experimenters than with Negro experimenters, while with younger subjects there was little difference in experimenter effectiveness. Second, during the reinforcement period white experimenters were (*a*) more effective than Negro experimenters when no feedback was given, (*b*) equally effective when criticizing, and (*c*) less effective when giving praise. Regarding (*a*), Allen *et al.* speculated that since the experimenter of the same race as the child was more familiar, her not providing feedback in a potentially evaluative situation aroused more anxiety. The interpretation of (*c*) was that it showed the special efficacy of "praise from a stranger," a phenomenon reported in previous studies. Allen *et al.* reasoned that their subjects probably had had less experience in receiving praise from Negro adults than from white adults in formal, evaluative situations, thereby enhancing the reinforcement value of the praise given by the Negro experimenters.

There is an implicit assumption that for this white midwestern sample of elementary school boys, the characteristics attributed to Negroes were not of such a nature as to counteract the favorable effect of praise from a stranger when a Negro adult appeared in that role.

D. INTIMATE BIRACIAL CONTACT

Yarrow's (1958) field study of children's social interactions in an interracial summer camp has already been mentioned. Comparable groups of Negro and white children of both sexes, from low-income homes in a border state locality, were observed in segregated and newly desegregated two-week sessions. An initial tendency for both white and Negro children to prefer white friends lessened during the two-week period studied. Satisfaction with the camp experience, as indicated by the percentage of children who expressed a desire that the camp session be extended, was somewhat higher in the integrated camps than in the segregated camps. However, there were also indications of social conflict and emotional tension associated with the integration process. In older groups (ages 12 and 13), white children initially directed almost twice as much aggression toward Negro cabin mates as toward white age peers. At the beginning of contact, 29% of all actions by white campers toward Negroes were hostile. On the other hand, Negro children of all ages aggressed more against one another than against whites. Overt manifestations of white prejudice tended to diminish during the two-week period. Nonetheless, tension symptoms appeared in almost twice as many white children in desegregated as in segregated groups (71% compared with 38%).

E. WHITE BEHAVIOR IN BIRACIAL WORK GROUPS

A few researchers have dealt with interpersonal behavior and perception in biracial working groups under various conditions. Mention was made earlier of a study done at a southern college by Burnstein and McRae (1962) in which five-man problem-solving groups, consisting of four naive white subjects and one Negro confederate, received either failure or success feedback. The failure feedback condition was regarded by the authors as a situation of shared threat. It was found that subjects evaluated the Negro partner more favorably on likeability and competence when shared threat was present than when it was absent. This was particularly true of subjects who initially were relatively high in anti-Negro prejudice. Amount of communication to the Negro was not affected by the feedback variable, but as already noted, it was related to prejudice. The total sample apparently sent just as many notes, proportionately, to the Negro confederate as to white group members.

Katz, Goldston, and Benjamin (1958) did an experiment on biracial work teams that employed both Negroes and whites as subjects, two situational variables, and a variety of tasks. Male students at a northern college were hired to work on cognitive and motor tasks for several two-hour sessions. All work groups consisted of two whites and two Negroes, operating under a shared or individual (but noncompetitive) monetary bonus setup and high or neutral group prestige.

It was found that whites initiated more communicative acts (verbal and nonverbal) than did Negroes over all experimental treatments. This was true for total communication on each of the five tasks and for most content categories on four of the tasks.

With regard to the targeting of remarks, white communicators were significantly biased in favor of white recipients on 7 out of 22 content categories, with two of the five tasks (logical problems and mechanical construction) accounting for almost all of the bias. (Negro communicators, on the other hand, favored white recipients in 16 content categories, representing virtually all types of recorded behavior in four of the five tasks.)

Turning to the effects of group *versus* individual reward and high *versus* neutral group prestige, these situational variables had little influence on the targeting of communications originating with either white or Negro subjects. However, group reward produced a greater *amount* of cooperative behavior in both white and Negro subjects, as shown by score differences on several types of communication content. Also, teams in the group reward condition worked better than those under individual reward on a motor task (ball-and-spiral) demanding close coordination of members' efforts. Thus, although there is evidence that the group bonus condition was conducive to cooperative interaction, it did not affect the tendency of white subjects to avoid talking to Negroes on some tasks, or the tendency of Negro subjects to prefer talking to whites.

The findings on white subjects' behavior across all treatments were recently reproduced by E. G. Cohen (1969), using samples of high school students in a northern California community. Groups consisting of two white boys and two Negro boys, loosely matched on social class and school adjustment, worked on a cognitive task in a standard setting. The data on social interaction revealed a clear status hierarchy associated with race: whites spoke more than Negroes and were more influential in group decisions; furthermore, members of both races favored white recipients when talking.

In a modified replication of the experiment by Katz *et al.* (1958) on biracial groups in different bonus and prestige conditions, Katz and Benjamin (1960) introduced an additional variable: the two white members of each four-man team were both either high or low on authoritarianism, as indicated by their scores on the California F scale. Special procedures were introduced to minimize real or apparent race differences in cognitive ability, thereby reducing a possible cause of Negro-white differences in communication: Negro and white team mates were matched on intelligence test scores, and were told they had been matched; furthermore, some of the group tasks were secretly rigged so that men of the two races would seemingly display equal cognitive ability.

It was found, as in the earlier study by Katz *et al.*, that whites tended to talk more than Negroes. Also, whites exercised more social influence than Negroes in group problem solving even though they were not more likely to have correct solutions. But in contrast to the data of the earlier experiment, whites did not talk more to one another, proportionately, than to Negro partners. (Negroes, however, continued to display a strong tendency to direct their remarks to whites.) In terminal ratings of team members, white subjects chose Negroes as future working companions as often as they chose one another, and ranked Negroes as high as themselves on task competence.

Group *versus* individual bonus, and high *versus* neutral prestige had little effect on white behavior. But authoritarianism was associated with a number of behavioral differences: on a two-man motor task requiring close coordination, authoritarians accepted more suggestions from Negroes and rejected fewer; on tasks requiring group decisions, authoritarians tended to be more compliant; authoritarians evaluated Negroes more favorably on personal traits. If it is assumed that the authoritarian subjects held anti-Negro attitudes, then these results contrast with Burnstein and McRae's (1962) finding that highly prejudiced subjects tended to avoid communicating with a Negro partner in the absence of shared threat. However, Burnstein and McRae's study was done in the South, while Katz and Benjamin's research was done at a northern university. The obtained effects seem understandable in terms of the low perceived power of authoritarians in the experimental situation. The unbiased behavior of the white experimenter, the university setting, and the role of equality of white and Negro subjects could have introduced strong restraints against open expressions of anti-Negro sentiment.

The reactions of northern white college students to a Negro partner of equal or less ability were studied by Katz and Cohen (1962). Biracial pairs of male subjects were given a large number of oddity discrimination problems to solve cooperatively. On most of the items initial disagreement was deceptively induced. In an experimental condition hidden arrangements caused the Negro to prevail over his white partner in half the instances of initial disagreement, thereby contributing equally to the team's attainment of a monetary bonus for accuracy. In a control condition the Negro partner was relatively compliant, enabling the white person to prevail even when he was wrong, so that no bonus was earned.

Pre- and post-measures were taken of social influence on another type of group decision task, administered under a standard condition in which there was no experimental manipulation of subjects' responses. On the pre-measure, the entire sample of whites tended to be dominant over Negro partners. The post-measure revealed that control-condition white subjects became even more dominant, while in the experimental dyads dominance tended to become equalized. However, the greater degree of role equality in the experimental condition, even though associated with attainment of a shared goal, seemed to have a negative effect on white subjects' attitudes. On a terminal questionnaire, whites in the experimental group downgraded the problem-solving ability of Negro partners and expressed less willingness to continue working with them than did control whites.

F.   AMBIVALENCE, AMBIGUITY, AND RESPONSE AMPLIFICATION

Interpretations of white subjects' behavior in the studies of biracial work groups must be tentative, since it usually was contingent upon the behavior of Negro partners. Still, it is noteworthy that the findings provide little support for the hypothesis put forth by Allport (1954), Deutsch and Collins (1951), Sherif (1958), and others that intergroup contact tends to reduce mutual alienation and hostility when it involves cooperative achievement of a shared goal in an equalitarian environment. In the experiments described above, the introduction of a shared goal (group bonus condition) did not increase white subjects' willingness to accept Negro peers' suggestions in group problem solving (Katz & Benjamin, 1960), nor reduce their tendency to favor one another as recipients of communications (Katz et al., 1958). Indeed, successful cooperation even had a negative effect on whites' acceptance of Negro partners when the latter's competence led to an equalization of social influence (Katz & Cohen, 1962). In another study, whites evaluated a Negro partner more favorably when groups received failure feedback than they did after success feedback (Burnstein & McRae, 1962).

These results suggest that the cooperative goal attainment hypothesis is based on an oversimplified model of race relations. Though undoubtedly correct under certain conditions, it appears to have limited heuristic value in research on face-to-face interactions. What seems to be required is an approach that takes full account of the cognitive predis-

positions that Negroes and whites bring to contact situations — predispositions that include not only racial attitudes and stereotypes in the usual
sense, but also assumptions about the motives of other-race actors in a
given interracial encounter. In this regard, Jones and Davis' (1965) analysis of attributional processes in person perception is highly suggestive,
particularly when it examines the influence of status factors. They point
out that cognitive-affective responses to low-status persons and groups
are often marked by *ambivalence*, with important behavioral consequences. Moreover, ambivalence appears to be a basic feature of white
America's attitude toward the black minority. It probably arises in part
from an awareness of the contradiction between racist practices and
democratic ideals — the "American dilemma" which Gunner Myrdal
(1944) saw as the key to an understanding of race relations in this
country.

Recent survey data provide some support for the ambivalence
thesis. Brink and Harris (1964), for example, have reported that fully
71% of a nationwide white adult sample, and even 56% of a southern
sample, acknowledged that Negroes were treated unfairly. Substantial
majorities believed that Negroes were discriminated against in jobs,
education, and housing. Brink and Harris observed that ". . . when
whites were asked how they thought it must feel to be discriminated
against as a Negro, they bristled with indignation and even outrage at
the thought of being treated like a Negro" [p. 147]. Yet questions about
integration elicited strong resistance. According to the investigators,
"[The] majority view of whites was clearly that the Negro was pressing
too hard, asking for too much." Two years later, Brink and Harris
(1966) found that 70% of a national adult sample thought that Negroes
were trying to move too fast.

These aggregate data are of course only suggestive, since the percentages mentioned do not indicate what proportion of individuals actually held inconsistent views. But they fit with other survey and field
data gathered over a long period of time.[3] Further, the notion of ambivalence is consistent with the results of social psychological experiments
showing that people may have a potent need to reduce inequity, even
when the inequity is advantageous to them (reviewed by Adams, 1965).

[3]A recent factor analytic study of whites' racial attitudes by Woodmansee and Cook
(1967) is suggestive. They found a large number of relatively independent components, all
of which discriminated criterion groups made up of persons with pro- and anti-Negro organizational affiliations. One item subscale, *sympathetic identification with the (Negro)
underdog*, had negligible correlations with 10 other item subgroups. Unfortunately, *sympathetic identification* was not included in the validity study. But looking at the 10 subscales
of known validity, it seems clear that a large proportion of the total sample must have held
inconsistent attitudes.

It is conceivable that ambivalence toward Negroes has had an *amplification* effect upon the white majority's reactions to black demands for equality during the past 15 years. These reactions have been marked by wide swings between accommodation on the one hand, and total resistance on the other. Consider, for example, the groundswell of popular support that made possible the civil rights legislation of the 1960's and the anti-poverty expenditures of the Johnson administration. Consider also the present move toward public and private retrenchment on most issues of equal opportunity. Of course demographic, political, and economic developments play a fundamental role in the shaping of the dominant group's behavior toward nonwhite minorities. What is being proposed here is that over and above the macro-level determination of this behavior, its seeming instability and polarity over relatively brief periods of time suggests the possibility of a psychological process of response amplification. This process might operate not only with respect to public policy formulation, but also in small-group racial interactions.

Amplification of both positive and negative responses to an ambivalently regarded stimulus person was demonstrated experimentally by Gergen and Jones (1963). They started with the psychoanalytic proposition, well supported in clinical literature, that emotional ambivalence is sometimes resolved by the suppression or repression of one affective component and enhancement of the other. Their experiment made use of attitudes toward the mentally ill, on the assumption that persons so categorized tend to arouse a basic emotional ambivalence in those who come in contact with them, a mixture of sympathy and concern on the one hand, and fear and abhorence on the other. Gergen and Jones reasoned that the ambivalence toward a particular mentally ill person would be "split" in a situation in which his behavior had clear positive or negative consequences for the perceiver. That is, the perceiver should like a psychotic person more than a normal person when the actions of both are beneficial to him, and dislike a psychotic more than a normal when the actions of both are detrimental to him. But in a situation in which the behavior of the stimulus person has little hedonic relevance for the perceiver, it was expected that affective reactions would be more a function of observed actions in the case of a normal person than of a mental patient. The second prediction followed from an assumption that the psychotic would be more or less "excused for" deviant or inadequate behavior so long as there were no painful consequences involved.

Gergen and Jones used a situation in which subjects had to predict the consumer preferences of a stimulus person who was described as mentally ill or normal. The choices were very hard or very easy to predict, and errors in prediction brought forth noxious or innocuous corrective feedback. It was found that subjects' pre- and postevaluations of the stimulus person supported the experimental hypothesis.

1. Theoretical Basis for an Amplification Hypothesis

The psychoanalytic proposition that guided the Gergen and Jones experiment is relevant to a large class of low-status outgroups which are perceived as disadvantaged, unfortunate, and perhaps victimized by social injustice, but which at the same time are stigmatized as inferior, deviant, and potentially threatening to the comfort and security of the dominant majority. Actions of these low-status persons that have beneficial consequences for a more advantaged perceiver run the risk of being interpreted as either externally caused (induced by the superior power of others) or manipulative (an attempt to control the perceiver through ingratiation). But when the circumstances surrounding the behavior do not favor these interpretations, the ambivalent perceiver may resolve his conflicting feelings toward the actor by emphasizing the benevolence of the latter's intentions. A similar process of conflict reduction may cause negative actions to be seen as highly malevolent.

The amplification hypothesis can also be derived from some of Jones and Davis' (1965) notions about the attribution process. They propose that the more favorable or detrimental are the effects of an action on a perceiver (i.e., the more "hedonically relevant" the action), the greater his tendency to see the action as intended to have that effect (i.e., the more "correspondent" the influence). Relevance is supposed to increase correspondence by reducing the number of unique effects of an action, the reduction coming about in two ways. First, effects which might at other times appear unrelated tend to become *functionally equivalent* when the perceiver's well-being is involved. Second, the number of unique effects may be further reduced by *assimilation* of more or less neutral effects to the predominant hedonic value. Hence, when nonrelevant effects of an action (avoidance of social censure, ingratiation, etc.) are not so obvious as to provide a sufficient explanation of why an action was chosen, a perceiver's evaluation of the actor will be influenced by hedonic relevance, through its tendency to increase correspondence.

In the case of low-status actors, hedonic relevance may sometimes have an especially strong influence on the correspondence of causal inferences, through marked reduction in the number of unique effects which are observed to follow their actions. Two biasing influences on the cognitions of dominant group perceivers could contribute to this phenomenon. First, they might take it for granted that they had special salience as initiators and recipients of social exchange with minority group members. Second, since it is well known that disadvantaged persons experience low fate control in their daily lives, high-status perceivers might assume that they were relatively lacking in autonomous needs and well-articulated goals. In social interaction situations, both assumptions would increase the tendency of perceivers to interpret the behavior of low-status actors as largely intended to affect them. Hence, if the action were seen as freely chosen (not induced by the superior power of others), the functional equivalence and assimilation influences of relevance would be especially strong.

However, the causes of actions that favor another person are often ambiguous, particularly when performed by individuals of low status (Jones, 1964; Jones & Davis, 1965). If the beneficiary were unambivalently hostile toward the outgroup in question, he would probably be strongly biased toward interpreting the behavior as either externally caused or manipulative in intent, thus greatly diminishing the likelihood of a correspondent inference (i.e., an inference of benevolent intention). He would probably lean toward this type of interpretation even when circumstantial evidence pointed in the opposite direction.

But the same beneficial action should receive a different interpretation from an observer who had both sympathetic and antagonistic feelings toward the low-status actor. Awareness of the actions' positive consequences should arouse friendly feelings, thereby strengthening the tendency toward correspondent attribution. Since actions of low-status persons are likely to be seen as directed toward the perceiver, the correspondence would be stronger than if the actor's status were similar to that of the perceiver. Once this process began, the need to reduce affective conflict could further amplify favorable evaluation of the actor.

With regard to actions having negative consequences, the ambivalent person should react as extremely, or perhaps even more extremely, than the person who was unambivalently hostile. Of course a basic premise of this discussion is that the average white person is ambivalent toward Negroes, rather than unambivalently hostile or friendly. Systematic investigation of the ambivalence hypothesis would be facilitated by the development of a scale for measuring individual differences in degree of racial ambivalence, as distinct from existing scales which measure prejudice as a single continuum.

2.   *Factors Relating to Ambivalence Effects*

a.   Frustration. The ambivalence hypothesis suggests that in frustrating situations not only might *negative* reactions be stronger against Negro than white group members, in accordance with the frustration-aggression hypothesis of Dollard, Doob, Miller, Mowrer, and Sears (1939), but also, under certain conditions, *positive* reactions to Negroes

might be stronger. Consider the earlier mentioned experiment by Burnstein and McRae (1962) in which failure at a group task led to greater
acceptance of a Negro partner than did success.

Findings from other studies are seemingly contradictory. Berkowitz
and Holmes (1959) and Berkowitz and Green (1962) found that college
students frustrated by an experimenter showed increased hostility
against a disliked partner. Further studies by Berkowitz (1959) and
Weatherley (1961) indicated that highly anti-Semitic college students
were more prone, after experiencing frustration, to aggress against a
neutral bystander and/or Jewish figures than less prejudiced students.

Given these results, how are those of Burnstein and McRae to be
explained? Shared threat can reasonably be expected to lead to increased acceptance of minority group persons when their actions result
in amelioration of the threat. But in this experiment, group action had no
mitigating effect upon failure feedback. To account for the increased
liking of the Negro partner it seems necessary to assume that he was
clearly visible as a helpful contributor to the team product even though
failure occurred. The assumption is supported by subjects' ratings of
team members' contributions in the shared threat condition, and is consistent with the fact that the Negro confederate had been trained "to attain maximum familiarity and skill with the type of problem to be used in
the experiment." When the team was successful, the Negro's contribution was evaluated relatively unfavorably, which could have been due to
its receiving less attention and/or to equally good performance on the
part of white group members.

Even though the Negro confederate's actions did not alleviate frustration in the group, both his intent and ability to help the group achieve
its goal were clearly perceptible. Just as apparent was the group's need
for his contribution. Hence his motives could have been perceived as
benevolent, with somewhat the same positive effect upon evaluations as
if his efforts had actually led to group success. The favorable reaction
apparently was an amplified one, inasmuch as the evaluation of the
Negro in the shared threat condition represented an improvement in his
ranking on various traits, relative to white team mates. It would be
worthwhile to replicate this experiment with a neutral control condition
(neither success nor failure feedback) so that the separate effects of success and failure could be measured against a single baseline.

As suggested above, the *visibility* of a Negro person's behavior may
be a critical determinant of evaluative response. In the Burnstein and
McRae experiment, if the Negro accomplice's contributions had been
less obviously good, scapegoating rather than increased liking might

have occurred. Probably, for relatively prejudiced whites, a high degree of behavioral clarity would have to be present before greater acceptance, instead of increased hostility, would occur.

Behavioral clarity or ambiguity should also be a determinant of evaluations of Negro and white individuals whose contributions have *negative consequences* for other group members. Jones and de Charms (1957) found that when a white accomplice's failure prevented white subjects from reaping rewards that were available, the tendency to de-value him as a person depended upon whether his poor performance was attributed to lack of ability or low motivation. Only in the latter instance was he rated as a less likeable person. It would be interesting to repli-cate this experiment using race of the accomplice, and possibly racial attitude of subjects, as independent variables, in addition to Jones' and deCharms' low ability *versus* low motivation manipulation.

   b. Personal threat. No doubt an important reason why successful interracial cooperation does not always have favorable attitudinal effects on white participants is that Negro behavior in the situation may be ex-perienced as personally threatening. Thus, in the Katz and Cohen (1962) experiment, when the assertiveness of a Negro partner led to successful cooperative problem solving, white subjects experienced (*a*) reduced influence over team decisions and (*b*) comparison with a Negro of equal mental ability. The threatening implications of (*a*) and (*b*) might have been the cause of the subsequent rejection of the Negro by whites in the experimental condition.

   M. Cohen (1965) carried out a study related to the threat interpreta-tion. He had white subjects individually administer a test that purport-edly measured intelligence to a Negro or white confederate, and then score it. Just prior to the testing session, half of the subjects were told by the experimenter that their scores on a different task indicated that they had very high ability of the sort tapped by the test they were about to administer. The other half of the sample were told that the two tests were unrelated. One of the interesting findings had to do with the sub-ject's expressed belief that the confederate had cheated on the test. Sub-jects who were *not* given an estimate of their ability on the intellectual test believed there had been relatively little cheating by the confederate. However, those who were informed that they had high ability on the test tended to see the Negro person, but not the white person, as having cheated a great deal. Since the test answers were identical in all treat-ments, it would seem that subjects who had a vested interest in the dis-criminative power of the test needed to deny the possibility of low-status individuals (i.e., Negroes) attaining validly high scores on it. While this is a *post hoc* interpretation, it is reasonable enough to encourage investigation of the effect on white subjects' affective reactions of real or anticipated cross-racial comparisons.

    c. Ingratiation. As mentioned earlier, beneficial actions tend to be much more ambiguous than harmful actions when it comes to deciding on the actor's true motives in the situation, because of the possibility that his ultimate objective is control of the perceiver through ingratiation. The suspicion of manipulative intent may be strong when the perceiver has higher status than the actor and controls resources that are important to the actor—a common feature of Negro-white interactions. Hence perceived dependency should be an important variable in Negro-white relationships. Positive, supportive behavior on the part of a Negro toward a white perceiver, such as agreeing with his opinions or adopting a cooperative game strategy, should have a more favorable attitudinal effect when the Negro actor is not dependent on the perceiver or does not stand to benefit from the latter's approval.

    d. Guilt. According to Myrdal's (1944) conception of the "American dilemma," the average white person is capable of feeling a considerable amount of guilt about racial inequities. It seems reasonable to assume that the arousal of racial guilt can bring about either increased hostility against Negroes or increased supportiveness, depending on the availability of opportunities for guilt reduction. Working within a cognitive consistency framework, and postulating a "need to believe in a just world," Lerner and Matthews (1967) obtained empirical support for the hypothesis that individuals would denigrate an innocent victim for whose fate they were made to feel marginally responsible. When responsibility was not present, the evaluations of the victim were relatively favorable. A replication of this experiment, using white subjects and varying the race of the victim, could be expected to reveal stronger denigration when the victim was Negro than when he was white. By the same token, a guilt-reducing opportunity to help the victim for whose suffering one felt responsible might bring about increased liking, especially if the other person were properly grateful. Again, an amplification of the evaluative responses would be predicted when the person helped was a Negro.

III. Studies of Negro Subjects

    As already stated, a crucial research area from the standpoint of developing an understanding of change processes in American race relations has to do with factors influencing Negroes' acquisition and utilization of competitive resources, especially intellectual-academic skills. This review will focus on features of biracial situations that appear to have important influences on Negro learning and performance. Personality and early socialization factors per se will not be included, inasmuch as the relevant experimental data are sparse and inconsistent. The topics to be covered are as follows: (a) the social reinforcer effectiveness of Negro and white experimenters, (b) emotional stress and inhibition in biracial peer interactions, (c) experimentally induced stress in Negro and white task environments, and (d) task situations varying with respect to the race of a peer norm, the race of an examiner, and the probability of success.

A.   Social Reinforcer Effectiveness of Negro and White Experimenters

Three published studies have examined the effect of verbal reinforcement from Negro and white adults upon the behavior of Negro children. An experiment by Allen, Dubanoski, and Stevenson (1966) was described earlier, with reference to white subjects. Female experimenters gave a marble dropping task to midwestern Negro and white boys of elementary school age under praise, blame, and control (no feedback) conditions. The tester effect on Negro subjects can be summarized briefly as follows: (a) during an initial base-rate period, response rates were higher with a white tester than with a Negro tester; (b) across all three reinforcement conditions, response rates increased more with Negro testers; (c) looking at particular types of reinforcement, Negro testers were more effective in the praise and control conditions, while Negro and white experimenters were equally effective when giving criticism. Thus, except in the initial period, Negro boys were more responsive to Negro women than to white women.

Generally more favorable responses to Negro adults were also observed by Kennedy and Vega (1965). Southern Negro elementary school children of both sexes were given an oddity discrimination task by male adults under praise, blame, and control conditions. Subjects performed better with Negro testers, especially in the blame condition. Similar results were obtained by Katz, Henchy, and Allen (1968) when Negro male school children in the Northeast were given a verbal learning task (paired associates) by male experimenters. Subjects received either approval or disapproval from the testers. The data showed better learning with Negro experimenters, and a more favorable effect of approval than of disapproval. Poorest performance was shown by boys having a relatively strong need for approval, as measured by the Marlowe-Crowne scale, who received disapproval from white experimenters. Thus, studies done in different regions of the country found Negro children fairly consistently responding more favorably to social reinforcement from Negro adults than from white adults. In comparison, it was seen earlier that the behavior of white subjects (Allen *et al.*, 1966) was not consistently influenced by the race of adult reinforcing agents. But the data on Negro children must be interpreted cautiously; since the adult experimenters were always strangers to the subjects, it should not be assumed that the race effect would have survived even brief periods of acquaintance. Moreover, it will be seen later that the effect of varying the race of an adult examiner on Negro college students' performance of cognitive tasks is not consistent with these findings on children.

B. EMOTIONAL STRESS AND INHIBITION IN BIRACIAL PEER INTERACTIONS

An extensive anecdotal and clinical literature documents the fact that Negro children and adults often experience debilitating emotional stress in biracial social encounters (e.g., Katz, 1964). Among the more systematic observational studies is one by Yarrow (1958) which was mentioned earlier. At an integrated summer camp for children from low-income homes, the behavior of older white boys and girls toward Negro cabin mates was initially very aggressive and became somewhat more friendly during a two-week period. However, throughout the entire camp session, Negro children directed most of their hostility against one another. Although the proportion of children of each race who showed signs of emotional tension was about the same (over two-thirds), Negro campers were more likely to manifest covert or internalized signs of distress (enuresis, fears, nightmares, withdrawal, physical symptoms) than more overt symptoms (fighting, generally disruptive behavior, obscene language, complaining). Of the Negro campers showing tension, 85% showed reactions of the covert type. For the white children showing tension, on the other hand, neither covert nor overt responses predominated. That Negroes were particularly fearful of white disapproval is suggested by their oversensitiveness in desegregation, to aggressive and dominative behavior in other Negroes, and their denial of such impulses in themselves. Both reactions are further evidence of a tendency to conceal tensions in the presence of whites.

Studies of small biracial working teams have already been described, mainly with reference to the behavior of white subjects. Recapitulating the findings in two experiments on male college students in the northeast (Katz & Benjamin, 1960; Katz *et al.*, 1958) and one experiment on male high school students in California (E. G. Cohen, 1969), behavior of both whites and Negroes tended to conform to a pattern of race-determined status differentiation with respect to amount, direction, and influence of communications. Variations of reward structure (group *versus* individual bonuses) and group prestige (high *versus* neutral) in the two college-student studies had little effect on the pattern of racial inter-action. In addition, there were the following results for Negroes: On a terminal questionnaire used by Katz and Benjamin (1960), Negroes (*a*) preferred one another over whites as future working companions; (*b*) ranked whites higher in ability, even on tasks that had been experimen-tally rigged to insure equal performance, and (*c*) expressed less satisfac-tion than whites with the group experience. [White subjects, however, gave no indication of racial bias on (*a*) and (*b*).]

Viewing Negro subjects' questionnaire responses in conjunction with their social behavior, it would seem that their passive orientation toward white partners could have resulted from feelings of intellectual inadequacy in a biracial problem solving situation. Testing this hypothe-sis, Lefcourt and Ladwig (1965) varied the expectancy of success of Negro male adults who played a competitive game requiring cognitive skill with a white stooge. Those in a "high expectancy" group, com-prised of jazz musicians who had been led to believe that the game was related to skills of musicians, persisted longer in the face of repeated failure than did control groups. Another possible explanation of Ne-groes' underperformance in the biracial work teams is that they were fearful of arousing white hostility through greater assertiveness. The Lefcourt and Ladwig results do not bear upon this interpretation, inas-much as subject and stooge were separated by a partition, so that per-sonal identities were concealed.

An earlier-mentioned experiment by Katz and Cohen (1962) was addressed somewhat to the issue of whether Negro passivity was caused mainly by low expectancy of success or social threat. Negro male col-lege students in the North were paired with white peers of equal ability on a cooperative task consisting of 50 oddity discrimination problems. Partners had to agree on an answer to each item, after which correctness feedback was given. Unknown to the subjects, most of the items were rigged so that one partner received an easy version and the other partner received an insoluble version. Each person received the easy version half of the time. In addition, there was an experimental variation which consisted of either deceptively forcing or not forcing the person with the easy form of the problem to propose his answer with a high degree of expressed confidence. In the "forced assertion" condition, the Negro subject usually prevailed in team decisions when he had the correct answer, thereby enabling the dyad to win a monetary reward for accuracy. But in the control condition, the white partner tended to prevail on *all* items, and the bonus was not attained. This happened despite the fact that subjects were required to write down their private answers before discussing each problem, so that when feedback was given, the person holding the easy version would know that his initial response was correct.

To ascertain whether the effect of the training experience would transfer to other situations, subjects were given a different type of group decision task in which there was no behavioral manipulation, before and after working on the oddity discrimination problems. On the pretest, all Negro subjects tended to defer to their white partners. On the posttest, Negro control subjects were even more deferential than before, while Negro experimental subjects attained equal influence over team decisions. Furthermore, on the post-measure, the latter subjects seemed to accept the white partner's influence on a given item largely on the basis of his demonstrated accuracy on prior items.

While Katz and Cohen's results do not permit a firm conclusion about the cause of Negro submissiveness in the control condition, it would appear that feelings of intellectual inadequacy were a relatively unimportant factor. Subjects were afforded compelling evidence that their private responses to the oddity problems were correct as often as were the partner's responses. Indeed, they were shown that when they *thought* they were correct (easy problems) they usually *were* correct. This, combined with the evidence of the disinhibiting effect, in the experimental condition, of being forced to disagree openly with the partner, suggests that the passivity of Negro subjects was due mainly to fear of instigating hostility in the partner.

C.   INDUCED STRESS IN TWO RACIAL ENVIRONMENTS

From the standpoint of clarifying the causes and effects of stress on Negroes in racially mixed performance situations, the foregoing studies have important limitations. Note that all-Negro teams were not included for comparison purposes; cognitive functioning, as distinct from overt behavior, was not systematically investigated; and such specific motivational influences as fear of derogation, hope of approval, and social comparison were not sorted out.

Katz and Greenbaum (1963) carried out an experiment that focused on the relationship between anxiety and level of cognitive functioning in two types of racial environment. They varied a specific stress factor—threat of electric shock—to determine whether Negro males were more vulnerable to debilitative effects when they were alone with whites than when they were with other Negroes. Students at a predominantly Negro college in the South were given a digit-symbol substitution task in the presence of two strangers who were both either white or Negro—an adult administrator and a confederate who pretended to be another student working on the same task. In order to minimize the amount of uncontrolled threat implicit in the white condition, after an initial meeting there was no further social interaction or visual contact between the Negro subject and his white peer and the task was described as a research instrument of no evaluative significance. Under the pretext of conducting an "investigation in psycho-physiology," each subject was told either that severe electric shock or very mild electric shock would be administered to himself and the "other subject" at random times during the task. No shocks were actually delivered.

The results showed that Negro students' scores on the digit-symbol task depended on the particular combination of stress and racial environment conditions under which they worked. When only mild shock was threatened, they performed better in the presence of whites than of other Negroes, indicating that the white environment was more motivating. But when told to expect strong shock, their efficiency in the Negro condition improved, while in the white condition it went down. Various alternative explanations of the reversal effect may be considered, including the hypothesis put forth by Malmo (1957), Duffy (1957) and others of an inverted U-shaped relationship between level of total drive, or arousal, and performance. According to this interpretation, the combination of low threat and Negro environment was *insufficiently* arousing for optimal performance, while the high threat-white environment treatment was *too* arousing.

Another relevant hypothesis is Bovard's (1959) notion that bodily emotional responses to threat are physiologically dampened by familiar social stimuli which have nurturant associations (in this instance, other Negroes). Consistent with both the arousal and the Bovard hypotheses was the finding that subjects reported experiencing greater "nervousness" in the high-threat-white-environment treatment than in any other treatment. Moreover, this situation was the only one yielding a sizable negative correlation between reported anxiety and task performance.

In a follow-up on the Katz and Greenbaum experiment, an attempt was made to simplify the racial environment variation, and to induce arousal in a manner more directly related to typical academic situations. The relevant features of this study (by Katz, Roberts, & Robinson, 1965) were as follows: male students at a southern Negro college were individually administered a digit-symbol code task either by a Negro or white experimenter, using either intellectual or nonintellectual test instructions. It was found that when the task was presented as a test of eye-hand coordination, the white experimenter elicited better performance than the Negro experimenter. But when IQ instructions were used, there was a tendency toward a reversal of this relationship. Thus, the effect of IQ instructions was similar to the effect of strong shock instructions in the Katz and Greenbaum study and lends itself to the same explanations in terms of arousal or anxiety.

But, perhaps, a more promising lead is provided by Atkinson's (1964) formulation of motivation in achievement situations as partly a joint function of the expectancy and incentive value of success. (Atkinson includes as a third factor a generalized success or failure orientation.) Assuming that a white experimenter has higher prestige for Negro college students than does a Negro experimenter, the prospect of being evaluated favorably by the white adult should be more attractive. It follows that when the likelihood of scoring well was the same, regardless of whether the tester was Negro or white (i.e., when the task was defined nonintellectually), the subject should have worked harder for the white person. Presenting the task as an intelligence test ought to have raised the incentive value of achievement in both racial conditions. But suppose that on the intellectual test the Negro subject saw very little likelihood of meeting the white experimenter's standard of excellence; unless the incentive strength of success increased enough to counterbalance the drop in perceived probability, there would have been a reduction in task motivation. As an additional source of impairment in the IQ test-white examiner situation, low expectancy of success could have aroused debilitating fear of earning the white examiner's disapproval. But when the subject had a Negro tester, there is no reason to assume that his expectancy of success would have been markedly lower in the IQ test condition than in the motor test condition (except in the case of highly test anxious subjects). In both situations, the racial identity of the tester would have suggested to the subject that he was to be compared with other Negroes. Accordingly, performance with the Negro tester should have been higher with IQ instructions than with motor instructions because of the greater incentive value of success.

D. VARIATIONS OF RACE OF NORM, RACE OF TESTER, AND
    EXPECTANCY OF SUCCESS

The foregoing suggests that there are at least two racial factors that can have motivational impact on Negroes in intellectual achievement situations: the race of the authoritative evaluator and the race of the peer group whose performance is implicitly or explicitly used as an evaluative standard. Put in terms of Kelley's (1952) distinction between two types of reference group processes, the two racial factors can be seen as tied, respectively, to the normative and comparative functions of social referents. That is, the white or Negro tester is a *normative* referent insofar as the subject accepts him as an authoritative evaluator and strives to gain approval or avoid disapproval by performing adequately; and the white or Negro peer group is a *comparative* referent insofar as it provides a standard for self-evaluation or evaluation by others.

Several experiments have dealt with the effect of variation in the race of peer comparison standards on performance of cognitive tasks presented as intellectual tests. In all studies, the subjects were male students at Negro colleges, and the task administrators were Negro male adults. Katz, Epps, and Axelson (1964) found at a deep south college that anticipated comparison with a Negro peer norm led to higher scores on a digit-symbol code task than did anticipated comparison with a white peer norm. However, three additional studies all showed higher performance scores in the white norm condition. This outcome was obtained on an arithmetic task at a deep south college with relatively high admission standards (Katz, Epps, & Perry, 1970c); on a code task at an upper south college (Katz, Atchison, Epps, & Roberts, 1970b); and on scrambled words and code at a northern college (Epps, Katz, & Runyon, 1970). Thus, except in the most depressed type of segregated educational environment (deep south nonselective college), anticipation of cross-racial comparison had a favorable motivational effect on Negro subjects tested by Negro experimenters. It would seem that even if the white standard was seen as more difficult to attain than the Negro standard, it was also perceived as being a more relevant (i.e., more informative) criterion of intellectual ability in American society.

Pulling together all of the foregoing experiments on race-of-tester and race-or-norm effects, three assumptions about the perceptions of most Negro students in situations of intellectual evaluation appear to be worthy of consideration: (*a*) white testers are seen as more authoritive (i.e., more powerful) evaluators, (*b*) white standards are seen as harder, and (*c*) white standards are seen as potentially more informative for self-evaluations of ability. Katz *et al.* (1970b) designed an experiment to test predictions from these assumptions. On the basis of these assumptions, they reasoned that simultaneous variation of race of tester and race of comparison norms should have an interaction effect on Negro students' task motivation. They predicted that on a cognitive task defined as an intellectual test, with Negro (i.e., easy) norms, a white (i.e., higher power) tester should occasion higher scores than a Negro (i.e., low power) tester, while with white (i.e., hard) norms a Negro (i.e., low power) tester should be better for performance. The investigators also predicted that setting probability of success (P_s) at a high level by providing fictitious feedback about prior performance should have a more favorable effect on Negro achievement in a white norm condition than in a Negro norm condition. They reasoned further that if Negroes perceive an important (white) standard as attainable, anticipated evaluation by a powerful authority (white tester) should be highly motivating. Hence, with white-norm instructions, setting P_s high should tend to have a more favorable effect upon performance with a white tester as compared with a Negro tester.

In the experiment, male freshmen at a Negro college in the upper south were first administered, *en masse*, a digit-symbol code task by a Negro male experimenter, with neutral instructions. A few days later subjects were again tested, this time in small groups. The tester, who was now either a white or Negro male, introduced himself as a psychologist from the "Southern Educational Testing Service," a fictitious organization. Subjects were informed that the earlier session had really been a practice tryout for the code test which they were about to take, and that test norms were available. For the white-norm condition, subjects were told that their scores would be compared with the average scores of students in all the colleges and universities of the state, and for the Negro-norm condition, the story was that they would be compared with the freshman average at their own college. The men were also told that immediately following the testing, the administrator would see each person individually, score the test, and explain what the score indicated about his intelligence and aptitude for college work. This was done to create a strong expectation of face-to-face evaluation by the adult authority.

To manipulate P_s, each subject was handed a letter, ostensibly from the "Testing Service," that stated the likelihood of his being able to achieve the average score of his age group, based upon his practice performance. The probabilities were either 10, 60, or 90% and had no relation to the individual's actual score on the pretest. In a control condition no letters were distributed.

Following the instructions, the code task that had been used in the pretest was readministered. (An arithmetic task was also administered at both sessions, always after the code task. Since the experimental instructions were not identical for the two tasks, results for arithmetic will not be discussed.)

The effects of the three independent variables on code performance were evaluated by an overall analysis of variance. Mean pre-post gain

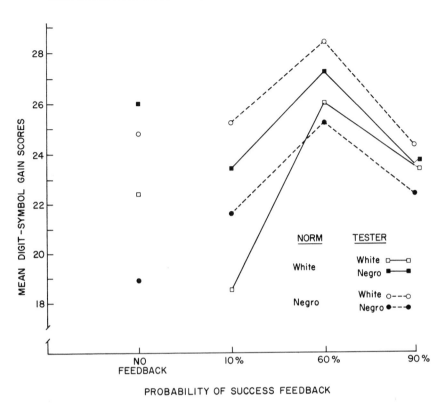

Fig. 1. Mean digit symbol gain scores for tester/norm/feedback groups.

scores of subjects (about 30 subjects per treatment) are shown in Fig. 1. First, there was a P_s main effect, in which scores for all tester-norm groups peaked in the 60% feedback condition. This finding is predicted by Atkinson's motivational model, if one makes the assumption that most subjects had a stronger general tendency to seek success than avoid failure. Second, the data supported the prediction of a tester x norm interaction: In the white norm condition, subjects performed better with a Negro tester than with a white tester, while the opposite pattern occurred in the Negro norm condition. These differences, it can be seen, occurred consistently across P_s feedback conditions. Finally, the predicted interactions of P_s feedback with race variables were not revealed by the analysis of variance.

However, Fig. 1 suggests that as P_s increased there was a convergence of white tester and Negro tester means in the white norm condition. As a further check on the reliability of the convergence effect, white norm groups were analyzed separately: The no feedback and 10% feedback conditions were combined and compared by means of a t test with the two high P_s conditions (60 and 90%). There was a significant difference between these high and non-high feedback groups in magnitude of the race-of-tester effect. For the difference in race-of-tester effects between the lowest P_s condition (10%) and the highest (90%), statistical significance was marginal. Thus, there was some evidence that in the white norm condition, high P_s had a relatively more favorable effect on performance when the tester was white than when he was Negro.

A terminal questionnaire provided data bearing upon the underlying theoretical assumptions. With regard to perceived difficulty of achieving the comparison standard, self-reports showed the following rank ordering of feedback conditions, from most to least difficult: 10%, no feedback, 60%, and 90%. There was no strong tendency for these self-reports of subjective P_s to be lower among white-norm subjects than among Negro-norm subjects, perhaps reflecting a phenomenon of defensive denial on the part of subjects. A consistent norm effect on reported "nervousness" suggests that fear of failure was indeed higher in the white norm groups, as initially assumed by the investigators.

It had also been assumed that subjects would perceive a white tester as a more potent, or authoritative, evaluator than a Negro tester. On three evaluative scales—capability, importance, and clarity of communication—the white tester received higher ratings. Since all testers gave identical instructions, it would appear that the differential ratings provided strong support for the assumption.

Insofar as the comparison group and the tester can be regarded as comparative and normative social referents, the experiment is relevant to Festinger's (1954) hypothesis that people are more likely to compare themselves with similar rather than dissimilar others. If level of task performance can be taken as a measure of responsiveness to opportunities for comparison, then the present data indicate that the preference for similar or dissimilar *comparison* referents can be influenced by characteristics of the salient *normative* referent. Specifically in this instance, degree of responsiveness to high-risk and low-risk comparisons on a positive characteristic—intelligence—was apparently determined by the status of an evaluator.

Since having a high-status evaluator is potentially more threatening than having a low-status one, the results can be viewed as similar to those obtained by Hackmiller (1966) in a study that used an attribute not involving ability—hostility. He created high and low threat conditions by describing the trait negatively or positively. In the high threat condition, subjects tended to choose a "defensive social comparison referent" that enhanced self-esteem, while in the low threat condition they preferred a comparison referent that was more informative for self-evaluation. In accord with this pattern, in the present experiment the threatening (i.e., high status, white) evaluator occasioned stronger response to the more self-enhancing (i.e., easy, Negro) standard of performance, while with the nonthreatening (i.e., low status, Negro) evaluator, stronger response was made to the standard that was riskier but more informative for self-evaluation (i.e., the hard, white standard).

If riskiness of the comparison standard was so important in determining behavior, it remains to be explained why setting P_s high experimentally did not produce a stronger tendency toward reversal of certain race effects, as predicted. What the investigators overlooked was that a person's expectancy of success at a given task is likely to be determined not only by objective information received in the task situation itself, but also by the more general expectations he brings with him to the task. Apparently, the expectations most Negro students bring to a situation of intellectual competition with whites would be likely to produce in them a tendency to displace objective P_s downward. As already noted, Katz and Benjamin (1960) observed a phenomenon of this sort in Negro students at a predominantly white college in the North. These subjects privately rated themselves below whites in ability on certain cognitive tasks, even after they had been provided with evidence of equal competence.

To investigate further how P_s feedback can influence Negro students' achievement efforts, Katz, Atchison, Epps, and Perry (1970a) did two experiments which were virtually identical, except that they were done at two colleges differing in academic standards of admission. The studies attempted to retest one of the predictions of the foregoing study (Katz et al., 1970b), to the effect that when a cognitive task is presented as an intellectual test, with a white-peer comparison standard, P_s feedback will interact with race of tester. That is, performance will be better with a Negro tester under low P_s, but better with a white tester under high P_s. The instructions used previously were modified to make high and low P_s feedback less extreme, hence more plausible. Also, the order of tasks was changed so that arithmetic (shown by pilot work to be perceived by Negro students as more diagnostic of academic aptitude) was always presented before the code. Finally, the P_s induction was fully reinstated between tasks.

One experiment was done at the same college as the earlier study, where standards of admission were relatively low. Results on both tasks fully upheld the prediction: Higher scores occurred with a Negro tester under low P_s and medium P_s, but the relationship was reversed under high P_s. Terminal questionnaire data tended to support the investigators' assumption that the white examiner would be perceived as a more stringent and threatening evaluator: With a white tester, subjects were more likely to report viewing both tasks as hard, feeling nervous, and thinking the tester would not be favorably impressed by their scores. (Since the questionnaire was given to subjects after they performed the tasks, the meaning of these response differences is somewhat ambiguous.)

The same experiment was done at a college having relatively high standards of admission. Here the outcome was unanticipated. The only findings for performance were that on both tasks subjects scored higher with a white experimenter. Two possible explanations come to mind: that the white norm was not seen by these highly selected Negro students as very risky, and/or that the white tester was a more attractive, but not a more threatening, authority figure than the Negro tester. There is some evidence in support of both possibilities. First, at both tasks, the selective college subjects, as compared with those at the nonselective college, were more proficient; and, on the terminal questionnaire, they were more likely to describe themselves as proficient and less likely to describe the items as "hard." While between-college comparisons do not really answer the question of whether the achievement situation was one of low risk for the selective college sample, they are clearly consistent with such an assumption. Regarding the possibility that selective college subjects viewed the white examiner more positively than the Negro examiner, their questionnaire responses showed that they were more inclined to believe that he would be favorably impressed by their test scores and more interested in seeing him afterward to receive his evaluation. (Again it must be noted that these perceptual responses could have been influenced by awareness of good performance.)

It should be mentioned that *within* each of the two colleges, ability, as defined by scores on academic achievement tests, was not predictive of experimental performance. But differences between the two college samples was not restricted to intellectual ability. One institution's selective admissions policy could have created an atmosphere of elitism that favorably influenced the self-confidence of all students enrolled there.

E. CONCLUDING REMARKS ON NEGRO BEHAVIOR

This discussion of Negro behavior has been mainly directed to the identification of biracial situational variables affecting achievement efforts. Starting with some empirical evidence of emotionality and constraint in face-to-face contacts with white peers, I have reviewed a body of research on stress, and normative and comparative referent influences, in various types of task setting. The experimental demonstrations of effects on Negro performance at relatively simple cognitive tasks must be regarded as only suggestive of underlying cognitive and motivational factors.

An obvious gap in existing knowledge is the achievement behavior of white counterparts. Replications on whites are needed to establish definitely that the observed cross-racial influences on Negro performance really reflect a basic status phenomenon rather than mere effects of novelty or unfamiliarity. While the studies of biracial work teams support the status assumption, the need for direct empirical verification still exists.

In addition, future research on the determinants of Negro performance should include the following: a broader range of achieving behaviors and motivational measures, analysis of situational factors determining the selection of social comparison and normative referents, and identification of critical personality dimensions.

Finally, a comprehensive approach to the problem of how Negroes can bring about social change would have to include the study of the development and utilization of pressure resources, such as the skills requisite for traditional and nontraditional political action. Here, theories and research techniques related to bargaining behavior, coalition formation, and mixed-motive games could probably be profitably applied.

REFERENCES

Adams, J. S. Inequity in social exchange. In L. Berkowitz (Ed.), *Advances in experimental social psychology*. Vol. 2. New York: Academic Press, 1965. Pp. 267-299.

Adorno, T. W., Frenkel-Brunswik, E., Levinson, D. J., & Sanford, R. N. *The authoritarian personality*. New York: Harper & Row, 1950.

Allen, S. A., Dubanoski, R. A., & Stevenson, H. W. Children's performance as a function of race of E, race of S, and type of verbal reinforcement. *Journal of Experimental Child Psychology*, 1966, 4, 248-256.

Allport, G. *The nature of prejudice*. Cambridge, Mass.: Addison-Wesley, 1954.

Amir, Y. Contact hypothesis in ethnic relations. *Psychological Bulletin*, 1969, 71, 319-342.

Aronson, E., & Golden, B. W. The effect of relevant and irrelevant aspects of communicator credibility on opinion change. *Journal of Personality*, 1962, 30, 135-146.

Atkinson, J. W. *An introduction to motivation*. Princeton, N.J.: Van Nostrand, 1964.

Berg, K. E. Ethnic attitudes and agreement with a Negro person. *Journal of Personality and Social Psychology*, 1966, 4, 215-220.

Berkowitz, L. Anti-Semitism and the displacement of aggression. *Journal of Abnormal and Social Psychology*, 1959, 59, 182-187.

Berkowitz, L., & Green, J. A. The stimulus qualities of the scapegoat. *Journal of Abnormal and Social Psychology*, 1962, 64, 293-301.

Berkowitz, L., & Holmes, D. S. The generalization of hostility to disliked objects. *Journal of Personality*, 1959, **27**, 565-577.

Blalock, H. M., Jr. *Toward a theory of minority group relations*. New York: Wiley, 1967.

Bovard, E. W. The effects of social stimuli on the response to stress. *Psychological Review*, 1959, **66**, 267-277.

Bray, D. W. The prediction of behavior from two attitude scales. *Journal of Abnormal and Social Psychology*, 1950, **45**, 64-84.

Brink, W., & Harris, L. *The Negro revolution in America*. New York: Simon & Schuster, 1964.

Brink, W., & Harris, L. *Black and white*. New York: Simon & Schuster, 1966.

Burnstein, E., & McRae, A. V. Some effects of shared threat and prejudice in racially mixed groups. *Journal of Abnormal and Social Psychology*, 1962, **64**, 257-263.

Clark, K. B. Problems of power and social change: toward a relevant social psychology. *Journal of Social Issues*, 1965, **21** (No. 3), 4-20.

Cohen, E. G. Interracial interaction disability. Unpublished manuscript, Stanford University, 1969.

Cohen, M. White students' reactions to the test performance of Negroes. Unpublished doctoral dissertation, New York University, 1965.

Cook, S. W. Desegregation: A psychological analysis. In W. W. Charters, Jr. & N. L. Gage (Eds.), *Readings in the social psychology of education*. Boston: Allyn & Bacon, 1963.

DeFleur, M. L., & Westie, F. R. Verbal attitudes and overt acts: an experiment on the salience of attitudes. *American Sociological Review*, 1958, **23**, 667-673.

DeFriese, G. H., & Ford, W. S. Open occupancy—what whites say, what they do. *Trans-Action*, 1968, **5**(5), 53-56.

Deutsch, M., & Collins, M. *Interracial housing: A psychological evaluation of a social experiment*. Minneapolis: University of Minnesota Press, 1951.

Dollard, J., Doob, L., Miller, N., Mowrer, O., & Sears, R. *Frustration and aggression*. New Haven: Yale University Press, 1939.

Duffy, E. The psychological significance of the concept of "arousal" or "activation." *Psychological Review*, 1957, **64**, 265-275.

Epps, E. G., Katz, I., & Runyon, E. Effect of race of comparison referent and motives on Negro performance: A Northern replication. Unpublished manuscript, University of Michigan, 1970.

Festinger, L. A theory of social comparison processes. *Human Relations*, 1954, **7**, 117-140.

Fishbein, M. The relationships between beliefs, attitudes, and behavior. In S. Feldman (Ed.), *Cognitive consistency*. New York: Academic Press, 1966. Pp. 200-223.

Gergen, K. J., & Jones, E. E. Mental illness, predictability, and affective consequences as stimulus factors in person perception. *Journal of Abnormal and Social Psychology*, 1963, **67**, 95-104.

Hackmiller, K. L. Threat as a determinant of downward comparison. *Journal of Experimental Social Psychology*, 1966, **2**(Suppl.), 32-39.

Harding, J., & Hogrefe, R. Attitudes of white department store employees toward Negro co-workers. *Journal of Social Issues*, 1952, **8**(No. 1), 18-28.

Harding, J., Proshansky, H., Kutner, B., & Chein, I. Prejudice and ethnic relations. In G. Lindzey & E. Aronson (Eds.), *The handbook of social psychology*. Vol. 5. Reading, Mass.: Addison-Wesley, 1969. Pp. 1-176.

Himmelstein, P., & Moore, J. C. Racial attitudes and the action of Negro and white background figures as factors in petition signing. *Journal of Social Psychology*, 1963, **61**, 267-272.

Hyman, H. H. Social psychology and race relations. In I. Katz & P. Gurin (Eds.), *Race and the social sciences*. New York: Basic Books, 1969. Pp. 3-48.

Insko, C. A., & Schopler, J. Triadic consistency: a statement of affective-cognitive-conative consistency. *Psychological Review*, 1967, 74, 361-376.

Iverson, M. A., & Schwab, H. G. Ethnocentric dogmatism and binocular fusion of sexually and racially discrepant stimuli. *Journal of Personality and Social Psychology*, 1967, 7, 73-81.

Jones, E. E. *Ingratiation*. New York: Appleton-Century-Crofts, 1964.

Jones, E. E., & Davis, K. E. From acts to dispositions; the attribution process in person perception. In L. Berkowitz (Ed.), *Advances in experimental social psychology*. Vol. 2. New York: Academic Press, 1965. Pp. 219-266.

Jones, E. E., & de Charms, R. Changes in social perception as a function of the personal relevance of behavior. *Sociometry*, 1957, 20, 78-85.

Kamenetsky, J., Burgess, G. G., & Rowan, T. The relative effectiveness of four attitude assessment techniques in predicting criterion. *Educational and Psychological Measurement*, 1956, 16, 187-194.

Katz, I. Review of evidence relating to effects of desegregation on the intellectual performance of Negroes. *American Psychologist*, 1964, 19, 381-399.

Katz, I., Atchison, C. O., Epps, E. G., & Perry, A. Factors affecting response to white intellectual standards at two Negro colleges. Unpublished manuscript, University of Michigan, 1970. (a)

Katz, I., Atchison, C. O., Epps, E. G., and Roberts, S. O. Race of evaluator, race of norm, expectancy, and achievement motive as determinants of Negro performance. Unpublished manuscript, University of Michigan, 1970. (b)

Katz, I., & Benjamin, L. Effects of white authoritarianism in biracial work groups. *Journal of Abnormal and Social Psychology*, 1960, 61, 448-456.

Katz, I., & Cohen, M. The effects of training Negroes upon cooperative problem solving in biracial teams. *Journal of Abnormal and Social Psychology*, 1962, 64, 319-325.

Katz, I., Epps, E. G., & Axelson, L. J. Effect upon Negro digit-symbol performance of anticipated comparison with whites and with other Negroes. *Journal of Abnormal and Social Psychology*, 1964, 69, 77-83.

Katz, I., Epps, E. G., & Perry, A. Effect of race of comparison referent and achievement motive on Negro cognitive performance. Unpublished manuscript, University of Michigan, 1970. (c)

Katz, I., Goldston, J., & Benjamin, L. Behavior and productivity in biracial work groups. *Human Relations*, 1958, 11, 123-141.

Katz, I., & Greenbaum, C. Effects of anxiety, threat, and racial environment on task performance of Negro college students. *Journal of Abnormal and Social Psychology*, 1963, 66, 562-567.

Katz, I., & Gurin, P. Race relations and the social sciences: overview and further discussion. In I. Katz & P. Gurin (Eds.), *Race and the social sciences*. New York: Basic Books, 1969.

Katz, I., Henchy, T., & Allen, H. Effects of race of tester, approval-disapproval, and need on Negro children's learning. *Journal of Personality and Social Psychology*, 1968, 8, 38-42.

Katz, I., Roberts, S. O., & Robinson, J. M. Effects of difficulty, race of administrator, and instructions on Negro digit-symbol performance. *Journal of Personality and Social Psychology*, 1965, 2, 53-59.

Kelley, H. H. Two functions of reference groups. In G. E. Swanson, T. M. Newcomb, & E. L. Hartley (Eds.), *Readings in social psychology*. (2d ed.) New York: Holt, 1952. Pp. 410-414.

Kennedy, W. A., & Vega, M. Negro children's performance on a discrimination task as a function of examiner race and verbal incentive. *Journal of Personality and Social Psychology*, 1965, **2**, 839-843.

Kutner, B., Wilkins, C., & Yarrow, P. R. Verbal attitudes and overt behavior involving racial prejudice. *Journal of Abnormal and Social Psychology*, 1952, **47**, 649-652.

LaPiere, R. T. Attitudes vs. actions. *Social Forces*, 1934, **13**, 230-237.

Lefcourt, H. M., & Ladwig, G. W. The effect of reference group upon Negroes task persistence in a biracial competitive game. *Journal of Personality and Social Psychology*, 1965, **1**, 668-671.

Lerner, M. J., & Matthews, G. Reactions to suffering of others under conditions of indirect responsibility. *Journal of Personality and Social Psychology*, 1967, **5**, 319-325.

Linn, L. S. Verbal attitudes and overt behavior: a study of racial discrimination. *Social Forces*, 1965, **44**, 353-364.

Malmo, R. B. Anxiety and behavioral arousal. *Psychological Review*, 1957, **64**, 276-287.

Malof, M., & Lott, A. J. Ethnocentrism and the acceptance of Negro support in a group pressure situation. *Journal of Abnormal and Social Psychology*, 1962, **65**, 254-258.

Mann, J. H. The effects of interracial contact or sociometric choices and perceptions. *Journal of Social Psychology*, 1959, **50**, 143-152. (a)

Mann, J. H. The relationship between cognitive, affective, and behavioral aspects of racial prejudice. *Journal of Social Psychology*, 1959, **49**, 223-228. (b)

Matthews, D. R. Political science research on race relations. In I. Katz & P. Gurin (Eds.), *Race and the social sciences*. New York: Basic Books, 1969. Pp. 113-144.

Matthews, D. R., & Prothro, J. W. *Negroes and the new Southern politics*. New York: Harcourt, Brace & World, 1966.

Mussen, P. H. Some personality and social factors related to changes in children's attitudes toward Negroes. *Journal of Abnormal and Social Psychology*, 1950, **45**, 423-441.

Myrdal, G. *An American dilemma*. New York: Harper & Row, 1944.

Pettigrew, T. F. Social evaluation theory: Convergences and applications. In D. Levine (Ed.), *Nebraska symposium on motivation*. Lincoln: University of Nebraska Press, 1967.

Pettigrew, T. F. Racially separate or together? *Journal of Social Issues*, 1969, **25**, No. 1, 43-69.

Porier, G. W., & Lott, A. J. Galvanic skin responses and prejudice. *Journal of Personality and Social Psychology*, 1967, **5**, 253-259.

Rankin, R. E., and Campbell, D. T. Galvanic skin response to Negro and white experimenters. *Journal of Abnormal and Social Psychology*, 1955, **51**, 30-33.

Reynolds, D., & Toch, H. Perceptual correlates of prejudice: a stereoscopic-constancy experiment. *Journal of Social Psychology*, 1965, **66**, 127-133.

Rokeach, M., & Mezei, L. Race and shared belief as factors in social choice. *Science*, 1966, **151**, 167-172.

Rossi, P. H. New directions for race relations research in the sixties. Paper presented at a conference on Research in Race Relations, New York, December 1963.

Saenger, G., & Gilbert, E. Customer reactions to the integration of Negro sales personnel. *International Journal of Opinion and Attitude Research*, 1950, **4**, 57-76.

Sherif, M. Superordinate goals in the reduction of intergroup conflict. *American Journal of Sociology*, 1958, **48**, 349-356.

Smith, E. W. L., & Dixon, T. R. Verbal conditioning as a function of race of the experimenter and prejudice of the subject. *Journal of Experimental Social Psychology*, 1968, **4**, 285-301.

Stouffer, S. A., Suchman, E. A., DeVinney, L. C., Star, S. A., & Williams, R. M., Jr. *Studies in social psychology in World War II.* Vol. 1. *The American soldier.* Princeton, N.J.: Princeton University Press, 1949.

Triandis, H. C., & Davis, E. E. Race and belief as determinants of behavioral intentions. *Journal of Personality and Social Psychology,* 1965, 2, 715-725.

van den Berghe, P. L. *Race and racism.* New York: Wiley, 1967.

Vidulich, R. N., & Krevanick, F. W. Racial attitudes and emotional response to visual representations of the Negro. *Journal of Social Psychology,* 1966, 68, 85-93.

Weatherley, D. Anti-Semitism and the expression of fantasy aggression. *Journal of Abnormal and Social Psychology,* 1961, 62, 454-457.

Westie, F. R., & DeFleur, M. L. Autonomic responses and their relationship to race attitudes. *Journal of Abnormal and Social Psychology,* 1959, 58, 340-347.

Williams, R. M., Jr. *Strangers next door.* Englewood Cliffs, N.J.: Prentice-Hall, 1964.

Williams, R. M., Jr. Social change and social conflict: race relations in the United States, 1944-1964. *Sociological Inquiry,* 1965, 35, 8-25.

Wilner, D., Walkley, R. P., & Cook, S. W. Residential proximity and intergroup relations in public housing projects. *J. of Social Issues,* 1955, 8(No. 1), 45-69.

Woodmansee, J. J., & Cook, S. W. Dimensions of verbal racial attitudes: their identification and measurement. *Journal of Personality and Social Psychology,* 1967, 7, 240-250.

Yarrow, M. R. Interpersonal dynamics in a desegregation process. *Journal of Social Issues,* 1958, 14(Whole No. 1).

FINDINGS AND THEORY IN THE STUDY OF FEAR COMMUNICATIONS[1]

Howard Leventhal
UNIVERSITY OF WISCONSIN

[1]This chapter is an expanded version of a talk presented at the Eastern Psychological Association meetings in the spring of 1966. The research and theoretical ideas have benefited from discussion with a number of individuals, in particular: James Dabbs, Jean Johnson, Neil Kornzweig, Patricia Niles, John Rosen, Robert Singer, and Jean C. Watts. Daniel Horn and Bernard Mausner have been helpful protagonists, and I am especially indebted to Sylvan Tomkins for many stimulating discussions of these ideas. I would also like to thank Richard Lazarus, Richard Nisbett, and Sidney Perloe for helpful comments on an early draft. Thanks also go to the editor of this series, Leonard Berkowitz, for his many helpful suggestions. Special thanks go to Mrs. Bonnie Simon whose diligent help made it possible to complete this chapter. The experimental work reported was supported by grants from the United State Public Health Service (CH 00371) and the United Health Foundation.

I. Introduction

This paper reviews the empirical results and theoretical underpinnings of studies of fear arousing communications. The discussion will focus on the interrelationship of emotional and instrumental behavior. As a consequence, theoretical and empirical problems similar to those confronted in discussions of two factor learning theory (N. E. Miller, 1951a; Rescorla & Solomon, 1967), punishment (Church, 1963; Solomon, 1964), eyelid conditioning (Spence, 1966), and the formation of conscience, (Aronfreed, 1964) will be dealt with. All of these analyses make clear that stimuli which provoke intense emotion have varied effects upon instrumental or problem solving activity. This review of the fear communication literature will also reveal that the outcomes are often influenced by complex contingencies. But despite the complexity, I shall make a serious effort to identify empirical regularities and will present a theoretical model to provide conceptual integration.

In working toward the above goals, I shall make the following points: (1) increases in fear generally increase persuasion, but there obviously are conditions where this is not so; (2) when high fear messages fail to persuade, the failure frequently reflects the subject's felt incapacity to cope with danger; (3) the predictions suggested by drive models, whether linear or curvilinear, are largely unsupported; and (4) the experimental data seem consistent with a general model which posits that both fear reactions and instrumental activities are under the control of external stimulation.

A. EXPERIMENT AND THEORY

In the typical attitude change study, the subject is exposed to a communication (written, verbal, pictoral), and questionnaires are used to assess the message's impact upon beliefs. On some occasions, although not as frequently as one might wish, behavioral measures are obtained along with the attitude measures. Many investigations in this area show that a wide range of variables influence the persuasive impact of a message (Hovland, Janis, & Kelley, 1953; Klapper, 1960). In an effort to order or systematize these variables, they are frequently classified according to a communication model, e.g., source, media, message, and recipient factors (Fearing, 1953; Hovland, 1954). This classification is useful in that it facilitates remembering and discussing results. It is unsatisfactory, however, in that it does not explain the process of persuasion. For this reason, investigators have attempted to view their findings in the light of a variety of theoretical models which allow one to interpret past findings and derive hypotheses for new observations.

To make it easier for the reader to follow my analysis of the literature, I shall present an overview of the key components of fear communication experiments and will introduce the two major theoretical paradigms that can be used to interpret the findings. The first and historically
most important of the paradigms is the fear drive model, a variant of the
classic drive reduction model used in many animal learning studies (N. E.
Miller, 1951a). It assumes that the emotional response of fear functions
as a drive which mediates belief change and behavior change. The second
paradigm, which I have called the parallel response model, was suggested
by the experimental data. This model assumes that the communication
produces both persuasion *and* fear; fear does not cause persuasion.
The scheme I will describe is basically an information processing analysis
that emphasizes the situational factors and cognitions leading to coping
behavior, and the situational factors and cognitions producing fear.
It also postulates that the organism's own behavior, its fear and its
coping reactions, can serve as information modifying subsequent decisions and actions. Thus, the model suggests that different informational
processes control specific types of behavior at particular points in time.

The Components of Fear Communication Experiments

Most studies of fear communication have dealt with dangers to the
body. These communications typically consist of two parts: (1) information describing a danger and (2) information (recommendations) on how
to avoid the danger. Further differentiations can also be made. Danger
can be divided into subcategories, such as information on causes of danger as distinct from consequences of danger, and each type of information
can be presented at different levels of vividness. For example, information on the causes of lung cancer can be factual and relatively unemo-
tional if we use schematic diagrams, bland verbal descriptions, and
movies of smoking machines extracting tars from cigarettes. These descriptions can be made especially vivid by using live models of lungs,
emotional language, and realistic simulations of the process of deposition
of tars in a lung. Another example of an emotion-provoking description
of a danger agent is seen in movies of controlled automotive accidents
(Leventhal & Trembly, 1968). The crashing of cars at high speeds is
emotion provoking and devoid of direct information on the consequences
of the accident. In most cases, however, the emotional part of the message consists of information on the consequences of the agent. Pictures
of a cancer on a laboratory animal, a cancerous lung, an operation removing a cancerous lung, etc., focus on the consequences of the danger and
arouse strong emotion.

Information on practices comes in many forms, such as the detailed descriptions of toothbrushes and brushing techniques used by Leventhal and Singer (1966) and the brief recommendations to stop smoking employed by Leventhal and Niles (1964). In most studies the fear provoking information is varied across experimental treatments while the information on the recommended practice is kept constant. Of course, the characteristics of both sets of information can be manipulated and their effects observed upon randomly assigned subject samples and upon specific subgroups of the sample.

The types of questions asked of the subjects are varied, but they can usually be placed in one of three classes: (1) manipulation checks; (2) measures of acceptance; and (3) checks for confounding. The first group of questions, manipulation checks, include measures of concern or worry about the danger (Janis & Feshbach, 1953), moods (Nowlis, 1965), reports of emotional symptoms (Leventhal & Niles, 1965), and questions about the fearfulness of the communication. Attitude questions measuring belief in the danger (smoking causes lung cancer.), evaluations of its magnitude (tetanus is serious.), and personal relevance (I believe that I am vulnerable to lung cancer.) are also used to check on the effects of the danger information. These items are treated sometimes as if they are measures of emotional arousal and at other times as measures of mediating processes. While there is no reason to assume that all of these questions assess a common intervening process, responses to them are frequently correlated.

The second class of measures, dealing with acceptance of the communication, is typically focused upon the subject's responses to the preventive action recommended by the communicator. The measures are of three types: evaluative (Does *S* feel the action is important?), intentional (Does he intend to take action?), and performance (Does he actually follow through in behavior?). The relationship between the attitudinal and behavioral measures provides an important challenge to attitude theory and research. Indeed, the frequent independence of these measures provides additional evidence for the assumption that evaluation, emotion, and action are often controlled by different variables and may have no intrinsic tendency to be in balance or to influence one another.

The third class of measures, checks for confounding, is used to demonstrate that the experimenter has equated his communication conditions on irrelevant but potentially important variables, anger, source credibility, etc. If high fear messages seem more or less credible, or arouse different levels of anger, these differences, rather than the variations in fear, might be the source of the resulting differences in persuasion.

In some cases, however, these unintended effects can probably be ignored. For example, one could not readily attribute the persuasive impact of a high fear message to credibility if the fear message seems *less* credible and is more persuasive. But when the high fear message is regarded as more credible and it is also more persuasive, one will have to entertain the alternative hypothesis that credibility rather than fear is responsible for the outcome.

While it may seem preferable to manipulate rather than to measure confounding variables, limitations of technology, of sample size, etc., may preclude their inclusion in a single experimental design. Thus, the assessment of such factors may be the best and, at times, the only way of evaluating their potential contribution to treatment differences. The need for these measures makes clear that the fear communication experiment is complex and that the experimenter may be uncertain as to which aspect of his message is responsible for attitude change. Of course, not all studies use all three classes of measures, nor will they all be discussed when they have been used.

B. THEORETICAL PARADIGMS

1. Fear as a Drive

The design of the typical fear communication study reflects the assumption that fear is a drive or a motivator of attitude change. The danger information in the message *starts* an emotional fear reaction, and the stimuli generated by this response are supposed to be drive producing (N. E. Miller, 1951a). The performance or rehearsal of the communicator's recommendations (actions designed to cope with danger) are expected to reduce or *stop* the emotional activity. When a response reduces fear, it is reinforced and becomes a part of one's permanent response repertory. Fear is the motor for instrumental activity, and the onset and termination of fear provide the signals (start and stop rules) for behavior change.

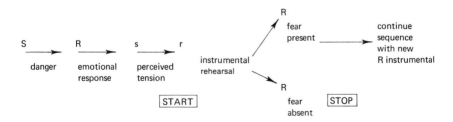

Fig. 1. The drive paradigm for acceptance.

It is important to note that the fear drive paradigm postulates a *serial process*, with later behaviors, such as attitude change, *functionally* dependent upon or mediated by the earlier (emotional) responses in the chain. Because of this, the fear reactions are the central explanatory concept in the paradigm. Other independent variables are supposed to influence attitude change by altering the mediating fear reactions. This use of the drive paradigm assumes that covert, symbolic, or anticipatory responses follow the same rules as overt responses (Berlyne, 1965). Thus, in the communication experiment the dangers are symbolic or pictorial in form, fear is anticipatory and usually not very intense, and attitude or covert verbal responses are typically the only possible reactions at the time of communications.

What does the fear drive paradigm say about the relationship between fear and persuasion? Do increases in fear increase acceptance of recommendations to stop smoking, take tetanus shots, etc. (a positive association), or does heightened fear decrease acceptance of recommendations to stop smoking, brush teeth after meals, etc. (a negative association)? The model suggests that more fearful messages should lead to greater persuasion (both attitude and behavior change) if the recommendations presented are in some degree fear reducing. But this prediction holds only when the rehearsal of the communicator's recommendations reduces fear; the reduction of fear is reinforcing. If fear is reduced by denying or ignoring the danger, there will be resistance to the communicator's recommendations.

The studies conducted by the author and his collaborators attempted to isolate specific variables that could integrate opposite findings (fear increasing persuasion and fear decreasing persuasion) into the drive schema. If fear is actually a key factor in mediating or determining the formation of beliefs, intentions, and actions, it is essential that the model suggest modifier variables that yield predictable interactions with fear level and that these effects be theoretically related to the process of fear reduction.

2. The Parallel Response Model

In the parallel model, emotional arousal is not a necessary antecedent of adaptation to the danger. Emotional behavior is seen as contemporary with adaptive behavior. As illustrated in Fig. 2a, both types of behavior, emotional and adaptive, are consequences of environmental stimulation. They do not cause one another.

The parallel model has certain interesting features. First, it raises the question of whether similar or different aspects of the stimulus situation elicit both types of response (see Fig. 2b). Second, it suggests that there

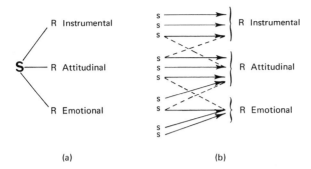

(a)   (b)

Fig. 2. The parallel response paradigm. (a) Depicts the stimulus dependence of the behavioral class. (b) Suggests that each class of responses may depend on partially overlapping stimulus elements.

is a correlation between emotional and adaptive behaviors, i.e., more serious threats elicit stronger coping responses *and* stronger emotional reactions. The model stresses the difference between a correlation and a causal or necessary relationship. Thus, some features of the situation may intensify or minimize fearfulness and have absolutely no effect upon the magnitude or the intensity of adaptive activity, while other aspects may intensify or minimize adaptive activity and not influence the intensity of emotional behavior.

A more elaborate version of the model can be seen in Fig. 3. It shows that reactions to situational stimulation are mediated by perceptual cognitive processes that encode and identify the environment threat. It is this encoding process that gives rise to fear and to adaptive behaviors.

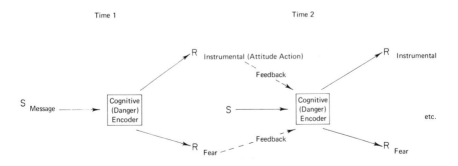

Fig. 3. A more elaborate version of the parallel model.

(It is not necessary to equate the encoding process with consciousness.) At later points in time the perceptual-cognitive system will also receive information from the organism's own behavior, including its emotional reactions and its coping behavior.

Both the evaluation of specific instrumental actions and the decision to act are dependent upon a problem solving process which we call *danger control*. The information guiding this process consists primarily of information from the external environment, but information respecting one's own coping behaviors and their effects upon the danger play an increasingly important role as problem solving proceeds.

Information can also be extracted from emotional behavior. There may be several steps to this process, including, perhaps, the interpretation of bodily cues as signs of fear. This may be followed by interpretations of the fear as a sign of inability to act, or the need to act, etc. When emotional behavior provides the cues for the selection and guidance of instrumental actions, the process involved is one of *fear control*. *Fear control* often may be independent of *danger control*, although the two processes should interact. Thus, many actions that are useful for controlling fear may have little or no effect upon the actual danger. *Fear control* behaviors of this sort include a wide range of avoidance reactions (including defenses) as well as acts that can control (or interfere with) components of the emotional response, e.g., eating and drinking to quiet (or reinterpret) internal signals and to dull awareness of external dangers.

The separation of the two processes, fear and danger control, leads to a variety of interesting predictions and helps us understand a number of frequently made observations. One of these is the fact that fear often is strongest *after*, rather than before or during, the successful avoidance of a danger. In such instances there may be little interference between fear control and danger control, and the responses used to control fear may be quite different from those used to control danger. On other occasions, the two types of control processes might be in competition with one another. For example, immediately after exposure to highly threatening warnings, fear will be strong and may motivate avoidance behaviors that could disrupt danger control and create resistance to persuasion. Conflict would also arise when one had to approach a danger in order to control it (e.g., have an X-ray taken and be operated on to eliminate lung cancer). The model also suggests that long term adaptive activity depends on a variety of cognitive variables related to danger control and is independent of the intensity of emotion at the time that behavioral intentions are formulated.

In summary, the two models raise different possibilities with regard to the types of interactions expected between emotional arousal and modifier variables. With respect to simple main effects, the parallel response model clearly leads us to expect that for the most part there will be positive associations between fear and persuasion. A highly threatening communication will produce multiple responses: a high level of fear, highly favorable attitudes toward protective acts, strong intentions to execute the acts, and a high probability that protective action will be taken. But the model also suggests that the strength of this association will change with the passage of time. The changes will depend on the presence or absence of various factors that stimulate fear and the presence or absence of factors that encourage danger control. Further speculation on these points will be presented along with the empirical findings.

II. Conflicting Effects and Experimental Hypotheses

Our review of the experimental literature begins with a simple question: Does increasing fear regarding a potential danger facilitate the formation of beliefs and the execution of behaviors recommended by the communication, or does strong fear interfere with belief formation and behavior change? After we have discussed this issue we will talk about interactions in which specific variables modify the relationship between fear level and persuasion. But why begin with the main effect question when it is clear that the interactions between fear level and modifier variables are the data that will lead us to accept or reject our alternative paradigms. In his discussion of simple monotonic relationships Janis (1967) has made this comment, ". . . is it the right question to ask? Does not this question take too much for granted by assuming a simple monotonic relation between the intensity of fear arousal and communication effectiveness?" [p. 167]. Should not investigators ". . . start looking for hitherto neglected variables that might be interacting with those under investigation?" [p. 168].

While it would simplify our exposition just to ignore main effect data, there are several reasons for not doing so. First, *there are actually very few studies showing negative relationships*. Second, there has never been a critical review of these discrepant studies. Third, investigators and secondary sources have put great emphasis upon main effects. Fourth, the low frequency of appearance of negative effects has important methodological implications and important consequences for the interpretation of positive effects (more fear-more persuasion).

A. EVIDENCE FOR NEGATIVE RELATIONSHIPS

A number of authors have attributed considerable importance to the negative relationship between fear and persuasion. Introductory textbooks of high quality (e.g., Hilgard & Atkinson, 1967; Krech, Crutchfield, & Livson, 1969) suggest that negative relationships are frequently found, although they do mention contradictory positive effects. Even recent social psychology texts state (some without qualification) that increasing fear decreases communication acceptance (Berelson & Steiner, 1964; Krech, Crutchfield, & Ballachey, 1962; Proshansky and Seidenberg, 1966, p. 108). Indeed, the emphasis upon negative main effects can be traced directly to the original Janis and Feshbach (1953) study. Although the authors stated that fear level and persuasion might not always be negatively related, the impact of this qualifying statement was weakened by the fact that they published the main effect (1953) and the interaction which underlay it in separate journals (Janis & Feshbach, 1954). Additional emphasis on the main effect also appears in the review of this study in the Hovland *et al.* (1953) volume. Let us examine this effect more closely.

A negative relationship between fear level and persuasion exists, of course, when a measure of acceptance (attitude, intention, or action) shows stronger responses among subjects exposed to a mild fear message than among subjects exposed to a high fear message. Emotional drive theory offers a variety of hypotheses to account for this outcome. All of them derive from a common assumption; when the communicator's recommendation does not completely reduce fear — turn off the drive — the organism will be motivated to make other responses and reject the persuasive message. For example, if there is a delay before behavior is possible, if the recommended protective act is viewed as imperfect, if the subject is high in self-esteem and sees himself as invulnerable to attack, or if he is neurotic and prone to deny threat, etc., high fear is likely to result in resistance to persuasion. (Each of these hypotheses will be discussed in the section on interactions.)

In their 1953 study, Janis and Feshbach presented the same set of recommendations on dental hygiene practices to three groups of junior high school students. Each experimental group received varying amounts of fear information on the danger of improper dental care. Immediately after exposure to this message, interest and reported fear were higher in the groups given the most threatening communication. Two weeks later there was a higher net proportion of subjects reporting favorable changes in dental hygiene practices in the *low* fear communication (36%) than in the moderate (22%) of high fear (8%) messages ($p < .06$; two-tailed).[2] The above data were supported by subjects' responses to a brief statement that was presented at the end of the questionnaire. The statement contradicted the earlier recommendation on the type of toothbrush that is most effective. Subjects previously exposed to the high fear communication were more willing to accept this counter propaganda. Both of the above relationships were linear. For various attitude measures there were no significant differences.

Janis and Feshbach suggested that the subjects exposed to high fear messages denied the personal relevance of the danger and were therefore resistant to persuasion. But the investigators had no independent evidence for such a denial interpretation. The hypothesis was made plausible by the negative results that were reported for other alternatives; there was no evidence that Ss exposed to high fear messages were inattentive and failed to learn the recommendations.

Unfortunately, the exclusion of one or two of a number of alternative hypotheses is not as satisfactory as a direct test of the denial hypothesis. Indeed, in a later study, which used a more sensitive test of the subjects' memory for the fear-producing information, Janis and Milholland (1954) did find differences in recall after high and low fear communications; more fear relevant material and less practical protective material was recalled after the high than after the low fear message. The authors then suggested that memory differences might be responsible for defensive avoidance and could cause the differential acceptance of high and low fear messages. But there is a serious problem inherent in their method which casts doubt on this thesis. Fear level was perfectly correlated with message length; the high fear messages were longer and subjects exposed to them had much more to remember. It is not surprising that they did less well, therefore, in remembering the recommendation material. Duke (1967) has also suggested that the slides which accompanied the verbal presentation may have distracted the audience and that distraction rather than fear led to forgetting. Duke found evidence in favor of his hypothesis; there was as much forgetting of the verbal content when

---

[2]While it is reasonable to use one-tailed probability values in testing hypotheses in specific experiments, it seems more difficult to justify their use in evaluating data from many experiments in which opposing results appear. Therefore, we shall use two-tailed probability values throughout our discussion. This takes into account the likelihood of either outcome, high fear more persuasive than low fear and low fear more persuasive than high. Where one-tailed values were reported in specific experiments, they will be doubled and therefore, will appear to carry somewhat less weight than they were given in the original publication. This is preferable to the procedure followed in Janis' recent theoretical article which reported both one- and two-tailed probability values but did not distinguish between them (e.g., Janis, 1967, pp. 197 and 204).

blank slides were introduced into the communication as when fear slides were included. While we cannot use these data to support the denial hypothesis, there is clearly a need for further work on the memory problem.

In a later study, Janis and Terwilliger (1962) offered a different explanation for the negative relationships. They suggested that high fear reduced the acceptance of antismoking propaganda by stimulating anger or aggression toward the communication and the experimenter. In a two-condition study they found that intense criticism of the high fear message was more frequent ($p < .05$) than intense criticism of the low fear message. Moreover, although net attitude change was greater in the low than in the high fear condition, this difference was clearly not significant ($p < .18$). The authors also did not indicate if critical reactions occurred more often in those Ss who disagreed with the communication.

The results of an experiment by Leventhal, Singer, and Jones (1965) are consistent with the idea that the expression of anger does not necessarily lead to resistance to persuasion. Their subjects expressed more anger (on a mood check list) and were more critical of a high fear message regarding tetanus than of a low fear communication. But the high fear message was more effective in strengthening intentions to take shots. In another study, Dabbs and Leventhal (1966) found both negative and positive correlations between intentions to take shots and expressions of anger. Negative correlations appeared after the subjects had received messages which portrayed the injections as painful and ineffective. When the shots were depicted as effective and painless, however, anger and intentions were positively associated. There were no differences in anger level between any of the experimental conditions. Thus, anger can accompany either message acceptance or message rejection.

The third hypothesis offered to account for negative main effects is that denial reactions develop only when there is a delay between the communication and the opportunity for action. When delay is eliminated there is no opportunity for denial to occur and there supposedly will be a positive relationship, with more fear leading to more persuasion (Janis & Feshbach, 1953, p. 87).

A study by Leventhal and Niles (1964) bears upon this last mentioned possibility. Using a sample of visitors to a health exposition at the New York City Coliseum, Leventhal and Niles measured verbal intentions to quit smoking and to take X-rays and also recorded whether Ss took an X-ray at a nearby health department mobile unit. There were three experimental conditions: a high and a moderate fear condition created by two versions of a movie on smoking and cancer, and a low fear control group. High fear was expected to increase the use of the mobile unit since this action could occur right away, but the high fear was also expected to be less effective in leading the subjects to formulate intentions to stop smoking as this response involved a commitment to an effortful, long-range course of action.

Contrary to this prediction, there were no differences among the fear conditions for either expressed intentions to take X-rays or the actual taking of X-rays; in short, high fear messages did not increase the frequency of these fairly immediate responses. On the other hand, intentions to quit or reduce smoking were strongest in the control group, in apparent agreement with the defensive denial hypothesis. But there was no significant tendency for reported intentions to stop smoking to be stronger in the mild than in the high fear group. This difference should have been significant as subjects in the high fear group were substantially more fearful than those in the mild condition. The fact that the control subjects were not exposed to a movie makes it still more difficult to interpret their intentions to stop smoking.

Additional analyses raised other questions about the defensive denial hypothesis. The high fear movies clearly strengthened the subjects' beliefs that smoking causes lung cancer, a change inconsistent with denial. In addition, within the high and mild fear conditions there were substantial positive correlations between reported fear and the acceptance of the recommendations. It would seem, therefore, that the data support the hypothesis that fear and acceptance of the communicated attitude are positively associated, but there is little support for the idea of an immediate facilitation of action by high fear. We shall return to this problem later on.

B. Evidence for Positive Relationships

In contrast to the relatively small number of studies reporting negative main effects (more fear less persuasion), there is a very large number of studies reporting *greater* acceptance of health and safety recommendations after high fear than after low fear messages. There are also numerous studies where the main effect may be positive in direction but is not significant statistically. These studies report the same positive relationships despite the differences between them in the topic of communication, the subject population sampled, and the conditions under which the data were collected. Most, though not all, were designed to detect interactions of fear level and other variables. Typically, some X factor was expected to produce a cross-over interaction; at one level of the X factor low fear would produce more acceptance than high fear and at the other level of the X factor high fear would produce more acceptance than low. Quite often, however, the outcome was a main effect, with more acceptance of the communication under high than low fear, and no evidence of an interaction of X and fear level. When interactions were present, they would generally show a greater difference between high fear and low fear at one level of X than at another level, but seldom, if ever, was there greater acceptance after low fear than high. A number of such studies are listed in Table 1, although the list is not exhaustive.

1. Studies of Smoking and Lung Cancer

Many experiments have been conducted to investigate the effects of fear communications upon intentions and reported behavior with respect to stopping smoking and taking chest X-rays. Communications on this topic have produced some of the strongest and most provocative interactions, threat level interacting with vulnerability of subject, immediacy of response, etc., and these interactions are discussed in the next section. The point to be made here is that despite the appearance of interactions, the overall picture presented by the data is for high fear messages to produce more persuasion than low fear messages. In general, the persuasion is greater on measures of attitude and intentions. While fear arousing communications often lead to reductions in smoking, subjects exposed to both high and low fear messages reduce their smoking more than do control subjects (see Leventhal, Watts, & Pagano, 1967). There are relatively fewer studies that show high fear messages leading to more smoking reduction than do low fear messages.

Some of the studies report no differences between treatments for attitudes or behavior, although they find correlations within treatment conditions. For example, Leventhal and Niles (1964) found positive correlations for smokers between reported fear and desire to stop smoking; in the high fear group between $r = .40$ ($p < .01$), in the mild fear group $r = .47$ ($p < .01$). The correlation between reported fear and stated desire to take X-rays was also positive ($r = .42$, $p < .05$) in the high fear condition and in the mild fear condition ($r = .40$, $p < .05$), and those who took X-rays were more frightened than those who did not. In a study by Leventhal and Watts (1966) there were also positive correlations within conditions, with reports of intense fear associated with stronger intentions to take X-rays ($r = .37$, $p < .05$) and stronger intentions to decrease smoking ($r = .40$, $p < .05$).

Niles' (1964) study using college students found the first clear main effect showing that high fear communications increased verbal acceptance of recommendations to stop smoking and take X-rays. But, the increase was strong only for those smokers who scored themselves as *low* (below the median) in vulnerability to cancer. A study by Insko, Arkoff, and

Insko (1965) reported that a high fear message strengthened nonsmokers' belief that smoking is dangerous, i.e., a cause of cancer. Smokers' belief that smoking causes cancer was also greater at high fear levels in the Niles' (1964) study and in the Leventhal and Niles (1964) experiment, although in the latter, there were no treatment effects for recommendation acceptance.

2. Smoking and Emotional Role Playing

In two recent studies, Janis and Mann (Janis & Mann, 1965; Mann, 1967; Mann & Janis, 1968) advanced the hypothesis that emotional role playing can break through defenses and stimulate a fear state which will facilitate rather than inhibit persuasion. The subjects in this procedure play the part of patients diagnosed as having cancer and are given information (X-rays) that encourage them to think about the consequences of the illness.

Janis and Mann (1965) compared role playing subjects and control subjects and found that the former reported a greater belief in the connection between smoking and cancer, stronger feelings of vulnerability to cancer, and stronger intentions to quit and/or modify their smoking. The authors stated that reductions in smoking were greater for role playing subjects than for control subjects and that the effects lasted for an 18-month period (Mann & Janis, 1968). The immediate effects are close to significance ($t = 1.84$, $df\,24$, $p < .10$) and the long-term effects exceed the $p < .05$ level in one of the three later comparisons. The scores used in the analysis involved the difference between smoking level at each of four points in time and the pretreatment smoking level. Because the initial level of smoking was higher in the role playing group than in the control group, each of the comparisons benefits from a potential regression effect.[3] Even without that problem, the greater change in the experimental groups brings it to only 2.5 cigarettes per day below the control group. This final difference is small and the same size as the initial nonsignificant ($p < .40$) difference.

The possibility that emotional role playing could contribute to a solution of the smoking problem merits our attention. The procedure is intrinsically fascinating and the authors describe it as ". . . an exceptionally successful means for arousing potentially adaptive fear reactions, breaking through the defensive facade that normally prevents many people from

---

[3]Questions also can be raised about the use of parametric procedures on nontransformed scores for the analysis of these data. Distributions of scores of change in smoking behavior are frequently skewed (see Leventhal et al., 1967) and the difference reported could reflect the fact that a few subjects quit smoking in the role playing condition.

taking account of their personal vulnerability to objective sources of danger" (Janis & Mann, 1965; p. 90; see also Janis, 1967, p. 22). But, while we may be tempted to ignore the problems with the data analysis of the first study, a later experiment by Mann (1967) shows no significant difference in smoking reduction between emotional role playing and information role playing (p. 343) groups. It is clear, then, that emotional role playing is one of a number of techniques that have some modest effect upon reported smoking behavior.

But there is another and perhaps more important point to be made: the role playing data neither suggested nor required an explanation different from that used in any experiment which showed more acceptance of the communication with high than with low fear. A main effect does not and cannot in itself show that role playing produces adaptive fear reactions by breaking through invulnerability defenses. The hypothesis requires that there be an interaction between a manipulation of these defenses and a manipulation of fear. Many researchers have devised special explanations for positive main effects, apparently assuming that the negative relationship is the typical state of affairs. But, since the positive relationship is actually the typical one, these explanations are nearly always superfluous. Indeed, with respect to vulnerability, a very large number of investigations suggest just the opposite of the Janis-Mann hypothesis; they show that persuasion is *facilitated by maintaining* rather than destroying invulnerability defenses.

3. Comments on Remaining Studies

There are a few points that should be mentioned about the other studies listed in Table I. First, in the tetanus studies (the last five cited in the table), high fear messages were clearly superior to low fear messages in changing attitudes. But high fear messages increased the taking of tetanus shots in only two (Dabbs & Leventhal, 1966; Kornzweig, 1967) of the five. An identical trend in a third study was not significant (Leventhal, Jones, & Trembly, 1966). The tetanus studies also illustrate the difficulties involved in obtaining interactions between fear level and other variables, instructions on how to get shots, the perceived effectiveness of the injections, etc. Attitudes were generally more favorable toward shots after high than after low fear messages, and this direction of difference was maintained across nearly all levels of the other factor.

Because more influence had been expected with low than high fear, at least under certain conditions, an *ad hoc suggestion* was offered by Leventhal (1965) and collaborators (Leventhal *et al.*, 1965) to account for the absence of these reversals. We suggested that tetanus inoculations appeared to be perfect protection against danger, reduced fear completely,

TABLE I
STUDIES IN WHICH HIGH FEAR MESSAGES WERE
MORE PERSUASIVE THAN LOW FEAR MESSAGES

Topic	Investigators	Acceptance measures
Atom Bomb testing	Haefner (1956)	Attitude
Automotive safety	Berkowitz & Cottingham (1960)	Attitude
	Leventhal & Niles (1965)	Attitude
	Powell (1965)	Attitude
	Simonson & Lundy (1966)	Attitude
Capital punishment	Evans, Rozelle, Lasater, Dein-broski, & Allen (1968)	Behavior
Dental hygiene	Haefner (1965)	Attitude and Behavior
	Leventhal & Singer (1966)	Attitude
	Singer (1965)	Attitude
Eye damage	Kraus, El-Assal, & DeFleur (1964)	Behavior report
Fallout shelters	Hewgill & Miller (1965)	Attitude
	G. R. Miller & Hewgill (1966)	Attitude
Intercollegiate sports and the admission of Red China	Lundy, Simonson, & Landers (1967)	Attitude
Political issues	Simonson & Lundy (1966)	Attitude
Smoking	Leventhal et al. (1967)	Attitude and Intention
	Niles (1964)	Attitude
Tetanus	Dabbs & Leventhal (1966)	Attitude, Intentions and Behavior
	Kornzweig (1967)	Attitude and Behavior
	Leventhal et al. (1966)	Attitude
	Leventhal et al. (1965)	Attitude and Intention
	Radelfinger (1965)	Attitude, Intentions and Behavior (n.s.)

and, therefore, always produced a positive relationship between fear level and persuasion. This hypothesis has been contradicted by the appearance of positive relationships for many other health issues, e.g., dental hygiene (Haefner, 1965; Leventhal & Singer, 1966; Singer, 1965) and automobile seat belts and car accidents (Berkowitz & Cottingham, 1960; Leventhal & Niles, 1965).

Two additional comments are in order, one on the studies by Haefner (1956) and the other on the investigation by DeWolfe and Governale (1964). Haefner compared the effects of messages producing high and low guilt and high and low fear. On his two measures of attitude change, high guilt was consistently less persuasive than low guilt. The fear messages, on the other hand, produced no effects for one measure, but, for the second measure, showed more attitude change for high than for low fear both immediately and two weeks after the communication. Contrary to the actual results, this study is occasionally referred to as supporting the superiority of low fear messages to high fear messages (e.g., Janis & Terwilliger, 1962; McGuire, 1968).

The study by DeWolfe and Governale (1964) found that nurses working with T.B. patients became more favorably disposed to their work the higher their initial fear scores ($r = .41$, $p < .01$). There was no such correlation in the control group. Since only the nurses in the experimental group associated with the patients, the correlation of fear and belief change might reflect the fact that the initially more fearful nurses experienced more dissonance when required to associate with patients who had a contagious illness.

C. SUMMARY OF EARLY ISSUES

The data reviewed clearly show a predominantly positive relationship between fear level and acceptance of the communicator's recommendations. Thus, the greater the fear stimulated by a treatment the more favorable the attitude toward the recommended practice. Moreover, the same generally positive relationship holds when correlations are computed within experimental conditions. The effects reported are stronger for measures of attitude than for measures of behavior.

Under these conditions, one might be tempted to be democratic and to choose between the two hypotheses by counting the number of studies on each side and declaring the one with the highest frequency the winner. Such a vote would imply that the studies involved a random sample of subjects, communication issues, threat levels, and settings, i.e., a random sample of experiments. Since it is indeed unlikely that we have such a sample, this vote could well be misleading.

The controversy could also be resolved by denigrating the evidence for negative relationships. Low fear messages are seldom found to be more persuasive than high, and, as with most experiments, these few studies can be questioned. For example, we can entertain reservations about the validity of the main effect originally reported by Janis and Feshbach (1953) because the effect is actually the product of an interaction between a personality factor and fear level (Janis & Feshbach, 1954) and because a large number of cases were omitted in the 1953 paper (7 of 57 in the low fear condition and 24 of 74 in the high fear group). Judging from the second article (Janis & Feshbach, 1954), it may be that the difference that was originally reported would be substantially reduced if these cases were replaced.

A more fruitful approach, in my opinion, is to accept the existence of both positive and negative relationships and to strive for a clear specification of the conditions and the processes which determine the outcome. In doing this, we must not overlook the following implications of the generally *positive* association: (1) Defenses are not easily observed when normal populations are exposed to realistic threats, and (2) special explanations are not called for in studies in which a high fear condition is more persuasive than a low fear condition. One cannot claim that a procedure obliterates defenses, bolsters coping, etc. without an interaction that simultaneously demonstrates resistance.

III. The Search for Interactions

In this section we shall review the evidence regarding interactions between the level of fear elicited by the communication and other factors such as personality variables and recommendation effectiveness. These other factors were chosen because they were expected to modify the fear-persuasion relationship by producing a fear reduction. Thus, each interaction is based upon the assumption that fear is the motivating or mediating process underlying acceptance. If the interactions fail to appear with regularity, or if the interactions produced are different from those anticipated by fear-drive hypotheses, the key assumption of the fear drive theory will be damaged. There may be some disagreement, however, regarding the relevance of different factors to the fear paradigm. But, as we shall see, a factor's apparent relevance to drive theory provides little or no assurance that it will interact with fear level.

After discussing each interaction from the perspective of the drive model, we shall also comment upon it from the point of view of the parallel response analysis. Since the bulk of the studies were not suggested by the parallel model, however, we can merely evaluate whether the results are consistent with the model. We will not, at any time, point to any new data generated by the model.

A.   Neurotic and Realistic Fear

1.   Neurotic Personalities

It has been suggested that high fear will *reduce* persuasion when fear is *neurotic* and will *increase* persuasion when the fear is *realistic*. Realistic or reflective fear reactions are described as stimulus bound, i.e., the magnitude of fear is supposedly appropriate to the magnitude of the threat and the appearance and disappearance of fear coincides with the onset and termination of the threat stimulus (Freud, 1926; Janis, 1958; Janis & Leventhal, 1965, 1968; Leventhal, 1965; May, 1950). Neurotic fear, on the other hand, is not tied to a stimulus, is not proportional to the danger, and does not disappear when the danger is eliminated. Neurotic fear reactions have a fixed quality because they are responses to past (infantile) threats that have been assimilated to the present danger situation. Manipulation of the present threat is insufficient, therefore, to alleviate the past danger. As a consequence the individual is still fearful even though he has thought of ways of resolving the contemporary crisis. The fear based upon the past danger can only be reduced by defensive behaviors. But the use of defense will produce distortion of reality and failure to accept realistic preventive recommendations. The realistic-neurotic fear dimension distinguishes somewhat different rules for the onset and cessation of fear motivation. It suggests that a variety of factors, particularly personality variables, will determine the occurrence of these different motives.

Janis and Feshbach (1954) reanalyzed part of their 1953 data to provide evidence for the hypothesis that neurotic fear is responsible for denial. They omitted their middle fear condition entirely and then used all of the subjects in their high and low fear conditions. They divided the groups on the basis of a previously administered questionnaire measuring neurotic anxiety. A subject was classified as high in neurotic anxiety if he was in the upper 40% of a distribution of responses to 12 questions on hypochondrial complaints and physical symptoms of chronic anxiety. Low neurotic anxiety was defined as the lower 60% of the distribution. The authors hypothesized that the neurotically anxious people would be most easily frightened and would show the strongest defensive reactions to the high fear communication.

The neurotically anxious subjects reported very little compliance with the recommended dental hygiene practices after the high fear message and much compliance after the low fear message. The neurotically anxious also resisted counterpropaganda (critical of the initial recommendations) two weeks after the low fear message, but showed little resistance to this opposing communication two weeks after the high fear message. The low or nonanxious Ss, on the other hand, were very slightly more accepting of the recommendation after the high fear message. Thus, the messages were about equally persuasive for the majority of subjects.

As we mentioned before, there is no direct evidence for a denial reaction on the part of the highly anxious subjects. It is also difficult to explain why the neurotic subjects were so easily persuaded by the low threat communication (the most persuasion occurred in this condition). Indeed, if this relatively great persuasion was produced by fairly strong fear, one could argue that being fearful to a low threat is even more unrealistic and neurotic than being fearful to a high threat. The conclusion would be that there is greater persuasion after the arousal of neurotic rather than realistic fears. The parallel response model suggests a somewhat different explanation. When the neurotically anxious Ss were exposed to the mild fear message they were motivated to control danger and responded rationally by changing their dental health practice. When they were exposed to the high fear message, on the other hand, they were motivated to control their fears rather than to control the danger. But, the neurotics' fears are recurrent, and the acceptance of protective recommendations provides only a temporary means of controlling their fear. The reappearance of fear renews motivation for its control and a search for new sources of reassurance. One consequence is the acceptance of the new recommendations given two weeks later. Unpublished evidence is reported by Radloff[4] which shows that neurotics respond to reassurance but then become fearful again and need new reassurance.

However plausible the interpretation, we must mention that the scale devised by Janis and Feshbach has been used in several studies and that none of them has replicated the original effect (Goldstein, 1959; Haefner, 1956; Millman, 1965; Niles, 1964; Singer, 1965). Three of the studies also used dental hygiene messages highly similar or identical to those used by Janis and Feshbach (Goldstein, 1959; Haefner, 1965; Singer, 1965). We cannot say, therefore, that the original result serves as evidence for either model.

2. Delay and Defense

The defensive denial hypothesis states that residual fear, fear which is no longer attached to any clear object, motivates the defensive denial. As Janis and Feshbach (1953) indicate, this hypothesis suggests an interaction of fear level and time; high fear messages would be more persuasive than low fear messages when action is taken immediately after the communication (before defense occurs) while the relationship will be reversed if action is delayed.

There is little evidence, however, in support of this reasoning. For example, Haefner (1956) measured acceptance immediately and two weeks after exposure to low and high fear messages. On one of his two attitude measures he found high fear more persuasive than low fear on both the immediate and delayed occasions. For the other measure, there

[4]Radloff (1963) interviewed visitors to an exhibit on cancer and its treatment. He found that anxious subjects were initially reassured but that this reassurance disappeared in about a weeks time.

was no significant effect of fear treatments. In a parametric investigation, Leventhal and Niles (1965) recorded fear reports and desires to engage in safe driving practices immediately, 2 hours, one day, and one week after fear messages dealing with automotive injuries. The communication groups consisted of four durations of exposure (8, 16, 24, and 32 minutes) to films of gory automotive accidents. Fear and intentions to follow safe practices were greatest immediately after exposure to these films and also following longer rather than shorter exposures. All differences disappeared, however, by the end of the week. Nevertheless, there was never any tendency for the shorter films to be more effective than the longer ones. Moreover, intentions to engage in protective practices were always weaker in the control condition where the Ss did not see a threat film.

The recent studies of dental hygiene practices also failed to show reversals in effectiveness over time. Neither Haefner (1965) nor Singer (1965) reported any trends for low fear to be superior to high fear for attitudes, intentions, reported dental practices, or behavior (getting toothbrushes or sending for booklets on dental care). This was true both immediately and one week after exposure to the communication program. At worst, the persuasive effects of high fear dissipated with time; at best, they remained constant.

While the evidence that has been presented on the delay-by-fear interaction offers no support for the drive hypothesis, it makes no positive suggestions about the parallel response model. There are, however, two additional studies that provide evidence relevant to time effects. In both cases, their results contradict drive predictions – or at least that version that suggests that high fear messages will be more effective if action is taken immediately after the communication.

In the first of these two experiments, Leventhal and Watts (1966) compared the degree of acceptance of two different responses, one made immediately after the communication (X-rays) and the other made after a delay (smoking). The investigators used improved versions of the communications from the Leventhal and Niles (1964) study. (Movies were used in low, medium, and high fear conditions.) The subjects, visitors to a state fair, were drawn from a broad cross section of the population. The high fear communication included a sequence of a lung cancer operation which showed a close-up (in color) of a lung removal. Subjects were then advised to stop smoking and to have X-rays taken. X-rays were available at a mobile unit located 40 feet from the movie theater. But *fewer* eligible smokers (eligible = 25 years of age and not X-rayed within the last two years) took X-rays after the high fear communication than after the low or medium fear messages. The sharpest drop occurred between the medium and high treatments ($p < .025$). Nonsmokers were equally willing to take X-rays regardless of the threat value of the communications.

The sharp decrease in X-ray taking with high fear is reminiscent of the original Janis and Feshback finding. It must be remembered, however, that these authors expect interference to occur for delayed responses; with an immediate reaction there is supposed to be less opportunity for defensive denial (Janis & Feshbach, 1953, p. 87). The data are inconsistent, therefore, with the hypothesis that a delay will increase resistance to acceptance. The simplest explanation is that when fear is most intense, immediately after the communication, it paralyzes coping skills. This interpretation follows from the idea that parallel responses can interfere with one another when one of them becomes very strong. The interference could go either way, of course; coping can disrupt fear and/or fear can disrupt coping. Additional data from the Leventhal-Watts study provide even more negative evidence respecting the defensive denial hypothesis. For example, the idea that "smoking causes lung cancer" was given a somewhat stronger (but statistically nonsignificant) endorsement after high than after low fear. A five-month follow-up questionnaire showed that in all conditions a very high proportion of subjects (82%) claimed some effort to cut down their smoking. Reports of success in smoking reduction were greater, however, in the high (79%) than the moderate (57%) or low (57%) fear groups ($p < .10$). The findings are qualified by the fact that only half the respondents returned the follow-up questionnaire. But this later sample did seem to be representative of the original groups; the proportion of returns was similar across conditions, and the negative relationship between fear treatment and X-ray taking (fewer X-rays taken after high than low fear) also held in these returns.

Drawing upon correlational data for additional supporting evidence, Leventhal and Watts suggested that a strong avoidance motive was elicited with respect to taking X-rays by the strong fear message because the required response, X-ray taking, leads to the detection of danger and is a necessary step toward surgery, a danger emphasized in the film. A similar hypothesis was proposed earlier by Hochbaum (1958) in order to account for people's failure to take X-rays in a tuberculosis screening program. In his sample, diagnosis and hospitalization for tuberculosis were seen as more threatening than the disease. The aspect of the findings that we wish to emphasize is that the avoidance appeared when the action could be undertaken immediately. The data strongly imply that the unpleasant feelings and ideas stimulated by the communication led to withdrawal behavior. The parallel response model suggests that subjects should be concerned with the control of fear rather than the control of danger when fear cues are very strong, immediately after exposure and when approaching the threatening cues. Danger control, i.e., acting to control threat, is more likely with delay since fear cues will fade while the danger cues may still be present. Indeed, smokers exposed to high fear report a greater amount of success with the long term problem of reducing smoking. Of course, these reports are merely suggestive and do not provide compelling evidence for a delay effect.

The comparison of delayed and immediate behavior in the above study is less clear than one might wish; Leventhal and Niles compared different responses as well as the same responses at different points in time. The immediate reaction itself is threatening and this threat, rather than the immediacy of the response, may be responsible for avoidance behavior. A recent study by Kornzweig (1967) is of special interest here. It compares the frequency with which people act on the same response, taking an antitetanus inoculation, at two different points in time.

Kornzweig (1967) recommended receiving a tetanus inoculation immediately or the day following the communication. He used high and low fear messages and a no-threat control. When shots were available immediately after the recommendation, there was an interaction between threat level and esteem. For high esteem Ss, a higher proportion took inoculations the more threatening the communication. For low esteem Ss, the relationship was the opposite; fewer low esteem Ss took shots as the message became more frightening. The esteem groups differed most in the no-fear control. There, all low esteem Ss took shots and few highs did.

When inoculations were available a day later, shot-taking declined for all experimental groups (delay = 46%; immediate = 86%). But both high and low esteem Ss took more shots after the high than after low fear message. The simplest interpretation of these results is that high threat led to a temporary paralysis of coping for low esteem Ss. This interaction appears similar to that obtained in the previously cited Leventhal and Watts (1966) study, although, in the present case, the threat of an inoculation is undoubtedly less than the threat of X-rays and potential surgery. Thus, inhibition of immediate action can occur after a high fear message without any strong threat associated with the action itself. Of course, the effect is restricted to low esteem Ss, people with presumably weak coping skills.

Neither of the above studies produced the immediate facilitation predicted by the Janis and Feshbach defensive denial hypothesis, that denial and avoidance occur only with delay. Indeed, there is no suggestion in these data that Ss deny their vulnerability when they do fail to act. But it should be made clear that neither the data nor the parallel response model preclude the appearance of defensive denial under other circumstances. Although we have yet to isolate the conditions that produce denial, this reaction seems most likely to occur when danger cues are weak or ambiguous. At this particular point, the findings regarding the effects of delay seem to be better explained by a loss of hope than by a denial process. In particular, Kornzweig's findings resemble some of those reported by Solomon and his co-workers (Rescorla & Solomon, 1967). These investigators found that dogs will not learn an avoidance response immediately after they have been subjected to several trials of strong, inescapable shock. But the introduction of a 24-hour delay between no-escape and avoidance trials permits successful avoidance learning. Apparently, the animals develop a fear-induced sense of hopelessness (Overmier & Seligman, 1967) which dissipates with time.

B.   COPING AND THE FAILURE OF INFLUENCE

In the previous section we suggested that inability to cope with fear was responsible for the avoidance reactions displayed and the observed failure to execute protective recommendations. In some of these studies the coping hypothesis was an after-the-fact interpretation of the findings, in others not. The studies described in the present section were all designed to test the coping hypothesis. The hypothesis suggests that individuals differ in their capacity to cope with stressful circumstances and assumes that these differences are responsible for variations in the inhibition of action following high fear messages. In only a few cases, however, have the investigators distinguished between the ability to cope with danger and the ability to cope with fear. Thus, one can place the coping hypothesis within either the fear drive paradigm or the parallel response paradigm. In the former, the hypothesis would be that fear stimulates coping and the two are dependent upon one another (drive model). In the latter, the hypothesis would be that the presence of danger stimulates both fear and coping (parallel model). Funkenstein, King, and Drolette (1957) preceded us in arguing for the latter interpretation. They found that the variables predictive of the intensity of acute emotional response to stress are different from the variables that relate to coping or the ability to master stress. Much of the available data tend to support the independence argument.

We shall deal with three types of factors that interact with the threat level: (1) personality traits involved in the coping disposition, (2) classifications of Ss which appear unrelated to personality factors but which appear to be related to possessing the resources for coping with health dangers, and (3) situational variables which are related to coping concepts.

1. Classification by Personality Factors

Goldstein (1959) reported an interaction between experimentally induced fear level and coping or defensive style. Subjects classified as avoiders (upper 25% on a word association test) proved less accepting of dental hygiene recommendations following a high fear message than following a low fear message. Subjects classified as copers (lower 25%) by contrast, showed equally strong acceptance after both messages. Goldstein failed to find an interaction between fear level and the classification of subjects on the Janis-Feshbach (1954) scale of neurotic anxiety. He concluded, therefore, that the personality characteristic of coping, as measured by a sentence completion test (Mainord, 1956), is different from the characteristic measured by the neurotic anxiety scale.[5]

Two studies dealing with tetanus inoculations also have suggested that in the face of vivid dangers some subjects may experience hopelessness and/or paralysis of their coping mechanism. Using a self-rating measure of esteem, Dabbs and Leventhal (1966) found that Ss high in self-esteem expressed stronger intentions to take tetanus shots after exposure to high than to low fear communications. Low esteem Ss, on the other hand, expressed a slight decrease in intentions with increased fear. Low esteem by threat level interaction was significant for the intention measure but not for the behavior measure.

The esteem scale was interpreted as a measure of coping, since past evidence suggested that Ss with high scores on this scale saw themselves as copers, were seen as such by others, and were more accepting of messages from coping communicators (Dabbs, 1964). Why the effect appeared for intentions but not for behavior was at the time unclear. It now seems that time of measurement could have been involved; the intention questions were completed immediately after the message while no subjects took shots until several days later. Thus, as in Kornzweig's study (1967), a reduction in expressed intentions could reflect a temporary disintegration of coping processes for low esteem Ss.

Another example of the esteem-threat interaction was reported by

---

[5]Janis (Janis & Terwilliger, 1962) has critized Goldstein's study because the post communication measures of fear showed no difference between the high and low threat conditions. The criticism is serious if the messages failed to elicit fear, which was the case in another early study by Moltz and Thistlethwaite (1955) which used army recruits as subjects. But Goldstein used school children as did Janis and Feshbach. Goldstein did, however, modify the communications by placing all recommendations in a group at the end, and all threat material in a group at the beginning of the communication. Leventhal and Singer (1966) have shown that this order can reduce the amount of fear reported at the *close* of the message without reducing the amount of fear reported at the close of the threatening portion of the communication.

Leventhal and Trembly (1968). These investigators began with a hypothesis which required that they compare two threat films.[6] One of the films depicted controlled or experimentally produced collisions of cars while the other showed victims of automotive accidents. Because the films varied widely in content, it would be difficult to interpret film effects. The investigators also varied the "intensity" of each stimulus by using very small (with low sound) and very large (with loud sound) screen images of each film. Stimulus content was constant across intensity levels.

The effects of these treatments were observed for Ss of either high, medium, or low self-esteem by dividing the distribution of esteem scale scores in equal thirds. The most important finding was an interaction between esteem and intensity. Going from the control condition (no film) to the small and then to the large image films, high esteem Ss obtained increasingly high scores for: (1) desires to take protective action (have car checked, drive slowly, etc.), (2) disturbing thoughts about automobile accidents, and (3) wishes to make others follow safe practices. These Ss also reported feeling less tired and fatigued when exposed to the bigger picture than when they had seen the smaller one. Low esteem Ss showed a different pattern. Their protective intentions, upsetting thoughts and desires to get others to act safely increased from the control to the low intensity stimulus but decreased after the large (high intensity) picture. After the larger picture, low esteem Ss also tended to report increased fatigue and deactivation.

The pattern of effects in the Leventhal-Trembly study, particularly the desire to avoid disturbing thoughts and fatigue, suggests that there may have been an avoidance reaction due to a breakdown in perceived coping ability. A potentially important aspect of these findings is the indication that the coping mechanism employed by low esteem Ss can be disrupted at low as well as at high levels of reported fear. The resistance to effective safety practices occurred after the intense (large picture) version of both films. For the large version of the film of accident victims, reported fear was high, while for the large version of the film of experimental car crashes, reported fear was quite low. The breakdown in acceptance, therefore, was not a simple correlate of fear intensity. It seems that the large image *per se* is critical. Perhaps it created the impression of a bigger-than-life world that is resistant to manipulation.

The Leventhal and Trembly results raise an important question about coping. Up until now we have interpreted the low amount of persuasion as a sign that subjects were responding to their emotional activity (i.e.,

[6]For details of this hypothesis the reader should consult the original article (Leventhal & Trembly, 1968).

were displaying *fear control*) which led directly to withdrawal and other reactions to control or minimize their fear. The new data suggest that a paralysis of control or coping can occur even when fear is low if the danger cues exaggerate the potency of the threat or its resistance to manipulation. Thus, failure to cope can occur both for inner fear cues and outer danger cues. Indeed, the same coping mechanism may be started or stopped by danger or fear control information.

2. *Resistance due to Past Behavior*

In the present section, we shall review data that show how the subject's past behavior, actions taken to prevent danger, or actions which expose him to threat (e.g., smoking heavily and driving a great deal) can facilitate or interfere with acceptance of the message's recommendations after threatening communications. According to the emotional-drive model, the more vulnerable a person feels to a threat the more likely is he to act protectively. But when high fear stimulates the subject to feel invulnerable to threat, he should show resistance to persuasion.

The experiments on vulnerability involve several different ways of classifying subjects. But regardless of the classification used, it is the vulnerable subject who shows inaction in the face of strong warnings of danger. In most cases the resistance seems to reflect an immediate or short-term effort to minimize strong or unpleasant affect (*fear control*). In other cases, however, the findings suggest the presence of long term cognitive changes, changes in perceived capacity to cope with danger. In these cases, warning communications appear to stimulate a sense of hopelessness, the feeling that one can avoid neither fear nor danger.

A vulnerability effect, and a completely unanticipated one, appeared when we compared reactions to tetanus communications by Ss who were already protected against the danger of tetanus and by those who were not. People who were not inoculated were objectively in greater danger and should have been more frightened and accepting of the tetanus recommendations (assuming that realistic fear is a motivator). The study by Leventhal, *et al.* (1966) found a difference between vulnerable (not inoculated) and invulnerable Ss; the unprotected Ss (vulnerables) were more frightened (in both low and high fear conditions) and generally were less persuaded of the value of tetanus shots. (This occurred oftener following high threat messages.) The pattern is similar but less strong in the earlier study by Leventhal *et al.* (1965).

In the smoking and lung cancer studies, comparisons were made between the more vulnerable smokers and the less vulnerable nonsmokers as well as between smokers who did not believe they were susceptible to lung cancer and smokers who did believe they were susceptible. For example, Niles (1964) divided subjects on the basis of their self reports of vulnerability to cancer, and compared their responses to threat films. She found that high fear communications increased acceptance of recommendations to stop smoking and take X-rays, but only for Ss scoring as invulnerables on the predispositional measure. Subjects scoring high (above the median) on the vulnerability measure showed essentially no differences between communications either in intentions to stop smoking or in intentions to take X-rays. The results, therefore, were similar to those for the tetanus study, although the subject classification is based upon a different operation. Additional analysis suggested that when vulnerable Ss were threatened, they felt they could not cope with the danger. The interpretation was based on the following evidence: (1) With more fearful messages high vulnerable Ss felt they would get lung cancer whether or not they tried to protect themselves; and (2) the vulnerability scale correlated negatively with our self-esteem measure, indicating that vulnerable Ss have negative self-evaluations and low perceived competency. The effect, then, is highly similar to the interactions discussed in the prior section.

There is a whole series of findings on vulnerability in the smoking studies. I previously discussed (under immediacy *vs.* delay) the Leventhal and Watts (1966) experiment which compared the responses of smokers and nonsmokers to high, mild, and low fear communications dealing with smoking and lung cancer. As mentioned earlier, the number of smokers taking X-rays sharply decreased as the communication became more fear arousing. By contrast, the same proportion (45%) of non-smokers took X-rays in each communication condition. Thus, resistance to action appeared in smokers, the group for whom the threat message was most relevant. But the defensiveness of smokers does not seem to reflect a long term cognitive change involving an irrational denial of their vulnerability. Smokers exposed to the high fear message did report greater success in smoking reduction several months later. The resistance to X-rays seemed to be motivated by an immediate need to control fear. It appears, therefore, that subsequent to a high fear message, people use discretion in deciding which of two recommendations they should follow. The response that bolsters a rational belief in personal invulnerability is accepted (stopped smoking) and the response that arouses fear of surgery, etc., is resisted.

Although the classification as a smoker or nonsmoker (vulnerable *vs.* nonvulnerable) is based upon Ss' prior behavior, one could argue that personality differences are associated with the frequency of smoking (see Eysenck, 1965; Matarazzo & Saslow, 1960) and with vulnerability beliefs. Thus, the personality variables, not the history of commitment to smoking, would be the cause of ignoring protective actions and failing to control danger. Certainly, both smokers and nontakers of tetanus shots may be more anxious, culturally deviant, etc., and the effects may be due to one or more of these characteristics. Fortunately, there is further evidence of the interaction of relevance and communication threat level in which personality variables seem less likely to be associated with the vulnerability classification factor. Berkowitz and Cottingham (1960) reported two studies on the effects of fear arousing communications upon attitudes toward the use of seat belts. Their Ss were subdivided in terms of the amount of driving they did, and the threat was expected to be more relevant to people who drive frequently. The results showed that high fear communications produced increasingly favorable attitudes toward seat belts among nondrivers. Regular drivers, however, were about equally favorable to the use of seat belts in high and low fear conditions. Unless regular drivers are lower in esteem or more anxious, the results indicate again that when a person's past behavior increases his vulnerability to danger, he is less likely to accept the protective recommendations when the communication is made more fearful.

While the factors that increase vulnerability appear to vitiate the positive impact of high threat messages, it is not clear that the resistance generated depends on a desire to minimize fear. The threat information, and not the fear itself, could conceivably be responsible for the interaction. Vivid information on the magnitude of danger could convince vulnerable Ss that the threat is uncontrollable. Moreover, as suggested by the Leventhal and Trembly (1968) study, one could possibly generate relatively extreme variations in vulnerability and/or uncontrolability of threat at high or low fear levels. In this way, breakdowns in coping and resistance to attitude change could be produced regardless of the fear level.

That resistance is in no way dependent upon high levels of threat is seen in recent work on selective exposure (Brock, 1965; Brock & Balloun, 1967). Brock and Balloun (1967) investigated the degree to which smokers and nonsmokers were willing to receive different messages on smoking and lung cancer. The investigators devised a very sensitive response measure, pressing a button to reduce momentarily the static level in a tape-recorded talk. The results showed that smokers worked harder to reduce the static for a message claiming that "Smoking Does Not Lead to Lung Cancer" than for a message saying that "Smoking Leads to Lung Cancer." (When compared to nonsmokers, the smokers pressed more frequently for the No Link message and substantially less often for the Link message.) There was a negative correlation between amount of smoking (commitment to the act) and tuning in to the "Smoking Leads to

Lung Cancer" message; for all subjects $r = -.20$ (n.s.), for males $r = -.47$ ($p < .05$). Heavier smokers also pressed the button more often than light smokers to eliminate static for the No Cancer Link message ($r = .26$; $p < .10$). The author's description of the five-minute communication suggests that its content is typical of low fear messages. Thus, the avoidance acts found with the relevance (or vulnerability) classification of *S*s do not appear to depend upon high levels of fear.

Despite the consistency of the findings, there is uncertainty as to whether perceived vulnerability, commitment to a prior response, or some other factor is responsible for the resistance. Smokers, drivers, and people who have not been inoculated may be more vulnerable to specific threats without seeing themselves as vulnerable. The smoker and the driver who does not use a seat belt have substantial support in reality for the idea that smoking is harmless and seat belts unnecessary. Thus, a regular smoker may have more evidence to contradict the idea that smoking is dangerous and, in addition, his habit may be older and more resistant to change. Moreover, his unwillingness to label smoking as dangerous and his resistance to change may appear together but may not be dynamically or causally linked. In short, the evidence up to this point is only correlational and we have no clear information regarding causal linkages.

3.   Experimental Manipulations of Vulnerability

If vulnerability is causally and not just correlationally related to resistance, it should be possible to produce resistance to a belief advocated by a fear-arousing message by an independent manipulation of the subject's felt vulnerability to the communicated danger. Watts (1966) conducted such a study using four experimental conditions: a no exposure control group, a group exposed to a vulnerability-manipulating communication, a group exposed to a fear communication (the surgical sequences used in the earlier studies), and a group exposed to both the vulnerability and the surgery films. Both the vulnerability film and the fear film (surgery alone) strengthened intentions to quit smoking and intentions to take X-rays. One week and one month later, subjects exposed to the single films (vulnerability alone, fear alone) were smoking significantly less than subjects in the control condition. Naturally, *S*s exposed to the surgery film had been far more frightened than *S*s who had viewed only the vulnerability message. When the vulnerability and fear films were combined the level of fear remained high (as in the fear only condition) but smoking reduction and postcommunication attitudes were similar to the control group; there were basically no changes in intentions and action.

Watts and Leventhal[7] prepared both color and black and white versions of the vulnerability and fear films used in the Watts' study. Preliminary data indicated that persuasion and behavioral compliance were nonexistant for the black and white version of the combined vulnerability and fear film. The color version was more successful, however. There is no way of accounting for the difference between the color and black and white films.

It should be emphasized that these data represented the first instance in which an experimentally created high fear communication (vulnerability plus fear film) was clearly less effective than a low fear communication (vulnerability alone) or than an equally frightening condition without vulnerability information (surgery alone). Moreover, common sense, early survey data (Hochbaum, 1958; Leventhal, Hochbaum, Carriger, & Rosenstock, 1960), and the fear drive paradigm (Janis, 1967) all predicted the opposite effect: that increased feelings of vulnerability and fear would increase attitudinal and behavorial compliance. Indeed, Janis and Mann (1965) had assumed that emotional role playing reduced smoking behavior by breaking down invulnerability defenses at the same time that it stimulated fear.

It was with great interest, therefore, that we examined the results of several recent studies of emotional role playing carried out by Bernard Mausner and his associate Ellen Platt. Mausner and Platt (1968) conducted a study comparing four groups: one in which the subject played the part of a patient with lung cancer; a second in which the subject played the part of a doctor who informs the patient he has cancer; a third in which the subject observed the interaction; and a fourth in which subjects were unexposed to information on smoking and cancer. Following the Janis and Mann (1965) model, it was anticipated that Ss enacting the patient role would be most directly involved and least able to defend against the implications of the information and, therefore, would be most likely to change their behavior. On the other hand, observers presumably would be least involved and most able to defend against the cancer threat. Subjects playing the role of the doctor were expected to fall in between.

The present analysis suggests a quite different outcome. The patient role player should show the smallest reductions in smoking since he was made to feel both highly vulnerable and highly threatened. Subjects playing the role of the doctor, or just observing the sessions, theoretically will experience less personal threat and should show substantial reduction in

---

[7]These data are unpublished.

smoking. When mean changes in smoking were examined, the results showed that the patient group (threatened and feeling vulnerable) changed no more than the control group that was not exposed to antismoking material. In accord with the present reasoning, the doctor and observer groups showed a substantial reduction in mean number of cigarettes smoked. The Mausner and Platt studies seem more definitive than the earlier investigation in that the sample was larger ($N = 135$), the differences reached more robust significance levels, and the treatment differences were the same for the proportion of Ss cutting down and for mean reduction in cigarettes smoked.

C. MANIPULATIONS DIRECTED AT THE COPING MECHANISM

Early in our research program, well before the formulation of the parallel response model, it became clear that S's belief in his ability to cope with danger was a crucial determinant in his acceptance of the recommendations given with fear arousing communications. Two classes of variables appeared relevant to the coping problem: (1) S's ability, understanding or readiness to execute specific protective actions, and (2) the perceived effectiveness of the particular remedies offered. The first type of variable was manipulated by means of informational factors that have been labelled "specific action instructions." The second, the effectiveness variable, was varied by changing the described efficacy of the recommendations. Both factors were expected to interact with drive level.

1. Specific Action Instructions

In his discussion of the World War II mass communication campaigns devised to stimulate bond purchases, Cartwright (1949) suggested that a person must not only be motivated to act and know action is possible, but must also know how, when, and where to respond. Difficulties in converting protective health attitudes into action, such as those exhibited by low self-esteem Ss, seem to involve failure to make specific responses to specific stimuli. It is not enough to know the final goal (get a tetanus shot at student health, stop smoking); one must also know how to perform the sequence of actions to get there.

In essence, the subject, like the scientist, must operationalize his beliefs. His desire must be construed as a series of specific acts, with each act attached to appropriate environmental cues. That this is a problem is attested to by the difficulty experienced by most people in completing actions which are not part of their daily life pattern. Successfully carrying out a nonroutine action, such as going to the credit union to buy bonds or going to the health service to get a tetanus shot, requires that the action be inserted into an already organized or chunked sequence of daily activities. Simply wanting to do something is not enough. One has to plan to do it at a certain time so as to insert it within a set of organized acts.

The idea of action instructions was suggested to me by a personal problem: getting to the bank to cash a check when I was down to my last nickel. The need for money became very strong. As a consequence, my intentions were clear and strong — "Go to the bank." No amount of swearing, self-criticism, or will power resulted in my getting to the bank. I forgot to go in the morning on the way to work, forgot to go before lunch, and forgot to go in the afternoon before the bank closed. Indeed, I invariably remembered the need when the time to satisfy it had passed. The problem seemed to involve difficulty in remembering the need at a time that was propitious for action. Thinking about this, I decided to try a behavioral instruction that would start me on the path to the goal. Upon arising, I instructed myself that while driving to work I should turn right at State Street. I knew I would pass State Street and hoped that when I saw it I would turn right and get to the bank. After giving myself the instruction I forgot about it. This was not unusual as for the past five days I had reminded myself upon arising that I had to go to the bank. I had not yet succeeded. But, on the drive to the office this morning I saw State Street and turned right. Even after I turned I was uncertain as to where I was going. Fortunately, and with the help of other environmental cues, I soon recalled that I was going to the bank. The action instructions cued the specific behaviors that would lead to the goal. Once the first act appeared it rearoused the intention and insured the completion of the act sequence.

The problem of communication for behavior change may require constructing such programs. Subjects often want to do something — to take a tetanus shot or quit smoking — but they may not remember their intention at the right moment, or may fail to remember what to do or say in order to carry out the intended act sequence. Instead, they resort to will power, which is frequently in short supply. In the first study using this variable, Leventhal *et al.* (1965) investigated the effects of fear level and action instructions upon attitudes, intentions, and the taking of tetanus shots. The fear section of the communication described a case history of tetanus. The high fear version used color photographs and vivid description of symptoms and indicated that the patient died. The low fear pamphlet used bland language and photographs and said that the patient lived. The specific instructions were a map of the local campus with the health service circled in ink. A variety of examples were given as to how one could pass the health service while changing classes and on route to and from various buildings. The student was asked to review his daily schedule and to locate within it a time that was convenient for action.

Four experimental groups were formed from the two experimental variables (fear level and specific instructions). It was predicted that *S*s would express stronger intentions to get the injections and would take more shots in the high fear than in the low fear condition and that this difference would be greatest when *S*s were given action instructions. Two control conditions were used. The first tested the effects of action instructions without danger information. The second recorded the number of *S*s taking inoculations in a sample of *S*s not exposed to any experimental materials. The results showed more favorable attitudes to tetanus inoculation and stronger intentions to get shots with high than low fear communications. Action instructions had *no* effects, however, on any of these verbal responses. For behavior, on the other hand, there was significant main effect for specific instructions; 29% of the *S*s in the high and low fear groups took shots if they had received action instructions. Only 3% of the *S*s unexposed to action instructions did so. But action instructions are not sufficient to produce action; no *S*s took shots in the action instructions control group. (No shots were taken in the unexposed control.) Both action instructions and motivation were necessary for shot taking to occur — alone neither led to action. But specific instructions did not interact with fear level! Thus, the factor has important effects upon performance, independent of amount of threat.

In a later study Leventhal *et al.* (1966) tried to see if an interaction between specific instructions and fear level would appear when a delay was introduced between the communication and the opportunity to act. It was predicted that specific instructions would help the subject to bridge the delay by giving a more permanent structure to the intentions generated by high fear. Unfortunately, the delay manipulation appeared to have been ineffective, and the results were similar to those in the Leventhal, Singer and Jones study; more *S*s took inoculations after receiving both the action instructions and threat information. Neither instructions nor fear was effective alone. The significance of the contrast between the specific and nonspecific groups was weaker than in the earlier study.[8]

It should be pointed out that the *S*s in these studies fit our anecdotal example very well; they wanted shots and they knew the location and hours of the student health service. But it seemed necessary for them to review the location of the health center and when they could pass it, to plan to do so at a particular time, etc., in order to integrate the action into their daily life patterns.

---

[8]There was some suggestion of a reactance effect in this study; under high fear and specific instructions eligible male subjects became less persuaded of the value of shots. But there is no reason to believe that this form of resistance is specific to fear (see Brehm, 1966).

Although action instructions facilitated the introduction of a new response into an otherwise established behavior pattern, an experiment was needed to establish the relevance of action instructions to changing established habit patterns. Leventhal *et al.* (1967) did this in a study that attempted to alter smoking behavior. Smoking could be monitored over a relatively long period of time and this would provide an opportunity to examine both the short and the long range effectiveness of action instructions at different fear levels.

The action instructions in the smoking study consisted of detailed recommendations on how to combat the smoking habit. Considerable emphasis was placed upon techniques for avoiding the onset of the behavior, including ways of avoiding the purchase of cigarettes. The fear messages were the movies used in the Leventhal and Watts (1966) study. There were four experimental groups (two levels of both fear and specific instructions) and a control group (receiving only action instructions). The findings showed that *S*s exposed to the high fear communications expressed significantly stronger intentions to stop smoking than *S*s viewing the less frightening movie. A week after the communication there were no differences in reduction of smoking between any of the experimental groups; all smoked significantly less than the controls exposed to action instructions only. However, both of the fear groups (high and low) given action instructions gradually separated from the fear groups not given instructions; one and three months later, the fear groups without action instructions were moving toward their pre-experimental smoking levels. Despite the significant instructions by time period interaction ($p < .025$), the mean difference in number of cigarettes smoked between instructed and noninstructed groups is relatively small. When we consider the proportion of *S*s cutting down, nevertheless, the differences between instructed and noninstructed groups are quite substantial. But with either measure, fear (high or low) combined with specific instructions was most effective for long term behavior change.

There was an indication that action instructions were more effective for high than for low fear messages, but the interaction was of marginal stability ($p < .10$), and appeared only in the analysis for number of cigarettes smoked. As in the tetanus studies, action instructions had no effects upon postcommunication attitudes or reported emotions. However, *S*s presented with action instructions did say that they felt less vulnerable to lung cancer. Thus, the subjects who reported low vulnerability were more effective in carrying out the smoking reduction. Although this result was not obtained in the tetanus studies, it is indeed suggestive of links to the vulnerability effects reported in the prior section.

Before exposing their subjects to communications on smoking and cancer, Leventhal *et al.* (1967) obtained self-ratings of esteem from the *S*s. Because of the small numbers per cell when the experimental conditions were further subdivided in terms of this measure, the analyses were not reported in the published paper. There was an indication, however, that action instructions were of most benefit to *low* rather than *high* esteem *S*s. For example, when action instructions were omitted, low esteem *S*s in the high fear condition showed absolutely no reduction in smoking at the end of one week. When action instructions were included, by contrast, both low and high esteem *S*s showed substantial reductions in smoking. Thus, individual differences in coping were irrelevant to performance when all subjects had guides for action. While this finding is precisely the effect needed to tie together the esteem and instruction studies, the results at this point are no more than suggestive. The data do seem to emphasize that the instructions influence coping reactions and that coping is itself unrelated to fear level.

In his national survey of smoking behavior Daniel Horn (1968) found that respondents who wish to quit smoking believe that smoking is dangerous and believe that it is of value to stop. But neither seeing smoking as a threat (fear level?) or as relevant to the self (vulnerability) was related to short term success (less than one year) in cutting down on smoking. Regarding oneself as able to control the habit was the main factor related to smoking reduction. In addition, there was a negative relationship between the perceived personal relevance of the threat and long term success. While Horn's data differ in some details from the experimental findings, the overall trends are similar; competency in controlling the danger (the specific instructions equivalent) is a key factor for behavior change, and making the threat excessively personal (high vulnerability) is detrimental to cessation.

The tying of attitudes to behavior through action instructions, whether experimenter devised or self-generated, should be a challenge to our theoretical and empirical ingenuity. We do not know what aspects of the instruction are necessary or sufficient for change. Factors such as improved cue and response identification could be involved along with the analysis of ongoing response sequences. To some degree the success of the instructions appears to depend primarily on a careful analysis of the individual's daily action pattern, locating natural chunks or subdivisions for the introduction of new behaviors, and locating the specific cues that initiate the action sequences that are to be eliminated. Of course, action instructions could function in a far simpler manner: as information to the subject that his attitude is supposed to lead to action! Indeed, the subject's assumption that he is supposed to act may be more important in some circumstances than the cue and response contents in the information. Whatever the key factors may be, it seems that this set of variables is likely to be of greater importance the more complex the action and the longer it extends in time. Action instructions should be less important and behavior and attitude measures should give increasingly identical results as both the verbal and the overt responses are made under more similar conditions and closer together in time (see Greenwald, 1965; Leventhal & Niles, 1964). The main problem presented by the "specific instructions" effect is the isolation of the mental operations, i.e., the cognitive contents that connect attitudes to action. Whatever these factors may be, it is reasonably clear that the subject's response to action instructions is fairly independent of fear level.

How easily can we accommodate the effects of specific instructions to the two paradigms? The fear model would seem to call for an interaction of fear level and specific instructions. The data suggest, however, that fear level at the time of communication is of little consequence. The parallel model, with its emphasis upon different stimulus factors controlling different responses, is quite at ease with the findings. But the latter model did not predict the effects. The data do lead to an important amplification of the control processes involved in the model, however.

2. Recommendation Effectiveness

The fear drive model predicts that communication acceptance will be greater with low fear than with high fear messages when the recommendations are seen as being relatively ineffective for dealing with threat and, therefore, are not completely fear reducing (see Janis, 1967; Janis & Leventhal, 1968). When the recommendations are viewed as very effective, on the other hand, there will be no residual fear, and high threat messages should be more persuasive. As mentioned earlier, this type of hypothesis was first advanced to account for the difference between the dental and the tetanus studies (Leventhal, 1965).

But do low fear messages tend to become more effective than high fear messages as one reduces the apparent effectiveness of the recommended protective actions? In a study of tetanus inoculations, Dabbs and Leventhal (1966) varied fear level and the perceived effectiveness of tetanus shots (two levels). Differences in the described effectiveness of the shots had no consequences for attitudes, intentions to take shots, or actual shot taking; there were neither main effects nor interactions with fear level. Dabbs and Leventhal indicate that the perceived difference in effectiveness, while statistically significant ($F_{1,170} = 105.85$), was relatively small. Thus, failure to locate an interaction could be due to the restricted range of the manipulated variable. But restricted or not, the findings do suggest a need for ". . . caution in using . . . (effectiveness) to reconcile divergent results of studies on fear arousal and persuasion" (p. 529).

The effectiveness variable extended over a much wider range in a study by Chu (1966). This investigator manipulated the perceived efficacy of a drug for roundworms by describing it as 90%, 60%, or below 30% in effectiveness. On a verbal measure of willingness to use the drug, Chu found considerably more acceptance of the recommendation with the high efficacy description ($\chi^2 = 13.67$, $p < .001$). But the key interaction between efficacy and fear level was only of borderline significance ($\chi^2 = 8.32$, 4 df; $p < .10$) even though 1043 Ss participated in the experiment.

The absence of a strong interaction between effectiveness and fear level is clearly counter to drive model predictions; a more effective recommendation apparently does not eliminate defensive denial and facilitate persuasion. Even if we accept the weak interaction obtained in the Chu study as reliable, the form of the interaction is inconsistent with the drive position. The drive-denial interpretation suggests that high fear messages should be less influential than low fear messages when the recommendation is regarded as ineffective. This, however, is not the case. At every level of perceived effectiveness Chu found more persuasion for high than for low fear messages. Even at the very lowest level of effectiveness, the small difference was in favor of the high fear message. The data appear to reinforce two of the suggestions made by Dabbs and Leventhal (1966); (1) Factors other than effectiveness account for the reversals in the positive association between fear and persuasion, and (2) "Unless a compelling deterrent exists, people who anticipate danger prefer to do something rather than nothing" (Dabbs & Leventhal, 1966).

The results are compatible with the cognitive emphasis on *danger control* in the parallel model. If subjects are reacting to their appraisal of the danger and to the information on the effectiveness of the preventive agent, it is perfectly reasonable to find more acceptance of effective than ineffective actions. The more effective the recommendation, the greater the acceptance, and this should be true regardless of how frightened the subjects feel. Of course, when a protective behavior is viewed as completely ineffective, there is no reason to try it even if the danger is extremely vivid or close. The result is the positive interaction reported by Chu, and no sign of acceptance being reduced by high fear.

D. FEAR REDUCTION AND PERSUASION

We have emphasized the drive theory assumption that the onset and continuation of emotional responses provides the motivating force for belief change and that cessation of the emotional response is reinforcing. A study by Leventhal and Singer (1966) made a direct effort to test the stop rule. The investigators prepared both high and low fear messages and a set of detailed recommendations for protection against dental disease. The fear reduction procedure involved different ways of pairing the fear material and the recommendations. In three pairs of conditions (consisting of high and low fear) the recommendations were included with the threat material: in one pair, recommendations came first, in another the recommendations and threat were intermixed, and in the third the recommendations came after the threat information. In a fourth pair of fear conditions the recommendations were omitted (two other controls were included). With recommendations omitted there presumably is little fear reduction and no clear knowledge of action alternatives. With recommendations before the fear stimuli, there theoretically is a chance to inhibit fear arousal, but this order does not effectively link thinking about recommendations with reducing fear (see Cohen, 1957). Recommendations made after the threat provide the best linkage to fear reduction; the subject has become frightened and can think about protective actions while his fear is gradually relieved. The drive model would predict more acceptance in the latter condition. Leventhal and Singer used both high and low levels of threat to be sure that the fear reduction effect appeared only with the high threat message. They reasoned that under low threat there would be little emotion to reduce and consequently, that the placement of the recommendations would not influence their impact upon attitudes.

The results showed that the variations in the position of the recommendation affected the level of reported fear for the high threat message. The subjects said they were most fearful when the recommendations were omitted, less fearful when recommendations were placed before the threat material, still less fearful when the recommendations were intermixed, and least fearful when the recommendations followed the fear stimuli. Despite these differences, the subjects were somewhat more accepting of the recommendations when they were presented in a solid block, either before or after the communication ($p < .10$). As this pattern held for both the low and the high fear messages, it appeared to be quite unrelated to fear. Contrary to the drive reduction hypothesis, acceptance was not improved by fear reduction. The findings are most easily interpreted as an effect of cognitive clarity; when the recommendations are in a block (first or last) they are better understood and more readily accepted.

However, one should not overlook the fact that there was a very strong positive association between fear level and persuasion; when the threat was strong (high fear messages) acceptance was greater than when the threat was low. There also was a substantial correlation across experimental treatments between the means of the dependent measures (fear and attitude change). How can this take place when the data are negative respecting the drive reduction hypothesis? The answer is that a correlation is not necessarily an indication of causation. This is true whether we correlate individual scores or group means.

The results fit the parallel response model rather well. Acceptance of protective actions varies as a function of knowledge of the threat and the clarity of the recommendations. Fear level is increased by the vividness of the threat stimuli and decreased by an opportunity to think about protection. As was stated in the original publication, "The data suggest that the acceptance of recommendations occurs in anticipation of later danger and before there is any reduction of the fear aroused by the communications ... Rather than fear serving as a drive, the awareness of danger in combination with the perception of effective preventive action may serve as the motivational basis for acceptance" (Leventhal & Singer, 1966). The parallel model is an extension of this idea.

IV. Theoretical Elaborations

A. EXTENSIONS OF THE FEAR DRIVE MODEL: THE CURVILINEAR HYPOTHESIS

The experimental findings led us to reject the drive model and propose in its stead the parallel response model. Other investigators have attempted to resolve the problems of the fit between data and theory by elaborating the drive paradigm. Most of the extensions have started from a single point: the observation that increased fear level is often found to be related to both increases and decreases in persuasion. The suggested change made by these writers is quite simple; there is a curvilinear relationship between fear level and persuasion. Increases in fear from very low to moderate levels increase the acceptance of persuasive messages, but increases from moderate to very high levels decrease persuasion. The curvilinear hypothesis has a long history (Bindra, 1959, p. 247; Freeman, 1940; Hebb, 1949; Kohler, 1925; Yerkes & Dodson, 1908; Young, 1961) and it should not come as a surprise that McGuire (1968) and Janis (1967) have extended the hypothesis to the fear communication data. Both maintain the basic idea of curvilinearity but differ in their suggestions as to how the curves are generated.

1. McGuire's Acceptance-Rejection Model

McGuire (1968) has hypothesized that increasing fear level strengthens two tendencies: an acceptance and a rejection process. It is hypothesized that the two processes increase in strength at different rates, with the rejection process having the steeper slope, and that the acceptance process is elicited at lower levels of fear. As a consequence, increases in fear first stimulate acceptance, but this acceptance is soon balanced and then exceeded by the rejection process. The net result is a curvilinear relationship between fear level and attitude or behavior change.

McGuire's proposal that there are two processes which accelerate at different rates is similar to the conflict model developed by Neal Miller (1951b) except that the conflict model assumes that the stimulus, and not the subject's fear, elicits both approach and avoidance tendencies. Indeed, if we applied McGuire's acceptance process to *danger control* and his rejection process to *fear control*, his model would be akin to the parallel model. By adding McGuire's rules about slope, we could then generate a variety of curves. Indeed, we did something similar to this in using the parallel model to account for resistance effects immediately after high fear.

There are many reasons, however, to hesitate in adopting a curvilinear model. The most important is the question we have raised as to whether fear actually mediates acceptance. If we take this question seriously, the primary task that faces us is the analysis of *danger control* (acceptance) and *fear control* (rejection) processes and the specification of the variables effecting each. The adoption of a curvilinear hypothesis will not solve this problem. Indeed, premature adoption of the curvilinear model may produce a false impression of synthesis and order that will distract investigators from the more important task. This point can be illustrated by a careful examination of Janis' (1967) curvilinear model, the most fully developed analysis proposed along these lines.

2. The Janis Family of Curves Hypothesis

Janis (1967) [see Jones (1960) for a similar model] suggests that the number of curves relating fear level to acceptance is infinite. These curves are generated by a variety of factors which interact with fear. For each curve there is an optimum point at which acceptance is greatest. Moreover, the amount of acceptance is greater when the optimum falls at higher fear levels.[9] The final model is represented in a three-dimensional

---

[9]If we accept this model we would conclude that given a common threat message, any variable which changes acceptance of recommendations has influenced the subjects fear level. The specific instruction data provide evidence counter to this hypothesis, as specific instructions change behavior but have no effect upon fear.

space; fear on the X axis, acceptance on the Y axis, and an amalgam of other factors on the Z axis. At that point on Z at which the other factors are unfavorable, a small increase in fear quickly brings acceptance to its maximum, and the maximum is relatively low. Further increases in fear, drop acceptance to zero or even below. When other factors are favorable, fear can reach very high levels before persuasion reaches its maximum and the level of persuasion will be high. But further increases in fear will again return persuasion to a zero level.

The complexity of the model will undoubtedly stimulate our curiosity and sustain our interest. But we may also wonder whether it is an explanatory and predictive model or a strictly post hoc descriptive schema. The key question is whether the model presents the theoretical constructs or variables that are necessary to generate its complex surface. Intensity of fear is important, but the position of the optimal point, the specification of the curve under consideration, is determined by other variables. These variables change the fear process and alter the need for vigilance and reassurance which lead to rejection or to acceptance of the communicator's recommendation. What are these other factors? The list is replete with the standard variables (recommendation effectiveness, invulnerability defense, immediacy of response and aggression at the experimenter), and predictions are made for these factors in terms of their success in reducing and directing fear motivation. Fear is still the motivator of acceptance. However, as our review has shown, the factors listed by the fear-drive model typically have either no effect or effects opposite to those expected. Unfortunately, there are no new specifications as to how these factors influence the acceptance curves, and there are no new suggestions for operational definitions of these variables. Thus, we are presented with a complex and precise quantitative surface but have neither equations, sets of variables, nor specific suggestions as to how the variables combine to generate the surface.

The pitfalls in using a very complex theory with many unspecified variables can be seen by a careful examination of Janis' (1967, pp. 210-215) effort to apply the model to the fear literature. For example, Janis says that the theory predicts interactions that are unspecified by other theories. Does this mean that the theory suggests new and unique variables that interact with fear? Does it mean that its predictions for familiar variables, such as immediacy, effectiveness, and invulnerability defense, are different from and more frequently supported than the predictions suggested by other theories? Neither of these statements is true, and it is not clear that they represent what Janis intended. What he does argue is that the curvilinear theory shows that only second or higher order interactions (those that are curvilinear) are worth examining; linear interactions are not. Thus, ". . . investigators have formulated their interaction hypothesis in an unnecessarily restrictive way, in terms of two contrasting monotonic functions (an ascending versus descending curve). As will be seen shortly, this type of formulation can be extremely misleading and is likely to generate experiments that provide incomplete and inappropriate data for testing the predicted interaction effects" (p. 112).

Janis refers to two studies to illustrate the incompleteness and inappropriateness of contrasting linear interactions. One of the investigations argues that fear level interacts with prior commitment to a response (Insko *et al.,* 1965). The other study claims that fear level interacts with the believability of the threat (Rosenblatt, 1962). Quite correctly, Janis points out that these researchers did not test their linear interaction predictions. Their studies use multiple levels of fear but only one level of the interactive variable, the level that was expected to produce a superiority of high to low fear. This reflects, however, the inadequacies of the particular experimental designs, and is in no way a shortcoming of the original linear by linear interaction predictions. In fact, there are many other examples of incomplete experimental designs which Janis could cite. For example, (1) Simonson and Lundy (1966) suggested that irrelevant fear, fear not related to the topic of the recommendation, will increase persuasion, but, nevertheless, used only irrelevant fear conditions; (2) Janis and Terwilliger (1962) assumed that high fear reduces persuasion because it elicits anger, but they did not separately vary anger and fear level; (3) Janis and Mann (1965) proposed that role playing undercuts invulnerability defenses, but they did not separate fear level from the presence or absence of defense.

The heart of Janis' point is obvious and important; an interaction cannot be tested when investigators use only one level of the interacting variable. But why did the experimenters make these errors in design? The most obvious explanation is that each of them accepted the generality and repeatability of the negative relationship reported by Janis and Feshbach (1953). That early study is used as a standard which supposedly is not in need of replication. Since the Janis-Feshbach study does not replicate, this position is actually quite untenable.

Janis goes on to state that "first order differences can tell us nothing about the interaction we are trying to test; the evidence can be confirmatory in either instance if the contrasting curve for the avoidance type of recommendation shows a relatively greater gain in acceptance" (p. 214). This statement is difficult to interpret but important to understand as it is supposed to define a special contribution of curvilinear theory. One problem in interpretation stems from the ambiguity of the terms first and second order. It is not clear if the first order effects refer to main effects or linear by linear interactions and if second order refers to two-way interactions or to interactions that are part of a quadratic effect. We shall assume that the reference is to a quadratic interaction, two functions curving at different rates. If this assumption is correct, one clear interpretation of the statement is that linear by linear interactions (two, straight, nonparallel arms) cannot be seen with a fundamentally curvilinear process.

In Fig. 4 we have drawn three curves (A_1, A_2, and A_3) that might describe the curvilinear relationship between fear level and persuasion. If our manipulations of fear level were within the regions of L_1 and L_2 (where all three curves ascend) we could not see any linear interactions of fear and variable A if the data produced followed curves A_2 and A_3. This is because the ascending slope of the curves are parallel. On the other hand, if the data followed curves A_1 and A_3, we could see an interaction since the slopes are diverging. Both arms of this interaction would show high fear superior to low fear. If we chose other points, the interaction would change in shape. For example, using curves A_3 and A_1 at fear levels L_2 and L_4, we would see an ascending arm (high fear superior to low) for A_3, and a descending arm (low greater than high) for A_1.

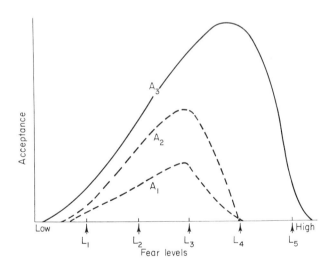

Fig. 4. If variable A and Fear produce curves A_1 and A_2 a 2 × 2 design could show interaction effects for a pair of fear levels between L_1 and L_3. If curves A_2 and A_3 are involved in the comparison, interactions could not easily be found for points between L_1 and L_3 or L_3 and L_5. An interaction could be found if the lowest fear level was between L_1 and L_3 and the highest between L_3 and L_4.

It isn't clear if Janis is really concerned with the problem illustrated by our first example where interactions cannot be seen because the slopes of the curves are parallel. We suspect not, as the issue would involve very precise quantitative assumptions about the slopes of his curves. Moreover, if we examine the figures in his paper (Janis, 1967), one shows curves with identical ascending slopes (p. 182) while another, as best one can tell, does not (p. 207). Thus, it is more likely that he is concerned with another problem illustrated by our example; linear interactions change their shape depending upon the level of fear. Thus, if the curvilinear model is true, which is unproven, we would have to know the fear level for the optimal points of any curves in order to predict whether both arms of the linear interaction would diverge while ascending or if they would diverge while one is ascending and the other descending. Moreover, the curvilinear model suggests that in any one experiment, the two arms comprising the interaction will never cross.

But regardless of these modifications, we still can see linear interactions with a curvilinear process. In fact, if an experiment uses fear levels that cross the optimum for one of two curves (e.g., L_1 and L_4), we would see a very strong linear by linear interaction. But none of the data reviewed shows interactions that require or suggest an interaction with a fear drive process. In addition, in experiments in which more than two fear levels are used, a necessary condition to detect a quadratic effect, there is not one in which an arm of the interaction shows that persuasion first rises and then falls. The variables identified by the theory certainly have not produced any suggestions of curvilinearity.

Using the theory as a post hoc synthetic device presents additional problems. Questionable, and at times untrue, assumptions are needed to fit past studies to its mold. For example, in order to organize divergent outcomes, Janis places different experiments at different points on the fear dimension. The procedure is defensible if the fear measures support specific placements. Thus, he argues that fear increased attitude change in the Berkowitz and Cottingham (1960) seat belt study because (in comparison to the Janis-Feshbach experiment) all of the communications were at low levels of fear. This assumption is untested and possibly false. It also ignores other results, such as those of Leventhal and Niles (1965), in which longer exposures to very threatening films on automotive accidents produced greater attitude change.

Janis also suggested that the communications used in the tetanus studies and the dental hygiene studies by Leventhal and Singer (1966) and Singer (1965) were less potent than those used in his dental study. This seems implausible given the fact that the communications used in all of the dental hygiene studies were extremely similar. Indeed, Haefner

(1964) used the same messages used by Janis and Feshbach and still found the high threat message more effective than the low. As for the tetanus communications, there are some indications that they are more, rather than less, frightening than the dental hygiene messages. Two subjects passed out while reading the high fear tetanus booklets (Leventhal *et al.*, 1965; Leventhal *et al.*, 1966), and no such strong reactions were ever observed or reported for the various dental hygiene studies. To argue his point successfully, Janis would also have to claim that the lung cancer movies, where the high fear messages were also more persuasive, aroused less fear overall than his dental slides. This is clearly not so. It would seem that the studies fit the curvilinear hypothesis only if one uses the amount of persuasion (the predicted effect) as a sign of fear (the mediator).

A second and more interesting procedure used to fit data to the curvilinear model involves rank ordering the cells of a factorial study so that the plot of attitude change against fear level is curvilinear. For example, Janis (1967, p. 199) placed the experimental groups from the Berkowitz and Cottingham (1960) study in rank order by assuming that for each communication, low and high threat, the amount of fear increased from low to moderate to high relevance subjects (defined by amount of driving). He then plotted attitude toward the use of seat belts and came up with a curvilinear function. Since Berkowitz and Cottingham did not report fear data for their second study, the one Janis used, we have no way of confirming the validity of his assumption respecting fear levels. But Berkowitz and Cottingham did report fear means in their first study and, in this instance, the fear scores did not agree with the *a priori* ordering of the relevance groups.

The same procedure is used for data from an experiment by Niles (1964); among *S*s seeing the high fear message the high susceptibles (on a self-report premeasure) are ranked as more frightened than the low susceptibles, and the same position is assigned to the subjects seeing the moderate fear message. Figure 5 presents the curve as Janis gives it along with another curve which we constructed from the same data. The two curves are obviously different, and the differences are due to two factors: (1) Our curve orders the groups according to their actual postcommunication scores on the fear measure, and (2) our curve includes the high and the low vulnerable subjects from the low fear condition.

The divergent treatments of the Niles' data provide a trenchant illustration of an inadequacy of the curvilinear theory; its variables are not sufficiently specific to allow us to choose between the two ways of ordering the data. If we actually use a measure of reported fear, we get no support for the hypothesis. If we use an *a priori* ordering and omit

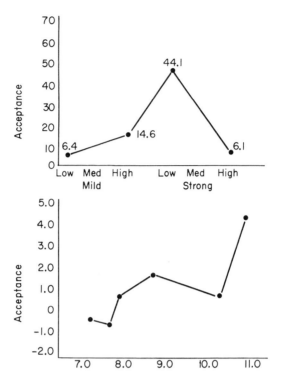

Fig. 5. Two plots of Niles (1964) data for intentions to quit smoking. The top figure follows the figure in Janis (1967) with the experimental conditions arranged according to fear communication (Mild and Strong) and perceived vulnerability to cancer (Low and High). The two low fear communication groups are omitted. The bottom figure plots the same Niles (1964) data but the experimental groups are ordered by means for reported fear, the two low fear conditions are included, and the acceptance scores are reported as in the thesis.

the low fear cells, things look a bit better. But if we use the *a priori* ordering, we are combining different levels of two different factors and assuming they form a common dimension called fear level. This is not justifiable if we believe the fear measure. Still, the idea of ordering cells upon a single dimension may be useful and could be a way of finding relevant underlying factors. Of course, even if such rankings repeatedly form smooth curves, there would be no way of telling if the underlying dimension is fear level. One could readily argue that we are plotting acceptance against perceived hopefulness and that perceived hopefulness is a function of proximity to threat (message threat) and coping resources (vulnerability and esteem). Fear emotion need not be the mediator of these relationships.

The curvilinear model is so flexible that it can fit any set of data that one can generate. This would be fine if the theory predicted the data beforehand or if the assumptions made in the post hoc fit could be followed consistently over a wide range of experimental findings. In our judgment the model does very poorly in this respect. A final example of this is seen in an interesting prediction about boomerang effects. (Janis, 1967, p. 205). Carefully following the implications of the curved surfaces, Janis suggests that at very high levels of fear, persuasion could drop below the zero point; at this point there would be movement away from the communicator's position. Confirmation of this interesting prediction is found in a study by Leventhal and Watts (1966). The critical finding is that very few smokers take X-rays at high fear levels. But the conclusion that this is a boomerang effect requires evidence that the proportion of smokers taking X-rays after the high fear message is less than the proportion taking X-rays in a group unexposed to any communication. To prove his point, Janis takes a baseline proportion from an earlier study by Leventhal and Niles (1964). The selection is unfortunate since the two samples and the situations are markedly different. The two most dramatic differences are that the baseline figure was obtained from a population that was visiting a health fair, and the health fair had about one-tenth of the visitors to the state fair (Leventhal & Watts, 1966). It was virtually impossible for the same proportion of people to have been X-rayed at the state fair (there were too many), and their interests in health were clearly less salient. Thus, this comparison does not demonstrate a boomerang effect in which high fear produces a level of X-ray taking below that expected on the basis of spontaneous action.

Another criticism of the curvilinear model concerns its failure to differentiate adequately between fear and arousal. Fear is presented as the key mediating variable. It is assumed to be a source of positive motivations, a force for attitude change and self protection, and it is also assumed to be a source of negative motivation, a force that inhibits change. But is fear the source of the curvilinear effect? Janis (1967, p. 178) presents an important figure which depicts the hypothetical relationship between what is labelled *emotional arousal* and acceptance; as arousal moves from a zero level to very low levels of arousal, acceptance shows a slight increase. Acceptance then remains stable from very low arousal, through middle, to high, and up to very high levels of arousal. Acceptance only drops at extremely high levels and does so through a very small change in arousal level. The changes, therefore, are restricted to the ends of the curve and the vast middle region is flat. The rise at the beginning appears to represent an energizing effect and the decline at the end appears to represent inefficiency or interference due to excessive arousal. But arousal is not the same as emotion, although arousal appears to contribute to emotional experience (Schachter & Singer, 1962). It seems important to distinguish the effects of arousal upon acceptance from the effects of fear. Janis' "family of curves" is supposed to represent the effects of fear upon acceptance and to account for changes in acceptance along the broad plateau or middle range of the arousal curve between wakefulness and panic. Of course, the parallel model claims that the events which occur in this middle range of arousal are changes in *decision*. It is in this middle region that the curvilinear and parallel models compete. The parallel model cannot ignore the ebb and flow of arousal. One cannot process a communication when sleeping or in rigid terror, but one should not confuse the arousal process with the decisional one. There seems to be little value in clumping together a variety of processes: attention, interference, fatigue, decision, etc., under the label fear. It seems more reasonable to examine the contribution of each of these variables to the persuasion process.

In summary, the objections to the curvilinear model are not based upon its suggestion of nonlinearity between acceptance and underlying processes. The theory is faulted on the following points: (1) It assumes without evidence that fear is the mediator of acceptance; (2) it treats fear as a unitary concept or entity when much research clearly questions this assumption; (3) it specifies few variables which change the optimal level of fear and does not adequately describe how these factors would operate; (4) where it specifically mentions a modifier variable, it is frequently inaccurate or incomplete in relating the variable to persuasion; (5) it ignores the problems in the measurement of fear and related variables; and (6) it seems to function primarily as a low order descriptive hypothesis, with arbitrary shifting of points to fit curves rather than concentrating upon the description and analysis of underlying process. The curvilinear model as presently constituted is an interesting surface without a generating equation.

B.   EXTENSIONS OF THE PARALLEL RESPONSE MODEL

A substantial number of problems arose in attempting to fit the drive model to the fear communication data, all deriving from the assumption that fear is the necessary causal factor in the process of persuasion. The parallel response model seeks to resolve this host of issues by making the fundamentally different assumption that emotional and adaptive acts are independent of one another. The hypothesis of independence also can be extended to the various acts usually classified within the categories of emotional and adaptive activity. Thus, verbal statements of attitude are not the same as verbal statements of intention, and neither are equivalent or necessarily perfect predictors of action.

There are two important and positive consequences of beginning with the independence assumption. First, to make statements about a specific response and about its relationship to any other specific response, we must measure both responses and examine their relationship to one another. Second, we must make a special effort to explain any relationship that is found; we cannot simply accept relationships as reflecting the natural organization of drives or other special forces in the nervous system. There clearly will be clusterings of behaviors, and the organization can be produced by a variety of mechanisms. The parallel model does not explain these mechanisms; in this respect it is highly abstract and more a frame of reference than a theory. But its use of concepts like *fear control* and *danger control* does suggest reasons for the clustering of reactions. Clusterings in this instance are based upon the assumption that external and internal sources of cues can provide separate guidelines for behavior.

In the following section we will attempt to draw a few of the implications of the model and relate them to existent research. In some instances the model seems a bit more powerful than one might expect since it accounts for findings that were not anticipated by the investigators. In other instances we can do no more than point to new problems which are in need of exploration.

1. Cognitive Control of Adaptation

The parallel model emphasizes the mutual independence and the stimulus boundedness of reactions; glandular response and motor activity may each be stimulus controlled and not influence each other directly. The application to the fear communication data emphasized that subjects adapt to a potential threat because they recognize danger as something to be avoided. They know danger whether or not they are frightened. The dangerousness of an object is a property of the object, not a property of their fear. Adaptive activity can be sustained by this knowledge. Of course, fear will increase and decrease with the magnitude of danger, proximity to danger, and success in coping with danger, and fear and coping behavior will continually interact with one another. The parallel model and the emphasis upon cognitive control of danger does not deny these problems. It is concerned with explaining them.

2. Internal Consistency Forces

One important theoretical implication of the parallel hypothesis is that the various behaviors classified under a common label will frequently be unrelated. Verbal responses affect physical responses (heart rate changes, GSR, etc.), and overt behaviors may respond to separate aspects of the stimulus situation. The emphasis upon independence is quite different from that seen in many theories of attitude change which assume a natural tendency toward balance or symmetry (Abelson & Rosenberg, 1958; Osgood & Tannenbaum, 1955; Rosenberg, 1960). The fear communication data give abundant examples of inconsistency. The model does not assume that affect, attitude, and action tend toward consistency. Additional examples in other areas can be found in a review by Insko and Schopler (1967).

The model also makes clear that the empirical presence of consistency is not sufficient evidence for balance or symmetry forces. A person may see a danger, evaluate it negatively, be frightened, and act to eliminate it. The result is a consistent set of actions. But each of these acts may be separately evoked by the external situation. There are more complex and less obvious cases in which it is also unnecessary to assume consistency. For example, if a person runs to avoid being hit by an on-rushing car we can assume that his knowledge of the consequences of being hit explains his action. But suppose that the same person feels anxious while he is crossing the street and because of this he begins to run. Do we need to postulate a consistency between affect and instrumental action, or can we simply say that affective responses are providing the cues for behavior (see Freud, 1961; p. 43, 58 & 59)? If we see the action as a response to a cue, we might decide to apply consistency principles only in cases in which the presence of both cues (external danger and internal affect) produces a response that is different than that made to either cue alone. Moreover, we might use the term consistency only for effects that show we are dealing with something other than simple averaging or addition of separate response tendencies. The notion of Gestalt or organization clearly implied something more than a summative process. Thus, the parallel model requires that we define precisely all conditions giving rise to consistency.

3. Hierarchical Processes

Contemporary neurophysiology suggests that independence and interdependence are compatible events. They are compatible with the view of the nervous system as a hierarchy. Even simple glandular reactions have separate control mechanisms, and these mechanisms appear to be capable of instrumental learning (N. E. Miller, 1969). But some systems function in a superordinate capacity and exert a degree of control over other systems nested within them. Thus, while emotional, cognitive and instrumental behaviors may be produced by a common external stimulus, some degree of integration may be imposed upon these separate response systems by the activity of higher order, neural integrators. The so-called perceptual-cognitive element in the parallel model would appear to serve this function.

A good example of inconsistency and consistency is seen in the concept of arousal. Many theorists (Duffy, 1962; Lindsley, 1951) claim that arousal is the key factor in motivation and learning. Lacey (1967) has pointed out, however, that the concept lacks the degree of unity attributed to it. The specific measures of arousal, such as EEG indicators, and behavioral alertness, simply do not show strongly consistent relationships. Indeed, Lacey discusses the dissociation of behavior systems and points out that organisms may be perfectly aroused in terms of cerebral activation and perfectly comatose in terms of behavioral activation. The inverse can also be produced. The two positions suggest that separate systems exist that are capable of higher order integration.

4. Stimulus Control of Parallel and Independent Reactions

The assumption that different aspects of a person's response to a communication are dependent upon stimulus elements has important implications. The idea suggests that salience of a response, attitude change, fear, protective behavior can be altered by changing specific aspects of the stimulus setting. For example, in fear communications it is likely that strong emotional behavior is stimulated by scenes of blood and human destruction. While these same scenes undoubtedly convey some information on the nature of the danger, it is questionable that they add as much to the viewer's knowledge as they add to his fear. He could be given essentially the same information about the danger in words or aseptic diagrams. For many people, the informational aspect may be sufficient to produce action, and increasing action-relevant information will produce compliance without raising fear.

The above analysis leads to practical prescriptions different from those emphasized by the drive model. The drive model concludes that at least a moderate amount of fear is necessary if people are to prepare for crises, e.g. preparation for the stress of surgery (Janis, 1958). Fear supposedly stimulates preparation by initiating the work of worry (Marmor, 1958). The parallel model suggests that the most important feature in preparation is instructing the patient to identify correctly internal and external cues and to prepare actions that are appropriate to these signals. It is not necessary, however, to stimulate fear. As seen in the studies of specific action instruction, the level of fear has no important effects upon the execution of the recommended behaviors. Recent data with surgical patients support this conclusion (Johnson, Dabbs, & Leventhal, 1970).

5. The Cognitive Operator and Its Sources of Information

The more complicated version of the parallel model (Fig. 6) makes clear that stimuli are encoded or interpreted before eliciting responses. The term "cognitive operator" refers to the variety of processes that are involved in interpretation. As the figure shows, the cognitive operator has three sources of information: (1) external stimuli (dangers), (2) internal bodily disturbances (which are labeled as affective or emotional), and (3) instrumental behaviors. In addition to dealing with separate inputs, the cognitive operator can simultaneously appraise information from combinations of cues.

The experimental literature contains studies of the effects of cognitive operations upon each of the three types on input. For example, Lazarus (1968) and his colleagues have demonstrated that the subject's set will change his interpretation of an external threat, a movie of a subincision rite. Changes in interpretation alter both verbal reports and physiological measures of disturbance.

Schachter and his co-workers (Schachter & Singer, 1962; Schachter & Wheeler, 1962) have investigated the effects of cognitive sets upon the encoding of internal states. They have suggested that internal cues are necessary for the judgment that one is emotional, but the internal information provides only one ingredient for this judgment. External information, the happy or angry behavior of a stooge, determines which specific label is applied to the internal state (Schachter & Singer, 1962). There are also several studies which claim that associating body states with irrelevant causes (such as a placebo pill) eliminates emotion, while associating body states with relevant causes increases emotion (Nisbett & Schachter, 1966; Ross, Rodin, & Zimbardo, 1969).

The parallel model raises a number of interesting questions about the Schachter studies. First, it is not clear that the subjects were responding to their body states. Indeed, when they were given accurate expectations and, therefore, were most likely to be aware of their body states, they failed to experience emotion. Thus, the results suggest that close attention to body cues may inhibit emotional arousal. Second, none of the studies has used a control group in which the subjects were prepared to identify their internal states and to attribute it to a *relevant* cause. Because of this, there is considerable ambiguity concerning the importance of awareness of internal cues.

Schachter and his colleagues also failed to distinguish consistently between the cognition of the environmental object (There is a dangerous situation.), the evaluation of the object (The situation is very dangerous.), and various emotional behaviors toward the object; autonomic, expressive and subjective (I am—or am not—frightened by X.). The parallel model stresses the need to distinguish among these reactions and suggests that evaluations are controlled by cognitive encoding of the external stimulus. Evaluations of the stimulus should not be easily changed by internal states. The Schachter and Wheeler (1962) study illustrates the importance of these distinctions. The investigators gave epinephrine and chlorpromazine, respectively, to two different groups of subjects. Both drugs were described as having properties other than their actual exciting or relaxing effects. In the absence of an explanation for the bodily changes, the exciting or relaxing effect of their drugs was expected to increase or decrease the subjects' enjoyment and evaluation of a funny movie. The drugs did affect expressive behavior; subjects given epinephrine laughed a great deal and subjects given chlorpromazine laughed very little. Control subjects given no drugs were between the other two groups. However, the changes in laughter had absolutely no effect on the subjects' judgments of the quality of the film. Indeed, the epinephrine subjects felt that they had laughed at an unfunny movie. Thus, expressive behavior was altered, but the property of the stimulus and the subjects' familiarity with it anchored his judgments.

In summary, it is not clear that subjects are typically responsive to their internal states, or at least it is not clear that awareness of their inner states is necessary for emotional experience to occur. What *is* obvious, however, is that inner signals are potential cues of threat and are exceedingly important for certain types of protective medical behavior. When people notice bodily symptoms, they are likely to wonder about their meaning. Establishing this meaning appears to involve a complex set of strategies which includes locating antecedents of the body symptom, isolating correlated symptoms, observing changes, and applying various (passive or active) forms of self-exploration. Leventhal and Quinlan have observed people's responses to symptoms (in a role play situation) and classified the acts involved in self-evaluation. They found that these classes were also correlated with the strategies used in the solution of standard perceptual and concept formation tasks. It is clear from some of these data, and from sociological studies of reactions to body change (Kutner & Gordon, 1961), that body signals are important determinants of instrumental and emotional behavior.

Finally, Bem and his associates (Bandler, Madaras, & Bem, 1968) suggest that an individual draws conclusions about the painfulness of a stimulus from observations of his instrumental escape behaviors; when the subject makes an escape response he rates a shock as more painful.

The parallel model suggests that the appearance of such a phenomenon depends upon the relative clarity of the informational inputs, a suggestion also made by the now old, new-look theories of perception (Bruner, 1957). Experimental data confirm this hypothesis (Klemp, 1969); when subjects escape a strong shock that is uniform in intensity, they tend to minimize rather than to exaggerate its painfulness.

6. Interrelatedness of Danger Control and Fear Control

When a person encounters a danger or a vivid warning of danger, many of the processes we have discussed are activated simultaneously within him. The individual is aware of external cues of threat, responds emotionally, becomes aware of his emotional behavior, responds instrumentally, and becomes aware of his instrumental reactions. It is exceedingly difficult, therefore, to determine which specific source of information is critical in producing particular types of behavior. However, there are situations that will allow us to see these separate processes.

We might take as an example the case of a car unexpectedly thrown out of control, an instance that I can all too easily reconstruct from my own experience. As the vehicle careened wildly along the highway, following its own momentum rather than my instructions, I became vividly aware of danger. The awareness of danger led to vigorous coping actions; hitting and the releasing the brakes, turning with the skid, allowing the wheel to spin, etc. The coping acts were highly elaborate and required specific plans and the coordination of arm and leg movement with changes in the visual field. While I was busy with these actions I was not frightened. At any rate my hands, feet, and consciousness were not frightened. My wife reported that my face was frightened, or at least that it had turned white. But I could afford to have a frightened face and a frightened stomach as neither was actively involved in contending with the danger.

When I finally brought the vehicle under control and could stop my coping efforts, I experienced intense fear. I became aware of the turmoil in my inner organs, and my hands and feet, since they were no longer involved in coping, began to be afraid and to tremble. I next had to think of ways of coping with my fear: Should I stop to relax, get a bite to eat, or just ignore my discomfort? In this instance, danger and fear led to quite different types of reactions. For certain systems, the two types of reactions proved to be mutually exclusive. Hands, feet, and consciousness were involved with danger at one point and with fear at another. This sequence is a good illustration of the fact that fear does not mediate coping reactions and that the responses stimulated by fear have little or nothing to do with the management of the danger situation.

The example also demonstrates how control processes may shift over time and, specifically, how the removal of a danger can lead to the dominance of fear control. Indeed, some authors suggest that interruptions in coping are a source of fear (Mandler & Watson, 1966). The foregoing example illustrates that interruptions may stimulate fear even when the danger has vanished.

Another important feature of the interplay of danger control and fear control concerns the degree to which they are mutually facilitative. It is easy to focus on those instances in which fear-motivated action interferes with the control of danger. But do avoidance behaviors have any value in controlling danger? The avoidance of X-ray taking by smokers seems totally irrational; it eliminates fear but makes no positive contribution to the control of danger. But suppose the smoker had to manipulate the X-ray machine and that he could give himself a dangerous overdose of radiation if he did it improperly. The possibility of such an error could increase when he is fearful. Temporary avoidance of the setting could then be a desirable strategy.

If one works in a dangerous setting it can be very useful to judge accurately one's ability to control one's fear. Thus, in sport parachuting (Epstein, 1967), underwater exploration (Radloff & Helmreich, 1968), and other such conditions, control of fear is necessary for the successful control of danger. Strong emotions increase the hazards in the setting. Epstein's skilled chutists seem to become progressively more adept at emotional control. They apparently experience peak emotion at the time of decision on the morning of the jump. Perhaps they are testing the strength of their fear or making sure that they have sufficient control over it so that it will not appear at jump time. It is clear that we need to know more about the various strategies people use to control affect.

7. Sequences of Cognitive Operations

In our discussion to this point we have made it seem that fear control is associated with internal cues and danger control with external cues. It is conceivable that individuals who respond to inner cues will inevitably choose behaviors aimed at fear reduction, responses such as hiding, eating, etc. But this may not necessarily be the case. High esteem subjects may show similar response tendencies to both internal emotional disturbance and external danger. Regardless of its source, high esteem subjects may interpret danger cues as signals for action. Indeed, one fruitful direction for inquiry would be to identify the various sequences of beliefs that appear under stress and to see which of them is associated with successful preparation.

Our knowledge of high esteem subjects suggests that regardless of

A. Overview of model

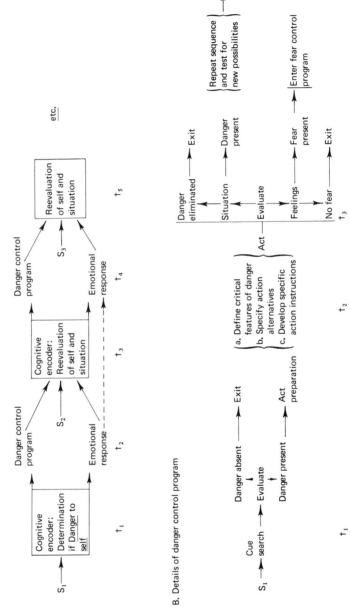

B. Details of danger control program

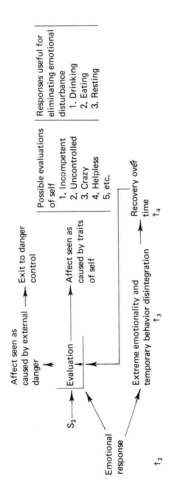

Fig. 6. Expansion of the parallel response model.

the source of danger, they go directly from awareness of danger to action. If this is true, then what does it mean if a high esteem subject fails to follow a recommendation? Because he has the competency needed to cope with both danger and emotion, the absence of action may reflect a break early in the belief sequence, such as failing to see himself as vulnerable to danger. When a low esteem subject fails to act there are many ways of accounting for his failure. He may not recognize that he is threatened. But even if he does, he may feel incapable of acting. In fact, the more personally involved or vulnerable he becomes the more difficult it may be for him to believe that he can protect himself. On the other hand, his failure to act may be due to avoidance generated by the need to control fear. If we can observe such cognitive sequences we may be able to pinpoint the determinants of inhibition of action.

8. Nature of Cognitive Operations

A final theoretical issue concerns the similarities and differences between the cognitive operations used to evaluate different types of danger cues, internal affect cues, cues from instrumental behavior, and external cues. As we have already suggested, it is doubtful that the organism functions at an equivalent level of sophistication for all inputs. Analytical or formal operational thinking would seem to be more likely with respect to external inputs and instrumental behaviors. Indeed the development of formal operations presumably requires the observation of interactions between motor actions and the external world (Piaget, 1967). A far lower level of cognitive sophistication will probably be seen with respect to internal emotional inputs as the individual has less opportunity for the observation, labeling, and manipulation of internal states (Bem, 1967).

The difference between so-called high and low esteem subjects could reflect differences in the sophistication of cognitive structures associated with emotional arousal. This suggests the interesting possibility that affect in high esteem subjects is largely a cognitive reaction. If this is indeed the case, high esteem Ss, when exposed to danger, would show little autonomic arousal and report considerable affect. This hypothesis is supported by a recent reanalysis of the studies by Lazarus and his colleagues (Weinstein, Averill, Opton, & Lazarus, 1968). This analysis shows that better adjusted (higher esteem) subjects report emotions but give relatively weak responses at the autonomic level.

A second suggestion is that low esteem or cognitively unsophisticated subjects would be readily persuaded by internal feedback. This hypothesis is strongly supported by Valins and Ray (1967), who show that emotional subjects are very influenced by false feedback respecting their emotional states. The emotional (low esteem) subjects treat an emotional communication, false feedback of heart pounding, as an accurate and highly authoritative statement of their likes and dislikes. It is unlikely that a direct communication from an external source could produce persuasion of this magnitude.

9. Methodological Implications

The parallel model has a wide range of methodological implications. Many of these stem from the model's focus on new problems; an example is the way people make judgments about bodily symptoms. It would be inappropriate, however, to deal with these factors in this general presentation. Nevertheless, there are some methodological issues that conform more closely to the central concerns of this paper. The first of these is the need to distinguish necessary or causal relationships from correlational ones. Spence (1944) cast this problem in terms of R-R versus S-R laws, the correlational law emerging from individual difference study and the S-R law from experimental study. The parallel model strongly suggests that we must separate R-R laws into two types, mediational (causal) and nonmediational (correlational), and devise ways of distinguishing mediational effects from S-R effects. In the mediational relationship one response provides a cue for another. In the latter it does not.

Mediational R-R laws are not tested by the usual method of observing treatment differences. For example, if Message A elevates fear and persuasion relative to Message B, we are dealing with a correlation across treatments of the means of the two dependent variables. What are the methodological requirements for isolating a mediational effect? One approach would be to rule out all potential alternative mediators. The question is similar to that raised about potential confounding variables. The investigator eliminates the potential confound by showing that it has no consequences for performance. But ruling out effects is slow and relies on negative instance. A positive technique is to develop what Garner, Hake, and Erickson (1956) call converging operations, different and independent ways of manipulating the same variable which should produce similar consequences. In the fear communication area, the problem reduces to developing ways of manipulating fear that are separate from manipulations of information about danger. As we have already suggested, one might try to define different types of information, facts on the agent, its means of operation, its consequences, etc., to see if some classes of information are more important in raising fear level while other classes are more important in influencing attitudes and/or action. Manipulations with drugs, etc., might also be useful in evaluating the importance of arousal in emotion-decision interactions.

Another significant methodological point stems from the idea that independent processes can be correlated if they are nested in a common hierarchical schema. This idea suggests that correlations between fear level and attitudes may be the product of a variety of higher order processes. For example, Horowitz (1969) has argued that inconsistent results in fear studies stem from the use of compulsory *versus* volunteer subject groups. When participation is voluntary, increased communication pressure (high fear) increases persuasion. When participation is required, increased communication pressure (high fear) decreases persuasion. Horowitz presents data that support his interaction hypothesis and then goes on to suggest that the results could account for past inconsistencies. But the demonstration of the interaction does not mean that the process which causes it is the same process as that which caused interactions in past studies. To demonstrate that the processes are identical, Horowitz must either show that volunteering differences are correlated with the variables which produced interactions in past studies, or that both variables effect identical mediational process. An example of such an analysis can be seen in a study by Dabbs (1964).

C. Value of the Paradigm

Our paradigm views the organism as an active decision maker. Belief change, emotional arousal, action, information rejection, etc., are complex processes that are extended in time. Each is dependent upon the specific kinds of information available to the problem solver, and each process is related to the others. The paradigm makes clear that information is extracted from observation of (1) the danger stimulus, (2) emotional behavior, and (3) the effects of coping acts upon the danger and emotional behavior. The model provides a framework, therefore, for research on both fear communications and stress. It is, in part, a linguistic device that seeks a closer association of concepts (such as fear and danger) with specific behavioral referents. It stresses the need to identify the separate processes subsumed under more global concepts and the need to recognize that these processes are often partially independent. It rejects the oversimplification of using the concepts of fear and fear dynamics (a chapter heading) as the primary intervening variable in adjustment to danger. Explaining resistance to or acceptance of fear communications as an aspect of fear dynamics makes eloquent propaganda but is not very much more useful than appealing to human nature.

The paradigm is more open to change than the various drive models. It makes visible the need for the conceptualization of danger detection processes and for the elaboration of structures connecting both affective and cognitive events to behavior. These structures may differ in complexity and mode of operation. The model also suggests a number of hypotheses respecting attention to fear or danger cues, the complexity of adaptive responses, etc., and suggests the need to experiment on mediators with adequate controls for parallel or correlated processes. It is an analytical model that directs us to differentiate and develop new concepts.

Finally, the model suggests that a multiplicity of mechanisms and adaptive processes (*fear control, danger control,* etc.) can co-exist and/or be used to different degrees on different occasions by the same or by different people. Thus, it will share features of conflict models and be hospitable to the analysis of sequential events and to shifts in process over time. The paradigm aims less at an axiomatic theory than at a simulation of adaptation to dangers. Unlike the curvilinear extension of the drive model, it does not call for a premature commitment to a particular function before we have identified the variables in the function. It is merely a first step toward structuring a theory, and it claims to be no more. It is interesting to note, however, the many points of convergence between this approach and that of other investigators (cf. Epstein, 1967; Lang, 1968; Lazarus, 1968; Rescorla & Solomon, 1967). Of course, the immediate value of the parallel hypothesis will depend upon its ability to stimulate research. But I would regard it as having real value only if it provides a more accurate description and understanding of this part of reality.

REFERENCES

Abelson, R. P., & Rosenberg, M. J. Symbolic psychologic: a model of attitudinal cognition. *Behavioral Science*, 1958, **3**, 1–13.

Aronfreed, J. The origin of self-criticism. *Psychological Review*, 1964, **71**, 193–218.

Bandler, R. J., Madaras, G. R., & Bem, D. J. Self-observation as a source of pain perception. *Journal of Personality and Social Psychology*, 1968, **9**, 205–209.

Bem, D. J. Self perception: an alternative interpretation of cognitive dissonance phenomenon. *Psychological Review*, 1967, **74**, 183–200.

Berelson, B., & Steiner, G. A. *Human behavior*. New York: Harcourt Brace, 1964.

Berkowitz, L., & Cottingham, D. R. The interest value and relevance of fear-arousing communications. *Journal of Abnormal and Social Psychology*, 1960, **60**, 37–43.

Berlyne, D. E. *Structure and direction in thinking*. New York: Wiley, 1965.

Bindra, D. *Motivation: A systematic reinterpretation*. New York: Ronald Press, 1959.

Brehm, J. *A theory of psychological reactance*. New York: Academic Press, 1966.

Brock, T. C. Commitment to exposure as a determinant of information receptivity. *Journal of Personality and Social Psychology*, 1965, **2**, 10–19.

Brock, T. C., & Balloun, J. L. Behavioral receptivity to dissonant information. *Journal of Personality and Social Psychology*, 1967, **6**, 413–428.

Bruner, J. S. On perception readiness. *Psychological Review*, 1957, **64**, 123–152.

Cartwright, D. Some principles of mass persuasion. Selected findings of research in the scale of United States war bonds. *Human Relations*, 1949, **2**, 253-267.

Chu, G. C. Fear arousal, efficacy, and imminency. *Journal of Personality and Social Psychology*, 1966, **4**, 517-524.

Church, R. M. The varied effects of punishment on behavior. *Psychological Review*, 1963, **70**, 369-402.

Cohen, A. R. Need for cognitions on order of communication as determinants of opinion change. In C. Hovland (Ed.), *Order of presentation*. New Haven: Yale University Press, 1957. Pp. 79-97.

Dabbs, J. M. Self-esteem, communicator characteristics, and attitude change. *Journal of Abnormal and Social Psychology*, 1964, **69**, 173-181.

Dabbs, J. M., & Leventhal, H. Effects of varying the recommendations in a fear-arousing communication. *Journal of Personality and Social Psychology*, 1966, **4**, 525-531.

DeWolfe, A. S., & Governale, C. N. Fear and attitude change. *Journal of Abnormal and Social Psychology*, 1964, **69**, 119-123.

Duffy, E. *Activation and behavior*. New York: Wiley, 1962.

Duke, J. D. Critique of the Janis and Feshbach study. *Journal of Social Psychology*, 1967, **72**, 71-80.

Epstein, S. Toward a unified theory of anxiety. In B. A. Mahrer (Ed.), *Progress in experimental personality research*. Vol. 4. New York: Academic Press, 1967. Pp. 1-89.

Evans, R. I., Rozelle, R. M., Lasater, T. M., Deinbroski, T. M., & Allen, B. T. New measure of effects of persuasive communications: a chemical indicator of toothbrushing behavior. *Psychological Reports*, 1968, **23**, 731-736.

Eysenck, H. J. *Smoking, health and personality*. New York: Basic Books, 1965.

Fearing, F. Toward a psychological theory of human communication. *Journal of Personality*, 1953, **22**, 71-88.

Freeman, G. L. The relationship between performance level and bodily activity level. *Journal of Experimental Psychology*, 1940, **26**, 602-608.

Freud, S. *Inhibition, symptoms and anxiety*. (1926). London: Hogarth Press & Institute of Psychoanalysis, 1961.

Funkenstein, D. H., King, S. H., & Drolette, M. E. *Mastery of stress*. Cambridge, Mass.: Harvard University Press, 1957.

Garner, W. R., Hake, H. H., & Erickson, C. W. Operationism and the concept of perception. *Psychological Review*, 1956, **63**, 149-159.

Goldstein, M. The relationship between coping and avoiding behavior and response to fear arousing propaganda. *Journal of Abnormal and Social Psychology*, 1959, **58**, 247-252.

Greenwald, A. Behavior change following a persuasive communication. *Journal of Personality*, 1965, **33**, 370-391.

Haefner, D. Some effects of guilt arousing and fear arousing persuasive communications on opinion change. Technical Report, August 15, 1956, Office of Naval Research, Contract No. N 6 ONR 241. (Abridgement of unpublished doctoral dissertation, University of Rochester.)

Haefner, D. Arousing fear in dental health education. *Journal of Public Health Dentistry*, 1965, **25**, 140-146.

Hebb, D. O. *The organization of behavior*. New York: Wiley, 1949.

Hewgill, M. A., & Miller, G. R. Source credibility and response to fear-arousing communications. *Speech Monographs*, 1965, **32**, 95-101.

Hilgard, E., & Atkinson, R. *Introduction to psychology*. New York: Harcourt, Brace & World, 1967.

Hochbaum, G. M. *Public participation in medical screening programs: a sociopsychological study*. Public Health Service Publication No. 572. Washington, D.C.: U.S. Government Printing Office, 1958.

Horn, D. Factors affecting cessation of cigarette smoking: a prospective study. Paper presented at the meeting of the Eastern Psychological Association, Washington, D.C., April, 1968.

Horowitz, I. A. Effects of volunteering, fear arousal, and number of communications on attitude change. *Journal of Personality and Social Psychology*, 1969, **11**, 34-37.

Hovland, C. I. Effects of the mass media of communication. In G. Lindzey (Ed.), *Handbook of social psychology*. Vol. 2. Cambridge, Mass.: Addison-Wesley, 1954. Pp. 1062-1103. 1062-1103.

Hovland, C. I., Janis, I. L., & Kelley, H. H. *Communication and persuasion*. New Haven: Yale University Press, 1953.

Insko, C. A., Arkoff, A., & Insko, V. M. Effects of high and low fear-arousing communication upon opinions toward smoking. *Journal of Experimental Social Psychology*, 1965, **1**, 256-266.

Insko, C. A., & Schopler, J. Triadic consistency: A statement of affective-cognitive-conative consistency. *Psychological Review*, 1967, **74**, 361-376.

Janis, I. L. *Psychological stress*. New York: Wiley, 1958.

Janis, I. L. Effects of fear arousal on attitude change: Recent developments in theory and experimental research. In L. Berkowitz (Ed.), *Advances in experimental social psychology*. Vol. 3. New York: Academic Press, 1967. Pp. 167-222.

Janis, I., & Feshbach, S. Effects of fear-arousing communications. *Journal of Abnormal and Social Psychology*, 1953, **48**, 78-92.

Janis, I. L., & Feshbach, S. Personality differences associated with responsiveness to fear-arousing communications. *Journal of Personality*, 1954, **23**, 154-166.

Janis, I. L., & Leventhal, H. Psychological aspects of physical illness and hospital care. In B. Wolman (Ed.), *Handbook of clinical psychology*. New York: McGraw-Hill, 1965.

Janis, I. L., & Leventhal, H. Human reactions to stress. In E. Borgotta & W. Lambert (Eds.), *Handbook of personality theory and research*. Chicago: Rand McNally, 1968. Pp. 1041-1085.

Janis, I. L., & Mann, L. Effectiveness of emotional role-playing in modifying smoking habits and attitudes. *Journal of Experimental Research in Personality*, 1965, **1**, 84-90.

Janis, I. L., & Milholland, H. C. The influence of threat appeals on selective learning of the content of a persuasive communication. *Journal of Psychology*, 1954, **37**, 75-80.

Janis, I. L., & Terwilliger, R. An experimental study of psychological resistances to fear-arousing communication. *Journal of Abnormal and Social Psychology*, 1962, **65**, 403-410.

Johnson, J., Dabbs, J., & Leventhal, H. Psychosocial factors in the welfare of surgical patients. *Nursing Research*, 1970, **19**, 18-29.

Jones, H. G. Learning and abnormal behavior. In H. J. Eysenck (Ed.), *Handbook of abnormal psychology*. New York: Basic Books, 1960. Pp. 488-528.

Klapper, J. T. *The effects of mass communication*. Glencoe, Ill.: Free Press, 1960.

Klemp, G. O., Jr. The meaning of escape and the perception of discomfort. Unpublished masters thesis, University of Wisconsin, 1969.

Kohler, W. *The mentality of apes*. (1925) New York: Humanities Press, 1951.

Kornzweig, N. D. Behavior change as a function of fear arousal and personality. Unpublished doctoral dissertation, Yale University, 1967.

Kraus, S., El-Assal, E., & DeFleur, M. L. Fear threat appeals in mass communications: An apparent contradiction. Mimeo, 1964.

Krech, D., Crutchfield, R. S., & Ballachey, E. L. *Individual in society*. New York: McGraw-Hill, 1962.

Krech, D., Crutchfield, R. S., & Livson, N. *Elements of psychology*. New York: Knopf, 1969.

Kutner, B., & Gordon, G. Seeking care for cancer. *Journal of Health and Human Behavior*, 1961, 2, 171-178.

Lacey, J. I. Somatic response patterning and stress: Some revisions of activation theory. In M. H. Appley & R. Trumball (Eds.), *Psychological stress*. New York: Appleton-Century-Crofts, 1967.

Lang, P. J. Fear reduction and fear behavior: Problems in treating a construct. In J. M. Shlien (Ed.), *Research in psychotherapy*. Vol. III. Washington, D. C.: American Psychological Association, 1968. Pp. 90-103.

Lazarus, R. S. Emotions and adaptation: Conceptual and empirical relations. In W. J. Arnold (Ed.), *Nebraska symposium on motivation*. Lincoln: University of Nebraska Press, 1968. Pp. 175-266.

Leventhal, H. Fear communications in the acceptance of preventive health practices. *Bulletin of the New York Academy of Medicine*, 1965, 41, 1144-1168.

Leventhal, H., Hochbaum, G. M., Carriger, B. K., & Rosenstock, I. M. Epidemic impact on the general population in two cities. In I. Rosenstock, G. M. Hochbaum, H. Leventhal, (Eds.), *The impact of Asian influenza on community life*. Public Health Service Publication No. 766. Washington, D. C.: U.S. Government Printing Office, 1960. Pp. 53-78.

Leventhal, H., Jones, S., & Trembly, G. Sex differences in attitude and behavior change under conditions of fear and specific instructions. *Journal of Experimental Social Psychology*, 1966, 2, 387-399.

Leventhal, H., & Niles, P. A field experiment on fear arousal with data on the validity of questionnaire measures. *Journal of Personality*, 1964, 32, 459-479.

Leventhal, H., & Niles, P. Persistence of influence for varying durations of exposure to threat stimuli. *Psychological Reports*, 1965, 16, 223-233.

Leventhal, H., & Quinlan, D. Perceptual and cognitive components of symptom testing: a model for the evaluation of danger. Mimeo, University of Wisconsin, 1969.

Leventhal, H., & Singer, R. P. Affect arousal and positioning of recommendations in persuasive communications. *Journal of Personality and Social Psychology*, 1966, 4, 137-146.

Leventhal, H., Singer, R. P., & Jones, S. Effects of fear and specificity of recommendation upon attitudes and behavior. *Journal of Personality and Social Psychology*, 1965, 2, 20-29.

Leventhal, H., & Trembly, G. Negative emotions and persuasion. *Journal of Personality*, 1968, 36, 154-168.

Leventhal, H., & Watts, J. Sources of resistance to fear-arousing communications on smoking and lung cancer. *Journal of Personality*, 1966, 34, 155-175.

Leventhal, H., Watts, J. C., & Pagano, F. Effects of fear and instructions on how to cope with danger. *Journal of Personality and Social Psychology*, 1967, 6, 313-321.

Lindsley, D. B. Emotion. In S. Stevens (Ed.), *Handbook of experimental psychology*, New York: Chapman & Hall, 1951. Pp. 473-516.

Lundy, R. M., Simonson, N. R., & Landers, A. D. Conformity, persuasibility, and irrelevant fear. *Journal of Communication*, 1967, 17, 39-54.

Mainard, W. A. Experimental repression related to coping and avoidance behavior in the recall and relearning of nonsense syllables. Unpublished doctoral dissertation. University of Washington, 1956.

Mandler, G., & Watson, D. L. Anxiety and the interruption of behavior. In C. D. Spielberger (Ed.), *Anxiety and behavior*. New York: Academic Press, 1966. Pp. 263-290.

Mann, L. The effects of emotional role playing on desire to modify smoking habits. *Journal of Experimental Social Psychology*, 1967, **3**, 334-348.

Mann, L., & Janis, I. L. A follow-up study on the long-term effects of emotional role playing. *Journal of Personality and Social Psychology*, 1968, **8**, 339-342.

Marmor, J. The psychodynamics of realistic worry. *Psychoanalysis & the Social Sciences*, 1958, **5**, 155-163.

Matarazzo, J. D., & Saslow, G. Psychological and related characteristics of smokers and nonsmokers. *Psychological Bulletin*, 1960, **57**, 493-513.

Mausner, B., & Platt, E. S. Role playing as a technique for changing cigarette smoking behavior. Paper presented at the meeting of the Eastern Psychological Association, Washington, D. C., April, 1968.

May, R. *The meaning of anxiety*. New York: Ronald Press, 1950.

McGuire, W. J. Personality and susceptibility to social influence. In E. Borgatta & W. Lambert (Eds.), *Handbook of personality theory and research*. Chicago: Rand McNally, 1968. Pp. 1130-1188.

Miller, G. R., & Hewgill, M. A. Some recent research on fear-arousing message appeals. *Speech Monographs*, 1966, **33**, 377-391.

Miller, N. E. Learnable drives and rewards. In S. S. Stevens (Ed.), *Handbook of experimental psychology*. New York: Wiley, 1951. Pp. 435-472. (a)

Miller, N. E. Comments on theoretical models illustrated by the development of a theory of conflict. *Journal of Personality*, 1951, **20**, 89-100. (b)

Miller, N. E. Learning of visceral and glandular responses. *Science*, 1969, **163**, 434-445.

Millman, S. H. The relationship between anxiety, learning and opinion change. Unpublished doctoral dissertation, Columbia University, 1965.

Moltz, H., & Thistlethwaite, D. L. Attitude modification and anxiety reduction. *Journal of Abnormal and Social Psychology*, 1955, **50**, 231-237.

Niles, P. The relationships of susceptibility and anxiety to acceptance of fear-arousing communications. Unpublished doctoral dissertation, Yale University, 1964.

Nisbett, R. E., & Schacter, S. Cognitive manipulation of pain. *Journal of Experimental Social Psychology*, 1966, **2**, 227-236.

Nowlis, V. Research with the mood adjective check list. In S. Tomkins & C. Izard (Eds.), *Affect, cognition and personality*. New York: Springer, 1965. Pp. 352-389.

Osgood, C. E., & Tannenbaum, P. H. The principle of congruity in the prediction of attitude change. *Psychological Reviews*, 1955, **62**, 42-55.

Overmier, J. B., & Seligman, M. E. P. Effects of inescapable shock on subsequent escape and avoidance learning. *Journal of Comparative and Physiological Psychology*, 1967, **63**, 28-33.

Piaget, J. *Six psychological studies*. New York: Random House, 1967.

Platt, E. S., Krassen, E., & Mausner, B. Individual variation in behavioral change following role playing. Mimeo, Beaver College, 1967.

Powell, F. A. The effect of anxiety-arousing messages when related to personal familial and impersonal referents. *Speech Monographs*, 1965, **32**, 102-106.

Proshansky, H., & Seidenberg, B. (Eds.) *Basic studies in social psychology*. New York: Holt, Rinehart & Winston, 1966.

Radelfinger, S. Some effects of fear-arousing communications on preventive health behavior. *Health Education Monographs*, 1965, **19**, 2-15.

Radloff, R. An evaluation of the exhibit "Man against Cancer." Mimeo, Public Health

Service, U. S. Dept. of Health, Education and Welfare, 1963.

Radloff, R., & Helmreich, R. *Groups under stress: Psychological research in Sealab II.* New York: Appleton-Century-Crofts, 1968.

Rescorla, R. A., & Solomon, R. L. Two-process learning theory: Relationships between Pavlovian conditioning and instrumental learning. *Psychological Review,* 1967, **74,** 151-182.

Rosenberg, M. J. Cognitive reorganization in response to the hypnotic reversal of attitudinal affect. *Journal of Personality,* 1960, 28, 39-63.

Rosenblatt, P. C. Persuasive value of threat and amount of attitude change advocated. Unpublished doctoral dissertation, Northwestern University, 1962.

Ross, L., Rodin, J., & Zimbardo, P. G. Toward an attribution therapy: The reduction of fear through induced cognitive-emotional misattribution. *Journal of Personality and Social Psychology,* 1969, 12, 279-288.

Rotter, J. B. Generalized expectancies for internal vs. external control of reinforcement. *Psychological Monographs,* 1966, **80.**

Schachter, S., & Singer, J. E. Cognitive, social and physiological determinants of emotional state. *Psychological Review,* 1962, **69,** 379-399.

Schachter, S., & Wheeler, L. Epinephrine, chlorpromazine and amusement. *Journal of Abnormal and Social Psychology,* 1962, **65,** 121-128.

Simonson, N. R., & Lundy, R. M. The effectiveness of persuasive communication presented under conditions of irrelevant fear. *Journal of Communication,* 1966, **16,** 32-37.

Singer, R. P. The effects of fear-arousing communications on attitude change and behavior. Unpublished doctoral dissertation, University of Connecticut, 1965.

Solomon, R. Punishment. *American Psychologist,* 1964, 19, 239-253.

Spence, K. W. The nature of theory construction in contemporary psychology. *Psychological Review,* 1944, **51,** 47-68.

Spence, K. W. Cognitive and drive factors in the extinction of the conditional eye blink in human subjects. *Psychological Review,* 1966, **73,** 445-458.

Valins, S., & Ray, A. Effects of cognitive desensitization on avoidance behavior. *Journal of Personality and Social Psychology,* 1967, 7, 345-351.

Watts, J. C. The role of vulnerability in resistance to fear-arousing communications. Unpublished doctoral dissertation, Bryn Mawr College, 1966.

Weinstein, J., Averill, J. R., Opton, E. M., & Lazarus, R. S. Defensive style and discrepancy between self-report and physiological indexes of stress. *Journal of Personality and Social Psychology,* 1968, **10,** 406-413.

Yerkes, R. M., & Dodson, J. D. The relation of strength of stimulus to rapidity of habit formation. *Journal of Comparative Neurology and Psychology,* 1908, 18, 459-482.

Young, P. T. *Motivation and emotion.* New York: Wiley, 1961.

PERCEIVED FREEDOM[1]

Ivan D. Steiner[2]
UNIVERSITY OF ILLINOIS

I. Introduction

During recent decades freedom has not been a very fashionable word among psychologists. Examination of popular textbooks suggests that people make decisions, satisfy their needs, avoid noxious stimulation, and indulge their egos. But they are rarely described as enjoying

[1]Work on this paper was supported by Grant # 1161-67 from the Behavioral Division, Air Force Office of Scientific Research (J. E. McGrath, Principal Investigator). The writer is indebted to G. Levinger and J. McGrath for comments concerning an early draft of the manuscript.
[2]Present Address: University of Massachusetts, Amherst, Massachusetts.

the state which Webster defines as "exemption from necessity in choice and action." When authors mention freedom it is generally in connection with statistical tests or association techniques, or with reference to threadbare philosophical arguments concerning the issue of free will. Sometimes the "illusion of freedom" is discussed and man's self-ascribed liberties are likened, in the manner of Spinoza, to the freedom of a stone which thinks, as it travels through space, that it determines its own trajectory and selects the place and time of its descent. Freedom is represented as a fantasy concocted by the human brain.

Such was the view of Freud who maintained that no behavior is uncaused, and that what seems to be a freely chosen course of action is in reality determined by an abundance of unconscious and coercive motives. Freud regarded "free association" as a powerful diagnostic technique precisely because associations are not free, and he described man's most personal beliefs and dreams as manifestations of compelling, and often ominous, internal forces. These notions are still central to the thinking of many psychologists.

Behaviorists have been no more hospitable to the view that man exercises a margin of freedom. From Watson to Skinner they have contended that human conduct is controlled by the environment and history of the individual, and that "an analysis which appeals to external variables makes the assumption of an inner originating and determining agent unnecessary [Skinner, 1953, p. 241]." According to this view, freedom is a "byword" (Skinner, 1957, p. 460) which pleases those who use it, but which contributes little to the understanding of human behavior.

It is not the purpose of this chapter to defend the utility or respectability of freedom as a psychological concept. Whether or not such a defense could be mounted is irrelevant to the discussion that follows. What *is* relevant is the fact that people often *believe* they enjoy freedom, and that this belief appears to affect their behaviors in a wide variety of situations. The focus of this chapter is on *perceived freedom* rather than on actual "exemption from necessity." Perhaps perceived freedom is an illusion, but it is at least an illusion with antecedents and consequences that deserve attention.

The potential importance of perceived freedom has been underscored by recent research in two areas. Investigators have noted that dissonance appears to be much more readily aroused when people believe their actions are self-determined than when they do not, and that observers are most inclined to attribute dispositional qualities to actors who are thought to enjoy freedom of action. Empirical studies dealing with a number of other social psychological issues can also be interpreted as reflecting the impact of perceived freedom.

II. A Conception of Perceived Freedom

An individual may believe he possesses either of two kinds of freedom. He may feel that he has a high probability of obtaining desired outcomes (outcome freedom). Or he may believe that he, rather than other people, fate, or the press of circumstances, selects the outcomes he will seek and the means he will employ in seeking them (decision freedom). Either of these perceived freedoms may occur without the other. Thus a person may feel that he has freely decided to pursue objectives he has little chance of obtaining, or that he has been coerced into seeking outcomes which are attainable and attractive.

A.   OUTCOME FREEDOM

As a first approximation we may assume that a person perceives himself to have outcome freedom if he believes he is able to obtain the outcome he desires. According to Heider (1958), a man believes he *can* row a boat across a river if his resources seem adequate to the task, and he believes he *may* do so if anticipated social reprisals are not prohibitively severe. Together the "can" and the "may" identify the man's "space of free movement." Lewin expressed a similar view. The individual's area of free movement was represented as a topological region encircled by other regions that were not accessible. Two types of factors were alleged to limit the accessibility of regions: lack of sufficient ability and social prohibitions. But Lewin (1948) contended that "one has to distinguish within the life space not only regions in which the person is entirely free to act and others which are entirely prohibited, but regions of an intermediate type: a certain activity may not be altogether prohibited, yet the person may feel somewhat restricted and hindered within this region" [p. 9]. Thus perceived freedom is not a dichotomous variable; it exists to the extent that one's desired activities and outcomes are thought to be unimpeded by the necessity to expend resources or endure social sanctions.

The views of Heider and Lewin may be translated, albeit somewhat loosely, into the language of exchange theory (Blau, 1964; Homans, 1961). A person believes himself to enjoy outcome freedom to the extent that he feels he can afford to incur the costs involved in obtaining the payoff he desires. If the costs are more critical to the individual than the outcome they promote, or if the individual lacks the resources with which to incur the required costs, he cannot be expected to credit himself with outcome freedom. As John Dewey (1922) noted, "To say that a man is free to choose to walk while the only walk he can take will lead him over a precipice is to strain words as well as facts" [p. 304]. To incur such costs for the privilege of walking would be to ignore "practicality of purpose," a quality that Whitehead (1933) identified as the essence of freedom. Writing in a similar vein, Simmel (1950) described obedience to a tryant as a matter of balancing costs against payoffs. An individual is not free to disobey if the price of his action is more than he is willing and able to pay.

Viewed in this light, perceived outcome freedom is a positive function of the *gain* the individual expects to experience from engaging in the transactions by which the desired outcome may be obtained. The individual will credit himself with very high outcome freedom when the anticipated payoff has extremely high valence and low costs are involved; he will perceive himself to have little freedom when the valence of the payoff is low and the costs are high.

The foregoing statements ignore an important consideration. In many real-life situations one cannot be completely certain that desired outcomes will actually be obtained even when one is willing and able to incur the anticipated costs. A man who can afford the best surgeon in the world realizes that a successful operation is not therefore assured, and every farmer knows that the extent of his crop depends upon the vagaries of nature as well as upon the quality of his land, tools, and agricultural practices. Almost all endeavors involve a degree of dependence upon factors the individual cannot hope to control, and a Sunday afternoon drive is sufficient to demonstrate that no man is absolute master of his own fate. In order to incorporate the element of uncertainty into our formulation, we shall assume, along with other theorists (e.g., Atkinson, 1957; Edwards, 1954; Rotter, 1954), that the attractiveness of an uncertain outcome depends not only upon its valence but also upon the probability that it will be obtained.[3] In accordance with incentive theory (Lawler, 1968; Vroom, 1964), valence and subjective probability are postulated to combine multiplicatively to determine *expected payoff*. Thus the gain an individual expects to experience from a transaction equals: (valence of payoff × subjective probability) − costs.

Because perceived outcome freedom is presumed to be a positive function of expected gain, the above formula may be regarded as a statement of the factors that determine an individual's perceived outcome freedom. The elements of the formula deserve careful attention.

---

[3]For ease of exposition, this chapter deals only with the comparatively simple case in which the individual either obtains the outcome he desires, or obtains nothing. Some of the models that employ the notion of subjective probability conceive outcomes to be continuous rather than dichotomous, and deal with negative as well as positive outcomes.

Depending on a number of considerations, subjective probability may be high or low. The individual may believe that attainment of his goal is controlled entirely by factors he cannot influence (e.g., by luck, or by nonmanipulable entities such as nature, the government, or a deity). An individual who holds this view may expect the controlling agents to be benign and helpful, or to be malicious and obstructive. In the former case, the subjective probability will presumably be high, but in the latter it will be low.

In many instances individuals believe that outcomes depend in part upon their own efforts. By behaving in the "proper" fashion they can increase the probability that the desired outcome will be granted. Goffman (1967) has reported that gamblers often assume they can exercise some margin of control over the decision of a roulette wheel, and M. Mead (1937) has noted that deities, at least in the western world, are conceived to be responsive to the behavior of the individual. Thus subjective probabilities are thought to vary in a manner that reflects the costs the individual incurs. Costs include all those expenditures of effort, time, social capital, money, or other resources that are believed by the individual to affect his probability of obtaining an outcome.

The correlation between perceived costs and subjective probabilities may be zero, as is the case when an outcome is thought to be totally controlled by external forces, or it may be strongly positive, as is true when a student believes that his chances of passing a test are directly proportional to the amount of work he does. In most instances the correlation probably falls somewhere between these extremes, the individual believing that he can influence probabilities of success, but cannot totally eliminate the effect of external factors.

Whenever the correlation between costs and subjective probability is zero (e.g., whenever outcomes are thought to be controlled entirely by external factors), people have no incentive to incur costs, and presumably incur none. But when the correlation is positive, an individual can increase his subjective probability by investing his resources. Whether or not he will do so depends on the fund of resources at his disposal, the strength of the relationship perceived to exist between investment and probability, the valence of the desired outcome, and the magnitude of the gains he believes he can obtain by investing his resources in other alternatives. The role of each of these considerations will be examined in the following paragraphs.

An individual who lacks the resources necessary to boost his subjective probability must, of course, settle for whatever chances of success are provided by external factors. Thus a man who cannot afford an air conditioner to cool his room must rely on the vagaries of nature, and a motorist without a spare tire is compelled to trust in the luck of the road. Even without the investment of resources, subjective probabilities are sometimes rather high.

When the correlation between costs and subjective probability is low, investment of resources will have only a slight effect on expected payoff. (Expected payoff equals valence × subjective probability.) On the other hand, when the correlation is high, investment may produce an increase in expected payoff that far exceeds the value of the incurred cost. This is most likely to be the case when the valence of the outcome is very high. Together, a high correlation between costs and subjective probability, and a strongly valued outcome, may offer the promise of considerable gain on one's investment.

Even when a small investment will produce a large increment in expected payoff, the individual may be unwilling to invest his resources in a specific outcome because other opportunities offer even larger returns. Like Thibaut and Kelley (1959), we assume that individuals attempt to maximize their total satisfaction, and thus endeavor to employ their scarce resources in exchanges that promise the greatest "marginal gain" per unit of investment. Consequently, an individual's freedom to obtain a specific outcome may be limited not only by his inability to incur the costs that will generate a high subjective probability but also by the fact that he may have to sacrifice other, more attractive, outcomes in order to do so. A starving man has little freedom to spend his last dollar on anything but food.

The above discussion has treated resources as though they were a completely homogeneous fund of assets, any one of which could be used for any purpose. But this is certainly not the case. Some resources can be used only for very specific purposes, whereas others can readily be employed to meet the costs associated with many different goals. Thus an ability to read hieroglyphics is extremely helpful if one wishes to understand the intricacies of early Egyptian culture, but is of little help in the pursuit of other ends. By contrast, money, good health, and mathematical skills are multipurpose resources that can be invested in a variety of ways. Highly specialized resources permit less "freedom of choice" than do those that are "legal tender" for the purchase of many goods. It should also be noted that some resources, such as intelligence and knowledge, are undiminished by use, and thus may be employed successively or even simultaneously in the service of many desires. People who possess such resources in great abundance may be able to incur the costs associated with many outcomes, and thus are likely to enjoy rather high outcome freedom.

An analogy will illustrate the impact of subjective probabilities, costs, and resources on outcome freedom. An individual enters a bizarre gambling establishment and discovers a multitude of strange slot machines. Each machine offers the possibility of obtaining a different kind of payoff, some dispensing material items, others entertainment, social approval, sexual satisfaction, peace of mind, etc. Furthermore, the coins one may insert in the slots are of varied denominations and carry labels such as time, energy, money, delay of gratification, etc. Different machines will accept different combinations of coins, and each is programmed to maintain a distinctive relationship between the inputs it receives and the probability that it will dispense the reward it controls. Some maintain almost perfect harmony between the value of the inputs and the probability of payoff, whereas others are equally likely to yield their bounty regardless of the investment one makes. Among the latter, there are some machines that almost never pay off and others that almost always do.

Machines that maintain a zero correlation between input and probability of payoff require no investment. The outcome freedom offered by such machines is entirely a function of the valence of the rewards they control and the rate at which they dispense those rewards. If a machine never pays off, it offers the individual no outcome freedom; regardless of how desirable the outcome may be, the subjective probability is zero and the outcome is unobtainable. However, some machines that maintain a zero correlation between costs and probability of payoff may offer the individual considerable outcome freedom. This is the case whenever the outcome is highly valued and the subjective probability is at least moderately high. Maximum outcome freedom will occur when a machine controls an extremely desirable outcome and always pays off regardless of whether or not the individual incurs a cost.

Machines that make outcomes contingent on the magnitude of the investment represent more complex cases. If the individual does not possess the particular resources needed to establish a high subjective probability, he must accept whatever fate is dictated by the machine's basic rate of payoff. Consequently, his outcome freedom is likely to be low. If the individual does possess the needed resources, he will find it profitable to invest them in a specific machine only if (a) the increment in expected payoff is greater than the value of the investment, and (b) the increment in expected payoff from the specific machine is greater than that offered by others that will accept the same scarce resources. Unless the individual's resources are unlimited, he will sometimes be compelled to accept low expected payoffs. He will have little freedom to obtain certain outcomes although his freedom to obtain others may be very high.

In the preceding discussion the term "investment" has been substituted for cost in recognition of the fact that the individual may elect to meet only some, or none, of the costs by which he could raise his subjective probability. Investment refers to the valence of the costs he decides to incur in order to raise the subjective probability of receiving a specific outcome.

Although the above analogy illustrates the impact of several factors on outcome freedom, it is less complex than the phenomena it is intended to represent. In real life the important parameters are unlikely to be clearly specified for the individual. Instead, he must rely upon uncertain and incomplete information when deciding whether the machine that controls a desired outcome maintains a positive relationship between investment and probability of payoff, and whether it usually or rarely delivers the desired outcome. Furthermore, he is unlikely to know which kinds of resources most affect the machine's behaviors, or whether its rules of conduct are constant from one moment to another. Consequently, the individual's private world of investments and expected payoffs is one he constructs for himself, drawing as he must on previous experience and training, but permitting hopes and fears to color his appraisal of the benign or malicious character of the machines that confront him. *Perceived outcome freedom is the individual's judgment of the availability and desirability of the outcomes he wishes to obtain.* Like other judgments, perceived outcome freedom may reflect a mixture of information and misinformation, but it is unlikely, except perhaps in the case of children or psychotics, to be based on sheer fantasy.

B. Decision Freedom

Perceived decision freedom refers to the volition the individual believes himself to exercise when he (1) decides whether or not to seek a specific outcome, or (2) decides whether to seek one outcome rather than another.

Consider the hypothetical case of a person who has only one desire in life. As noted earlier, this person's perceived outcome freedom is a positive function of the gain he expects to receive by seeking the desired objective. If his expected payoff (valence × subjective probability) is substantially greater than his anticipated investment, his perceived outcome freedom is high. But his freedom to decide whether or not to seek the outcome is another matter. The greater the expected gain, the less readily the individual can decide against seeking it; the greater the expected loss, the less freely he can elect to seek it. Maximum decision freedom should occur when the anticipated investment equals the expected payoff (i.e., when the expected gain is zero). The relationship between perceived outcome freedom and perceived decision freedom should be curvilinear, moderate levels of the former producing the highest levels of the latter.

In real life people generally desire many different outcomes, and no single decision is likely to seem independent of all others. Contingencies are created by the individual's belief that some outcomes are inconsistent with, or reduce the attractiveness of, certain others, or by the individual's realization that resources expended in the pursuit of one goal will not be available for the pursuit of another. Thus the law permits a man to have but one wife at a time, the purchase of one automobile reduces the marginal utility of another, and time and effort spent studying for examinations cannot also be used to promote one's physical fitness. Social rules, limited resources, and the character of the environment conspire to compel the individual to choose among desired outcomes as well as to decide whether specific outcomes are worth the investments they entail.

Whenever an individual must choose between two or more available alternatives, decision freedom should be a negative function of the discrepancies between the gains offered by the available options. If expected gains are approximately equal, the individual can feel that he controls the decision. But if the gain expected from one alternative far exceeds that offered by others, the individual should experience little decision freedom; his choice should appear to be controlled by factors external to himself. This view of decision freedom closely parallels the arguments of Brehm and Cohen (1962, pp. 201-203) who have suggested that people experience more self-determination or volition when they choose between alternatives that are about equal in value than when one alternative is regarded as being much inferior to another. Brehm and Cohen were not explicitly concerned with subjective probabilities or perceived costs because they were dealing with situations in which these factors were likely to be relatively constant, but their conception of perceived decision freedom can easily be expressed in the language of this chapter. Perceived decision freedom is greatest when expected gains are approximately equal.

According to this view, it is the comparative, rather than the absolute, magnitudes of one's outcome freedoms which determine one's perceived freedom to choose among alternatives. People with very different degrees of outcome freedom may experience the same amount of decision freedom, and the correlation between the two kinds of freedom may be rather low. However, to the extent that a single type of resource can be used to pay the costs associated with a variety of different outcomes, a positive correlation may be anticipated. Possession of multipurpose assets such as money, general intelligence, a liberal education, high social status, or good health should not only encourage the perception of high outcome freedom but also permit the individual to feel that he can choose which of many outcomes he will pursue. By contrast, a person whose resources cannot be readily employed to obtain many different outcomes is likely to find that only a few alternatives offer high gains. A skilled angler probably has high freedom to obtain fish for his breakfast table, but he may have little freedom to choose bacon instead; a wealthy person may elect to exchange money for either. Thus, although high perceived freedom to obtain a specific outcome may be accompanied by either high or low perceived freedom to choose among alternatives, some of the resources that encourage the former also promote the latter.

Of course, resources are not the only determinants of decision freedom. Anything that produces gross inequality among the gains expected from mutually exclusive outcomes will reduce the individual's freedom to choose. Brehm (1966) has explored the impact of telling people that one of several attractive outcomes has suddenly become unavailable due to chance factors or to the behaviors of other people. In situations of this kind, the individual can expect to gain nothing whatever by choosing the "blocked" alternative; consequently, he is presumed to experience a reduction of decision freedom. Brehm's data suggest that individuals often tend to raise their evaluations of the unavailable option, a reaction that was predicted many years ago by Lewin (1935).

Decision freedom may also be restricted by a feeling of "commitment" that is generated when one takes the initial steps toward achievement of an objective. According to C. A. Kiesler and Sakumura (1966), a sense of commitment is likely to be generated to the extent that one's initial actions are public, unambiguous, irrevocable, and seemingly voluntary. Behaviors of this kind are said to reduce one's freedom to shift from one alternative to another (Walster, Walster, Abrahams, & Brown, 1966). Thus a nation may persist in a war because many lives have already been lost and because a change of policy would imply that inappropriate decisions have been made in the past. A student may continue his efforts to become a psychologist because he has already invested important resources in the endeavor and does not wish to admit to himself or others that he really prefers to become an artist or a philosopher. In the language of this chapter, commitment is a state of affairs in which one cannot afford to relinquish one objective in favor of another because to do so would involve the loss of one's investment and the necessity to incur other costs such as "loss of face." One's own actions have accentuated disparities between the gains expected from the chosen and nonchosen alternatives.

Freedom to change one's mind is often restricted by the rules of nature or of society. The decision to commit suicide is, after certain steps have been taken, irreversible, and the same may be said about the decision to commit murder or incest. Other decisions can be reversed only at great cost. Business practices sometimes prevent a customer from exchanging a purchase for another item he finds more attractive, and most societies make it difficult to exchange one wife for another. Such restrictions on decision freedom have been found by Lowe and Steiner (1968) to affect the kinds of information people seek and the appraisals they make of chosen and nonchosen alternatives.

Regardless of the specific circumstances that limit decision freedom, the underlying dynamics seem always to be the same. Decision freedom exists to the extent that alternatives are believed to offer approximately equal gains. Anything which alters the valence, subjective probability, or perceived costs associated with an outcome may affect the individual's perceived freedom to obtain that outcome (outcome freedom) and his perceived freedom to decide whether or not he will attempt to obtain it (decision freedom). The two kinds of perceived freedom are conceptually interrelated, but are not necessarily highly correlated.

III. Expected Relationships among the Elements of Perceived Freedom

It is evident that learning plays an important role in determining one's perceived freedom. Since the days of Watsonian behaviorism, experimenters have repeatedly demonstrated that the valence of an outcome can be altered by associating it with other outcomes. Probabilities are also learned (Estes, 1957; Rotter, 1954). Several experimenters (Estes, 1957; Grant, Hake & Hornseth, 1951; Humphreys, 1939) have shown that under certain laboratory conditions, subjective probabilities are brought into close accord with experimentally established probabilities. Early studies of problem solving, and more recent investigations of behavior modification, have indicated that people also learn what they must do (the costs they must incur) in order to achieve positively valenced outcomes. Consequently, all three of the elements that determine perceived freedom are influenced by learning experiences. However, as cultural anthropologists have repeatedly affirmed, learning experiences may differ greatly from one society or subsociety to another. Moreover, Skinnerians are quick to point out that members of the same family may be subjected to quite different patterns of reinforcement. In contemporary society even young children are likely to exercise some margin of discretion in selecting their models and reinforcing agents, and thus tend to determine which of many sets of valences, subjective probabilities, and costs they will learn. Few become modern Don Quixotes whose behaviors are guided by completely atypical values and assumptions, but the diversity of outlooks represented by a group of college-age adults is sometimes bewildering. Under these circumstances, to say that the elements of perceived freedom are learned adds little to our understanding of the phenomenon. More important, perhaps, is the fact that learning experiences often involve the three elements in patterned relationships to one another. In many instances positively valenced outcomes are, in fact, uncertain outcomes, and whether or not they occur depends in part on the costs one incurs. Moreover, parents and other agents of socialization teach the growing child to anticipate certain relationships among costs, subjective probabilities, and valences. Thus, for example, the story of the little red hen, or of the locomotive that could, express a theme that is repeated many times in our written and spoken literature. Kardiner (1945) and McClelland (1951) suggest that the lessons taught by other societies may convey a different picture of the critical relationships, but that the educational process is no less ubiquitous.

As a consequence of contact with his environment and with people who tell him about its basic rules, the individual may be presumed to learn a schema (Bartlett, 1932; Woodworth, 1938) that influences his subsequent appraisals of the elements of perceived freedom. When situational cues concerning valences, subjective probabilities, and costs are ambiguous, this schema guides the individual's perception of the situation he faces. Consistency theorists have amassed considerable evidence that people attempt to maintain "preferred relationships" among their cognitions, and sometimes distort seemingly unambiguous happenings in order to do so.

The discussion that follows examines experimental and "common sense" evidence bearing on the relationships that people attempt to maintain among valences, subjective probabilities, and costs.

A. VALENCE AND SUBJECTIVE PROBABILITY

Theorists have expressed contrasting views of the relationship between valence and subjective probability. Edwards (1954) and Rotter (1954) treated the two variables as though they were independent, but others (Atkinson, 1957; Lewin, Dembo, Festinger, & Sears, 1944) assumed an inverse relationship, low subjective probabilities being associated with highly valent goals.

Empirical evidence indicates that valences are indeed affected by subjective probabilities, but the shape of the function is not entirely clear. Feather (1967) confronted college students with a series of hypothetical situations in which an individual's success was said to depend entirely upon chance factors. Probabilities were systematically varied, and subjects were asked to rate the attractiveness of stated outcomes. Unlikely (low probability) successes were judged to be more attractive than likely (high probability) successes. Thus rated valence was negatively correlated with manipulated subjective probability.

Similar results were obtained by Brehm (1966) in a series of studies in which experimental subjects found that one of several attractive alternatives had suddenly become unavailable to them. Brehm took great care to explain that denial of the critical option was due to adventitious factors and completely unrelated to the subject's abilities or behaviors. Consequently, the experimental manipulations may reasonably be interpreted as having lowered subjective probabilities from a comparatively high level to approximately zero. Under these circumstances, a slight increase in the rated valence of the unavailable option was observed. Brehm suggests that "reactance effects" are dependable consequences of arbitrary restraints on decision freedom.

Mischel and Masters (1966) obtained results that parallel those of Brehm. Sixth-grade children watched a movie which was suddenly interrupted at an exciting point in the narrative. The interruption was said to be caused by a burned out fuse for which (a) there definitely was no replacement; (b) there was a 50-50 chance of obtaining a replacement, or (c) there definitely was an available replacement. Children told there was no chance the movie could be resumed (subjective probability = 0) increased their ratings of the film whereas those informed that the chances were 50-50 or 100% did not. These findings indicate that the immediate effect of a complete and arbitrary blockage of goal attainment is an enhancement of valence.

Evidence to be reviewed later (see Section VI of this chapter) suggests that the long range effects of goal blockages are quite different. Individuals who see little chance of obtaining desired outcomes tend eventually to lower their appraisals of such payoffs. The immediate reaction upon discovering that a subjective probability is low may well be an increase in valence (what fate and my limited resources deny me is better than that which I can actually obtain). But as one continues to confront the frustrating prospect of failure, valence is reduced to a level which makes one's unhappy plight more tolerable. We should expect such reductions to occur most markedly when subjective probabilities are very low and when there is little prospect they can be raised. [Perhaps devaluation of goals occurs only after a period of time because people are not, at the outset, really convinced that probabilities *are, and will remain*, low. Bettelheim (1943) noted that concentration camp prisoners viewed their early experiences in the camp as unreal, and came to accept their fate only after considerable exposure to it.]

It seems appropriate to conclude that improbable outcomes are highly valued over short periods of time, especially if the individual believes that luck and resources may still combine to deliver the desired goal.

Evidence concerning the effect of valence on subjective probability is often difficult to interpret because costs, and the individual's ability to incur them, are not carefully controlled. However, it is apparent that gamblers expect high payoffs to carry adverse odds. Indeed, Griffith (1949) and McGlothin (1956) found that racetrack bettors are not only willing to accept very low odds on "long shots," but are more attracted to them than the official odds would suggest they should be. Stoner (1967) documented the inverse relationship between valence and subjective probability in a different context. His subjects recommended acceptance of lower odds on Choice-Dilemma items (Wallach & Kogan, 1959) when the attractive payoff was deemed important than when it was not. Moreover, subjects in level-of-aspiration studies estimate that they have less chance of achieving highly valent outcomes than of obtaining less attractive ones (Worell, 1956).

Although there is evidence indicating that individuals sometimes overestimate their chances of obtaining highly desired goals, the studies cited above suggest that people tend to expect highly valent outcomes to carry low subjective probabilities, and expect easily obtained goals to be less valuable than more uncertain outcomes. This inverse relationship may prevail only so long as people believe they have a meaningful chance of obtaining the desired outcomes.

B. Perceived Costs and Expected Payoffs

If perceived costs are high, will the expected payoff (valence × subjective probability) also be high? Do people believe that hard work, heavy financial investment, and the application of knowledge and skill generate a high probability of obtaining attractive goals? When achievement of a highly valued goal is assured, do people tend to credit themselves with having worked hard, borne heavy financial costs, or employed unusual knowledge and skill? Tradition and casual observation offer affirmative answers to each of these questions, but evidence from well-controlled studies is sparse.

As Ralph Barton Perry (1944) has noted, the Puritan ethic leaves little room for doubt: good things come with high certainty to those who are diligent and competent; and the fact that good things have come to a man indicates that he has been diligent and competent. Good things cost much; and things that cost much are good. But it is not only the Puritan ethic and the writings of Horatio Alger that maintain this stance. Blau (1964), for example, contends that love and approval that are easily gained tend to be lowly valued, and Lewin (1948) asserts that barriers to a goal region sometimes enhance the attractiveness of the goal. Anthropological reports suggest that societies in which costs are believed to be only very loosely related to payoffs are rare indeed, and they risk disintegration and turmoil (e.g., see the analysis of Alorese society in Kardiner, 1945).

1. Perceived Costs and Valences

Lerner (1965) has reported experimental evidence that people allow their estimates of costs to be influenced by the valence of payoffs. College students listened to two experimental accomplices as they worked together on an anagram task. The subjects were aware that accomplice A would receive $3.50 for his service while B would receive nothing, but believed that neither A nor B knew which would be paid. Although the two accomplices contributed equally to the solution of the problem, the one who was thought to be in line to receive payment was judged by the subjects to have made the greater contribution. In another study, Lerner and Simmons (1966) had college students observe a peer while she received what appeared to be severe electrical shocks during an experiment on memory. The students lowered their ratings of the victim's attractiveness after observing her painful experience, a finding Lerner and Simmons interpret as indicating that observers want to believe that people deserve what happens to them. This conclusion is reminiscent of earlier contentions by Freud (1949), Takashi (1951), Rosenman (1956), and Wolfenstein (1957) that even utter disasters such as floods and hurricanes are often judged by observers and victims alike to be punishment for the victims' sinful behavior or blundering ineptitude.

Laboratory evidence that people expect heavy costs to lead to attractive payoffs has been provided by Feather (1967) in a study already cited in another context. College students reacted to hypothetical situations in which outcomes were represented as being due to skill and intelligence. They rated success more attractive when the task was difficult (i.e., involved heavy costs) than when it was easy. In other studies Feather (1959a, 1959b) determined that the positive relationship between attractiveness of success and task difficulty was more pronounced in a test situation than in a game situation. In the former case success was presumably a more accurate measure of the costs individuals incurred.

Research dealing with coalition formation (reviewed by Gamson, 1964) also reveals a tendency for people to expect payoffs to be positively associated with costs. Although the findings have been somewhat inconsistent, they reveal the operation of a "parity principle": People tend to expect that the payoffs obtained by a winning coalition will be divided among the members in a fashion that reflects the resources they have contributed. A similar conclusion is suggested by equity theory (reviewed by Adams, 1965) which maintains that people prefer that the ratio of their own outcomes to their own inputs be approximately equal to that of other persons.

Some of the research conducted by dissonance theorists reveals a strong propensity for people to employ cognitive strategies that support the belief that payoffs are commensurate with costs. Several studies (Brehm & Cohen, 1959, Freedman, 1963; Weick, 1964) have indicated that persons who receive small rewards for performing onerous duties tend to say the tasks have not been very exacting or disagreeable. Another line of investigation (Aronson, 1961; Aronson & Mills, 1959; Gerard & Mathewson, 1966) suggests that people who are required to work inordinately hard or to endure uncomfortable circumstances in order to obtain a goal tend to evaluate the payoff more highly (after it is obtained) than do those who are not required to incur such heavy costs. There is also evidence (Adams, 1965; Arrowood, 1961) that people who believe they are being overpaid for rendering a service work harder, at least for a short period of time, than do those who believe their remuneration is less adequate.

Brehm (1956) and Brehm and Cohen (1959) conducted studies in which the major cost of obtaining a chosen payoff was the necessity to forego a nonchosen but attractive alternative. Subjects were asked to rank a set of 10 or 15 objects, and then to indicate which of two of them they preferred to receive as a gift. Finally, after their choices had been made, subjects re-evaluated all of the objects. Some subjects were permitted to choose their gift from among two options they had ranked approximately equal in attractiveness, whereas others chose from two unequally ranked alternatives. Thus the former were confronted by a situation in which perceived costs were very nearly equal to expected payoffs (high decision freedom) while for the latter subjects the perceived cost of one option was considerably smaller than the expected payoff. After making their choices, subjects for whom initial perceptions of costs and payoffs were almost equal tended to raise their evaluations of the chosen object (the payoff) and to lower their appraisals of the nonchosen object (the cost). Comparable shifts were not observed for the other subjects. These findings are consistent with the notion that people believe high costs should yield high payoffs.

None of the studies cited above as bearing on relationships between costs and valence included a measurement or manipulation of subjective probability. However, it is reasonable to presume that all or most of these investigations involved conditions in which subjective probabilities were very high. In many of them, the proffered payoffs were actually delivered before the data were obtained; and in others, subjects were given little reason to doubt that experimenters would, in fact, deliver the rewards they had promised. On the assumption that these procedures produced a fairly rigorous though unintended standardization of subjective probabilities, we have interpreted the experimental results as indicating relationships between perceived costs and valences. When subjective probabilities are held approximately constant at high levels, perceived costs and valences are positively correlated. Experimental manipulation of either produces a concomitant variation in the other.

2. Perceived Costs and Subjective Probability

A few investigators have manipulated costs while measuring changes in subjective probabilities. Yaryan and Festinger (1961) found that subjects who were induced to make difficult preparations for a possible examination believed more strongly than did those asked to make easy preparations that they would be chosen (by lot) to take the exam. Arrowood and Ross (1966) demonstrated that merely telling subjects they would be required to make difficult or easy preparations was sufficient to produce effects on subjective probabilities comparable to those reported by Yaryan and Festinger. Johnson and Steiner (1965) failed to support Yaryan and Festinger's findings but obtained evidence indicating that subjects who perceived an experimenter to be incurring large costs in their behalf were especially inclined to believe that random selection procedures would result in their taking the test. These studies suggest that heavy costs imply high subjective probabilities. Unfortunately, none of these investigations measured the value of the payoff to the subjects, or determined whether valences changed in response to the manipulated costs.

Naturalistic observations seem consistent with experimental results.

Festinger, Riecken, and Schachter (1956) noted that members of a religious sect who had divested themselves of material goods in preparation for the end of the world appeared to gain confidence that the final hours were at hand. According to these authors, awareness that they had incurred heavy costs would have been dissonant with a belief that the anticipated event might not actually occur.

That subjective probability affects the costs people are willing to pay is evident from observations of gambling behaviors. When valence (monetary payoff) is held constant, gamblers are more inclined to bet (incur costs) on high probability options than on those they believe to have little chance of materializing.

C. INTERRELATIONSHIPS AMONG THE VARIABLES

The previous discussion has examined relationships between pairs of variables, and has concluded that perceived costs tend to be positively correlated with valence and with subjective probability. The relationship between the latter two variables is less clear: valence and subjective probability seem to be negatively correlated over moderate time periods during which people have not concluded that their resources and luck are totally insufficient to deliver highly valent goals. But continued failure to achieve desired objectives may eventually force a devaluation of unattainable goals and generate a positive correlation between valence and subjective probability (the things I know I can never have are not really good after all).

One is tempted to attribute these findings to the operation of a single, sovereign principle enunciated by Lerner and Simmons (1966). According to these authors, people have a need to believe in an orderly world that maintains an "appropriate fit between what they do and what happens to them — their outcomes" [p. 203]. Thus one might contend that people have a compelling desire to believe that payoffs are a positive function of costs. Such a conception can readily accommodate and "explain" all the trends noted above except, perhaps, the positive relationship between valence and subjective probability that seems to emerge after prolonged frustration. Thus an increase in perceived costs should generate a compensating increase in valence and/or subjective probability, and an increase in valence should promote an increase in perceived costs and/or a decrease in subjective probability, etc.

However, there are reasons to doubt that cognitive adjustments uniformly follow the course suggested by this principle. The available evidence is badly fragmented in that it concerns relationships between pairs of variables; no single study has clearly demonstrated that the fragments are actually parts of the larger pattern of interrelationships implied by the model. Furthermore, even if the larger pattern is a valid representation of the way the fragments fit together, there is no assurance that it accurately depicts the cognitive processes of any specific individual. What is true of many people considered collectively may be untrue of most people considered individually. Thus it is reasonable to surmise that subjective probabilities are of minor importance to some people, and that perceived costs play an extremely small role in the thinking of others. The orderly world of the Puritan extremist was one in which almost everything was rigorously determined: costs were to be incurred and payoffs would be received (valence $= f_+$ perceived costs). On the other hand, residents of the modern ghetto sometimes assert that the costs one incurs bear no relationship whatever to the payoffs one receives. For these people the critical orderliness of the world may lie in the belief that good things are less likely to happen than bad things (valence $= f_-$ subjective probability). Considered collectively, the Puritan determinist and the ghetto resident provide support for the contention that valences, perceived costs, and subjective probabilities interact in a compensatory manner, but neither person may, in fact, be guided by the logic of the total model.

The attitudes and beliefs that influence perceptions of freedom are not independent of one another. They reflect both the individual's actual experiences with his environment and his judgments concerning the patterned orderliness of the world. Different persons may have quite different conceptions of what is orderly.

D. PERCEIVED LOCUS OF CONTROL

It is possible for an individual to explain his successes and failures in two very different ways. On the one hand, he may believe that by incurring high costs he diminishes the role of fate (i.e., the relationship between costs and subjective probability is strongly positive). Given this view, he should interpret successes and failures as consequences of his own ability and willingness to incur costs. On the other hand, the individual may believe that the relationship between costs and subjective probabilities is comparatively low, and thus conclude that his outcomes are largely determined by forces over which he has little control. Evidence that individuals do, in fact, differ in the degree to which they employ these two contrasting logics has been reviewed by Rotter (1966) and Lefcourt (1966).

A rapidly accumulating series of studies have employed paper-and-pencil tests to evaluate perceived "locus of control," and have linked scores on such instruments to behaviors in laboratory and real-life situations. The items employed in tests of this kind require subjects to indicate whether their own and other people's successes and failures appear to be determined by effort, ability, and personal resources, *or* by chance and uncontrollable external factors. Rotter has called subjects who favor the former interpretation "internals," and those who lean toward the latter "externals." Somewhat similar distinctions have been expressed by deCharms' (1968) "origin-pawn" dimension, by Levin and Baldwin's (1959) references to a "public-private" dimension, and by Riesman's (1950) popular distinction between inner and outer directed persons.

People whose scores on paper-and-pencil instruments identify them as internals or externals tend to manifest behavior patterns resembling those of subjects who are experimentally induced to believe that their outcomes in a specific situation are internally or externally controlled. Rotter (1966) has reviewed a number of studies in which success may readily be interpreted as due either to chance or to ability. When told by an experimenter that their outcomes depend upon their own behaviors (rather than on chance) subjects show greater attentiveness to cues that may facilitate task performance, are more inclined to adjust their levels of aspiration to harmonize with past performance, and are more concerned with achievement. People whose test scores identify them as internals have also been found to be especially attentive to relevant cues. Thus, for example, Seeman (1967) found that internally oriented prisoners learned material pertinent to obtaining a parole more rapidly than did externally oriented prisoners, but showed no superiority in learning nonachievement-related materials. James (1967) demonstrated that subjects who score toward the internal end of the continuum are more likely than those who do not to alter their expectations following successes and failures and to generalize their expectancies from one task to another. Several studies reviewed by Rotter indicate that internal subjects are also more achievement oriented than are those whose scores mark them as externals. In general, the results obtained when internality-externality is treated as a personality variable are in fairly close accord with the findings of studies in which perceived locus of control is experimentally manipulated. Apparently some people are prone to interpret their successes and failures as consequences of their own effort and worth whereas others more characteristically invoke luck, fate, or external events as explanatory concepts.

Considerable evidence suggests that people who possess the resources needed to incur heavy costs tend to be internal. As Lefcourt (1966) has noted, all of the pertinent studies report that internality tends to be associated with high status within society. Negroes are found to be less internal than whites, and lower class people are less internal than higher class people. College students, who generally combine moderately high status with high intelligence, tend to be more internal than randomly selected populations. Crandall, Katkovsky, and Preston (1962) found scholastic achievement among children to be associated with a high sense of internal control, and obtained a positive correlation of .52 between intelligence and the internality scores of their male subjects. A. R. Cohen (1959) suggested that high self-esteem implies partial immunity from external controls, and research on conformity behavior (see Allen, 1965) has repeatedly demonstrated that people who believe they are extremely competent on a task are not readily induced to alter their behaviors or beliefs. Heider (1958) and Jones and Davis (1965) have noted that the actions of powerful and resourceful people are more likely to be viewed as internally prompted than are those of persons whose resources are severely limited.

The previous paragraph suggests that an individual's propensity to emphasize internal *vs.* external control tends to reflect his own supply of resources and to mirror his experiences with nature. People who can afford to incur few costs realistically perceive their outcomes to be strongly influenced by external factors, whereas those with an abundance of resources are inclined to believe that outcomes reflect investment.

It should not be concluded that internals necessarily credit themselves with greater outcome freedom than do externals. An external who believes his destiny is determined by a benevolent deity, dictator, or boss may feel highly confident of his capacity to satisfy desires, and an internal who questions the adequacy of his own resources may harbor grave doubts about his ability to obtain desired outcomes. The greater tendency of internals to base expectations on past experiences should mean that they are more likely than externals to believe they have high freedom to obtain outcomes they have successfully sought in the past, and low freedom to obtain outcomes that have previously eluded them. If this is the case, internals may tend to enjoy less decision freedom than do externals. However, it should be noted that internals have been found to be especially prone to forget evidence suggesting personal inadequacy (Phares, Ritchie, & Davis, 1968), and it is possible that this dispositional quality permits them to avoid extremely low estimates of their own freedom.

Atkinson (1957) and Feather (1959a) have contended that negative outcomes that are believed to depend upon an individual's skill and resources tend to be interpreted as personal failures. According to this view, externals are spared an important psychological cost that is levied against internals whenever desired outcomes are not forthcoming. Consistent with this notion, both Lefcourt (1966) and Rotter (1966) have suggested that an external orientation may be a defensive reaction to demonstrated incapacity. Thus people who believe they are unable to succeed on the basis of their own efforts may deliver themselves into the hands of a protective force, such as God, nature, or King. In this way the individual escapes the costs of failure and, depending upon the perceived benevolence of the protective agent, may actually increase his anticipated outcome freedom.

Available evidence does not permit firm conclusions concerning relationships between locus of perceived control and perceived freedom. As Riesman (1968) has recently asserted, inner-directed people are not necessarily more autonomous than their outer-directed counterparts, though the two types of persons are presumably sensitive to different kinds of restraints on their autonomy.

IV. Perceived Freedom and the Attribution Process

According to Kelley (1967), "attribution refers to the process of inferring or perceiving the dispositional properties of entities in the environment" [p. 193]. The qualities that are inferred may range from the rectangularity of a table (most accurately inferred on the basis of observations made from several vantage points and at different points in time) to the honesty of an individual (inferred by observing his behaviors in a variety of situations). Attribution involves the use of available information (which may itself be the product of attribution) to generate new "information" about people or things. The new information may, of course, be incorrect because it is based on faulty knowledge, or because it is illogically derived from accurate knowledge.

Strictly speaking, perceived freedom is not a dispositional property. Unlike personality traits, physical dimensions, and intelligence, it may change rapidly as situational variables are altered. Furthermore, perceived freedom is often highly selective, the individual crediting himself with great freedom to obtain some outcomes and little freedom to obtain others, or great freedom to choose between certain alternatives and little freedom to choose between others. Perceived freedom refers to the individual's judgment of the gains he (or someone else) can expect to receive by pursuing desired objectives, or his judgment of the comparative gains offered by several different objectives. Like other judgments, perceived freedom reflects both dispositional and situational factors.

It is appropriate to discuss the attribution process in a review of research and theory dealing with perceived freedom. A rapidly expanding body of literature suggests that the amount of freedom an individual is thought to possess tends to determine whether or not his behaviors are interpreted as revealing his dispositional properties. Perceived freedom influences the conclusions individuals reach concerning both their own and other people's attitudes and personality traits.

A. ATTRIBUTION TO OTHERS

As noted earlier, Heider (1958, p. 85) employed the concepts of "can" and "may" in defining the scope of activities a person has the ability and social franchise to perform. Within this space of free movement, an actor's behaviors reveal his dispositional characteristics, but what he does or fails to do because he lacks essential resources or social support is unlikely to disclose his motives, preferences, or sentiments. Viewed in this light, the attribution process involves inferring answers to two critical questions: Is an observed act freely produced by the individual? and, if so, which of many possible internal states (motives, needs, personality traits) is responsible for the behavior?

In a recent review of research dealing with the attribution process, Jones and Davis (1965) present a theoretical structure that parallels the notions expounded by Heider. According to Jones and Davis, an observer attempts to infer the intention that has guided an actor's behavior, and then regards the inferred intention as evidence of the existence of a dispositional attribute. Thus an observer may infer that John Doe intended his kind words to win social approval, and may then conclude that Doe is an ingratiating individual. Jones and Davis are much more systematic than Heider in their consideration of the cues that determine which of several plausible intentions an observer will impute to an actor, and in their examination of the circumstances under which intentions are presumed to reveal stable personality characteristics. But, like Heider, they insist that perceived ability and absence of coercive environmental restraints are preconditions for the assignments of dispositional qualities. Unavoidable actions are not indicative of characterological properties.

According to the foregoing arguments, observers should be more prone to attribute dispositional characteristics to persons they believe to have acted freely than to those whose behaviors appear to have been dictated by personal inabilities or external constraints. A partial test of this proposition was conducted by Steiner and Field (1960) who asked groups of three college students to discuss the "desirability of desegregation of public schools." In half of the groups an accomplice was publicly assigned the role of a "typical southern segregationist," while two naive subjects were instructed to present the views of a N.A.A.C.P. member and a Northern clergyman. In the other groups no roles were assigned but participants were collectively urged to make sure that the beliefs of these three kinds of persons were fully presented in the discussion. Regardless of whether or not the accomplice was assigned the segregationist role, he always endeavored to defend the same prosegregationist position. At the conclusion of the discussion, subjects in groups that received role assignments were less certain that they knew the accomplice's true opinion of desegregation than were subjects in groups that received no role assignments. The former had observed the accomplice's behaviors under circumstances that clearly restricted his freedom of action, and thus they were unable to make confident inferences concerning his attitude.

Jones and Harris (1967) have reported three experiments that support the findings of the Steiner and Field study. College students read speeches concerning desegregation or Castro that had allegedly been written by a member of the debating team at a nearby university. Some subjects were told that the writer had been arbitrarily assigned to defend a specific point of view, whereas others were informed that the writer had decided which side of the issue he would support. In all three experiments writers who had been "assigned" were judged to be less strongly in favor of the views they espoused than were writers who were believed to have enjoyed freedom of choice. However, even the assigned writers were thought to be somewhat in favor of the positions they defended, possibly because they were presumed to have had some degree of decision freedom (they could have refused to write the speech) and because the speeches contained rather cogent and convincing arguments.

A parallel study was performed by Jones, Davis, and Gergen (1961). Male undergraduates listened to tape-recorded "job interviews," knowing that the interviewee had been instructed to present himself as a person whose dispositional characteristics qualified him for the job he was seeking. Some subjects heard the interviewee adhere scrupulously to his assigned role (e.g., he presented himself as an obedient, cooperative, friendly, and gregarious person when applying for the job of submariner), whereas others heard the interviewee express sentiments that deviated from role requirements. Four tape recordings were used to reflect two degrees of role compliance by persons seeking each of two different jobs, but no subject heard more than one tape. After listening to the interview, subjects rated the interviewee on a number of personality variables, and indicated their confidence in their ratings. Subjects who heard the interviewee violate his role confidently inferred that he possessed qualities other than those needed for the job, whereas those who heard the interviewee conform to his assigned role were far more uncertain of his true character. These findings suggest, as do those of Steiner and Field, that behaviors which conform to role requirements are seen as uninformative about the individual's personal qualities. But deviations from role expectations provide information that permits the attribution process to operate.

Role requirements specify a course of action from which the individual can deviate only by incurring costs (e.g., the criticism and possible punitive sanctions of other people). Consequently, roles restrict the individual's freedom to decide in favor of certain options, and a person who abides by his role may do so in order to avoid costs rather than because he attaches high valence to the actions he is taking. But a person who knowingly deviates from his role requirements presumably values his deviant expressions very highly; otherwise he would settle for the less attractive and less costly actions prescribed by his role. According to this line of reasoning, subjects in the studies described above interpreted role assignments as costly restraints on freedom, and thus evaluated in-role behaviors as indicating little more than the actor's ability to avoid potentially heavy costs. But actors who were observed to deviate sharply from their imposed roles were judged to value their personal preferences so highly that they were willing to incur the costs associated with expressing them. Such an interpretation is consistent with Jones and Davis' (1965) contention that perceivers assume that an actor chooses a course of action in spite of, rather than because of, the negative effects it will have, and that the presence of negative effects leads the perceiver to conclude that the actor strongly values the positive consequences.

Of course, an actor's apparent freedom may be limited by factors other than role assignments. He may, for example, be confronted by people who clearly disapprove the actions he would most like to take, although his preferred behaviors are not prohibited by an explicitly prescribed role. The criticism he would receive were he to defy the preferences of his audience represents a cost which may deter the actor from expressing his true sentiments. Consequently, when an actor behaves in a fashion that pleases his audience, an observer may refrain from concluding that his conduct reflects his genuine beliefs. But when an actor incurs the costs entailed in disagreeing with his audience, an observer should be inclined to attribute action-congruent attitudes to him. Mills and Jellison (1967) asked college students to read a five-page speech strongly advocating tripling the tax on trucks. Half of the subjects were told the speech had been delivered before a meeting of truckers, and half were told it had been presented at a meeting of railway men. The former instructions were designed to create the impression that the speech was unpopular with the audience while the latter instructions were intended to create the opposite impression. When the speech was thought to be unpopular, subjects rated the speaker as being more sincere, honest, impartial, and likable than was the case when the speaker told his audience what they preferred to hear. In another study Eisinger and Mills found that speakers who took an extreme position on an issue were judged to be more sincere than speakers who advocated more moderate views resembling those the subjects themselves supported. Eisinger and Mills (1968) suggest that "since it is likely that most people assume that the typical or modal position is close to their own position, a communicator with an extreme position on the opposite side is likely to be perceived as taking a more unpopular position and subjecting himself to more social disapproval than a communicator with a moderate position on the opposite side" [p. 225]. Presumably a communicator who expresses an unpopular view is strongly committed to the position he espouses; otherwise he would avoid the costs of social disapproval by advocating a more popular view.

A study by Walster and Festinger (1962) may be relevant to the above contention. Subjects were found to be more strongly influenced by a message when speakers were thought to be unaware that they were being overheard than when they were known to realize that subjects were present. In the former case speakers probably were regarded as having greater freedom to speak candidly and to express their true beliefs. A subsequent study by Brock and Becker (1965) suggests that "overheard" messages are no more effective than "intentional" ones if they argue *against* the audience's favored position. Perhaps the fact that a speaker disagrees with his audience is, in itself, sufficient proof that he is a sincere and discerning person.

The freedom a speaker is presumed to exercise may also be critical to an interpretation of research reported by Aronson and Linder (1965). Female college students "overheard" a conversation in which they were evaluated by a colleague. In some cases the evaluations were uniformly positive, or uniformly negative, but in other instances the first few comments were negative and the remainder became progressively more positive, or the first few were positive and the remainder were negative. The data indicated that the evaluator was liked most when her generally positive appraisals were preceded by a few negative ones, and was liked least when her predominately negative evaluations followed some positive views. Aronson and Linder offered a number of possible explanations of their findings, one of which assumes that evaluators who express both favorable and unfavorable appraisals are perceived to be more discerning than are those who make only favorable or only unfavorable comments. In a subsequent study (Landy and Aronson, 1968) this assumption was partially confirmed: evaluators whose appraisals were entirely favorable were judged to be less discerning than those whose comments were entirely or partly negative. (As we have suggested above, the fact that a speaker *opposes* the views of his unintended audience may be sufficient to indicate that he is a discerning person.) A slightly revised interpretation of the Aronson-Linder findings postulates that a critic who expresses both positive and negative views demonstrates his *freedom* to say what he believes, as well as his capacity for discernment. A discerning critic without freedom to report his true feelings is a "yes man" whose counsel may not be taken seriously.

An actor's freedom may also appear to be restricted by his lack of resources. When such is the case, an actor whose behaviors have unpleasant consequences for an observer may be pardoned for his wrongdoing. But an actor whose disagreeable behaviors are thought to be freely and deliberately produced is likely to become the target of retaliatory actions (cf. Berkowitz, 1962). As Heider (1958) has noted, when an individual is believed to be resourceful, his behaviors are thought to be determined by his dispositional qualities.

Burnstein and Worchel (1962) found that an accomplice who repeatedly interrupted a group discussion received more aggressive treatment, and was rated more negatively, when he did not wear a hearing aid than when he wore one and pretended that it was not working. In the latter condition his inappropriate behaviors were presumably excused as being due to inability to hear what others were saying. Lanzetta and Hannah (1969) reported that poor performance by trainees who were believed to lack ability evoked less punitive reactions from a trainer than did similar performances by trainees who were presumed to possess high ability. Wiggins, Dill, and Schwartz (1965) found that a group member who had demonstrated high competence but subsequently impeded the group's progress was more strongly rejected than a member whose frustrating behaviors were not preceded by a demonstration of high competence. Several investigators (Berkowitz, 1962; A. R. Cohen, 1955; Pastore, 1952; Rothaus & Worchel, 1960) have indicated that disliked behaviors that are thought to be due to unavoidable error, illness, or lack of information evoke less resentment and less aggressive responses than do disliked behaviors that are believed to be deliberate.

The studies cited above suggest that an observer's reactions to an actor's *harmful* behaviors depend upon the amount of freedom the observer imputes to the actor. Other research indicates that parallel conclusions can be drawn concerning an observer's reactions to an actor's *helpful* behaviors. Thibaut and Riecken (1955) found that voluntary acts of benevolence were appreciated more than those thought to be the inevitable result of environmental circumstances, and Goranson and Berkowitz (1966) observed that subjects were more inclined to reciprocate a "voluntary" favor than one portrayed as "compulsory." On the other hand, Gouldner (1960) contended that people feel more indebted to a benefactor whose freedom to render assistance is limited than to one whose freedom is not restricted. Consistent with Gouldner's view, Tesser, Gatewood, and Driver (1968) found that gratitude for a favor was a positive function of perceived cost to the benefactor. These findings imply that beneficial actions are appreciated less when they are demanded by the situation than when they are not, and that they are most deeply appreciated when they occur *in spite of* restraints that make them costly to the actor who produces them. There is one probable exception to the latter conclusion. When an actor deviates from his role in order to render a favor, his actions may be disapproved (S. B. Kiesler, 1966) because they are interpreted as an effort on the part of the actor to ingratiate himself with the recipient (Brehm & Cole, 1966; Jones, 1964).

Many of the studies mentioned in previous paragraphs provide only inferential evidence concerning the attribution process. They indicate that the affective reactions evoked by an actor's harmful or helpful behaviors depend upon the amount of freedom the actor is presumed to have. But they do not explicitly identify the qualities an observer attributes to the actor and which presumably mediate the observer's response to the actor's behavior. A study by Olberz (1968) focuses more directly on the attribution process. Male college students responded orally to a series of factual questions while in the presence of an experimental accomplice who also announced his answers orally. The subject responded to half of the questions before hearing the accomplice's replies, and to the other half after learning the accomplice's views. Because the accomplice was familiar with the answers the subject had given during a previous, private session, he was able to agree (or disagree) with the subject's preferred response even when the subject answered last. The findings of the study indicated that, when the accomplice answered first, the agreeing *vs.* disagreeing character of his responses had little effect on the qualities attributed to him. But when the accomplice answered last and expressed disagreeing views, he was judged to be significantly less friendly, flexible, cooperative, dependent, and helpful than was the case if he agreed with the responses he had heard the subject announce. Olberz suggests that, when answering first, the accomplice was perceived to have little freedom to agree with the subject; consequently, his announced judgments were not interpreted as indicating his dispositional qualities. But when the accomplice was free to agree with the subject's position (i.e., when he answered last), whether or not he did in fact agree became a critical determinant of the ratings he received from the subject.

B. ATTRIBUTION TO SELF

It may be argued that the process by which one infers one's own dispositional qualities roughly parallels that by which the qualities of others are inferred. This view has been championed by Bem (1965) who contends that "an individual's beliefs and attitude statements and the beliefs and attitudes that an outside observer would attribute to him are 'inferences' from the same evidence; the public events that the socializing community originally employed in training the individual to make such self-descriptive statements" [p. 200]. When asked whether or not he likes brown bread, the individual may assert that he guesses he does because he is always eating it. According to Bem, this response reveals the essential aspects of the attribution process: individuals observe their own behaviors (or those of other people) and conclude that they (or the other people) are predisposed to do whatever they are regularly observed to do. However, it is clear that people sometimes do things for purely monetary reasons or because they are influenced by compelling reinforcements. Bem refers to such actions as "mands" (Skinner, 1957), and acknowledges that they, unlike "tacts," provide a poor basis for inferring either one's own or anyone else's dispositional qualities. Although there is no room in the behavioristic jargon for a concept of perceived freedom, Bem's application of Skinnerian thought recognizes that "when attempting to infer a speaker's 'true' beliefs and attitudes, the listener must often discriminate the mand-tact characteristics of the communication" [p. 201].

If self-knowledge and knowledge about other people are obtained in similar ways (though not necessarily in the manner described by Bem), studies bearing on the attribution process should be equally applicable to both kinds of impression formation. Thus individuals should learn little about themselves when their behaviors and outcomes are thought to be determined by sheer luck or by compelling external circumstances. Research reviewed by Lefcourt (1966) and Rotter (1966) suggests that people do in fact avoid drawing conclusions concerning themselves when their outcomes are believed to be capriciously determined, and Jucknat (1937) found that tasks that are extremely easy or difficult do not prompt feelings of success or failure. Brehm and Cohen (1959) have argued that postdecisional dissonance is unlikely to be experienced unless the individual feels that he possesses decision freedom, and Gerard, Blevans, and Malcolm (1964) and Malewski (1962) have demonstrated that dissonance is most readily experienced if the individual believes he has the *ability* to make the required decision. Apparently self-attribution occurs only (or most uniformly) when people believe that they exercise considerable control over their own fate. In this connection it is interesting to note that Piaget (1930) concluded that lack of control is associated with the "not-self."

G. H. Mead (1934) and Cooley (1902) argued that self-attribution involves a process quite different from that suggested by Bem. According to these authors, the individual learns about himself by observing the responses he evokes in others rather than by analyzing his own behaviors. Thus one's self-concept is conceived to consist primarily of one's stimulus value for important other people, and to be revealed by a social looking glass. Much of the controversy surrounding this view of self-attribution has concerned the mechanisms by which other people's reactions are translated by the individual into meaningful information about himself, and the reasons why he treats one group rather than another as the mirror in which to see himself reflected. In the present context it is sufficient to note that a usable mirror is likely to be one that is free to transmit a variety of evaluative messages. One presumably learns little about one's self by observing the reactions of associates whose behaviors are severely restricted by role prescriptions or by other social pressures. Thus, for example, Ring (1964) found that people who agree with the ideas expressed by a powerful person provide that person with little information about the quality of his ideas; they are not free to render any other verdict.

Regardless of which of the above theories of self-attribution is most nearly correct, it is clear that an individual's conclusions concerning his own dispositional qualities are mediated by the freedom he ascribes to himself and/or to others.

V. Perceived Freedom and Interpersonal Influence

Much of contemporary social psychology is concerned with the processes by which people influence one another. Norms, social power, ingratiation, and "forced compliance" are but a few of the phenomena receiving widespread attention. The interaction process itself is commonly depicted as one in which each participant exercises control over the behavior of others. Such interpersonal influences may be presumed to affect the freedom an individual believes himself to enjoy, and to be affected, in turn, by the individual's perceived freedom.

A. Norms

According to Homans (1950), a norm is "an idea in the minds of the members of a group, an idea that can be put in the form of a statement specifying what the members or other men should do, ought to do, are expected to do, under given circumstances. . . . A statement of the kind described is a norm only if any departure of real behavior from the norm is followed by some punishment" [p. 123]. Thibaut and Kelley (1959) express a similar view, and suggest that norms serve as implicit agreements regulating the costs and payoffs individuals create for one another. Thus they are rules specifying what a person may expect from others and what he must give in exchange. Such rules simplify interpersonal transactions in that they provide needed stability and predictability of behavior, permit people to avoid renegotiating rights and duties each time they interact, and protect all parties from the capricious exercise of power. Norms are said to take on the characteristics of a moral obligation, becoming internalized rules that are regarded as one's own.

Relationships between norms and perceived freedom are revealed when one examines a model proposed by Jackson (1960). Individuals who enforce norms upon one another are assumed to operate like slot machines that are programmed to dispense varying amounts of reward or punishment depending upon the behaviors of their customers. Thus a student in a classroom may incur the wrath of his peers by speaking too much or too little, and he may receive their approval by participating at an intermediate level. Figure 1 shows a "return potential curve" depicting the payoff schedule that might guide the reactions of a group of norm-enforcers. It is to be noted that several different options fall within the range of "tolerable or approved behavior," although some are more highly rewarded than others. Jackson suggests that the entire curve, and not just the portion that rises above the point of indifference, represents the norm.

Jackson's model is designed to depict the payoffs an individual will actually receive for various behaviors. Many other theorists have dealt with "perceived norms"—the payoffs individuals expect to receive for specific actions. According to the latter approach, the individual is presumed to attribute a "return potential curve" to people who control important rewards and punishments. A perceived norm is an implicit statement of expected relationships between costs and payoffs; it is the individual's personal equation for predicting what he must give to others in order to receive specific outcomes from them.

When treated as a model of perceived norms, Jackson's formulation parallels the conception of perceived outcome freedom developed earlier in this chapter. Both theories envision a bargaining relationship in which

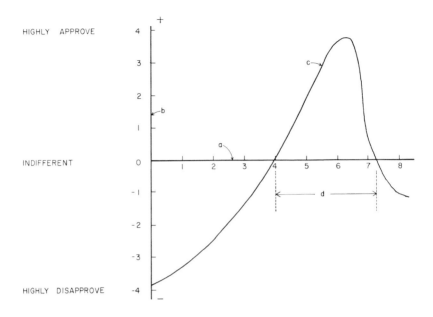

FIG. 1. Schematic diagram of Jackson's return potential model for representing norms. (a) A behavior dimension; (b) an expectation dimension; (c) a return potential curve, showing the distribution of approval-disapproval among the members of a system over the whole range of behavior; (d) the range of tolerable behavior.

costs must be incurred in order to obtain desired outcomes, and the individual's perceived freedom to achieve a specific goal should depend upon his ability and willingness to conduct the required transaction. However, Jackson's model does not deal explicitly with subjective probabilities, and it regards outcomes as a continuous rather than a dichotomous variable. For ease of exposition the present chapter treats negatively valenced outcomes as costs, and deals with only two degrees of outcome; the individual either receives the desired payoff or he does not. Although these differences reflect contrasting assumptions concerning the importance of variables, and concerning the manner in which variables can most readily be represented, the two conceptions are by no means incompatible. On the contrary, they seem complementary, and a complete model would presumably be a composite of both.

However, Jackson's model is designed to reflect only one class of considerations that influence perceived freedom. The payoffs depicted by the "return potential curve" include only the approving and disapproving reactions of the norm-enforcing agency (a group, society, or, in the case of an "internalized" norm, one's own conscience). The fact that people sometimes elect to behave in ways that invite reprisals from these agencies suggests that other payoffs may be more important than those summarized by the return potential curve. Thus, for example, a man may neglect his parental duties because the rewards he expects to receive from other preoccupations greatly outweigh the costs he expects to incur by displeasing the enforcing agency. Normative costs and payoffs enter into the calculations by which options are evaluated and freedom is appraised, but they are only part of the total picture. Were this not the case norms would presumably evoke utter obedience from all of us – or, at least, from all of us who have the ability to do what is most positively sanctioned.

A norm may be likened to a system of taxation in which some kinds of income-producing activities are taxed, others are exempted, and still others are subsidized by a negative tax. Such a system will undoubtedly restrict people's freedom to obtain certain outcomes and augment their freedom to obtain others. Consequently, it will affect decision freedom. But this pattern of taxation will function as only one of many determinants of perceived freedom. Unless the valence of the tax is very strong, and unless the tax is highly enforcable (subjective probability equals approximately 1.00), its impact may be less critical than that of other factors. The valences and subjective probabilities associated with many norms are not very high.

When seen from another perspective, norms may be regarded as having an overall effect on freedom that is generally positive. Since the days of Hobbs, a number of writers (Bales, 1950; Green, 1956; McIver & Page, 1949; Thibaut & Kelley, 1959) have contended that norms evolve because they provide the kind of stable and orderly interpersonal environment in which individuals can expect to obtain desired outcomes. Without norms even the most powerful persons would be uncertain of the reactions their behaviors would evoke in others, and subjective probabilities might be so low that nobody could enjoy a high degree of outcome freedom. According to this view, people accept the notion that certain outcomes ought to involve prohibitive costs in order that subjective probabilities associated with other outcomes may be fairly high. The costs of burglary ought to be so great that a homeowner has a good chance of finding his furniture when he returns from the theater. The penalties for fraud should be severe enough to permit a customer to believe he will receive the outcomes for which he has bargained.

Thus, although norms obviously restrict the individual's freedom to pursue certain objectives, their overall effect may be an increase in outcome freedom. However, Allport (1954) has argued that norms often favor the "haves" over the "have-nots." Whether they augment the outcome freedom of all persons is a debatable issue.

B. POWER

Power may be viewed as the capacity of one agent (person or group) to induce another to incur costs. French and Raven (1959) have described three bases for power that are especially pertinent to the arguments developed in this chapter. An agent that is believed to control the outcomes desired by an individual will ordinarily have reward power over him. The extent of this power is said to be a positive function of the magnitude (valence) of the rewards the agent is believed to control *and* the probability that the rewards will be delivered if the individual does what the power agent requires. Coercive power stems from the individual's expectation that the power agent will permit him to escape noxious outcomes if he incurs certain costs. The strength of the agent's coercive power is a positive function of the negative valence of the noxious outcomes multiplied by the probability that the agent, when properly appeased, will withhold those outcomes. Legitimate power involves a more complicated set of relationships. The power agent may not exercise direct control over the individual's rewards and punishments. But the larger society, an institution, or God is believed to have endowed the agent with the "right" to require that the individual incur certain, often narrowly defined, costs. If the individual does not accede, he exposes himself to the punitive reactions of the legitimizing body or to the coercive power of his own conscience. French and Raven do not specify a rule for assessing the strength of legitimate power, but it presumably varies as a function of the negative payoffs disobedience is expected to evoke from the legitimizing body.

Schopler (1965) has discussed a number of other conceptions of power, some of which focus on the agent's ability to control the individual's payoffs rather than on his ability to induce the individual to incur costs. Although the former ability often implies the latter, the two versions of power are not identical. A slot machine that maintains no relationship between the coins it receives and the payoffs it yields exercises control over the payoffs of its patrons, but it has little ability to induce them to incur costs. Such a machine has "fate control" (Thibaut & Kelley, 1959) but very little "behavior control." As Thibaut and Kelley note, human power agents often convert the former into the latter; in order to achieve behavioral control, they make their payoffs contingent on the costs people incur in their behalf. In the present discussion power is equated with behavioral control.

An agent's power reflects his ability to offer expected payoffs that are more valuable then the costs he asks people to incur. (In the case of legitimate power, the payoffs may be administered by a third party at the behest of the agent.) In effect, the power agent exercises his control by creating conditions that *promote* the individual's perceived freedom to obtain a specific outcome. In the case of reward power, the agent offers the opportunity to obtain either of two kinds of desired payoff: (*a*) a positively valenced outcome or (*b*) escape from a noxious state of affairs created by nature or by persons other than the power agent. ("I will give you a dollar if you will do it." "If you use the deodorant I am selling your friends will stop avoiding you.") Coercive power is like the second of the above examples, except that the power agent himself creates, or threatens to create, the noxious condition from which he offers the privilege of escape. ("Do this or I will have you fired.") Regardless of whether reward or coercive power is employed, the successful agent offers an expected payoff that is more valuable than the cost he asks his target person to incur. The greater the margin by which the value of the expected payoff exceeds the required cost, the greater is the target person's freedom to obtain the desired outcome.

A study reported by Brehm and Cohen (1959) suggests that the more distasteful the condition from which the agent of coercive power permits his target to escape, the greater is the target person's freedom *to do what the agent demands*. Fraternity pledges were told that they would be required to copy random numbers for 3 or 4 hours, and that if they did not comply the experimenter would ask the fraternity to impose (*a*) a moderate punishment in the form of extra duty hours or (*b*) a severe punishment, perhaps including expulsion from the fraternity. Before beginning the boring task (which was never actually performed) subjects rated the volition they experienced in complying with the request that they copy the numbers, and their satisfaction with the assigned task. The critical findings are that subjects offered an opportunity to escape very severe punishment reported significantly greater volition and satisfaction than did those for whom noncompliance would have brought only moderate punishment. The more a subject stood to gain by doing the task, the more willingly he agreed to do it.

The above finding should not be construed to indicate that the target of power experiences an increase in *decision* freedom. When the agent augments the target's freedom to obtain one outcome, he almost inevitably blocks or decreases the target's freedom to obtain other outcomes the individual might be able to purchase with his limited resources. In particular, the agent decreases the target's freedom to decide against doing what the agent wants him to do. The successful power agent induces the target to believe there is more to be gained by investing as the agent desires than by hording his resources or by investing them in other options.

Although the major impact of power is a reordering of the target person's outcome freedoms, power also affects the target's total freedom. In the case of reward power, the target is offered an opportunity that is more attractive than others in which he might invest his resources, and the expected payoffs exceed the required investment. Consequently, the net effect is an increase in total outcome freedom. But coercive power always confronts the target with the necessity to choose between two evils: the noxious condition and the burden of incurring costs in order to escape that condition. Thus coercive power decreases the target's *total* perceived freedom. French and Raven (1959) suggest that target persons come to dislike agents of coercive power but are attracted to people who employ reward power.

Power is a dyadic phenomenon that should be viewed from the perspective of the agent as well as that of the target. The agent of power must incur costs in order to induce the target to comply; he must offer rewards or administer punishments, and in many cases he must monitor the target's reactions to his power-inducing maneuvers. In exchange for these costs the agent expects to receive a payoff the attractiveness of which equals the valence (to the agent) of the target's compliant act times the probability that the target will produce the act (valence × subjective probability). It is evident that power, far from being one-sided, is an arrangement in which both participants incur costs and expect to receive gains. To be sure, when power is coercive the target's expected gain will leave him worse off than he was before, but he at least expects to receive immunity from an outcome that is even more aversive than the loss of his investment. In the case of reward power, both participants stand to gain positive outcomes they believe to be more important than the costs they incur.

The foregoing discussion implies that an agent who possesses the resources needed to purchase the compliance of a target person may refrain from exercising his power because the required investment is too great. Freedom to induce compliance, like freedom to obtain other outcomes, is a function of valences, subjective probabilities, and perceived costs.

The effect of power on the agent's total outcome freedom depends, of course, on the comparative values of the compliance the agent expects to receive and the costs he must incur. Individuals sometimes decline to accept "positions of power" on the grounds that the role is too restrictive or that compensations are incommensurate with responsibilities. As Fromm (1941) has noted, the institution of slavery binds both the master and the slave, and the long-run effects of the exercise of power may be detrimental to the agent as well as the target. But the agent would presumably be unwilling to wield his power if he did not expect to profit by doing so. Consequently, it seems safe to conclude that usable power contributes to the *perceived* freedom of the agent, at least until the time it is employed.

Because power is a double-edged sword and a potential threat to everyone's outcome freedoms, it tends to become the object of social regulation. Norms prescribe appropriate rates of exchange, and permit individuals to believe they are likely to receive certain outcomes from others provided they incur the required costs. But, as noted above, norms generally legitimize a number of different actions, rather than a single one. And actions that are disapproved may evoke only mild social reprisals. Consequently, the norms that limit the exercise of power often leave a rather wide margin of discretion to the individual.

C. Decision Freedom, Ingratiation, and the Breadth of Power

Whenever the "machine" that controls a desired outcome maintains a positive correlation between costs and payoffs, the individual who incurs costs increases his chances of receiving the outcome. Thus, although it would be correct to say that the individual's cost-incurring behaviors control the machine, one might also contend that the machine invokes compliance from the individual. Each takes orders from the other. The individual accepts this arrangement because the gain he expects from his investment is greater than that he anticipates from other uses he might make of his limited resources.

1. Ingratiation

Under circumstances such as those described above, the individual may attempt to cheat the machine by inserting counterfeit coins into its money slot or by giving it coins of the wrong denomination. In either case, the individual's aim is to obtain the desired outcome without incurring the costs that are normally required. When the machine that controls an individual's payoffs is a human being, there is another way of cheating. The individual may endeavor to convince the controlling agent that he is a special case and deserves a more favorable rate of payoff than is accorded ordinary mortals. "Because I am special you should give me a break; you should reward me for my attractive attributes, even though I do not incur all the costs you normally impose." Such tactics are called ingratiation.

The distinction between ingratiation and other types of cheating concerns the intention of the person who performs the act. An individual who inserts improper coins into the machine intends to convince it that he has incurred the required costs, whereas the ingratiator intends, through the use of flattery or other deceptive maneuvers, to persuade the machine to deviate from its normal rate of payoff. Jones (1964) suggests that three major tactics are commonly employed to accomplish this end. One is called "other enhancement" and involves flattering the human machine that controls the desired payoff. Another is conformity to the views of the controlling agent on issues that are not normally relevant to the transactions by which the desired outcome is obtained. A third consists of presenting one's self to the agent as an especially competent, worthy, or attractive person. In all three varieties of ingratiation the individual misrepresents himself in an effort to obtain a payoff for which he has not incurred the prescribed costs.

Several conditions must exist before ingratiation will occur. The individual will not ingratiate unless he desires the outcome controlled by the machine, and unless the normal cost of assuring himself a high subjective probability is rather high by comparison with the individual's available resources. Even if these conditions are met, an individual is unlikely to ingratiate unless he believes that his tactics are likely to have the desired effects. As Jones has noted, ingratiation is a potentially dangerous ploy, for if the controlling agent suspects that it is being employed, he is unlikely to provide the desired outcome and may, instead, administer some form of punishment. Consequently, ingratiation may involve high perceived costs and yield only moderate subjective probabilities.

One further condition must exist before an individual will risk ingratiating himself. The controlling machine must be thought to enjoy some margin of freedom to decide whether or not to grant the desired outcome. If the agent is believed to be rigidly programmed to follow an inflexible course of action, there is no point in convincing him that one is worthy of special consideration.

An agent's decision freedom may be limited by a number of factors. He may be under very strong normative controls that make any deviation from standard behavior extremely costly to himself. This will be the case if the return potential curve described earlier in this chapter is very steep and carries severe reprisals for all but a single kind of action (or offers strong rewards for only a single kind of action). The agent's decision freedom may also be restricted by a dictatorial boss or foreman who employs rewards and punishments in a manner that makes one course of action much more profitable than any other. Or the agent may need a particular kind of input so badly that he cannot afford to reinforce an ingratiator for providing other kinds. ("I like you and enjoy your company, but I will go broke if I pay you for anything but the work you have been asked to do.") In all of these instances the agent's behaviors are so thoroughly overdetermined that he is unlikely to be viewed as having any appreciable decision freedom.

An example will illustrate the hypothesized effect of attributed decision freedom on ingratiation. A man accused of murder may be quite willing to ingratiate himself to the jury which can find him innocent or guilty, or to the judge who can impose a moderate or severe sentence. But, when awaiting execution, the man will have little desire to ingratiate himself to the hangman who has no option but to spring the trap when the appointed moment arrives. The jury and the judge decide; the hangman merely follows orders.

Jones (1964) has reported a series of studies indicating that laboratory subjects are prone to ingratiate themselves to authority figures (usually experimental accomplices) who are believed to have decision freedom. Thus, for example, Jones, Gergen, Gumpert, & Thibaut (1965) found that subjects were more inclined to represent themselves as strong and competent persons when a "supervisor" who controlled their payoffs was free to modify the standards by which performance was judged than when the supervisor did not possess this freedom. In a similar investigation, Kauffmann and Steiner (1968) found that the amount of ingratiation elicited from subjects depended not only on the agent's decision freedom but on the joint impact of other variables as well. When high perceived decision freedom was combined with other variables to create a situation in which ingratiation was an extremely salient (visible) behavioral option, less ingratiation actually occurred than when ingratiation was only a moderately salient means of obtaining the desired payoff. These findings appear to support Jones' contention that ingratiation is a dangerous activity and tends to be avoided when the probability of detection is high. If a situation makes the use of ingratiation seem too obvious, a subject will expect the agent to be on guard against deceptive practices. Thus a student is unlikely to bring his teacher an apple just before examination time, although he might do so (or employ a more subtle ingratiation technique) earlier in the semester. Students are presumably more inclined to ingratiate if the teacher has high decision freedom (e.g., gives essay tests) than if he does not (e.g., if he give "objective" tests).

2. Decision Freedom and the Breadth of Power

An agent who is believed to enjoy decision freedom can exercise discretion in giving or withholding the outcomes he controls, whereas one who lacks such freedom cannot. The former may need to be appeased, flattered, or cajoled; the latter needs only to be given the "standard" price for his services. Consequently, an agent with high decision freedom should be able to induce individuals to incur a wide variety of costs; he can demand that individuals remain in his good graces if they wish to receive the payoffs he administers. On the other hand, an agent who is constrained to deliver rewards and punishments in a rigid fashion must grant his favors to anyone who pays the established price. Whether the former agent has greater total power than the latter may be a debatable issue, but the one with decision freedom should have the ability to control a wider range of the individual's behavior. Corrupt office holders are able to collect a variety of favors from the citizenry because they exercise far more decision freedom than the laws and norms actually bestow upon them (Merton, 1957), and capricious deities appear to command more constant attention from their followers than do those that are thought to abide by fixed rules of exchange (M. Mead, 1937). Much of the research on ingratiation provides experimental evidence of the effect of decision freedom on breadth of power. However, ingratiation represents a special case in which the agent *unintentionally* evokes a wide variety of costly and deceptive responses from individuals. Parallel studies are needed to document the effect of an agent's decision freedom on his power to command open and undisguised compliance across a range of situations.

Studies employing the prisoner's dilemma paradigm suggest that agents who always reward subjects for compliance, and always punish them for noncompliance, are successful in producing high levels of cooperative behavior. Rapoport (1964), for example, found that a tit-for-tat strategy generated more cooperation than any other pattern he examined. Bixenstine and Wilson (1963) and Lave (1965) reported that agents who always reward their associates regardless of the responses they make tend to be exploited, and those who never reward their associates evoke little cooperative behavior. These findings appear to indicate that subjects yield to the power agent when rewards are highly contingent on their doing so, and are less likely to comply when past experience indicates a low correlation between yielding and subjective probability. But research of this kind deals only with power to induce a single kind of response, and has little to say about breadth of power. It may be hypothesized that agents who employ a strategy of partial reinforcement are more likely than those who reinforce continuously to be viewed as enjoying decision freedom. If this is the case, the power of the former to elicit *unreinforced* responses should be greater than that of agents who employ 100% reinforcement. Unfortunately, the great mass of research on partial and continuous reinforcement is not very directly relevant to this contention. Most of it has involved infrahuman subjects who are probably incapable of deriving inferences concerning an agent's decision freedom, or human subjects whose understanding of laboratory procedures almost certainly prevents them from concluding that an experimenter ever exercises very much decision freedom. (Human subjects, and especially college students, are likely to realize that experimenters are highly programmed.)

In spite of these limitations on available research, Baron (1966) and Baron, Robinson, and Lawrence (1968) have reviewed a number of studies suggesting that subjects who experience marked changes in reinforcement rate manifest "negative affective arousal with concomitant activation of various self-presentations designed to eliminate such disparities" [Baron, 1966, p. 530]. Baron's own work provides inferential evidence that moderate rates of reinforcement provide an agent with broader power than do very high rates. Subjects who received 33% reinforcement following a period of 100% reinforcement were more willing to participate in an unpleasant future experiment than were subjects who had been shifted from 33 to 100% reinforcement. But studies explicitly linking reinforcement rates with subjects' conceptions of an agent's decision freedom and with the breadth of the agent's power seem not to have been performed.

Outside the laboratory, communication processes permit individuals to form impressions of the decision freedom enjoyed by teachers, policemen, parents, and other power agents. In such situations the agent's actual reinforcement strategy may not be very highly influential in determining the decision freedom he is believed to have. More important, perhaps, are the things people tell one another about the freedom of such agents, or about the past performance of a particular agent.

D. Decision Freedom and Stress

Freedom is sometimes regarded as a determinant of the stress people experience in interpersonal situations. Since the days of Hobbs and Locke it has been contended that people accept restraints on their liberties because unlimited freedom is a threat to everyone. Simmel (1950) argued that man strives to maintain a comfortable ratio between freedom and law, and, in a review of research dealing with group processes, Stogdill (1959) concluded that "excessive degrees of freedom are observed to result in indecision, confusion, and malco-ordination" [p. 283]. Norms and role systems are commonly depicted as instruments for reducing the burdens of decision making and information processing which might otherwise overwhelm the individual. Fromm (1941) suggested that man sometimes attempts to escape from freedom.

In evaluating these contentions it should be noted that social power, laws, norms, and role systems tend to be highly selective. The pursuit of certain goals is punished, as is the use of certain means of obtaining goals. But the individual is subsidized for seeking other goals and for employing socially prescribed means. The consequence of this selectivity is a severe limitation of decision freedom, but the individual's overall outcome freedom may actually be increased. To be sure, some outcomes are rendered prohibitively expensive, but the increased predictability and benevolence of the social environment make other outcomes more readily accessible. The freedom from which people "escape" or which they are at least willing to relinquish in exchange for other advantages, is decision freedom.

That decision freedom can become a burden is suggested by theorists (e.g., Brehm & Cohen, 1959; Pallak, Brock, & Kiesler, 1967; Weick, 1964) who contend that people who freely choose one option rather than another are likely to experience dissonance whereas those whose choices are dictated by external circumstances, by the grossly unequal expected payoffs of available options, or by perceived incompetence to decide (Gerard, Blevans, & Malcolm, 1964; Malewski, 1962) are not. Decision freedom implies personal responsibility for one's behaviors, and it exposes the individual to the dangers of criticism and self-reproach for having deliberately elected to pursue a foolish or immoral course of action. As noted earlier, people tend not to hold themselves or others personally accountable for behaviors that are thought to reflect little decision freedom. Thus, when an individual's actions are guided by strong normative pressures, by the commands of an authority figure, or even by his own ignorance, he tends to be absolved from blame and recrimination.

Berlyne (1960) and Garner (1962) have reported evidence that conflict and decision time increase with the number of alternatives among which the individual chooses. However, C. A. Kiesler (1966) and Hendrick, Mills, and Kiesler (1968) have noted that individuals who are permitted to choose among many different alternatives of approximately equal expected value tend to make rapid choices. These authors suggest that the complexity of such situations is so great that people feel unable to make discerning judgments; extremely high decision freedom confronts people with a seemingly impossible task from which they are inclined to escape by choosing in a perfunctory manner.

That high decision freedom may promote stress is also suggested by research indicating that suicide occurs more frequently among people who are largely immune from normative pressures than among those whose choices are regulated by social constraints (Durkheim, 1951; Henry & Short, 1954). Army officers, who clearly enjoy greater decision freedom than do enlisted men, also have higher suicide rates, and white have higher rates than do Negroes. Suicide is rare among extremely oppressed captives (Henry & Short, 1954). Although cross-species generalizations are perilous, the work of Brady (1958) and Brady, Porter, Conrad, and Mason (1958) deserves mention. These experimenters found that rhesus monkeys who exercised control over a painful stimulus developed ulcers, while their partners who were linked in series connections and passively received the same electrical shocks did not.

Unfortunately, the above studies compare cases which probably differ with respect to outcome freedom as well as decision freedom. Consequently, it is not entirely clear that the latter was the factor that promoted stress and resignation. However, it is very difficult to conceive high outcome freedom (perceived ability to obtain strongly desired outcomes) as a cause for anxiety, suicide, or ulcers, but very easy to believe that high decision freedom might have such consequences.

The previous discussion has ignored individual differences. In a review of organizational research, Forehand and Gilmer (1964) noted that individuals appear to differ from one another in their preferences for "constraining versus free environments." Vroom (1960) reported that high- and low-authoritarian workers expressed significantly different levels of satisfaction with their freedom to make work decisions. In a study cited by Stern (1962), Patton found that authoritarian students had high drop-out rates at the University of Chicago and that they frequently complained of the permissive atmosphere which permitted students to smoke in classrooms and did not require attendance.

The available evidence suggests that very high decision freedom exposes the individual to severe conflict, criticism, and self-recrimination, especially when the options among which he can choose involve low outcome freedom. Freedom to choose among options, all of which offer high outcome freedom, may be less troublesome.

E. COMPLIANCE AND ATTITUDE CHANGE

Some of the more intriguing and controversial research of recent years has examined the effects of behavioral compliance on attitudes (see reviews by Brehm & Cohen, 1959; Elms, 1967; Kelley, 1967). Subjects in this type of study are induced to produce a counterattitudinal speech or essay, to eat a food they dislike, or to otherwise behave in a manner that is inconsistent with their preferences. A common outcome of such investigations is the finding that subjects tend to bring their attitudes into increased accord with the actions they have been induced to take.

The two major explanations of this phenomenon make opposite predictions concerning relationships between the valence of the inducements subjects are offered and the amount by which subjects' attitudes will change. According to incentive theories, strong inducements to perform an unpleasant task serve as strong reinforcers, and thus tend to increase the attractiveness of the task and the attitude it implies. (That which is associated with a good thing tends, as a consequence of the association, to gain valence.) Consequently, large inducements should produce more attitude change than small inducements. But, according to dissonance theory, the opposite relationship should prevail. An individual who behaves in a manner that contradicts his own beliefs is presumed to experience dissonance, *unless* he sees strong justification for his actions (e.g., unless he has been offered a very large reward for performing in a counterattitudinal fashion). This line of reasoning suggests that maximum dissonance, and maximum attitude change, will occur when inducements are barely sufficient to gain compliance. The reviews cited above indicate that there is an abundance of evidence favoring both theories.

Attempts to reconcile the contradictory findings have focused on the subject's perceived freedom. Thus, several investigators (Brehm & Cohen, 1959; Brock & Becker, 1967; Linder, Cooper, & Jones, 1967) have reported evidence suggesting that dissonance is generated only (or mainly) when the individual feels he has freely decided to perform the counterattitudinal act. If the situation is such that the subject feels he had no real choice, reinforcement effects may occur. In the discussion that follows, decision freedom will be conceived to be only one of several factors that influence the outcomes of compliance studies.

It may be doubted that subjects in this kind of experiment ever feel very free to decline to do what the experimenter asks. That the payoff for compliance is more highly valent than the costs is demonstrated by the fact that even the subjects in the low-payoff groups almost invariably do what is requested of them. But what the experimenter tells them about their freedom to decline may influence their interpretations of the proffered payoffs and the costs they are asked to incur. As Kelley (1967) has noted, experimenters who have obtained strong dissonance effects have assured their subjects in a variety of ways that they were completely free to decline. When such assurances are coupled with payoffs that greatly exceed costs, subjects may be pardoned for wondering what the experimenter's aims really are.

The payoff promised by an experimenter may be interpreted either as a bribe for doing a somewhat despicable act, or as a symbol of approval for performing a commendable deed. If the experimenter wants his subjects to draw the former conclusion he should probably offer the reward at the same time as he makes his request, imply that other people may not be willing to do what he is asking, and suggest that he does not personally sanction the behavior he is asking the subject to produce. In addition, it may be helpful to make the payoff seem inordinately large. Studies that have yielded the dissonance effect appear to have followed these prescriptions rather closely. Without exception they have specified the payoffs and costs before subjects committed themselves to comply. Furthermore, subjects have been told that they were completely free to decline, a step which probably suggested that other people were not uniformly willing to cooperate and that the experimenter harbored doubts about the propriety of the behavior he was requesting. ("I want you to do it but I won't say you should do it; maybe you shouldn't.") Finally, the monetary payoffs employed in some of the studies have been rather high.

If a payoff is seen as a bribe, how might its magnitude affect the attitude of the person who accepts it? If the bribe is barely sufficient to induce compliance, the recipient can conclude that what he has done is not really very bad, and, in fact, he may convince himself that his real motives are quite pure. He did not sell out for a small bribe; on the contrary, his performance reflects his true beliefs. A large bribe should make such dissonance-reducing rationalizations less necessary, and, at the same time, more difficult to sustain. Dissonance theorists contend that a large payoff justifies a counterattitudinal act, so little dissonance is created. According to the view presented here, a large bribe may also imply that the experimenter expects the subject to disagree with the position he has been induced to defend. Otherwise the experimenter would presumably have offered a lesser reward, or none at all. Thus the often documented desire of subjects to please experimenters (Orne, 1959; Orne & Evans, 1965; Sarbin & Chun, 1964) should encourage little if any attitude shift following high bribery.

If an experimenter wishes his subjects to interpret payoffs as evidence of positive sanction he would be well advised to offer the reward after subjects have committed themselves to compliance. Furthermore, the experimenter should avoid telling subjects anything which implies that either he or other persons doubt the propriety of the requested behavior. Certainly he should not assert that the subject is completely free to decline when the subject knows full well that his freedom to do so is limited. Probably the investigator should avoid payoffs that are incommensurate with costs. Studies that have produced results consistent with reinforcement theory have not uniformly followed these prescriptions, but they have generally avoided allegations that the subject is free to decline and they have sometimes offered the payoff after the subject indicated his willingness to comply.

If the payoffs are interpreted as evidence of approval, high payoffs should provide the subject with stronger sanction for his behavior than should low payoffs. Thus high payoffs should generate more attitude change than low payoffs because strong positive sanctions serve as more potent reinforcers than do weak sanctions and/or because strong sanctions more clearly reveal the experimenter's expectations to the subject.

The strongest confirmation of the foregoing arguments has been provided by Linder et al. (1967). Groups of subjects were offered either $.50 or $2.50 for writing a short counterattitudinal essay, and were twice assured that they were completely free to decline to do so. Subjects in two other treatment groups were simply asked to write the essay and were not told they could decline. After the latter subjects had indicated their willingness to comply, they were promised either $.50 or $2.50 for their services. The findings of the study are exceptionally clear. When the monetary reward was an explicit part of the bargain and subjects were told they could decline, attitude change was an inverse function of amount of payoff. But when subjects were not told they could refuse and when payment was not a part of the bargain, attitude change was a direct function of amount of payoff. Thus a single study produced both the dissonance and reinforcement effects. Freedman (1963) has also reported evidence indicating that dissonance effects occur when the payoff is specified as part of the initial bargain, and that reinforcement effects are produced when the payoff is announced after compliance has been obtained.

Although the present interpretation of compliance research is based in part on the insights of Kelley (1967) and Linder et al. (1967), it involves a very different assumption concerning the impact of telling subjects they are free. When expected payoffs greatly exceed perceived costs, we assume that a subject's freedom to avoid the costs is very limited, and that it is unlikely to be increased when the "machine" that controls the payoffs says he may abstain from investing. Thus, unlike the authors cited above, we do not conclude that the experimenter's admonitions actually induced decision freedom.

1. Consequences of Attributed Decision Freedom

When an experimental subject produces a counterattitudinal message, he ordinarily addresses it to someone other than the experimenter who instructed him to produce it. Investigators have generally neglected this audience, choosing instead to concentrate their attention upon the amount and kind of inducements offered the subject, and the subject's apparent decision freedom. In studies of this kind the subject may believe that his audience realizes he is exercising little decision freedom (e.g., that he is role playing at the behest of an experimenter), or he may believe that the audience assumes he is behaving freely. The freedom a subject believes others are attributing to him may affect his interpretation of his behaviors and his tendency to bring his attitude into accord with his actions.

Helmreich and Collins (1968) made video tapes of subjects arguing a counterattitudinal position. Some subjects were permitted to explain at the end of their performances that they did not really subscribe to the view they had advocated, whereas other subjects were not. The former manifested significantly less pro-speech attitude change than did the latter.

Steiner and Darroch (1969) induced students to compose and deliver short counterattitudinal speeches opposing draft deferments for college students. Relationships between the quality of counterattitudinal performance and the amount of pro-speech change were found to depend upon whether the audience was thought to agree or disagree with the position being advocated and whether the audience was thought to realize that the subject had little decision freedom (i.e., had been assigned to speak against draft deferments). When speaking to an "agreeing" audience there was virtually no relationship between subjects' appraisals of their performances and the extent to which their attitudes changed. But when the audience was thought to oppose the advocated position, there were substantial correlations between these variables. For subjects who addressed a disagreeing audience that was thought to attribute decision freedom to the speaker, the correlation was $-.44$; for those whose disagreeing audience was believed to realize the speaker had been arbitrarily assigned, the correlation was $.60$.

These two studies indicate that the freedom an individual believes others attribute to him is a critical variable. Unfortunately, it has not yet received widespread attention.

2. Induced Compliance in Laboratory Research

Much of the research conducted by social psychologists involves a liberal smattering of "induced compliance." In the interest of science, or in exchange for research credit, human subjects are impelled to perform tasks that must seem unpleasant, monotonous, or utterly nonsensical to them. They endure shock, deliver painful stimuli to associates, belittle themselves, learn useless materials, throw "acid" in the face of another person, or suffer the indignities of unfair criticism. These things and many more they do because they are told to do them. Orne and Evans (1965), after imposing a wide variety of onerous tasks upon college students, concluded, "We still have not found an aspect of behavior which is sufficiently safe to request of a subject, and which a subject will refuse to carry out if the expectation of compliance is communicated to him" [p. 199].

The role of the subject is one in which decision freedom is denied and the individual does what his instructions demand. Sometimes his behavior is shaped by "non-verbal instructions" communicated to him by the experimental manipulations, or by subtle and unintended advice. As Edwards (1961) and Rosenthal (1966) have noted, when proper behavior is not explicitly defined, numerous cues tell the subject what is expected of him.

It is probably safe to conclude that subjects in many social psychological experiments feel that they enjoy little decision freedom, and realize that the experimenter himself is programmed to follow an inflexible role. Thus the distinction between studies that profess to examine induced compliance and those which do so inadvertently is sometimes difficult to discern. In either case, the subject's behavior is unlikely to be indicative of his dispositional qualities, and the subject probably experiences much less involvement in his performance than would otherwise be the case. Laboratory research has undoubtedly revealed far more about behaviors that occur when decision freedom is lacking than it has disclosed about behaviors that occur when it is present.

VI. Speculations Concerning Satisfaction with Perceived Freedom

Earlier sections of this chapter have dealt with perceived freedom to obtain specific outcomes, and with the individual's freedom to choose which of several outcomes he will seek. It seems appropriate at this point to speculate about the individual's "total perceived outcome freedom," and to offer tentative suggestions concerning his satisfaction with the total outcome freedom he believes himself to possess. History suggests that people who possess little outcome freedom sometimes seem comparatively satisfied with their lot, and that high (or increasing) levels of outcome freedom are occasionally accompanied by intense dissatisfaction.

Perceived freedom to obtain a single outcome has been described as a positive function of the gain the individual anticipates receiving from the pursuit of that outcome.

(1) $\dfrac{\text{Expected}}{\text{gain}}$ = (valence × subjective probability) − investment.

As a first approximation, total outcome freedom may be conceived to be a function of the *sum* of all the gains the individual anticipates receiving. It reflects the total gain he expects to receive as a consequence of his many investments and as a result of the operation of factors he cannot control.

(2) $\begin{array}{l}\text{Total}\\ \text{expected}\\ \text{gain}\end{array}$ = Σ[(valence × subjective probability) − investment].

This formulation is designed to summarize the individual's expectations; it focuses on what he *expects* to happen. But it ignores what he would like to see happen. The individual's satisfaction with his overall outcome freedom presumably reflects the relationship between expectation and desire. An index of satisfaction may be obtained by expressing expected gain as a proportion of desired gain:

(3) $\begin{array}{l}\text{Satisfaction with}\\ \text{total perceived}\\ \text{outcome freedom}\end{array} = \dfrac{\text{total expected gain}}{\text{total desired gain}}.$

In order to derive the denominator of the above ratio we may assume that people want to receive all positively valenced outcomes and to avoid all costs (negatively valenced outcomes). Consequently, the desired gain from any option equals the valence of the positive outcome. Total desired gain from all options equals the sum of the valences of all positive outcomes. In effect, we are proposing that people prefer a state of affairs in which they are certain to receive all of the outcomes they desire and are required to incur no costs in order to do so.

(4) $\begin{array}{l}\text{Satisfaction with}\\ \text{total perceived}\\ \text{outcome freedom}\end{array} = \dfrac{\Sigma[(\text{valence} \times \text{subj. prob.}) - \text{investment}]}{\Sigma \text{ valences}}.$

The magnitude of the denominator of this ratio depends, of course, upon the number of outcomes that are desired and the intensity with which they are desired.

It may be argued that the denominator of the above ratio is inappropriate because what people really want is not to receive "everything for nothing," but to receive "everything for whatever resources they are able to invest." If this is the case, the denominator should equal Σ(valences − investment). This alteration will not appreciably affect the conclusions we will reach in subsequent paragraphs.

If there were no limits on human desires, a realistic appraisal of resources and subjective probabilities would undoubtedly lead all of us to be dissatisfied with our freedom. But desires are not unlimited. They are restricted by ignorance and by our propensity to devalue outcomes we know we cannot have. Nineteenth century man might want a horse, or even a bicycle, but he probably did not desire an automobile, an airplane, or a rocket ship. The legendary noble savage may have craved a number of outcomes, but his aspirations did not include modern medical care, Saturday afternoon at the ballpark, or a guaranteed annual wage. As the defenders of contemporary advertising often say, people must know about a product before they can really want it. Perhaps this is an exaggeration; thoughtful people may conceive of desirable outcomes that have never occurred, but it is probably safe to say that they do not desire that which they are unable to conceive.

Fortunately, people do not want all the potentially attractive outcomes they are capable of imagining. Outcomes that are clearly unattainable either because the individual lacks necessary resources or because subjective probabilities are very low and nonmanipulable, tend not to be desired − or, at least, tend not to be desired very strongly for very long. Hyman (1953) concluded that lower class persons devaluate goals they have no chance of securing, and thus spare themselves the psychological conflict engendered by harboring unattainable aspirations. In a similar vein, A. Cohen (1955) has argued that delinquent boys abrogate blocked goals, and substitute less utilitarian but attainable objectives. Inferential evidence that extremely low probability payoffs tend eventually to lose their positive valence is provided by Bettelheim's (1943) account of the experiences of concentration camp prisoners. At the outset of the prison experience, captives were, of course, aware that they could obtain certain valued payoffs (e.g., avoidance of humiliating encounters with the guards) by paying the supreme cost (death). Some elected that option, but the majority continued to survive in an environment where payoffs were not noticeably contingent upon any costs they could afford to incur. Under these circumstances prisoners tended eventually to see their lives controlled by fate, luck, or unmanageable external forces, and many renounced the values they had held since childhood. A few are even reported to have espoused the contrary goals reflected in the behavior of their Nazi captors. Bettelheim comments that prisoners who had reached the stage of renunciation appeared to suffer less from the deprivations of camp life than did those who had not.

As Lerner and Simmons (1966) have remarked, "It seems obvious that most people cannot afford, for the sake of their own sanity, to believe in a world governed by a schedule of random reinforcements" [p. 203]. One way of escaping from such a chaotic world is to deprive uncontrollable reinforcements (or, at least, those that are unachievable) of their reinforcing value — to reduce their valences to zero. This appears to be what happened in the instances cited above, and also in certain cases of "anomie." Thus Bakis (1952) described the apathy of displaced persons following World War II as a consequence of continuous thwarting of desires. In the face of insurmountable obstacles, many people are reported to have lost interest in almost all goals, including some they might reasonably have expected to attain.

It should be noted that social norms sometimes support the renunciation of low-probability outcomes. Thou shalt not covet is a familiar commandment, and religious teachings extol the virtues of poverty and humility. To be sure, in contemporary American society such face-saving guidelines tend to be obliterated by an avalanche of advertising and exhortation designed to make everyone dissatisfied with his lot. But in other times and places the social definition of what is right and proper has often favored acceptance of what is available and rejection of what is not. Even in America, high school counselors advise students to pursue realistic aims, and parents recognize that not everyone can be President or a master plumber.

According to the formulation presented above, any increase in the attractiveness of outcomes (valences) entails an increase in outcome freedom *provided the corresponding subjective probabilities are greater than zero and do not decline.* But an increase in valences will necessarily augment the denominator of the satisfaction ratio regardless of what happens to subjective probabilities. And unless an increment in valence is accompanied by a parallel increment in subjective probability, satisfaction will decrease even though perceived outcome freedom increases. Thus people who are encouraged to seek new goals, or whose existing desires are intensified, may be less contented than those whose aspirations are stable. It is not difficult to cite instances in which increasing outcome freedom appears to have generated intense dissatisfaction.

Fromm (1941) has described the plight of the serf when the feudal system was replaced by new agricultural and industrial practices. For centuries the serf and his forebears had occupied roles that guaranteed certain minimal rights and provided a very modest but comparatively secure livelihood. However, the serf's opportunities to obtain outcomes other than those offered by his role were virtually nil, and his aspirations were mercifully limited to the narrow realm of the possible. The gambling establishment in which he played out his life's strivings contained many machines that never paid off regardless of the costs he might incur, some that paid off almost regardless of costs, and a few that yielded their booty only when he invested his available resources. Machines of the first type were ignored, and their unobtainable payoffs were devaluated. The serf's freedom ratio was high because his desires were few and carried high subjective probabilities.

With the breakup of the feudal system, new opportunities were opened, and the serf could aspire to obtain outcomes that were formerly unavailable to him. Payoffs that had been unattainable, and hence not actively sought, now became available and desirable. But the machines that controlled these newly desired outcomes made rewards contingent on costs. And the ex-serf gradually discovered that his resources (knowledge, skill, capital) were often insufficient to provide a high subjective probability of obtaining these rewards. At this stage the ex-serf's desires greatly exceeded his expected gains, and his satisfaction ratio was low. According to Fromm, the consequences were self-doubt, hatred, behavior that was destructive of the environment or self, and efforts to restore the authoritarian rule that had formerly limited the serf's opportunities. The latter reaction is described as an attempted "escape from freedom," and is said to have been motivated by a desire to regain earlier satisfactions.

In an analysis of revolutions, Brinton (1938) noted that cries of "liberty, equality, and fraternity" are likely to come from those whose opportunities have expanded and who have glimpsed the vision of unlimited horizons. Thus the American and French Revolutions, and the English Revolution of the 1640's, were sparked by upwardly mobile persons who saw their future progress blocked by what they came to regard as an unjust system. In each case the outbreak of hostilities was preceded by a period during which speakers and pamphleteers assailed the masses with propaganda arguing that numerous unavailable outcomes were rightfully the property of all men. As a result, new desires were stimulated and disparities between aspirations and expectations were accentuated. The widespread clamor for liberty that presaged the coming of the revolutions was thus a consequence of a diminishing satisfaction ratio; it led eventually to violent attempts to alter the machines that controlled the payoffs.

A somewhat similar theme is expressed in the Report of The National Advisory Commission on Civil Disorders (1968). Among the factors contributing to the riots of 1967 was a "revolution of expectations" in which Negroes, encouraged by civil rights legislation, by local successes, and by widely publicized assurances of white leaders, concluded that vastly expanded opportunities were soon to become available. When the actual progress experienced by the rank and file lagged far behind the pace they had been led to expect, a period of disillusionment followed. Although the Commission does not explicitly describe this disillusionment as a diminution of subjective probabilities, it is pictured as leading to a demand for "Freedom Now!"

The events preceding the riots of 1967 probably stimulated an initial and rather short-lived increase in subjective probabilities. Developments during the late 50's and early 60's kindled sparks of hope where little hope (and, therefore, limited desire) had existed. Rightly or wrongly, many deprived persons apparently concluded that society was about to atone for past injustices by causing many slot machines to pay off regularly and without regard for the costs patrons incurred. But the payoff behaviors of most machines were not actually changed very much; a few that had rarely yielded their rewards to Negroes became more generous, and others were adjusted to deliver their outcomes to anyone (regardless of color) who could incur high costs — costs which many Negroes could not afford. As these facts became increasingly apparent, subjective probabilities fell rapidly, whereas valences probably declined slowly, if at all. The result was a decrease in the satisfaction ratio and, in some cases, a desire to destroy the machines.

A year after the riots, Cromley (1968) observed that "studies of the riots to date indicate that the most dissatisfied among the Negroes seem to be those very men who have begun to rise in society, not those remaining at the bottom." As was true of the revolutions reviewed by Brinton, rising expectations intensified desires. When expectations were undermined, desires were not immediately extinguished, and the disparity between expected and desired payoffs generated intense feelings of oppression. Changes in valence appeared to lag behind changes in subjective probability. Whether this was in fact the case, and whether it is typical of episodes involving rapid social change, are issues that deserve careful investigation.

VII. Summary and Conclusions

Perceived freedom has been identified as the individual's judgment of the gains he can expect to receive by pursuing desired objectives (outcome freedom), or his judgment of the comparative gains offered by several different alternatives (decision freedom). Expected gain has been defined as the margin by which the expected payoff (valence × subjective probability) exceeds the investment the individual feels he must make. This conception of perceived freedom combines the insights of the exchange theorist with the probabilistic reasoning of certain decision theorists.

It is apparent that the cognitive elements that determine an individual's judgment of freedom are not completely independent of one another. Valences and subjective probabilities are often negatively correlated, and many people are inclined to associate costly investments with high subjective probabilities and/or highly valent outcomes. There are reasons to believe that some persons ("externals") are prone to see little relationship between investments and expected payoffs, whereas other persons ("internals") maximize this relationship. A society or subsociety can presumably teach its members to stress any of the linkages in the total formulation, but the variable experiences of members of a single society may be responsible for substantial individual differences.

Researchers have seldom attempted to make direct evaluations of individuals' perceptions of freedom, and few studies have measured or manipulated all of the elements that are believed to affect such perceptions. Consequently, available evidence linking the notion of perceived freedom with other concepts is badly fragmented, and conclusions can be drawn only by making an uncomfortably large number of assumptions concerning missing data. But during recent years authors have shown an increasing willingness to make such assumptions and to conclude that perceived freedom (or volition or self-determination) is a critical determinant of many human behaviors. Research reviewed in this chapter suggests that individuals' evaluations of their own or other people's freedoms influence the attribution process, the use of ingratiation techniques, the exercise of power, compliance with the demands of associates, and affective reactions to harmful and helpful deeds. Perceived freedom also appears to mediate the arousal of dissonance and to determine, in part, the degree of stress engendered by situations in which outcomes are denied. Moreover, there is tangential evidence that perceived freedom is one of many factors determining whether people will mount a riot, commit suicide, or apathetically resign themselves to their fate.

If perceived freedom has even a few of the consequences suggested above, it deserves far more careful attention than it has so far received. Its potential as a conceptual tool with which to unify diverse strands of social psychological theory and research should be explored and its practical implications for current social problems should be exploited. Programatic research into the relationships between valences, subjective probabilities, and investments should be undertaken with a view to determining both the situational and personality variables that influence people's propensities to emphasize one *vs.* another determinant of freedom. In particular, existing literature on perceived locus of control should be connected more explicitly to research on socialization procedures, and should be refined in a manner that recognizes that external controlling agents may be viewed as capricious, malicious, benevolent, or aloof. It is equally important that systematic research be conducted to reveal the complex effects of power, norms, and role systems on the scope of freedom people ascribe to themselves and to others, and that the resources that contribute most heavily to a perception of freedom be identified. Above all, it is imperative that satisfactory techniques for assessing perceived freedom be developed so that inferences concerning the impact of situational and personality variables can be tested more directly.

This review leaves many questions unanswered, and certain critical assumptions remain unsupported by empirical evidence. If two alternatives offer equal expected gains [expected gain = (valence × subjective probability) − investment], are they, in fact, regarded as equally available? Is the decision freedom experienced by an individual a simple function of the equality of the gains expected from alternatives, or does it also depend upon the absolute magnitudes of the expected gains? Under what circumstances will an individual reduce the valence of an improbable but highly desirable outcome, and when will he, instead, autistically elevate his subjective probability or lower his appraisal of the required investment? What kinds of reinforcement schedules are most likely to generate high correlations between investment and subjective probability, or between investment and valence? Will the use of a more complex model in which expected payoffs are conceived to reflect probabilities of obtaining negative as well as positive outcomes greatly improve the accuracy of predictions? How can "ego-defensive" motives, such as fear of failure and need for achievement, best be handled within a model of perceived feedom? To what extent, and in what fashion, does high decision freedom compensate for low outcome freedom? Does the individual employ substantially the same cues when judging the freedom of others as he uses when appraising his own freedom? Is there a "strain toward consistency" in the perception of freedom, the individual perferring to believe that his many outcome freedoms are approximately equal? In what way does social comparison influence the freedoms an individual believes he does or should possess? Answers to all of these questions can be obtained only through additional research.

REFERENCES

Adams, J. S. Inequity in social exchange. In L. Berkowitz (Ed.), *Advances in experimental social psychology.* Vol. 2. New York: Academic Press, 1965. Pp. 267-299.

Allen, V. L. Situational factors in conformity. In L. Berkowitz (Ed.), *Advances in experimental social psychology.* Vol. 2. New York: Academic Press, 1965. Pp. 133-175.

Allport, G. W. The historical background of modern social psychology. In G. Lindzey (Ed.), *Handbook of social psychology.* Cambridge, Mass.: Addison-Wesley, 1954. Pp. 3-56.

Aronson, E. The effect of effort on the attractiveness of rewarded and unrewarded stimuli. *Journal of Abnormal and Social Psychology,* 1961, **63**, 375-380.

Aronson, E., & Linder, D. Gain and loss of esteem as determinants of interpersonal attractiveness. *Journal of Experimental Social Psychology,* 1965, **1**, 156-171.

Aronson, E., & Mills, J. The effect of severity of initiation on liking for a group. *Journal of Abnormal and Social Psychology,* 1959, **59**, 177-188.

Arrowood, A. J. Some effects on productivity of justified and unjustified levels of reward under public and private conditions. Unpublished doctoral dissertation, University of Minnesota, 1961.

Arrowood, A. J., & Ross, L. Anticipated effort and subjective probability. *Journal of Personality and Social Psychology,* 1966, **4**, 57-64.

Atkinson, J. W. Motivational determinants of risk-taking behavior. *Psychological Review,* 1957, **64**, 359-372.

Bakis, E. The so-called DP-apathy in Germany's DP camps. *Transactions of the Kansas Academy of Science,* 1952, **55**, 62-86.

Bales, R. F. *Interaction process analysis.* Cambridge, Mass.: Addison-Wesley, 1950.

Baron, R. M. Social reinforcement effects as a function of social reinforcement history. *Psychological Review,* 1966, **73**, 527-539.

Baron, R. M., Robinson, E. L., & Lawrence, S. The effectiveness of social reinforcement as a function of changes in rate of reinforcement. *Journal of Experimental Social Psychology,* 1968, **4**, 123-142.

Bartlett, F. C. *Remembering.* Cambridge, Eng.: Cambridge University Press, 1932.

Bem, D. J. An experimental analysis of self-persuasion. *Journal of Experimental Social Psychology,* 1965, **1**, 199-218.

Berkowitz, L. *Aggression: A social psychological analysis.* New York: McGraw-Hill, 1962.

Berlyne, D. E. *Conflict, arousal, and curiosity.* New York: McGraw-Hill, 1960.

Bettelheim, B. Individual and mass behavior in extreme situations. *Journal of Abnormal and Social Psychology,* 1943, **38**, 417-452.

Bixenstine, V. E., & Wilson, K. V. Effects of level of cooperative choice by the other player on choices in a Prisoner's Dilemma game: Part II. *Journal of Abnormal and Social Psychology,* 1963, **64**, 237-238.

Blau, P. *Exchange and power in social life.* New York: Wiley, 1964.

Brady, J. V. Ulcers in "executive" monkeys. *Scientific American,* 1958, **199**, 95.

Brady, J. V., Porter, R. W., Conrad, D. G., & Mason, J. W. Avoidance behavior and the development of gastroduodenal ulcers. *Journal of the Experimental Analysis of Behavior,* 1958, **1**, 69-72.

Brehm, J. W. Post-decision changes in the desirability of alternatives. *Journal of Abnormal and Social Psychology,* 1956, **52**, 384-389.

Brehm, J. W. *A theory of psychological reactance.* New York: Academic Press, 1966.

Brehm, J. W., & Cohen, A. R. *Explorations in cognitive dissonance.* New York: Wiley, 1962.

Brehm, J. W., & Cole, A. M. Effect of a favor which reduces freedom. *Journal of Personality and Social Psychology,* 1966, 3, 420-426.

Brinton, C. *The anatomy of revolution.* New York: Norton, 1938.

Brock, T. C., & Becker, L. A. Ineffectiveness of "overhead" counterpropaganda. *Journal of Personality and Social Psychology,* 1965, 2, 654-660.

Brock, T. C., & Becker, L. A. Volition and attraction in everyday life. *Journal of Social Psychology,* 1967, 72, 89-97.

Burnstein, E., & Worchel, P. Arbitrariness of frustration and its consequences for aggression in a social situation. *Journal of Personality,* 1962, 30, 528-540.

Cohen, A. *Delinquent boys.* Glencoe, Ill.: Free Press, 1955.

Cohen, A. R. Social norms, arbitrariness of frustration, and status of the agent of frustration in the frustration-aggression hypothesis. *Journal of Abnormal and Social Psychology,* 1955, 51, 222-226.

Cohen, A. R. Some implications of self-esteem for social influence. In C. I. Hovland & I. L. Janis (Eds.), *Personality and persuasibility.* Vol. II. New Haven: Yale University Press, 1959. Pp. 102-118.

Cooley, C. H. *Human nature and the social order.* New York: Scribner's, 1902.

Crandall, V. J., Katkovsky, W., & Preston, A. Motivation and ability determinants of young children's intellectual achievement and behaviors. *Child Development,* 1962, 33, 643-661.

Cromley, R. Nixon bases slum attack on raising Negro hope. *The Springfield Union,* 1968, 105(No. 287, Dec. 2), 6.

deCharms, R. *Personal causation: The internal affective determinants of behavior.* New York: Academic Press, 1968.

Dewey, J. *Human nature and conduct.* New York: Holt, 1922.

Durkheim, E. *Suicide.* (Transl. by J. A. Spaulding & G. Simpson) Glencoe, Ill.: Free Press, 1951.

Edwards, W. The theory of decision making. *Psychological Bulletin,* 1954, 51, 380-417.

Edwards, W. Costs and payoffs are instructions. *Psychological Review,* 1961, 68, 275-284.

Eisinger, R., & Mills, J. Perception of the sincerity and competence of a communicator as a function of the extremity of his position. *Journal of Experimental Social Psychology,* 1968, 4, 224-232.

Elms, A. C. Role playing, incentive, and dissonance. *Psychological Bulletin,* 1967, 68, 132-148.

Estes, W. K. Of models and men. *American Psychologist,* 1957, 12, 609-617.

Feather, N. T. Subjective probability and decision under uncertainty. *Psychological Review,* 1959, 66, 150-164. (a)

Feather, N. T. Success probability and choice behavior. *Journal of Experimental Psychology,* 1959, 58, 257-266. (b)

Feather, N. T. Valence of outcome and expectation of success in relation to task difficulty and perceived locus of control. *Journal of Personality and Social Psychology,* 1967, 7, 372-386.

Festinger, L., Riecken, H. W., and Schachter, S. *When prophesy fails.* Minneapolis: University of Minnesota Press, 1956.

Forehand, G. A., & Gilmer, B. Environmental variation in studies of organizational behavior. *Psychological Bulletin,* 1964, 62, 361-382.

Freedman, J. L. Attitudinal effects of inadequate justification. *Journal of Personality*, 1963, **31**, 371-385.

French, J. R. P., & Raven, B. The bases of social power. In D. Cartwright (Ed.), *Studies in social power*. Ann Arbor: Research Center for Group Dynamics, University of Michigan, 1959. Pp. 150-167.

Freud, S. *Civilization and its discontents*. London: Hogarth Press, 1949.

Fromm, E. *Escape from freedom*. New York: Holt, Rinehart & Winston, 1941.

Gamson, W. Experimental studies of coalition formation. In L. Berkowitz (Ed.), *Advances in experimental social psychology*. Vol. 1. New York: Academic Press, 1964. Pp. 81-110.

Garner, W. R. *Uncertainty and structure as psychological concepts*. New York: Wiley, 1962.

Gerard, H. B., Blevans, S. A., & Malcolm, T. Self-evaluation and the evaluation of choice alternatives. *Journal of Personality*, 1964, **32**, 395-410.

Gerard, H. B., & Mathewson, G. C. The effects of severity of initiation on liking for a group: A replication. *Journal of Experimental Social Psychology*, 1966, **2**, 278-287.

Goffman, E. *Interaction ritual*. New York: Doubleday, 1967.

Goranson, R. E., & Berkowitz, L. Reciprocity and responsibility reactions to prior help. *Journal of Personality and Social Psychology*, 1966, **3**, 227-232.

Gouldner, A. W. The norm of reciprocity: A preliminary statement. *American Sociological Review*, 1960, **25**, 161-178.

Grant, D. A., Hake, H. W., & Hornseth, J. P. Acquisition and extinction of a verbal conditioned response with differing percentages of reinforcement. *Journal of Experimental Psychology*, 1951, **42**, 1-5.

Green, A. W. *Sociology: An analysis of life in a modern society*. New York: McGraw-Hill, 1956.

Griffith, R. M. Odds adjustment by American horse-race bettors. *American Journal of Psychology*, 1949, **62**, 290-294.

Heider, F. *The psychology of interpersonal relations*. New York: Wiley, 1958.

Helmreich, R., & Collins, B. E. Studies in forced compliance: Commitment and magnitude of inducement to comply as determinants of opinion change. *Journal of Personality and Social Psychology*, 1968, **10**, 75-81.

Hendrick, C., Mills, J., & Kiesler, C. A. Decision time as a function of the number and complexity of equally attractive alternatives. *Journal of Personality and Social Psychology*, 1968, **8**, 313-318.

Henry, A. F., & Short, J. F., Jr. *Suicide and homicide*. Glencoe, Ill.: Free Press, 1954.

Homans, G. C. *The human group*. New York: Harcourt, Brace, 1950.

Homans, G. C. *Social behavior: Its elementary forms*. New York: Harcourt, Brace & World, 1961.

Humphreys, L. G. Acquisition and extinction of verbal expectation in a situation analogous to conditioning. *Journal of Experimental Psychology*, 1939, **25**, 294-301.

Hyman, H. The value systems of different classes: A social psychological contribution to the analysis of stratification. In R. Bendix & S. M. Lipset (Eds.), *Class, status and power*. Glencoe, Ill.: Free Press, 1953. Pp. 426-442.

Jackson, J. The dynamics of instructional groups. In N. B. Henry (Ed.), *Fifty-ninth yearbook of the National Society for the Study of Education*. Part II. Chicago: University of Chicago Press, 1960. Pp. 136-163.

James, W. H. Internal versus external control or reinforcement as a basic variable in learning theory. Unpublished doctoral dissertation, Ohio State University, 1967.

Johnson, H. H., & Steiner, I. D. Effort and subjective probability. *Journal of Personality and Social Psychology*, 1965, 1, 365-368.

Jones, E. E. *Ingratiation*. New York: Appleton-Century-Crofts, 1964.

Jones, E. E., & Davis, K. E. From acts to dispositions: The attribution process in person perception. In L. Berkowitz (Ed.), *Advances in experimental social psychology*. Vol. 2. New York: Academic Press, 1965. Pp. 219-266.

Jones, E. E., Davis, K. E., & Gergen, K. J. Role playing variations and their informational value for person perception. *Journal of Abnormal and Social Psychology*, 1961, 63, 302-310.

Jones, E. E., Gergen, K. J., Gumpert, P., & Thibaut, J. W. Some conditions affecting the use of ingratiation to influence performance evaluation. *Journal of Personality and Social Psychology*, 1965, 1, 613-625.

Jones, E. E., & Harris, V. A. The attribution of attitudes. *Journal of Experimental Social Psychology*, 1967, 3. 1-24.

Jucknat, M. Leistung, Anspruchsniveau and Selbstbewusstsein. *Psychologische Forschung*, 1937, 22, 89-179.

Kardiner, A. *The psychological frontiers of society*. New York: Columbia University Press, 1945.

Kauffmann, D. R., & Steiner, I. D. Some variables affecting the use of conformity as an ingratiation technique. *Journal of Experimental Social Psychology*, 1968, 4, 400-414.

Kelley, H. H. Attribution theory in social psychology. In D. Levine (Ed.), *Nebraska symposium on motivation*. Lincoln, Neb.: University of Nebraska Press, 1967. Pp. 192-240.

Kiesler, C. A. Conflict and number of choice alternatives. *Psychological Reports*, 1966, 18, 603-610.

Kiesler, C. A., & Sakumura, J. A test of a model for commitment. *Journal of Personality and Social Psychology*, 1966, 3, 349-353.

Kiesler, S. B. The effect of perceived role requirements on reactions to favor-doing. *Journal of Experimental Social Psychology*, 1966, 2, 198-210.

Landy, D., & Aronson, E. Liking for an evaluator as a function of his discernment. *Journal of Personality and Social Psychology*, 1968, 9, 133-141.

Lanzetta, J. T., & Hannah, T. E. The reinforcing behavior of "naive" trainers. *Journal of Personality and Social Psychology*, 1969, 11, 245-252.

Lave, L. B. Factors affecting cooperation in the prisoner's dilemma. *Behavioral Science*, 1965, 10, 26-38.

Lawler, E. E., III. Effects of hourly overpayment on productivity and work quality. *Journal of Personality and Social Psychology*, 1968, 10, 306-313.

Lefcourt, H. M. Internal versus external control of reinforcement: A review. *Psychological Bulletin*, 1966, 65, 206-220.

Lerner, M. J. Evaluation of performance as a function of performer's reward and attractiveness. *Journal of Personality and Social Psychology*, 1965, 1, 355-360.

Lerner, M. J., & Simmons, C. H. Observer's reactions to the "innocent victim": Compassion or rejection. *Journal of Personality and Social Psychology*, 1966, 4, 203-210.

Levin, H., & Baldwin, A. L. Pride and shame in children. In M. R. Jones (Ed.), *Nebraska symposium on motivation*. Lincoln, Neb.: University of Nebraska Press, 1959. Pp. 138-173.

Lewin, K. *A dynamic theory of personality*. New York: McGraw-Hill, 1935.

Lewin, K. *Resolving social conflicts*. New York: Harper, 1948.

Lewin, K., Dembo, T., Festinger, L., & Sears, P. S. Level of aspiration. In J. McV. Hunt

(Ed.), *Personality and the behavior disorders.* Vol. 1. New York: Ronald Press, 1944. Pp. 333-378.

Linder, D. E., Cooper, J., & Jones, E. E. Decision freedom as a determinant of the role of incentive magnitude in attitude change. *Journal of Personality and Social Psychology,* 1967, **6**, 245-254.

Lowe, R. H., & Steiner, I. D. Some effects of the reversibility and consequences of decision on postdecision information preferences. *Journal of Personality and Social Psychology,* 1968, 8, 172-179.

MacIver, R. M., & Page, C. H. *Society: An introductory analysis.* New York: Rinehart, 1949.

Malewski, A. The influence of positive and negative self-evaluation on post-decisional dissonance. *Polish Sociological Bulletin,* 1962, **34**, 39-49.

McClelland, D. C. *Personality.* New York: Sloane, 1951.

McGlothlin, W. H. Stability of choices among uncertain alternatives. *American Journal of Psychology,* 1956, **69**, 604-615.

Mead, G. H. *Mind, self, and society.* Chicago: University of Chicago Press, 1934.

Mead, M. *Cooperation and competition among primitive peoples.* New York: McGraw-Hill, 1937.

Merton, R. K. *Social theory and social structure.* Glencoe, Ill.: Free Press, 1957.

Mills, J., & Jellison, J. M. Effect on opinion change and how desirable the communication is to the audience the communicator addressed. *Journal of Personality and Social Psychology,* 1967, **6**, 98-101.

Mischel, W., & Masters, J. C. Effects of probability of reward attainment on responses to frustration. *Journal of Personality and Social Psychology,* 1966, 3, 390-396.

Olberz, P. D. Effects of response order on reactions to interpersonal agreements and disagreements. Unpublished master's thesis, University of Illinois, 1968.

Orne, M. T. The nature of hypnosis: Artifact and essence. *Journal of Abnormal and Social Psychology,* 1959, **58**, 277-299.

Orne, M. T., & Evans, F. J. Social control in the psychological experiment. *Journal of Personality and Social Psychology,* 1965, 1, 189-200.

Pallak, M. S., Brock, T. C., & Kiesler, C. A. Dissonance arousal and task performance in an incidental verbal learning paradigm. *Journal of Personality and Social Psychology,* 1967, 7, 11-20.

Pastore, N. The role of arbitrariness in the frustration-aggression hypothesis. *Journal of Abnormal and Social Psychology,* 1952, **47**, 728-731.

Perry, R. B. *Puritanism and democracy.* New York: Vanguard Press, 1944.

Phares, E. J., Ritchie, E., & Davis, W. Internal-external control and reaction to threat. *Journal of Personality and Social Psychology,* 1968, **10**, 402-405.

Piaget, J. *The child's conception of physical causaltiy.* (Transl. by M. Gabain) New York: Harcourt, Brace, 1930.

Pruitt, D. G., & Teger, A. I. The risky shift in group betting. *Journal of Experimental Social Psychology,* 1969, 5, 115-126.

Rapoport, A. Research in the systems sciences. *Mental Health Research Institute,* 1964, pp. 54-71.

Report of the National Advisory Commission on Civil Disorders. New York: Bantam Books, 1968.

Riesman, D. *The lonely crowd: A study of the changing American character.* New Haven: Yale University Press, 1950.

Riesman, D. On autonomy. In C. Gordon & K. J. Gergen (Eds.), *The self in social interaction.* New York: Wiley, 1968. Pp. 445-461.

Ring, K. Some determinants of interpersonal attraction in hierarchical relationships: A motivational analysis. *Journal of Personality*, 1964, **32**, 651-665.

Rosenman, S. The paradox of guilt in disaster victim populations. *Psychiatric Quarterly Supplement*, 1956, **30**, 181-221.

Rosenthal, R. *Experimenter effects in behavioral research.* New York: Macmillan, 1966.

Rothaus, P., & Worchel, P. The inhibition of aggression under non-arbitrary frustration. *Journal of Personality*, 1960, **28**, 108-117.

Rotter, J. B. *Social learning and clinical psychology.* Englewood Cliffs, N. J.: Prentice-Hall, 1954.

Rotter, J. B. Generalized expectancies for internal *versus* external control of reinforcements. *Psychological Monographs*, 1966, **80** (Whole No. 609), 1-28.

Sarbin, R. R., & Chun, K. T. A confirmation of the choice of response hypothesis in perceptual defense measurement. Paper read at the meeting of the Western Psychological Association, Portland, Oregon, 1964.

Schopler, J. Social power, In L. Berkiwotz (Ed.), *Advances in experimental social psychology.* Vol. 2. New York: Academic Press, 1965. Pp. 177-218.

Seeman, M. Powerlessness and knowledge: A comparative study of alienation and learning. *Sociometry*, 1967, **30**, 105-123.

Simmel, G. *The sociology of Georg Simmel.* (Transl. by K. H. Wolff) Glencoe, Ill.: Free Press, 1950.

Skinner, B. F. *Science and human behavior.* New York: Macmillan, 1953.

Skinner, B. F. *Verbal behavior.* New York: Appleton-Century-Crofts, 1957.

Steiner, I. D., & Darroch, R. K. Relationship between quality of counterattitudinal performance and attitude change. *Journal of Personality and Social Psychology*, 1969, **11**, 312-320.

Steiner, I. D., & Field, W. L. Role assignment and interpersonal influence. *Journal of Abnormal and Social Psychology*, 1960, **61**, 239-246.

Stern, G. G. Environments for learning. In N. Sanford (Ed.), *The American college.* New York: Wiley, 1962. Pp. 690-730.

Stogdill, R. M. *Individual behavior and group achievement.* New York: Oxford University Press, 1959.

Stoner, J. A. F. Risky and cautious shifts in group decisions: The influence of widely held values. Unpublished working paper of the Alfred P. Sloan School of Management, Massachusetts Institute of Technology, Cambridge, Mass., 1967.

Takashi, N. *We of Nagaski.* New York: Duell, Sloan, & Pearce, 1951.

Tesser, A., Gatewood, R., & Driver, M. Some determinants of gratitude. *Journal of Personality and Social Psychology*, 1968, **9**, 233-236.

Thibaut, J. W., & Kelley, H. H. *The social psychology of groups.* New York: Wiley, 1959.

Thibaut, J. W., & Riecken, H. W. Authoritarianism, status, and the communication of aggression. *Human Relations*, 1955, **8**, 95-120.

Vroom, V. H. *Some personality determinants of the effects of participation.* Englewood Cliffs, N. J.: Prentice-Hall, 1960.

Vroom, V. H. *Work and motivation.* New York: Wiley, 1964.

Wallach, M. A., & Kogan, N. Sex differences and judgment processes. *Journal of Personality*, 1959, **27**, 555-564.

Walster, E., & Festinger, L. The effectiveness of "overheard" persuasive communications. *Journal of Abnormal and Social Psychology*, 1962, **65**, 395-402.

Walster, E., Walster, B., Abrahams, D., & Brown, Z. The effect on liking of underrating and overrating another. *Journal of Experimental Social Psychology*, 1966, **2**, 70-84.

Weick, K. E. Reduction of cognitive dissonance through task enhancement and effort expenditure. *Journal of Abnormal and Social Psychology*, 1964, 68, 533-539.

Whitehead, A. N. *Adventures in ideas*. New York: Macmillan, 1933.

Wiggins, J. A., Dill, F., & Schwartz, R. D. On "status liability." *Sociometry*, 1965, 28, 197-209.

Wolfenstein, M. *Disaster: A psychological essay*. Glencoe, Ill.: Free Press, 1957.

Woodworth, R. S. *Experimental psychology*. New York: Holt, Rinehart & Winston, 1938.

Worell, L. The effect of goal value upon expectancy. *Journal of Abnormal Social Psychology*, 1956, 53, 48-53.

Yaryan, R. & Festinger, L. Preparatory action and the belief in the probable occurrence of future events. *Journal of Abnormal Social Psychology*, 1961, 63, 603-606.

EXPERIMENTAL STUDIES
OF FAMILIES[1]

Nancy E. Waxler and
Elliot G. Mishler
HARVARD MEDICAL SCHOOL
AND
THE MASSACHUSETTS MENTAL HEALTH
CENTER

[1]This work was partially supported by the National Science Foundation, grant #1225, and the National Institute of Mental Health Research Scientist program, award #K2-38,842.

I. Introduction: Methodologies and the Need for Complex Models

There has been growing interest during the past twenty years in the application of experimental methods for investigating small groups to the study of families. A variety of theoretical perspectives are included in these studies and the problems dealt with range from evaluating the effectiveness of family therapy to testing hypotheses derived from general sociological and social psychological theory. It seems useful at this point to review these studies and to compare them with those from the more traditional body of experimental studies of *ad hoc* groups.

In the course of making these comparisons we will demonstrate the ways in which the experimental method strengthens the study of families. In some instances an extension of experimental methods to families opens up new substantive areas of family study. In others, experimental investigation serves to clarify both family and group process theories. Finally, the application of experimental methods to families requires that attention be paid to assumptions about structure and process that have in the past remained unexamined and untested. Each of these issues will be examined through a selective review of the experimental literature.

Experiments with *ad hoc* groups are reported as far back as the early 1900's. In these early studies the major concern was with the conditions under which high productivity could be reached (e.g., see Gates, 1924). In the 1930's, experimental work expanded both in size and in scope, and some researchers became interested in natural groups and particularly in groups of children (Beaver, 1932; Greenberg, 1932). However, it was not until the period after World War II that parent-child and husband-wife pairs were conceived of as a type of small group and were subjected to experimental investigation using methods already available (Bishop, 1951; Strodtbeck, 1951). Since that time, experiments using family members as subjects have multiplied, and both method and theory have become more sophisticated.

Family experimentation in the short period since the early 1950's seems to have recapitulated the history of small group studies. Historical trends are similar, with family studies showing a lag perhaps ten years behind issues that are the foci of other small group studies. A brief outline of historical trends in family experimentation will provide an overview of the major issues in family research at the present time.

A. Trends in Family Research

The first apparent trend reflects a historical change in much small group experimentation. There has been a shift from theories and studies centered on dyadic relationships to those in which family structure is central. The early dyadic approach examined ways in which one family member interacted with another (usually the mother and the child, as represented by Bishop, 1951); if there were any interest in the family as a whole, it was assumed that the family consisted of summed dyadic relations. Questions that followed logically from this perspective had to do with the quality of interaction, under specified conditions, between each pair of family members. Recent family studies have shifted from theoretical focus on the individual toward concern with the structure of the family group using sociological concepts such as family role, power structure, norms, and sanctions as guiding concepts. In fact, at present, not only are aspects of family structure measured but they are also experimentally manipulated and used as major independent variables.

A second change in family experimental work — a methodological one — also follows historical developments in small group studies. The first family experiments relied on observation of family interaction, without experimental intervention. Thus, in Kenkel's studies of married couples' discussions (Kenkel, 1957), the experimenter intervened only in the sense that a discussion task and an observer were imposed. Recent studies involve some degree of experimental intervention in natural family groups. For example, families have been asked to communicate in highly structured ways such as transmitting written messages and using abstract symbols (Reiss, 1967), experimenters have trained parents to play specified roles with their own children (Patterson, 1965) and artificial "families" have been constructed in order to measure effects of certain structural patterns (Leik, 1963).

These changes in theoretical focus and experimental method are directly related to the third historical development. Early family experiments measured only relatively undifferentiated qualities of the family's behavior while recent studies test precisely defined hypotheses derived from abstract theory. The earlier approach, in which the "whole family" was investigated, is currently represented largely by the group of researchers interested in family therapy and problems of pathology who argue that a method that abstracts one aspect of family structure from the family system is useless in understanding real families (see Framo, 1965, for this point of view.) However, for other investigators, theoretical questions have moved from the global (for example, Does the interaction of parents affect the personality development of the child?) to the specific (How is the distribution of power between the parents related to the child's choice of an object of imitation?). With increased experience with experimental intervention, this latter specific hypothesis is open to clear experimental test by creating artificial families with a variety of "parental" power structures and examining the child's behavior (Bandura, Ross, & Ross, 1963). The recent trend is, therefore, toward a series of well-controlled experiments each designed to shed light on one specific aspect of family structure or process and each related to a broader theory of families or groups.

While recent developments in the area of family experimentation have tended toward concern with family structure, toward the testing of explicit hypotheses related to a theory, and the introduction of experimental interventions and manipulations, the content of these experimental studies is relatively limited. A large proportion of family experiments focuses on the family groups as the socialization agent for the child; there is much less interest in the economic or religious functions of the family or even in the husband-wife role relations. The explanation of relationships between variables is usually in terms of how a particular kind of family may have produced a child with a certain characteristic. Within the set of studies that focus on the family as a socialization agent are a large number of experiments concerned with the part a family may have had in the development of a deviant child, for example, a delinquent child, one with schizophrenia, or with some other "maladjustment."

Other questions asked by family experimenters are less directly related to the general concern with socialization. Some studies have focused, at a rather descriptive level, on relationships between dimensions of family structure. They attempt to provide concrete descriptive material about how families are organized rather than data on some "outcome" of the family's interaction. For example, Kenkel's studies on role patterns are concerned with such things as whether the high power member is also the expressive member in most family groups (Kenkel, 1957.)

Some attention has also been given to questions about relationships between the family's social and cultural context and its internal structure. Most family experimenters control for these context variables by sampling families with homogeneous backgrounds. The few that have measured the influence of cultural context on family structure and organization have shown clearly the enormous effects of such variables as ethnicity, religion, social class, or race.

A final question asked by family experimenters has to do with family process, that is with the changing patterns of interaction within the family that may occur as a result of the changing family situation. While there are relatively few experiments of this type, the ones that predominate examine changes in interaction occurring over a short period of time—perhaps the experimental hour. Only a few experimenters

have been concerned with changes in family processes that may be related to the full life history of the family.

B. The Concept of "Family Structure"

Through these questions runs a common concern with the structure
of the family. Basic to the concept of "family structure" is the idea that
the family group is an organized system in which there are two or more
status levels, roles are differentiated, and norms or internalized rules for
behavior have developed about who may take each status position and
what kind of role behavior is appropriate. The organization or structure
of the family is maintained not only through adherence to the norms but
also because family members believe that it is appropriate and right to
apply certain sanctions to members who deviate from the norms.

The idea of family structure and the concepts of status, role, norm,
and sanction will be used to organize our discussion of issues in family
and small group experimentation. First, we will examine studies in
which family structure is the dependent variable, explained by the social
and cultural background of family members. It is here that individual
personality characteristics or cultural context of the family are used to
predict the internal organization of the group. Second, we will look at
experiments in which one dimension of structure (role, status, norm) is
the independent variable that predicts to another dimension of structure,
or to the behavior or development of the child. Most family and small
group experimentation falls within this general area. Finally, we will
look at experiments in which family structure is less central and there is
greater concern for explaining process and change.

These three general issues — background, structure, and change —
serve an organizing function for our discussion of family experiments. In
many instances we have imposed the concepts of family structure upon
a study that uses another conceptual framework; we do not intend that
the problem and theory original to the study should be ignored. Instead,
the ideas about family structure are used only to permit comparisons
between experiments that, on the surface, appear to be relatively dissimilar yet at a more abstract level attack the same general problem.

II. Personality and Cultural Background: Relationships to Family Structure

No new group is compelled to negotiate every detail of its own organization. Instead members bring to the group certain conceptions
about how a group should or could be organized, certain experiences in
role-taking, and certain understandings of the behavior of other group

members. These expectations and experiences form the basis upon which the new group is built. For example, past experience may predispose a member to feel comfortable in a particular role or to value one form of decision making over another. An individual's personality needs may also push him to behave in a specified way or to perceive others idiosyncratically. Thus, the structure that develops in a new group is to some extent related to or a result of the cultural background and personalities of individual members.

Is the same true for families? Family theories and more general sociological theories predict that it is. Personalities of parents and the subcultural context of the family are both central to theoretical formulations of family structure and particularly to theories about the socialization of the child. These theories have been extensively investigated using nonexperimental techniques, for example, self-report questionnaires, interviews of children or parents, or psychological tests. Yet, as we will see in our examination of the experimental family literature, the nature of the effects of personality and cultural context on structure remains largely an assumption rather than an empirical fact. The same conclusion holds for most of the experimental studies of *ad hoc* groups. It is assumed that personality and cultural background explain many aspects of group structure even though there are relatively few experiments designed to investigate this issue.

A. Personality and Family Organization

Small group experiments provide some evidence that personalities of group members are predictive of their roles, or that certain combinations of individual personalities are predictive of certain group structures or outcomes. For example, Schutz (1958) has shown that a group whose members all have similar levels of need for interpersonal affection (either a need to give and receive a high level of affection or a need to give and receive a low level of affection) has a high rate of productivity in contrast to a group in which the need for affection is mixed. Haythorn, Couch, Haefner, Langham, and Carter (1956) demonstrated that groups in which all members have authoritarian personalities develop cultures different from those composed of equalitarian personalities. These experiments and the few others that examine personality as an independent variable, suggest personality dimensions that are closely related to aspects of group structure and outcome.

Theories of the family and socialization also provide guide lines for experimental investigation of the relationship between personality and family organization. Several socialization theories that have developed out of psychoanalytic theory rest on the assumption that the quality of parental personalities is vital to the development of the child's identity. While these theories vary in their specification of the mechanisms of this relationship, all claim that the personality of the parents is significant for the child's development. Parental personality factors are also predicted to be related through specific child training practices to the development of the child's morality, to the ways in which the child expresses aggression, and so forth (see Hoffman & Hoffman, 1964, for reviews of this material). Other theoretical perspectives on the family take personality into account as well; for example, Winch (1958) explains mate selection and, further, marital success, by using personality variables.

1.   The Importance of Intervening Behaviors

With personality of parents as a major theoretical focus, one might expect that this variable would have been extensively examined experimentally. This is not true. Instead, empirical work has largely been in the form of interviews, questionnaires, or tests of parents that are then statistically correlated with some quality of the child. Seldom has the behavior of parent with child been observed directly. Therefore, most conclusions from empirical studies about the relationship between parental personality and child development have assumed, as Hoffman (1960) points out, "that it is sufficient to obtain parent data at the personality level since this underlies overt behavior" [p. 140]. The assumption that personality measures are identical to behavioral measures is often not supported, however, when parent-child interaction is examined empirically. For example, Hoffman predicted that a parent with an authoritarian personality would be most likely to use "unqualified power assertions" in disciplining his child and that this form of discipline would be related to certain behavior of the child. Yet he showed (in a working class sample) that it is not the personality of the mother (measured by the F scale) but, instead, the personality of the father that predicts the mother's reported behavior toward her child. In order to explain this relationship between "personality of father" and "behavior of mother toward child" one must postulate certain behavior relationships between the parents, thus adding an intervening explanation that can be tested by direct observation and measurement. The Hoffman findings show clearly the necessity of examining family interaction empirically in order to specify the relationship between personality and child development or other "outcome" variables.

Direct observation and measurement of family behavior alone is not the solution to this problem. Techniques of data analysis must also be carefully selected in order for observations of parental behavior to be made relevant to the question about personality. Hoffman shows that direct correlations between parental personality and child development leave out the complexities of the intervening behavioral process. In order to understand this process, even after the behavior is actually observed, one must examine the empirical relationships between all three sets of variables: personality, family behavior, and outcome. Instead, many family experimenters follow the analytic model used by nonexperimental investigators, that is, they relate all variables (personality or behavior), taken one at a time, to outcome. Stabenau, Tupin, Werner, and Pollin (1965) in their examination of interaction in families having schizophrenic, delinquent or normal children, serve as an example of this methodological problem. Individual personality measures were obtained for each family member using a variety of tests; also, families' discussions were recorded and coded. The analysis of data took the form of comparing the three types of families in average scores on personality tests or average behaviors in the interaction situation.[2] For example, the individual's ability to abstract was measured by the Object Sorting Test. Implicit in the theoretical approach is the hypothesis that unclear conceptualization on the part of parents may be related to the conceptualization difficulties found in schizophrenic patients. Stabenau shows that, indeed, the schizophrenic patients and their parents (along with the delinquent children and their parents) have significantly impaired ability to abstract. The questions raised by the Hoffman example may be raised here: Is impaired conceptualization evident in interaction between parent and child? Do the parents with the most impaired ability interact in a disorganized or fragmented (or "impaired") way with their children? and, if so, Are these children more impaired than others? or, Is there an even more complex relationship between parental impairment, parental interactions, and child qualities?

When an experimenter asks the questions dealing with the way in which personality is related to behavior, if Kenkel's (1961) findings are representative, he is likely to discover that the relationship is a complicated one. Kenkel observed married couples in their homes (no children were present) who were asked to discuss how to spend a gift of $300; interaction was classified with Interaction Process Analysis categories (Bales, 1951) and a measure of influence on the final decision made. A personality inventory developed by Brim was also administered individually to obtain measures of dominance, persistence, and self-confidence.

In contrast to the prediction that there is a high linear correlation

[2]Essentially, this technique of analysis makes the same assumptions as does the method of ecological correlation. It has the same pitfall as well. While mean scores of groups are compared, it is tempting and not legitimate to conclude that the correlation holds at the level of individuals as well (see Riley, 1963, for a discussion of this and related issues).

between personality and behavior, Kenkel found that this relationship depended on the sex of the family member. Husbands who had "dominant" personalities were indeed more influential in interaction with their wives than were the "submissive" husbands. However, wives with high "dominance" scores were less influential than wives who were "submissive" personalities. Of the latter wives, 80% were more influential than were their husbands while only 53% of the "dominant" personality wives were more influential than their husbands. Kenkel found the personality quality of "persistence" to be unrelated to behavior of either husband or wife while differences in level of self-confidence were related to behavior only for wives, with the self-confident woman being more influential than their husbands. Kenkel pointed out in his discussion the limitations of sample size and mode of analysis, particularly the fact that the effects of combined personality qualities of husbands and wives were not examined. Even with these limitations, however, his study provides one model for investigating "personality" as an independent variable and his findings provide evidence that concepts such as "role expectations" (in this instance, "sex role expectations"), "cultural values," or "interpersonal behavior" must be introduced in order to explain the relationship between personality and family structure or outcome.

The statistical interaction between personality, social expectations, and family role, exemplified by Kenkel's findings, raises a general question implicit in almost all experimental work on families. Which came first? Did the personality of the individual determine his role? Did his role alter his personality? Or was there a circular and constantly shifting relationship between the two? When families who have a long history of intimate interaction are the object of study this question is both serious and difficult to answer. However, there are a few experiments on *ad hoc* groups that provide models applicable to family groups.

Berkowitz's experiment is one of these (Berkowitz, 1956). He was concerned with the relative effect of personality and social role on a member's behavior, the same question that Kenkel's findings on families raises. The study design is such that personality and role are varied independently, so that the effects of each can be examined separately as well as in combination. Members, classified as either high or low on "ascendence," the personality variable, were placed either in central or peripheral role positions (determined by the number of people with whom it was possible to communicate). Dependent variables included the member's rate of communication, time taken to complete a task, amount of information transmitted, as well as post-meeting questions regarding satisfaction with the member's role. Berkowitz (1956) reports that, for the first group task, the personality variable is most important in determining behavior; members low in ascendence who find themselves in a central role behave passively, as their personality scores would suggest. However, by the third group task, demands of the central role seem to dominate and "low ascendence" personalities are "significantly more 'active' than the high ascendence subjects in the periphery" [p. 221]. Berkowitz shows, for *ad hoc* groups, that over a short period of time role effects come to predominate over personality effects, yet the effects of personality are not completely lost since, in peripheral positions, ascendent personalities continue to be more active communicators than those low in ascendence.

Berkowitz provides a model for investigating the relative effects of personality and other variables through manipulation of group membership. Naturally, this model is not directly applicable to real families because selection into roles has occurred in the past. However, since there is now evidence that it is possible for an experimenter to compose "artificial families," or groups having some of the abstract qualities of a family, this provides the opportunity to manipulate "parental personality" experimentally in order to test the effects of personality on parental roles and on child behavior.

As yet, no family experimenter has used this technique to examine the effects of parental personalities. However, following from the questions raised by Kenkel's findings and using the experimental group composition technique the relationship between "parental" personalities, "parental" behavior and "child" behavior might be examined. Let "expected family role" be indicated by the sex and age of the group member; let "personality" be indicated by a score for dominance on an individually administered personality test. Then compose four types of groups:

	Female Member	
	Dominant	Submissive
Dominant		
Male Member		
Submissive		

Place a child with each of these pairs of adults and measure the behavior of all three along relevant dimensions, e.g., influence, participation, expressiveness, imitation, and deviation. Following from one theoretical perspective, one might expect that the child will imitate (or "identify" with) the dominant "parent," without regard for his sex role. The socialization theories that include personality qualities as central dimensions might also be examined using the same experimental model. For example, Lidz and Fleck (1965) suggest that the degree to which an adult has resolved the Oedipal conflict is related to his ability to carry out the parental role. This quality of personality might be used as an independent variable for composition of "parental" pairs who are then required to interact with a child. Lidz and Fleck might predict "schizophrenic-like" behavior on the part of the child placed with the "conflicted" parents. The strength of these designs comes from control over the independent variables and the assumption that other important variables have been randomized; neither of these is possible when real families are used.

B. CULTURAL BACKGROUND AND FAMILY STRUCTURE

Everyone knows that families belonging to particular subcultures have qualities in common that set them off from families with other affiliations. While the "Jewish mother" or the "Irish father" or the "middle-class family" are stereotypes, the fact that such stereotypes have developed suggests that differences are real, if more complex, than indicated by these phrases. Our examination of studies of *ad hoc* groups and family groups will show how powerful subcultural membership is in predicting individual and group behavior.

While the mechanism through which personality affects family behavior is not clearly specified in most of the family theories, there is somewhat greater agreement on the way in which cultural background affects family structure. The intervening process is assumed to be one in which the member of the subculture (religious, ethnic, class) is socialized very early in his life to value certain family organizations, to expect that particular people will take particular roles, to learn that some behavior is right. These learned values lead him to interact in his own family and in other groups according to the subcultural expectations.

Experimental studies of *ad hoc* groups point to cultural background variables that are clearly related to group structure and they also suggest aspects of structure most likely to be influenced by culture. All of these experiments have similar designs; a cultural background variable (or two of them) is treated as the independent variable and the behavior of members, or the outcome of the group interaction is examined. Thus, Strodtbeck, in his series of jury studies, has shown that social class membership is a predictor of the role a member will take on a jury (Strodtbeck & Mann, 1956). For example, many more members of the highest occupational levels are elected jury foremen than would be expected by chance. This may be partially explained through the concept of "expectations" brought by members to the jury from earlier socialization experiences, specifically the expectation by lower class members that a higher class member will lead. Katz, Goldston, and Benjamin (1958) have demonstrated the differential effects of race on group structure, in this instance in groups composed of two whites and two Negros. Here the pattern of speech reflected a high-participation coalition between the white pair, with each of the Negro members talking more to white members than to each other. Again, expectations about role seem to be carried into new groups and the subcultural experience re-enacted. We would also expect that other subcultural affiliations such as religion might predict to the group behavior of a member. Milgram (1964) reported that Roman Catholics, assumed to value a dependent role, were more likely than members having other religious affiliations to be influenced by a group to carry out behavior that they did not personally value, in this case giving another person an electric shock.

If the subcultural expectations about group structure and roles are originally learned within the family then one would expect even clearer differences between family groups of differing subcultural background. Yet, there has been relatively little interest in measuring the effects of these differences; instead, many family experimenters control or match on these variables, some ignore the issue entirely.

We know from nonexperimental research on families that subcultural membership is related to socialization practices, to the nature of parental roles, to values about the child's future, to ways children are expected to behave (see N. W. Bell & Vogel, 1960). Experimental examination of these families provides the additional opportunity to show if and how verbally stated values are actually carried out in interaction in the family. When the cultural affiliation variable has been experimentally examined, its power to predict structural and interactional differences is apparent. The prototype of this approach is Strodtbeck's study of husband-wife decision making in three cultures (Strodtbeck, 1951). Three sets of husband-wife pairs were selected to represent three subcultures differing in values about the role of men and women. As expected, Protestant-Texan couples showed relative equality in influencing the final decision on the revealed differences task; Navajo women, from a matriarchal society, took precedence over their husbands; Mormon men, from a subculture having written prescriptions about male dominance, were more powerful than were their wives. While the Strodtbeck experiment provides a model, both in design and task, the data were not analyzed so as to show the internal structural patterns; for example, we are not told how a Navajo wife interacted with her husband in order to insure her influence. This limitation was overcome in a related experiment (Strodtbeck, 1958) on Jewish and Italian family triads in which adolescent sons were included in the decision making, and the relationships between internal family structure and the sons' need for achievement were of major importance. Family power relationships, indicated by a "who won the decision" measure, were related to cultural expectations; the Italian father was more powerful than both wife and son while the Jewish parents were equally powerful and more powerful than their son. But, in contrast to predictions, there were no differences between Italian and Jewish families in "expressive" role taking (nor on any of the other measures derived from Interaction Process Analysis). This latter finding provides concrete evidence that the observation of family behavior is important in understanding how cultural values are implemented; support for the stereotype of the "smothering" Jewish mother is clearly not evident in the data.

Since the early Strodtbeck work, other experimenters have examined ethnic/religious variation in family interaction. Haley's experiment is particularly interesting, not only because it looks at Japanese-American families but also because the dependent variable measures depart from the usual "who influences whom," "who speaks to whom," or "who is instrumental" (Haley, 1967b). Instead, the only data collected are the sequence of speakers in the experimental session; the only question asked is the following: Does the sequence of speakers deviate from a random one? While we will be concerned in a later section with this measure of "family process" the focus here is on ethnic family patterns. Haley found that the Japanese-American families deviated more from a random sequence than did American families examined in an earlier study (Haley, 1964, 1967a). This suggests somewhat greater rigidity or formality in the Japanese-American family, perhaps consistent with verbally stated values about how family members should behave. However, no pair of family members followed each other more often than other possible pairs. This lack of differences is important since some students of the Japanese family might have predicted a low rate of father-child interactions, consistent with the value on social distance between the two.

Straus' family experiment exemplifies a more complex experimental design in which two social classes are examined within each of three cultural groups: Indian families, Puerto Rican families, and American families (M. A. Straus, 1968). The extent to which families differ across cultures is fully apparent in Straus' reports that the experimental task originally planned was "... too strange and difficult for the [Indian] families . . ." [M. A. Straus, 1968, p. 421]. This task, a puzzle in the form of a game in which family members were asked to discover the rules of the game by playing it, had to be greatly simplified for use with both middle- and working-class Indian families. Here cultural differences between families are so great that a task requiring communication and the sharing of cognitive skills is apparently not within the range of experience or mode of organization of the Indian family. Social class differences, however, are strong and consistent across cultures. Middle-class families are more able to solve the problem and the author traces this to greater communication among members of these families than among working-class family members. While cultural and class differences are evident in the Straus experiment, no data are presented on internal family structure, for example, on communication patterns between husband and wife or parent and child within the middle-class families or on the quality of these communications.

One experiment that does examine the internal family structure in order to understand subcultural differences was carried out in Hong Kong by Liu (1966). He compared local Chinese families with those that had recently emigrated from the Chinese mainland. The effects of the acculturation process are shown in his findings that in the refugee family the father has a powerful position which is supported by deference rather than agreement by his son. The local families presented a set of relationships similar to those expected in Western families; the father is most powerful, yet he is also high on warmth; the family consensus also appears to be based on true agreement rather than simply on respect.

These investigations of the effects of cultural background have indicated, first, the importance that subcultural membership has for family structure. There are clearly different power relationships, rates of communication, and agreement patterns that depend on cultural expectations. Second, the experimental method gives the investigator the opportunity to examine specific ways in which cultural expectations are actually carried out in family members' behavior. It is evident from several of the studies cited that there is no clear positive correlation between cultural expectations about family structure and the family structure indicated by interaction measures, just as there is no clear correlation between personality of parents and the parents' behavior.

C. SUMMARY

Both personality and cultural background have been examined here as causal variables that are assumed to predict to aspects of family structure and outcome for the child. There is, however, relatively little experimental evidence supporting this assumption, particularly in the personality area. When there is experimental evidence, that is, when the family's behavior or modes of interaction are measured along with personality/culture variables and other dependent variables, two conclusions may be drawn. First, the theoretical model of the family must be stated in a much more complex form than most family investigators originally stated it. Neither personality nor cultural background of the parents fully explains empirical differences in family structure; instead, the intervening behavioral process must also be accounted for and theory revised so as to represent the statistical interactions between personality/background, behavior, and outcome variables.

Secondly, as soon as an investigator opens up the question of relationships between background and family structure by examining how family members interact with each other, the assumption of causality is also open to question. When families are observed in interaction in order to link parental personality to child's behavior through parental behavior-with-child, questions about which came first, and the relative effects of each, become important. For this reason an experimental design in which the causal variable is controlled by the experimenter becomes useful. Establishing synthetic or artificial family groups by selecting members to represent the major control variables makes the time order of variable effects clear and allows for a more precise statement of the relative importance of these background variables for family structure.

III. Aspects of Family Structure

Most family experimenters have been concerned, either explicitly or implicitly, with the internal structure of the family. "Structure" here refers to the organization of the family group, that is to the different statuses and roles in the family and to the set of norms that govern this organization. We will use these three general structural concepts — status, role, and norm — to organize the large body of experimental work that falls in this area.

One source of variation in these experiments is whether the structural dimension is taken as the independent or dependent variable. In some studies, one aspect of family structure is the independent variable that is experimentally manipulated and then related to a "family outcome" measure such as the child's identification with his parents (Bandura et al., 1963; Hetherington & Frankie, 1967). In other studies, one aspect of family structure is treated as the independent variable and another aspect as the dependent variable; for example, the organization of family statuses may be experimentally controlled and related to family role-taking (Scott, 1962). In the latter approach the experimental goal is to understand the interrelationships between dimensions of family structure at one point in time. In a third type of experiment, the structural variable is the dependent variable and a quality of the child is controlled, thus treating this quality in the experiment as the independent variable (Lennard, Beaulieu, & Embrey, 1965). We will be concerned in this section only with studies that use a structural dimension as an independent variable, and will discuss the third approach in a later section on outcome studies.

A. FAMILY STATUS STRUCTURE

A central proposition in sociological theories about group structure is that all groups differentiate into two or more status levels, each status having different prestige and responsibilities (Bales, 1951), just as a *sine qua non* of family theory is the assumption of status differentiation based on generation.

A status in a group, or in a family, is a position that is relatively higher or lower than other positions in terms of its prestige, rewards, and responsibilities. In contrast to the hierarchical conception of family status, the concept of "role" will be defined here in terms of the quality of behavior expected of the role player. In a family one would expect several roles to be associated with one status level; theoretically both parents, for example, take a high status position *vis-a-vis* their children yet the role behavior expected of each is quite different in quality.

A large number of experiments on *ad hoc* groups have investigated the division of labor and status differentiation. Some have looked at the process through which status differentiation takes place; for example, Hopkins (1964) showed that initial high participation rate is related to high status which, in turn, is associated with high power role-taking. It is important to note that these are not one-to-one relationships, and particularly that some high status members are not powerful. In studies in which status has been experimentally controlled, the status indicators most often used are age, sex, and task ability. J. C. Moore (1968) manipulated status experimentally leading some subjects to believe that their subject-partner was from a higher (or lower) status school than they themselves came from. It was assumed that status outside the group would generalize to status inside the group, and that this would affect the power roles (in this case, influence) inside the group. Findings supported these predictions even in the case of groups in which status "differentiation has no obvious or direct bearing on the task confronting the group" [J. C. Moore, 1968, p. 47]. Just as in the Hopkins' study, the high status member is likely to become the most influential role player.

1. Status Differences as the Independent Variable

There are relatively few experimental studies of families in which status differences are treated as the independent variable, yet family theories place great importance on the differentiation of statuses. Especially for researchers concerned with socialization, child development, and clinical problems of children, the status structure of the family is a central theoretical dimension. Families that deviate from the expected pattern (in which parents have high status and children low status) are predicted to socialize their children in deviant ways and to provide inadequate models for identification (Lidz, Fleck, & Cornelison, 1965; Wynne & Singer, 1963). These theories are a rich source of hypotheses about the effects of family statuses on role-taking and child development, yet these hypotheses remain largely unexamined by experimental methods.

One reason for the dearth of experimental studies investigating family status structure as the independent variable is the difficulty in selecting an indicator of status that is both theoretically meaningful and measurable. The variable selected must not be confounded with "role"; that is, it must stand for a family member's prestige relative to other members, rather than for a member's typical or expected behavior. Furthermore, in order to select families on the basis of differences in status structure, the indicator must be a quality that is relatively easily observable or measurable from outside the family. Because of these problems of selection and measurement, the indicators of status most often used to investigate effects of status structure on other dependent variables such as role-taking are the age and/or generational structure of the family.[3] An alternative solution to the selection and measurement problem is the creation of artificial families, experimentally composed on the basis of status structure.

Scott's experiment investigating the effects of different status structures on interaction in natural family groups exemplifies the first alternative (Scott, 1962). She selected families on the basis of generational patterns; three-person families (husband, wife, and one elderly parent), four-person families (parents, one grandparent, and one adolescent child) and five-person families (parents, grandparent, and two children) and

---

[3]However a two-stage study may be used in which the first stage is deisgned to obtain the measure of status; see Hetherington (1965), for an example of this approach.

examined power roles within each type of family. While family theories such as Parsons' (1955) would predict that status is positively related to power role, Scott shows that this relationship is a much more complicated one that is dependent on the specific status structure present in the family.

For example, only in the four-person family does the husband have the most powerful role (measured by rates of initiation); in the three-person family it is the wife who is most powerful and in the five-person family it is the oldest child. Furthermore, Scott's findings are not consistent with predictions and findings from studies of *ad hoc* groups that show age (as an indicator of status) to be a predictor of power.[4] In fact, here the grandparents are consistently powerless, whether measurement is based upon rate of interaction, rate of support, or both.

Not only did Scott examine the relationship between the status structure and individual power roles but she also looked at the patterning of power roles in each type of family group following the model provided by Mills (1953). Mills showed that the "solidary" coalition pattern (in which a pair of numbers gives each other high rates of support and there is mutual rejection between the isolate and the pair) is most stable and perhaps is more basic in *ad hoc* groups. Scott found in the three-person family that the "solidary" two-against-one pattern is common, with one important difference. The isolate is given support at a greater rate than is the isolate in Mills' *ad hoc* groups. This may be a major difference between families and *ad hoc* groups that have no history and little future. While a family member may be of low status, have little power, and take no part in decision making, he may still receive the emotional support necessary to maintain him as a member.

Mills suggests that over time, particularly in families, the power structure will tend toward the solidary or conflicting patterns; Scott shows that in approximately one-fourth of the families examined this prediction is not upheld. Furthermore, types of status structure were correlated with the power role patterns of the family. The contending or dominating power patterns are more likely to be found in large families having more adolescent children. One might hypothesize that with changes in status structures (here, the addition of a third generation of nearly adult members) not only does the power distribution shift but the power structure itself changes.

Although family theory has been relatively unspecific about the relationship between status and role patterns, usually focusing on an ideal-

---

[4]Ziller and Exline (1958) showed that age is directly related to influence, but only in groups of men.

type four-person family, it is clear from this examination of natural family groups that theory must be specified in order to account for other types of family organization. Further, questions are raised about how relationships in the family are developed and maintained in these non-typical families. If in three-person families, solidary coalitions between two members against the third exist yet the third member stays in the family, what does the powerful coalition do to maintain its position without alienating the third member? If adolescent children in some families are members of the powerful coalition what influence strategies do they use, especially in the face of normative support for powerful parental roles?

2. Status in Synthetic Families

The use of natural family groups, exemplified by Scott's study, has inherent limitations. The investigator cannot be assured of the time order of the variables and thus cannot draw conclusions about causal relationships. In these experiments we know nothing of the way in which each of these patterns developed, only that some seem to occur together. The second type of experiment is designed to solve this problem; here the status structure of a family is varied experimentally by creating types of artificial families and assuming or assuring that all other differences between families are random.

The experiment carried out by Bandura *et al.* (1963) is an excellent example of this approach. While the problem was set within the framework of theories of identity development, the independent variable may be restated in group structure terms as "family status." Two types of artificial family were constructed, one in which the child was clearly of low status (not only was he the youngest, but he received few rewards from the "parents") and the other in which the child was of mixed status (he was youngest, but he received more rewards from the high status "parent" than did the other "parent"). The adult male and female who played the "parent" roles were rotated across the high and low status positions. Bandura's question was this: With whom does the child identify, the parent who gives rewards or the one who receives, and does identification depend on the sex of the parent? The dependent variable measures centered on the degree to which the child imitated certain standard behaviors of each of the "parents." In general, findings show that the child imitates the high status "parent," regardless of who receives the rewards. Furthermore, cross-sex imitation occurs, particularly for girls, who are likely to imitate the male adult if he is the high status "parent." Bandura points to the possible effect of the distribution of power between parents, particularly to the effect of reversed parental roles, on the child's identity development.

It is clear that the use of "artificial families" in experimental situations has definite advantages for the study of family structure. Bandura's experiment allows us to examine certain family organizations that are important to family theory yet difficult to sample. We know from clinical evidence that some families have status structures quite deviant from the expected patterns but since these differences are not indicated by variables that can easily be seen from outside the family it is difficult to sample them. Second, the use of artificial families not only allows us to be clear about the direction of the effects of these variables, but also about the process through which the effect occurs. In natural families the effect occurred in the past; in artificial families the effect occurs in the experimental room and can be observed and measured. Bandura provides an interesting example of this latter advantage. While most of the children imitated the high status adult, a few did not; examination of these deviant cases showed that several children superimposed a cultural expectation about adult males on the situation and their imitative behavior was a response to this cultural expectation in combination with the experimental variable. These children reported that the low status male was really powerful anyway, reasoning that "He's the man and it's all his because he's a daddy. Mommy never really has things belong to her" [Bandura, *et al.*, 1963, p. 533].

3. *Real and Synthetic Families*

The fact that similar issues of status have been examined in similar ways (using age and sometimes sex as status indicators) in both *ad hoc* groups and families has led to questions about the differences between groups and families and has guided some investigators to select this question as the central one for empirical study. Underlying specific questions about the relationship between status structure and other variables in families and other groups is the more general question: Are family groups and *ad hoc* groups different from each other only along the dimension of "length of group history" or are there basic structural differences between them that lead, perhaps, to contradictory hypotheses and to theories based on distinctly different parameters?

Leik's (1963) experiment compares real families having known status structure with synthetic families having the same status structure; age and sex of the participants are the indicators of status. (A third set of groups is homogeneous with regard to both age and sex). Findings suggest that status is predictive of instrumental and expressive role playing in both types of groups but that predictions vary depending on whether the group is a real family or an artificially constructed family having the same status structure (i.e., a group composed of a father, mother, and daughter unrelated to each other). For example, the high status female member plays a different role in the two groups. With an artificial family she takes the emotional role and avoids the instrumental role; with strangers she behaves in the way that the common culture expects a "mother" to behave. But with her own family her role changes significantly; here she takes on much more of the task activity, equal to that of her husband, but at the same time has a high rate of emotional activity. Her daughter is low on task activity within her own family. Thus, in the artificial families it is sex that is most important in predicting role playing; in the real families it is age.

Bodin's (1965) experiment is similar in design and supports Leik's findings. Real and synthetic families do not differ in modes of accommodation to solve a game problem; each type of "family" group used more coalitions and forms of compromise than did *ad hoc* groups composed of equal status members. However, mothers in the real family situations compromised significantly less than did "mothers" in artificially constructed families. Again, there is a suggestion that adult women are likely to take a more powerful or instrumental role in their own families than in *ad hoc* groups. Ryder's (1968) findings on husband-wife dyads suggest, in general, that there are few differences in role playing between real and artificially constructed dyads. "The differences between married and split dyads seem much better described by noting that *S*s treat strangers more gently and generally more nicely than they do their spouses" [Ryder, 1968, p. 237]. Since no child was present in these latter groups, it is not possible to test the relative effects of sex and age on role playing.

An interpretative thread seems to run through the empirical studies comparing real with synthetic family groups. Relationships between status and role playing may be understood in the two groups by introducing ideas of "cultural expectations," "expected behavior with strangers," and other explanations that rest on the fact that real and artificial families differ in length of acquaintance. It is assumed that individuals in a new group bring with them a set of norms for group behavior that are initially used to organize interaction. One such norm might be the following: Women are supposed to be "followers" and to play expressive roles. Over time these norms are modified and perhaps altered on the basis of experience within the group. For example, the modified norm might be: High status women have an equal part, with men, in the group decision. If one were to compare artificial families having a long history (for example, using work groups or therapy groups with the status structure of families) with real families, then, following the above argument, the artificial, long-term families and the real families should not differ in role or norm patterns. The conclusion that seems to underlie explanations of the findings in these comparative studies is that the structure of family groups and *ad hoc* groups may both be explained by the same theory. Only the dimension of "time" need be included to predict the family *vs.* group differences.

B. FAMILY ROLES

A central concern, for both small group and family theorists, is with the development and differentiation of roles. A member role is the set of behaviors and relationships that the group and the individual taking the role expect the role player to carry out. A person taking the role of "mother," for example, is expected to have both a controlling and a warm relationship with small children in the family, and she has internalized this expectation. A committee chairman is expected to take charge and a committee member to follow his lead. Within any prestige or status level there may be a number of roles, each with specific expected relationships.

While theorists have predicted that role structure of the family is related to other dimensions such as the child's identity development, experimental work on family roles seems not to have kept pace with theoretical formulations. Instead the major empirical question has been, what is the nature of the role relationships within the family, and particularly between the parental pair? Therefore, a major portion of this section will be devoted to experimental studies in which family roles are the dependent variable. Only recently have the parameters of family role structure become clear enough that role could be introduced experimentally as an independent variable and its effects examined. At the end of the section, two experiments using role as the control variable will be presented as models for further work.

1. Parsons and Bales Theories of Role Development

The major theories of role development in *ad hoc* groups and in families, those of Bales (1951) and Parsons and Bales (1955) are obviously closely related. However, there seems to be at least one major theoretical difference that would lead to differing predictions for role development in the two types of groups. Bales links the group's differentiation into instrumental and expressive roles to the two systems problems imposed on all groups: (1) the requirement that groups adapt to externally imposed tasks and at the same time (2) maintain the group as a group or deal with the integrative needs of the members. The inherent need to handle both problems leads to differentiation of roles into two speci.ilties, task and emotional, that are assumed to be "complementary and supporting in the long run but in the short run tend in some degree to conflict with each other in a way that makes it difficult for the same man to be top specialist on both" [Parsons and Bales, 1955, p. 298]. In its most general sense, then, the theory predicts that roles will differentiate into expressive or instrumental specialties and that these two special roles will not be played by the same individual.

Parsons' theory of family role structure begins with the same assumptions as Bales' theory of group development (Parsons and Bales, 1955). Because the family as a system must deal with both adaptive (economic, political, and other extrafamily) relationships and integrative (internal) family relationships, presumably it must develop a division of labor in which instrumental and expressive roles become specialized. For the same reasons as in all groups, these special roles cannot be taken by the same individual. However, the Parsonian theory of the family adds a further qualification. Family roles are allocated according to sex, with the father taking the instrumental role and the mother the expressive role. This addition is necessary because Parsons assumes that the major function of the family is to socialize the child, and, following psychoanalytic theory, the socialization process rests on the identification of the child with the same-sex parent. Thus, if parental roles are not clearly differentiated, and further, if they are not clearly related to the sex of the parent, the child's identity will be impaired. Therefore, the theory predicts that family roles differentiate into instrumental and expressive specialties, that one individual cannot take both roles, and that the delegation of roles is based on sex.

2. Research Findings Bearing on the Theories

These theories of role development in families and groups have provided guide lines for research over a relatively long period of time. Yet there are few instances in which the theories, as they stand, are supported empirically. Until relatively recently, Slater's test of Bales' theory of role differentiation in *ad hoc* groups (Slater, 1955) stood as its major empirical support. In his groups there was clear evidence that members perceived and expected someone to be a task leader and another member to be an emotional specialist. However, as Slater points out in a later publication (Slater, 1961), the correlation between instrumental and expressive role activity was positive rather than negative as the theory would predict. This finding suggests that the major hypothesis must be qualified. It is even more difficult to find support from experimental studies of families for the Parsonian theory of family role differentiation. There are no experimental studies in which the theory is confirmed in an unqualified way.

Instead, empirical evidence from *ad hoc* group experiments indicates that the proposition that instrumental and expressive roles are taken by separate members must be modified. Burke (1968) points to group size, task orientation, legitimacy of the leader, and acceptability of the task behavior as necessary qualifications. Turk (1961) has shown that one member could be both the task leader as well as the best liked person in instances in which the task of the group is highly valued by the whole group. In groups of student nurses doing work together that they felt to be interesting and worthwhile the differentiation between instrumental and expressive leadership did not occur, perhaps because the tension raised by the task leader's instrumental activity was not so great that it could not be allayed by her own expressive acts. Burke's (1968) experiment, methodologically much more rigorous, supports the Turk findings. Role differentiation is mediated by the group members' acceptance of the "task ethic." *In groups where the task is not accepted, the members' instrumental activities are negatively correlated with the liking they receive. There is no task-liking correlation in the groups accepting the task; in these latter groups, instrumental and expressive role playing may be carried out by the same person.*

Several family experiments have indicated also that the separation between instrumental and expressive role taking, while theoretically expected, occurs only under special conditions. Kenkel (1957) in one of his series of experiments on husband-wife decision making measured "influence" (by whose idea was finally adopted by the couple), "task acts" (by Interaction Process Analysis categories), and "expressiveness" (in the same way). Husbands did give the higher proportion of task acts and wives performed most of the social emotional activity; however, the wives who were most expressive were also most influential and the least expressive wives were least influential. This latter finding suggests that one must qualify the prediction that "expressiveness" and "power over decisions" do not occur in the wife role. Leik's findings, already reported (Leik, 1963), also suggest qualifications of the theory. In real families both parents are high on task activity, and the mother and daughter are both specialists in emotional acts. Mothers therefore specialize in both task and emotional areas.

If we could stop with the Kenkel and Leik findings we might assume that the family theory should be qualified so as to account for the extension of the mother role into both instrumental and expressive areas, perhaps to be explained by the decreasing importance of the father in socialization. However, experimental findings reported by M. A. Straus (1967) add further complications. Family triads were asked to work on the task previously used in Straus' cross-cultural study. Parental power was measured by counting directive acts to other members (e.g., "Shoot the ball now") and expressiveness was measured by supportive encouraging statements. As expected, fathers were more directive of their children than were mothers; however, they were also much more supportive of children as well. But even more significant for the parental role-taking theory is the finding that "the husbands [were] predominant in both the expressive and instrumental role in the conjugal interaction sphere as well as in the parent-child sphere" [M. A. Straus, 1967, p. 18]. In the Straus study, therefore, it is the father whose role combines both major areas of role playing.

3. Role Differentiation Contingent on Situational Conditions

These experiments on *ad hoc* groups and families suggest that instrumental and expressive roles may not be inherently incompatible, and that, if there are temporary incompatibilities, groups and families develop methods for avoiding or resolving them. Freilich's discussion of the universal triad (Freilich, 1964) describes a number of situational factors which, if they are used to modify the role differentiation theories, may result in much more accurate descriptions of role playing in real families and other groups.

The prototype for the "situational" effect on role differentiation (described by Freilich, 1964) is the primitive family in which the parents' instrumental and expressive roles are played in different subsystems, thus serving to avoid the basic incompatibilities. For example, in a patrilineal family system, a father is an instrumental leader in relation to his own child but an expressive leader in relation to his nephew, allowing him to switch roles only when switching objects.

Such clearly defined situational rules do not seem to be available to families in modern society. However, the sex of the child may be one variable worth investigating in this regard. Nonexperimental literature suggests that the instrumental or expressive role chosen by the parent is dependent on the sex of the child with whom the parent interacts. Bronfenbrenner (1961) reports that in lower class families parents punish children of the same sex and indulge children of the opposite sex. O'-Rourke's (1963) experimental study, shows that fathers with female children are more expressive than mothers with female children. Since in the latter study, the parents of female children are not the same as those with male children, and since no parents were observed interacting with a male and a female child at the same time, we have little information of the process of role switching or what the child might do to elicit the switch.

The O'Rourke (1963) experiment points to a second "situational" variable that predicts the quality of role differentiation in the family. He compared a set of three-person families observed in an experimental laboratory with the same families observed in their own homes. When the family is placed in the more "artificial" laboratory surroundings, role differentiation follows the Parsonian predictions, with fathers taking the instrumental role and mothers the expressive role. At home, fathers drop in instrumentality and mothers increase; the opposite change occurs in expressive role taking.

Another situational variable that seems to be related to the selection of instrumental and expressive roles by parents is the cultural definition of the task. March (1954), in his study of political discussions between husbands and wives, used Interaction Process Analysis categories to show that instrumental and expressive role playing depended upon the cultural definition of the discussion topic as a "male" or "female" concern. When issues of foreign policy were discussed, the husband was the dominant instrumental leader; when the topic was of local politics, the wife's instrumental role became more prominent. Unfortunately, measures of expressiveness were not reported so that it is not at all certain that role differentiation actually changed form when the cultural definition of the task changed.

These experimental findings show that the clear division between instrumental and expressive roles of parents predicted by Parsonian theory must be modified, and, further, that several aspects of the parents' situation seems to be predictive of the role division. Role sharing may be associated with the sex of the child present, the cultural definition of the task, and the degree of "artificiality" of the situation.

This last dimension, "artificiality," seems to be an important one in both *ad hoc* group and family experiments. In real families there is little evidence of the instrumental and expressive role differentiation associated with the sex of the members, as is predicted by Parsonian theory. However, when families are examined under somewhat more artificial conditions (either in the laboratory rather than the home, as in O'-Rourke's (1963) study, or as artificially composed families, as in Leik's (1963) experiment, there is greater support for the Parsonian theory that relates role-playing to the sex of the parent. In *ad hoc* groups having none of the structural qualities of a family and having an even greater degree of artificiality, role differentiation is most clearly related to the sex of the group member. Strodtbeck and Mann (1956), for example, report in one of their jury studies that women exceed men in positive expressive reactions and men exceed women in attempted answers. Thus as the group becomes more artificial and *less* like a family in its structure, role differentiation becomes *more* clearly related to sex, and the Parsonian theory of family role structure more clearly supported. *Ad hoc* groups may use sex of the members as the determinant of role differentiation because of its visible and agreed-upon quality. When the group has developed specific norms of its own and when the integrative problem becomes crucial — usually this occurs when the group has its own history and has plans for a future — roles are shared, and instrumental and expressive roles become detached from the sex of the member.

4. Role as Independent Variable

Most of the preceding studies of role structure have centered on instrumental and expressive role playing and have been concerned largely with finding the parameters of family role structure and with describing the empirical patterns of roles. Few have gone on to examine role as an independent variable in order to understand the effects of different role structure on other variables such as the development of the child or the content of family norms. However, studies by Hetherington and Frankie (1967) and Mussen and Parker (1965) may serve as useful models for further experimental work in this area. Each uses some quality of the role of parent as the independent variable and asks how this role is related to the child's identification with the parent, measured in terms of imitation of parental behavior. One question that may be asked, following this model, is, if parental role differentiation is not based on sex, what are the implications for the identification of the child?

Hetherington and Frankie sampled parents on the basis of "dominant," "warm," and "conflictful" interaction with each other in an experimental situation (these measures indicate some dimension of instrumental and expressive role-taking) and then used the parents as "experimenters" in the sense that they were asked (individually) to play a role with their child that had been defined by the researchers. The dependent variable was the extent to which the child imitated the experimentally specified behavior of his mother or father. This approach falls between the artificial family method and the use of the real families since, here, there is experimental control of the independent variable (the parent role) and yet implicitly present in the parent-child interaction is the previous history of the family with all its unique qualities.

Findings show the importance of varying "parental role" experimentally and examining the effects of role on the child's behavior. The greater the warmth of the parent the greater the imitation by the child. However, when sex of the parent and sex of the child are taken into account "maternal warmth affects the girl's imitation more than it does the boy's." Also, the major prediction that—in homes in which there is high conflict between parents and little warmth from either of them, the child will identify with the dominant (aggressor) parent—is upheld; under these conditions both boys and girls imitate the dominant parent regardless of sex. However, if conflict is lower or if one parent is warm there is less tendency to imitate the dominant parent. This is true except for boys with dominant fathers; these fathers are imitated by the boys no matter whether mothers are nurturant or not. For girls, the warmth of the mother is salient for imitation.

One finding from the Hetherington study reflects on the question raised by the descriptive studies of role differentiation: If parental role differentiation is not based on sex, what are the implications for the child's identity development? In instances where the mother was the dominant parent, rather than the father, both girls and boys imitated the mother. The boys in these families may, therefore, be the ones whose identity development is impaired.

A second experiment in the same tradition adds an interesting finding that relates parental role-taking to the child's behavior. Mussen and Parker (1965) selected "nurturant" and "non-nurturant" mothers (measured by an open-ended interview) and asked each of them to take an "experimenter" role with the child. Findings showed that the degree to which the mother is nurturant (or expressive) is unrelated to the child's improvement on the task (a Porteus Maze). However, nurturance of the mother is significantly related to the child's imitation of his mother's incidental (non-task) behavior. For example, the greater the nurturance the more are irrelevant comments of the mother repeated by the child.

Once family researchers produce findings showing that parental roles are not simply divided between instrumental and expressive types, and not simply allocated at all times in all situations according to the sex of the parent, then an abstract theoretical model may be constructed to take into account these complex relationships between variables. These patterns can then be examined concurrently, either by sampling real families or by constructing artificial families, in order to test their effects on other qualities of the family or the child. The Hetherington and Mussen experiments are excellent models for investigating complex role structures in a clear and interesting way.

C. FAMILY NORMS AND SANCTIONS

Knowledge of a family's status structure and patterns of role differentiation provides the framework for understanding interrelationships between family members. However, this structural framework shows only the skeleton of the family and tells us little about the quality of family interaction, the climate of feeling in the family, what kinds of behavior are expected and what kinds avoided or punished. The concepts that underly this latter concern are "norms" and their accompanying "sanctions." Norms are rules for behavior that regulate the family members' conduct and that function to make interaction predictable for its members; they apply, naturally, to role-taking but affect other facets of interaction as well. When family norms are broken, or when they are particularly well followed, the norms call forth positive or negative sanctions to reinforce the family's normative system.

The clinical and descriptive literature on families best exemplifies the importance of family norms in predicting other aspects of the family. Wynne, Ryckoff, Day, and Hirsch (1958), for example, describe the normative structure of families who have produced a schizophrenic child and tie these peculiar norms to the problems the child has in forming an identity. A norm found commonly in these families is that "there is to be no hostility, disagreement, or other expression of negative feelings." Sanctions that support this norm are extreme, consisting of mass denials of behavior or feelings, and family myths that threaten catastrophe if the norm is not followed. The child growing up in this family finds it difficult to perceive accurately both his own feelings of hostility and hostile feelings of others, thus isolating him from relationships outside the family and limiting the possibility of identifying with qualities of non-family members.

Wynne's use of the family norm concept implies that family norms are rules for behavior known by the members (at some level) and carrying with them a sense of moral obligation. Family members feel that it is right and good to behave in a certain way and to punish those members who do not. However, there is an alternative definition of the concept, important because it leads to quite different measurement techniques. This second conception of "norm" does not imply knowledge by members nor a sense of obligation, but instead centers on the predictability or patterning of family behavior; if a family's behavior over time is consistent then it is assumed that its interaction is governed by norms.

1. Norm as Moral Obligation or Behavioral Consistency

The particular conception of "norm" used by an investigator sets limits on the ways in which norms are investigated. When the concept implies a moral obligation known by the family member, then two experimental techniques have generally been selected to examine the relationship between family norms and other variables. Members have been asked to predict others' behavior and the accuracy of the family's predictions used as a measure of their agreement on the family norms. The more common technique, taken from earlier experimental studies of *ad hoc* groups, consists of examining sanctioning acts and inferring the nature of the norm being violated.

In contrast, when norm is understood as a consistently patterned behavior, then measurement usually involves comparing interactions across a period of time. Experiments on *ad hoc* groups provide a model for this approach. For example, Heinicke and Bales (1953) examined consistency in interaction over four meetings for a set of student groups, using Interaction Process Analysis categories as the dependent variables. Interaction in the task, or instrumental, area did not change significantly over this period, but there was a significant increase in the level of solidary and tension release acts. While we could assume a norm for instrumental acts, the norms about level of expressiveness either changed over time, or were in the process of development. It is apparent here that conclusions about norms drawn from time samples are tenuous.

Do families have consistently patterned behavior? Two experimenters have followed the Heinicke-Bales model in examining families experimentally. M. Moore (1967) asked normal and "clinic" families to interact twice across an eight to ten week period, and rated their interaction on variables such as anger, tension, warmth, cohesiveness. Correlations ranged from .12 to .74, averaging .41. Moore concludes ". . . there exists a core of interaction consistency over time for both experimental groups" [pp. 4564-4565]. The fact that the average correlation is low and the range large suggests that much more interesting normative variation hides behind the correlation values.

Ferreira and Winter (1966) also examined normal and clinic families across a six month time period, asking members to discuss "revealed differences" items. They found no significant differences across time on levels of spontaneous agreement, decision time and choice fulfillment. Here, the mode of family decision making seems to be governed by normative rules.

These measures of behavioral consistency, while clearly important in evaluating the validity of findings from the usual family experiment in which each family is measured at only one point in time, are only introductory to the more interesting and specific questions about family norms. For example, are there some behavioral consistencies that, if interrupted call forth sanctions, and others that do not? Do families differ in the scope of their norms? Is there variation within a family in the degree to which norms are internalized by its members? If there is variation in understanding (or following) of family norms, does this variation affect other dependent variables for example, the development of the child? Each of these questions calls for more specific questions about knowledge of the norms, agreement on the norms, and strength of the norms. Thus, using the "consistency of behavior" studies as background, a few experimenters have moved on to examine the rules for behavior that are obligatory and understood by the group members.

2. Relation between Normative Structure and Other Group Aspects

It is surprising that there are so few experimental studies of *ad hoc* groups that deal directly with the problem of internally developed, obligatory group norms and the relationship between normative structure and other aspects of the group. The experiments that can be said to investigate norms usually examine the conditions under which group members "conform" to an experimentally-imposed norm, such as the group norm represented by the set of trained subjects who report inaccurate line lengths in the Asch-type experiment. In none of these experiments can one assume that the norm has naturally arisen as a result of group interaction over time.

However, a recent field study of small groups is an exception to the usual focus on experimentally-imposed norms. Feldman (1968) asked children in 61 groups at a number of camps to answer questionnaire items about the norms in their groups; content of the questions was developed by pre-testing a larger number of items and, presumably, selecting those that some groups reported to be naturally developed norms of the group. Major concerns of the study are the degree to which a group is normatively integrated and the relationship between normative integration and other qualities of the group. Normative integration is the extent to which each member's report of the norms coincides with the average report of the whole group. Thus, in our terms, it is a measure of the extent to which all members can accurately report the unique norms of their group.

Feldman reports that normative integration varies significantly depending on the sex of the group members, with girls' groups having greater agreement on the norms. But, further, he shows how agreement on norms is related to other qualities of the group as a whole. Norm agreement is related to the interpersonal integration of the group, that is to the extent to which members give and receive liking choices. Thus, with greater agreement on the rules there is greater reciprocal liking. However, normative agreement is not significantly related to functional integration, that is, to agreement among group members that three separate roles are being taken by members. While we might have predicted that agreement about group norms should be directly related to agreement about role differentiation, this does not seem to be the case, at least in Feldman's groups of children.

The Feldman study is not an experimental one, yet it provides a set of methods for measuring group norms as well as a complex set of findings suggesting that the quality of the group norms is related to other aspects of group structure.

One family experiment provides for a similar conclusion. Ferreira (1963) asked: Do family members accurately perceive the amount of rejection that other members direct toward them? In other words, in the family group is there agreement about the amount of rejection that is being expressed and thus is there agreement about the norms for rejection? Further, he asked, is this agreement related to other qualities of the family group?

Normal and "clinic" family members worked alone, coloring drawings and, later, choosing or rejecting the drawings of other members of the family. Not only was each member asked to reject others' drawings but he was asked to predict who would reject his. "Rejection" and "expected rejection" measures were obtained for each whole family and for each family member. One relevant finding is that there is less agreement on norms for rejection in the clinic than in the normal families. Ferreira also reports that children are more accurate perceivers of rejection than are adults in the family. This interesting finding, that in families where norms are misperceived, and where there is a clinic patient present (usually, but not always, the child) it is the child who is the most accurate perceiver. Thus, it is not simply that children who misperceive the norm are abnormal, or that children who are abnormal misperceive the norm. Instead, the parents are more likely to be the misperceivers, and this raises the question of the effect of lack of understanding or lack of consensus about family norms on the developing child. Further, what is the consequence of lack of normative consensus on family role structure? These are questions that might be investigated more systematically with the use of "artificial" families and experimentally introduced normative consensus.

3. Responses to Deviations from Norms

Several experimental studies of ad hoc groups provide another model for investigating the family norms. Here, group sanctions are observed and their effects measured; in most instances the experimenter insures that sanctions will occur by introducing a role player who plays a deviant role. Schachter's (1951) early experiment on deviation and communication indicated that a member whose opinion deviated considerably from the modal opinion was sanctioned first by group pressure to change, and later by being ignored. Other experimenters have built on this model and have asked more specific questions about sanctioning. Sampson and Brandon (1964) placed deviant members in experimentally constructed groups but varied the type of deviance; in some groups the role player differed from members only in her opinion about a group issue; in other groups, the role player deviated in terms of her social background and previous experience. Thus "opinion" and "role" deviation represent different degrees of deviation and the findings can be understood in these terms. A mild deviator (the opinion deviant) receives more communications, and especially more hostility and questions than do conformists and extreme deviants. The group attempts to understand his position and pressures him to change his opinion. The role deviant, whose differences are seen as more pervasive and long-term, is not the target of communication or hostility, but instead is simply ignored. Sampson and Brandon suggest, "Perhaps, like the stigmatized individuals to whom Goffman refers, the role deviate is permitted to exist as long as we, the normals, the role conformants, do not have to look at him" [p. 281].

Wiggins, Dill, and Schwartz (1965) investigated another dimension of sanctioning by groups, again by introducing deviance experimentally and examining the resulting behavior. They found that the extent to which a deviant is rejected is related to the extent to which deviance threatens the attainment of the group goal as well as to the status or importance of the deviant member. A high status member is punished less for a minor deviation but more for a major deviation, perhaps because he is not felt to be subject to the norms of the group.

Each of these experiments on sanctioning in *ad hoc* groups raises questions and problems relevant to families. In a family group, is extreme deviation sanctioned by ignoring the family member? If this member happens to be the child, what effect do these sanctions have on the child's role or development? Is it true, as Wiggins *et al*, might predict, that a high status family member is not sanctioned for minor deviations? Does this imply that the hostility aroused in the family will be displaced from the parent to a lower status member? Or, does this pattern of sanctioning change when the group has the age and sex structure of a family?

4. *Effects of Parental Sanctions*

These questions on sanctioning in families have only recently been put to experimental test. While the small group experiments that we have reviewed here deal with several aspects of deviance and sanc-

tioning—degree of deviation, type of deviation, and status of deviants—
the family experiments have looked only at the effect of sanctions by
parents on the child. In some instances the parental sanctioning is
known to reflect the real family interaction patterns; in others, sanctioning methods are imposed by the experimenter.

Stevenson, Keen, and Knights (1963) investigated the effects of
positive sanctions administered by parents as compared with strangers,
on the behavior of their own young children. While children transferred
marbles from one box to another the adult present gave verbal rewards
("That's very good," etc.) Stevenson found that the strangers had a
greater effect on the child's production (number of marbles transferred)
than did his own parents; only girls rewarded by their own mothers increased production. With strangers, all children increased production
except for boys with male strangers. Stevenson does not relate these
experimentally defined positive sanctions to the specific mode of sanctioning used by each of the parents at home.

Patterson's (1965) experiment took this latter factor into account by
selecting parents according to their use of punishing sanctions in the
home and then asking them to serve as "experimenters" and to follow
standard "punishing" behavior in the experimental situation. From interviews with mothers only, the child's home was judged, using rating
scales, to be warm or hostile, restrictive or permissive. A parent was
then cued by earphones to make a critical or negative comment on his
child's performance on a task similar to that used by Stevenson. The
effect of these comments on the child's performance was found to be
contingent on the usual modes of sanctioning used by the parent at
home. The greater the restrictiveness in the home the more the child
changed his behavior as a result of negative sanctions by his parent.
However, this applies only to boys; there are few significant differences
for girls. Futhermore, the degree of warmth reported in the home is unrelated either to boys' or girls' responses to punishment. The effects of
combinations of warmth and permissiveness on the punishment of the
child are not examined. These more complex relationships could be of
great interest in understanding the effects of preferred mode of sanctioning of children by parents.

As we have pointed out the major experimental concern has been
largely with sanctions directed from parent to child. Recent theoretical
interest in the effect of the child's behavior on the parents (Bell, 1968)
and the use of sanctions by all family members to maintain a particular
normative system (Wynne et al., 1958) has not reached experimental
test. However, it is clearly a simple step to extend the above experi-

mental techniques to other family relationships. Patterson has shown that it is possible to take into account the unique family norms and sanctioning patterns and to reproduce them experimentally in order to examine their effects. The small group literature provides considerable technical help in operationalizing sanctions and measuring effects; however, with the exception of some descriptions from group therapy, it is the clinical analyses of families that describe normative content and the sanctioning strategies in detail and these may be most fruitfully examined with experimental methods.

D. Summary

In the course of examining small group and family experiments concerned with structural dimensions there are several points at which findings reflect back upon a general issue: Are families and *ad hoc* groups simply two sub-types of a general type, "group?" Findings from several of the experiments comparing status structure in families and groups suggest that status is related to other variables in similar ways in both types of groups, with the empirical differences that occur explained by "length of acquaintance" or "situational" variables. A similar issue is raised, but not resolved, in the experiments on role-playing. There we noted that the theoretical formulation of family role-taking seemed to be a better explanation of role-taking in *ad hoc* groups than in the family; while expressive and instrumental roles are allocated on the basis of sex in the *ad hoc* groups this differentiation seems to break down in families, perhaps replaced by a role structure negotiated on the basis of the unique family situation and composition. An important empirical question, as yet unanswered, is whether or not a similar change in role structure occurs in long-term *ad hoc* groups.

Just as was the case in the experiments on social background and personality, when family structure is examined by looking at behavior in a controlled situation rather than simply by using interview or test data to infer structure, the resulting theory must be much more complex and specific. This is clearest in the experiments on family role-playing where it was found that a number of additional concepts must be included in the theory in order to explain the fact that parental roles are not neatly divided into instrumental and expressive types. Once the theory becomes more specified and includes behavioral concepts, then it is possible to put these specific hypotheses to the test in artificial families or through experimental intervention into the family system.

IV. Family Process

While experimental studies of families have provided a complex picture of family structure at one point in time there has been little concern with change. Yet as one looks at families interacting, either in the laboratory or under natural conditions, it is clear that change constantly occurs. Roles are switched, the balance of power shifts, sanctions are imposed, and family members learn new strategies and techniques for interacting with each other. Furthermore, these changes are not random ones but, instead, seem to be related to other variables such as the imposition of a new task on the family, the maturation of the child, or the loss of a member.

Experiments on family structure attempt to control for "change" variables by examining families at comparable points in the family history and under well controlled conditions. Suppose, however, that change or process were the major theoretical variable; how could it be approached experimentally? The few family experimenters concerned with this issue examine it in two different ways. The first reflects an interest in macro-process. Families are seen from an historical perspective and questions have to do with structural changes throughout the life cycle of the family. The second approach is through examination of micro-process, or change within an experimental session. Here the concern is with how one member's interaction affects a second and how the second, in turn, affects the first. Not only is there interest with whether change occurs, but also with exactly how this change comes about at the level of discrete behaviors.

A. FAMILY MACRO-PROCESS

Longitudinal and clinical studies of families suggest that major structural changes come about as a result of normal development (aging of parents, maturation of the children, changes in the extended family) as well as from less predictable circumstances (illness). At first glance it might be assumed that these long-term changes are not amenable to cross-sectional experimental methods and would be more appropriately tested in a longitudinal study. A sample of families might be examined over the course of the family history and changes in structure related to other variables. R. Q. Bell (1959-1960) discusses the difficult problems of longitudinal, or prospective, studies of families and also suggests an alternative technique in which the time required is telescoped by use of matched samples of families each of which is seen at only two points in its history. If theoretical concern were with the changes in family structure occurring when children reach adolescence and then begin to leave home, and if change were assumed to occur throughout this entire time period, a valid picture of change during this ten-year period in the family's history could be obtained in the following way: One sample of families might be examined when the child is 12 and again at age 14; another matched sample is examined when the child is 14 and again at 16, and so on. If samples are appropriately matched then conclusions can be drawn about the nature of the full-sequence of structural changes and the variables that predict these changes; further specific within-family changes may be measured and described.

Another technique that avoids some of the problems inherent in longitudinal studies consists of selecting families at particular "crisis" or change periods and examining them at several points in time during this relatively short period in the family history. Rapoport's study of families during the "engagement through first child" period (Rapoport & Rapoport, 1964) may allow conclusions about structural change and methods of handling it that can be generalized to other points in the family history as well.

Neither Bell's accelerated longitudinal method nor the "crisis" sampling technique has been used in combination with an experimental method to examine family process. However in a few instances appropriate sampling has been used as a substitute for the time dimension. Scott's (1962) experiment exemplifies a design in which cross-sectional materials are used to draw conclusions about structural changes in the family over a relatively long period of time. While her experiment was not specifically designed for this purpose the selection of family groups might be ordered so that cells of the experimental design stand for periods in the life history of a "family." The four-person family (parents, one child, and one grandparent) may be assumed to stand for an early point in the family history; a later stage of development is represented by the five-person family, the family having an additional child. In discussing this study earlier we suggested that differences in power structure between types of families may be related to the normal changes expected when an adolescent child matures. Scott reports that while parents are high power members in the smaller family it is the adolescent child who is high power in the larger, five-person family. If this experimental study had been specifically designed to examine the developmental process, a number of methodological requirements would have had to be met: one would want accurate matching of families on all variables assumed to be related to structure as well as careful selection of experimental groups on the basis of their "stage of family development."

A second experimental approach, taking an even longer historical perspective, asks about the relationships between family structure

across three generations of related families. Borke (1966-1967) selected
a small sample of families and collected interactional data from all three
generations. Interaction profiles were compared and conclusions drawn
about the ways in which motivations for acting might be transmitted
from one generation to another. While an attempt was made to observe
families under relatively standard conditions and while objective measures were applied to their interaction, the fact that each of the families
was seen at a different point in its own history means that one must assume the stability of family structure over a long period of time in order
to draw conclusions about the effects of socialization from one generation to the next.

The cross-sectional experimental methods represented by Scott's
and Borke's work is designed to answer questions about gross changes
in family structure over time. It does not tell us how these changes might
have come about. For example, if the adolescent child does become a
powerful member of the family, perhaps replacing the parent in some
situations, we know only that this occurs, not how the adolescent takes
over the role nor how the parents respond. It is the experimental studies
of micro-process that add to our understanding of these mechanisms of
change.

B. FAMILY MIRCO-PROCESS

The studies of micro-process in families, in most cases, examine the
relationship between one act and the response that immediately follows
it. Thus, findings about "change" or "process" refer to very short periods of time relative to the family's history, yet the conclusions drawn
from process findings may contribute to our understanding of how families go about maintaining or altering structural patterns throughout their
entire history.

In this area there are few precedents in small group theory or measurement from which family experimenters may draw. The vast majority
of small group experimenters has collapsed the process of interaction
into an aggregate measure for the whole experimental session. Then,
from the total proportions of certain kinds of actions investigators sometimes draw inferences about the sequence of actions between group
members; the sequence itself usually remains unmeasured.

In his early work on equilibrium in groups, Bales (1953) discussed
techniques for measuring micro-process and provided a theoretical ra-
tionale for interest in the minute sequences of actions. Using his proac-
tion-reaction method each act is examined and the question asked, what
is the quality of the next action? These two-act sequential patterns are

then summed for the whole group session and the proportions compared. For example, Bales reports that for experimental groups of students, when an act of antagonism occurs the act that will most probably follow is a tension-releasing act (laughter, joking). This sequence is seen as one that functions to maintain the equilibrium of the group.

While Bales does not spell out in detail the relationship between specific sequences of interactions and the maintenance of equilibrium in the group, the theory seems to assume that sequential patternings of acts will follow rules similar to other equilibrium-maintenance mechanisms on other theoretical levels. Just as role differentiation serves to maintain the equilibrium of a group so do particular sequences of acts, and the specific content at these two levels should be the same. Instrumental acts tend to elicit more instrumental acts, just as an instrumental role player tends to carry on this role over time. If the instrumental act does not elicit another instrumental act it will most likely elicit a positive expressive act, in the same way that an instrumental role player is complemented by an expressive role player who functions to restore positive interpersonal relationships among members.

In the history of small group experimentation this concern with micro-process seems to have dropped out, probably as a result of the difficulties of measurement and analysis. Not until computers were able to take over the job of counting sequences or even of coding interaction into categories (the General Inquirer is an example of the latter technique; see Stone, Dunphy, Smith, & Ogilvie, 1966) was there a return to the issue. And as yet the return is largely in terms of problems of measurement and analysis, not more abstract theoretical development.

Raush's (1965) field study of groups of normal and hyperaggressive boys living on an inpatient hospital ward is one important model for studies of family micro-process. He reports findings that show clearly the theoretical relevance of examining interaction sequences and demonstrates statistical techniques for handling measurement of behavior contingency patterns. The boys' interactions were sampled by selecting time periods and their actions coded as either "friendly" or "unfriendly." Measures derived from information theory were used to ask several questions about the sequential patterning of interaction. In one analysis, longer chains of interactions were measured, and theoretically expected sequential patterns were compared with actual sequences.

The relevance of this method to theories of equilibrium is apparent in some of the findings. In the group of hyperaggressive boys, hostile responses increase in successive steps; "more interesting is a suggested trend for hostility to increase beyond its expected theoretical course" [Raush, 1965, p. 495]. These children appear to have no corrective ability, no techniques that will turn off the hostility once it has begun. In contrast, among normal children "the chain of interactive events . . . would be expected to wind up in a friendly fashion more than half the time. . . . At each successive step, the normal boys showed greater friendliness than would be expected from the hypothetical curve based on the initial transition matrix" [p. 496]. Raush suggests that the group of normal children had a fund of strategies for switching the tone of its interaction and, furthermore, knew at what point in time to use them. For example, shifts of topics, recognitions of others' feelings, conventional encouragements are used by normal children to alter the direction of group processes. Raush's findings show that the examination of micro-process is useful for understanding behavioral contingencies, for discovering the implicit rules of response, and for examining the conditions under which these rules are modified. The application of methods like these to family groups should provide a way for determining the unstated norms for behavior, that is, the behavioral mechanisms used to maintain equilibrium, as well as a method for determining how structural changes occur.

Two groups of family experimenters have examined interaction at the micro-process level. Each asks the question, is the behavior of one member contingent (in specified ways) on the behavior of another member? Further questions that may be asked are: Under what conditions are contingency patterns changed? How? Who does it? Perhaps these questions may lead back to an issue raised by Scott's study, namely, how does the adolescent child gain a powerful position in his family? How do parents respond to these attempts? How does a new power equilibrium get worked out in these families?

Haley (1964, 1967a) asked about family micro-process by examining only one quality of the sequence of interaction, a non-content one. From samples of three and four-person families in laboratory discussions, he obtained the sequence of speakers, i.e., who follows whom. He then asked to what extent the actual speaker-responder sequence departed from a random sequence and assumed that departure from randomness stands for the use of a family rule about who should respond to whom. In three-person families (some normal and some having a psychiatric patient member), all families deviated from the random pattern; that is, for all there was a relatively predictable "process" of interaction. Furthermore, deviation from randomness was greater for the abnormal than the normal families. When four-person families were examined the departure from randomness was greater for both types of families yet there were no differences between the normal and patient family types. It was the normal families' sequences that become more predictable when a second child was added. The addition of a fourth member (or perhaps a second child) thus seems to be one of the conditions under which family equilibrium and structure is changed (see Waxler & Mishler, 1970, for a discussion of problems of measuring sequences of speakers).

Haley's experiment opens up the possibility for micro-process measures of family interaction that extend far beyond the simple sequence of speakers. Is the content of interaction patterned? Do families have patterned processes for handling power strategies? Does a family respond with a predictable set of actions to disagreements? One experimental investigation of family micro-process that concerns itself not only with the sequence of speakers but also with the predictability of certain types of interactions was carried out by Mishler and Waxler (1969). Here families with schizophrenic children and families with normal children interacted in a controlled experimental situation; each speech was classified with a number of content analysis systems (methods are reported in Mishler & Waxler, 1968b). In the micro-process study adjacent speeches were coded according to which family member made the speech, which family member responded to it, and the degree to which the response "acknowledged" the immediately preceding speaker. As in the Raush study, techniques of multivariate informational analysis were used to examine the predictability of sequential acts.

The investigators found significant differences between the normal and schizophrenic families in the extent to which it is possible to predict the second speaker's acknowledgment from the knowledge of who that person is and to whom he is responding. The level of patterning or predictability of acknowledgment, or responsiveness, is greater in the families with schizophrenic children than in the normal families, yet neither of these types of families has a predictability level that departs from chance. (Both types of families, however, have patterns deviating from a purely random one and thus these findings confirm those reported by Haley.) The schizophrenic-normal differences in predictability reflect on certain theories about schizophrenic family structure; for example, Wynne and Singer (1963) suggest that the rigidity of the family system is one factor pushing the child into inadequate identity development, and perhaps schizophrenia.

Mishler and Waxler go beyond the question: "Are there specific contingency patterns in family interaction?" to ask "Does the level of predictability change across time?" Time here is limited to the time the family is seen in the experimental session. Therefore the question is, does the patterning in family process shift during the experimental hour? For example, with regard to the sequence of speakers, while the schizo-

phrenic families were shown to have a more predictable process of acknowledgment, they were also shown to shift more quickly and more
often into and out of high levels of patterning of speaker sequences than
did the normal families. In contrast the normal families, whose overall
levels of predictability were relatively low, maintained longer sequences
of high level predictability of speaker sequences once it had been
reached. The schizophrenic family's erratic and perhaps fragmented interaction, within the context of a rigid patterning, recalls a number of
clinical observations of these families. While Raush showed that the
hyperaggressive boys seem not to have the skills or capacities for
stopping actions once they had begun, the schizophrenic families seem
not to have the mechanisms for maintaining a predictable sequence of
events. Normal families are able to keep a predictable process going for
a longer period of time even though their general norm is for flexibility
and change.

Once this question regarding the shifts of predictability within the
experimental hour has been asked, then one may ask which variables
cause the change in process. As yet this question has not been asked
empirically. However, the method represented by the Raush, Haley,
Mishler and Waxler studies, provides the appropriate technique for
obtaining the answer.

C. Summary

The methods for examining family macro-process, that is, changes
that occur throughout the long history of a family, center on appropriate
sampling techniques that may be combined with observation of family
interaction in an experimental situation. Some experimenters, however,
have chosen to examine change in microcosm in order to investigate
questions originally raised by theorists concerned with long-term family
development. If Bales is right (Bales, 1953) in assuming that each of the
theoretical levels of group analysis involves the same basic conflicts and
the same ways of resolving them, then we might hypothesize, for example, that families that alter the patterning of sequential acts as a result of
an increase in power acts by a low-power member will alter family structure in comparable ways when an adolescent child matures. Thus, perhaps long-term changes in family structure may be fruitfully examined
in microcosm, at the level of discrete act sequences.

V. Family Structure and Outcome

A large proportion of family experiments have as their explicit concern possible causal linkages between family structure and some out-

come variable. The outcome of most interest is the development of the child. Further, with the exception of a few experiments relating family structure to the child's attitudes or values, all are concerned with linkages between family structure and the child's illness, his identity development, or his cognitive style.

A. THE PROBLEM OF DIRECTION OF CAUSATION

A brief summary of one of these experiments will serve to raise the major methodological issue that appears when questions about the outcome of family interaction are raised. Stabenau *et al.* (1965) asked families of three different types to interact in an experimental situation. The families were selected on the basis of characteristics of one child member; the child was either schizophrenic, a juvenile delinquent, or normal. In selecting the dependent variables Stabenau was concerned with the qualities of family structure and the characteristics of interaction that may or may not have led to the development of schizophrenia. Thus, the quality of the child was the major independent variable and the normal and delinquent families were included as control groups with the assumption that if families with a schizophrenic child differed in modes of interaction from the other two types these patterns of interaction might be causal agents in the schizophrenia. Stabenau *et al.* (1965) conclude, after presenting findings, "These data support, but do not prove, the hypothesis, that differing patterns of interaction between parents and child are causally related to the development of psychopathology and the establishment and maintenance of mental health" [p. 59].

But isn't it equally likely that the pattern of family interaction found, measured after the fact of the child's illness, is a response to the illness and not in any sense a causal agent, or even a stable pattern that existed prior to the illness? Inherent in the experimental study of natural groups is this problem of the time-order of the variable effects and the problem is magnified when the major concern is with a cause-effect relationship that may have taken place in the past. In contrast, experimental studies of *ad hoc* groups avoid this difficulty by constructing new groups of known structure at $Time_1$ and examining the outcome of interaction at $Time_2$. Only recently have family experimenters followed this lead by constructing artificial families and using other experimental interventions to assure that the time-order is clear (this issue is discussed further in Waxler, 1970).

Of the experiments relating family structure to the child's illness the largest number examine families having schizophrenic children (see Caputo, 1963; Cheek, 1965; Farina, 1960; Lerner, 1965; Mishler & Waxler, 1968b; Reiss, 1967; Sharan, 1966). Similar questions have been asked experimentally about families with a child diagnosed as having childhood schizophrenia (Lennard *et al.*, 1965), families with a disturbed child (Hutchinson, 1967), or with a non-adjusted child (O'Connor, 1967). Within this set of experiments the way in which the time-order problem is handled ranges from simply assuming that the family's structure is stable and was causal in the child's illness to attempting a direct test of this question.

Within the limits set by the choice of real families as experimental subjects, two design strategies have been used to shed light on the time-order of family effects. One consists of the selection of appropriate control groups with which to compare the experimental family type. Specifically, the strategy involves using a type of family having a known outcome and having a known time order for the "family structure" and "child outcome" variables. For example, O'Connor (1967) chose families with mentally retarded children as the control group with which to compare families having "adjusted" or "non-adjusted" children, the second control and experimental group, respectively. In the mentally retarded group (assuming clear diagnosis) there is reasonable assurance that the child's illness existed prior to deviations from "normal" family structure. Farber's work on families having mentally retarded children suggests that these families are pressed to alter the family system in *response* to the handicapped child (Farber, 1960). Therefore, in the mentally retarded control group the time-order of the "family structure" and "child outcome" variables is known. If the experimental group of families of "non-adjusted" children is shown to have structural and interactional patterns no different from the control group of retarded families and both are different from the "adjusted," or normal, group then the most parsimonious explanation of the findings must be that the "non-adjustment" of the child has existed prior to, and may have called forth, the changes in family structure.

Unfortunately the findings are not so clear. O'Connor found that on most family structure variables the mentally retarded families fell between the other two. Thus, if we assume that an essentially "normal" family has been forced to respond differently to a mentally retarded child, we might also conclude that a "non-adjusted child" family has been forced to respond in an even more abnormal way to the non-adjusted child. However, since the non-adjusted families also differ significantly from the mentally retarded families it is equally likely that other effects are operating, and perhaps that the family structure has caused the adjustment problems of the child.

The selection of appropriate control groups for comparison purposes is, as the O'Connor experiment shows, only a partial solution to the tangle of cause-effect relationships that may have occurred in the family's past. A second, partial, solution consists of the addition of a different type of control, the observation of parents in interaction with a well sibling of the sick child. Mishler and Waxler (1968b), Reiss (1967), and Stabenau *et al.* (1965) use this technique, each in somewhat different ways, and in combination with other control groups, to ask whether the family system is the same with all children. This question reflects on the assumptions about stability of the family structure across long periods of time; if the structure is dependent on which child is present then it is precarious to assume that the structure seen at present, when the sick child interacts with his parents, reflects a much earlier pattern. However, if the family structure is "different from normal" only when the sick child is present then one may limit further questions about cause and effect to one, rather than all, children in the family.

In the Mishler and Waxler experiment (1968b) in which parents of two types of schizophrenic children (those having good and poor premorbid adjustments) and parents of normal children were asked to interact, each set of parents was seen once with the sick child and once with a well sibling of that child. The general trend of the findings support the notion of the specificity of patterns. On many of the measures of interaction in the experimental situation, parents interacting with their sick child differ from normal parents with their normal child. Further, the parents of schizophrenic children, when interacting with a normal child in their family, behave like normal parents. The "abnormal" structure of the schizophrenic family is, in general, limited to the relationship between parents and the one schizophrenic child.

This led the investigators to ask questions about possible time relationships between the family structure and the schizophrenia variables. One explanation, the etiological one, suggests that, since the parents' interaction patterns are different only when the sick child is present, they may have preceded and possibly caused the child's illness; this explanation follows some clinicians' speculations that parents "select" one child in the family to become the schizophrenic and all further pathological relationships are limited to that child. A second explanation, the responsive one, concludes that, since the parental differences occur only with the sick child present, that child may have elicited these differences by his pathological behavior.

It is clear that neither the addition of control groups nor the addition of control subjects to an experimental design is likely to provide positive evidence that the family structure did or did not precede the child's developmental problem or illness. Inferences may be drawn from the findings and some explanations reasonably ruled out, yet no clear conclusions can be drawn.

B. EXPERIMENTAL TESTS OF CAUSATION DIRECTION

Experimental construction of artificial families and the introduction of experimentally controlled variables into a family may be better solutions to these questions of family outcome. Groups having the abstract qualities of a "family" may be formed, asked to interact, perhaps in a specified way, and the effects on the child measured. Turning the question around it is also possible to investigate the effects of the child on family by controlling the child variable and examining the resulting behavior of the parents. If the theoretical framework is clear and concretely framed, it is thus possible to test the effects of family on child, or child on family, in such a way that generalizations may be made about real families.

We have previously referred to the work of Bandura et al. (1963), who constructed "families" with varied status distributions and asked which "parent" the child imitated, or identified with. In this instance family structure is the causal variable. Bandura found that the child generally imitates the high status adult, regardless of the reward structure in the "family." The experimental model could easily be expanded to include "parental affective relationship patterns, differences in participation of "parents," and varied distributions of instrumental and expressive roles, all of which have been singled out as important in the development of the child's personality.

It is also possible to test the effects of child on parents in an experimental situation. An experiment by Siegel and Harkins (1963) asked if it is reasonable to conclude that family structure may change as a response to a sick or deviant child. Here the child's behavior is the independent variable and "parental" behavior the dependent variable. An institutionalized retarded child was placed in an experimental room with a housewife (not his mother) and the housewife was asked to teach the child to do a puzzle; there was an unstructured time period as well. Whether the child was known by the housewife to have "high" or "low" verbal ability had no effect on her level of verbal interaction with the child; thus her response to the child was not simply a result of a label having been attached to the child. Instead, when data were combined with those from a previous study there was considerable evidence "suggesting that the actual verbal level of the children . . . may have been the crucial determinant of adult verbal behavior." Adults interacting with these children consistently use lower type-token ratios with the "low verbal ability" children than with the "high ability" children. Thus it is reasonable to conclude that one aspect of mental retardation in the child—restricted vocabulary usage—elicits specific responses from an adult, and thus, presumably, from the child's own parents.

The relationships between family structure and outcome for the child may be estimated, as we have shown, by comparing the real families in question with control groups for which the time-order is known, or by constructing artificial families and experimentally introducing the "family structure" or "child outcome" variables. One family experiment, now in process, is designed to combine the advantages of these two approaches (see Haley, 1968, for a related experiment). In this study (Waxler, 1967) natural family groups, rather than experimentally trained role players, are used, yet experimental manipulations are introduced so as to insure that the time order of the family structure and child outcome variables is known. The problem follows directly from findings of the earlier experiment on families having schizophrenic children (Mishler & Waxler, 1968b).

In the present experiment, families having schizophrenic, normal and chronically ill children (the latter with non-psychiatric illness) are sampled. For the same reason that O'Connor (1967) included the families of mentally retarded children, the medically ill families are included here; it is assumed that the illness preceded any "abnormalities" in family structure. Following the sampling of family types, artificial families are created by pairing parents of one type with a child of another type. Schizophrenic parents interact with a normal child and at another time with a schizophrenic child (not their own) or with a medically ill child. Normal parents and medically ill parents also interact with different types of children. (The control situation in which parents interact with children of the same type as their own, but not their own, is designed to standardize degree of acquaintance between parents and child for all interaction situations.)

The logic of this experimental design allows one to ask which is most likely to stand as a causal variable, the child's schizophrenia or the parents' modes of interaction. If, for example, the schizophrenic child's behavior remains the same across different parents and the normal parents' behavior moves toward the "abnormal" when interacting with that schizophrenic child, then it is reasonable to conclude that the schizophrenic child may have elicited "abnormal" responses from parents. If, on the other hand, the schizophrenic parents' behavior remains stable across children and the normal child with whom they interact changes his behavior in the direction of the schizophrenic, we could conclude that the schizophrenic parent can elicit "abnormal" responses from the normal child. Within the design itself there is no way in which findings will reflect on the true cause-effect relationship in the past family history; findings may, however, suggest which relationship is more likely and thus which theory and experimental strategy to focus on in the future.

C. Summary

One of the major questions raised when the experimental method is used to investigate the effects of family interaction on certain "outcome" variables is which came first, the structure or the outcome? This problem becomes most obvious at this point, where the sequence of events is a crucial part of the theory; however, time-order is also an issue in all of the earlier experimental studies in which real families are used. Our discussion here has centered on solutions involving experimental designs. When real families are used, certain control groups or control subjects are added in order to provide a comparison group having a known time-order. When artificial families are used, the effect of "parent" on "child" or "child" on "parent" may be measured by experimentally controlling the causal variable, either the "parent" or the "child" role, and allowing the effect variable to vary.

There are, however, strategies other than the creation of special experimental designs to investigate the cause-effect relationships within a family. One consists of a particular mode of data analysis applied to interactions in real families, where, by their very nature, the cause and effect in which one is interested has occurred in the past. The microprocess analysis described in the section on change is one example. The investigator may examine the relationship between one act and the next and may assume that each preceding act is the "cause" of the following act. He may then look for cause-effect patternings in the family's interaction during the course of the experimental hour and may draw conclusions about the effect of parent on child, or child on parent, that may also be relevant to the earlier cause-effect relationship that occurred in the family's past.

VI. Conclusion

In the course of reviewing selected experimental studies of families we have pointed a number of times to two recent methodological trends, the tendency toward greater experimental intervention into the family system and the use of synthetic family groups as sources of data on the family. The movement in this direction carries with it certain implications for further study of the family which we will discuss here.

Experimental intervention into the family system was most apparent in family outcome studies. There intervention offers one solution to the problem of the time-order of structure and outcome variables. However, increasing experimental control over the family's situation and interaction was also apparent in other conceptual areas. As we have reported, some experimenters have asked real family members to interact with strangers (Bodin, 1965; Leik, 1963; Ryder, 1968; Waxler, 1967); others have trained parents to play an experimentally defined role with their own child (Hetherington & Frankie, 1967; Mussen & Parker, 1965; Patterson, 1965; Stevenson et al., 1963); and some families have been asked to interact in artificial and unusual situations (Reiss, 1967; Haley, 1968). This variety of experimental interventions insures that the independent variable is clearly controlled and standard in all experimental treatments. Further, intervention may serve to control some aspects of the family situation so as to allow for more exact and clearer measures of other aspects. Findings from the experiments that have been reviewed suggest that, when hypotheses warrant them, that experimental manipulations of families generate findings permitting more precise statements of relationships than can be derived from the correlational findings of observational studies. Particularly when theoretical concerns move from the description of family structure to examining how it is formed or changed (i.e., to the understanding of cause-effect relationships), experimental intervention into the family system is a valuable approach.

The second major trend, the use of artificial or synthetic families, is apparent in almost all content areas. "Families" with defined status structures have been composed and the effect on the child measured (Bandura et al., 1963); "families" having a deviant child have been examined and the parental response to deviance observed (Siegel & Harkins, 1963). The obvious advantages of this approach—experimental control over the important variables and the assurance that other variables are randomly distributed, permitting more direct tests of cause-effect hypotheses—have been discussed earlier. A question often raised, however, is whether findings from artificially composed families have any relevance to real families. In particular, investigators who have had clinical experience with families, wonder whether it is possible to generalize to processes in real families when the people observed are strangers without the long, intimate experience with each other that is unique to the family.

No experimenter assumes an identity between real and experimentally constructed families; in fact a number of experiments have been designed to investigate differences between them (Bishop, 1951; Bodin, 1965; Leik, 1963; Ryder, 1968). Instead, findings from artificial families are assumed to be relevant to an abstract theoretical conception or model of the family. Findings from experimentally composed families serve to test and to modify the abstract theory just as do findings from real families. Neither real nor artificial families meet all of the theoretical requirements of a model and thus, for both, variations from what the model would predict must be accounted for by introducing other dimensions thus further complicating the model. For artificial families one might, for example, introduce the dimension of "acquaintance," while for real families one might introduce such dimensions as "developmental level" or "position in the economy" to explain variations from the abstract model. Thus, those experimenters who have worked with experimentally composed families do so, in most instances, with the awareness that they are contributing to the specifications of a theory of interpersonal relations in families and other groups rather than to empirical generalizations about "real" families.

These trends toward the use of synthetic families and intervention into the real family system are representative of the more general methodological changes in experimental family study. These changes were briefly outlined in the introduction of this paper. Now that the family experiments have been reviewed it is clear that such methodological changes have more general implications for family theory and research. When a researcher chooses to test an hypothesis in an experimental situation the evidence presented here suggests that the addition of behavioral data forces family theorists to add concepts and qualifications to the original family theory. The most common effect on theory consists of clarification of the behavioral processes that intervene between a quality of a member, or of the whole family, and some structural or outcome variable. Thus, for example, the predictions about the relationship between generally valued and expected role differentiation between parents and a certain outcome for the child may vary depending on the demands of particular situations; whether the situation is public or private is one source of variation.

In addition to this impact on theory, the experimental technique has led to greater concern with all aspects of measurement. In this paper we have stressed issues of experimental design and particularly the logic of control group comparisons and have not dealt directly with problems of measurement; however the decision to test hypotheses experimentally forces greater attention to the theoretical relevance of and the scientific adequacy of measuring instruments. One general trend has been a decreased reliance on measures taken directly from *ad hoc* group studies (for example, Interaction Process Analysis) and a movement toward the construction of interaction codes and other outcome measures that indicate concepts found in theories of family structure (see studies by Farina, 1960; Mishler & Waxler, 1968b; Riskin, 1964; for theoretically derived interaction coding systems). Also, many of the hypotheses being tested are centered on the processes or mechanisms that occur in families and seem to explain the relationship between a quality of the family and some outcome measure. Because of this increasing focus on family processes, measurement has moved from the use of global ratings or single outcome scores to codes of ongoing interaction. Thus, instead of judging who "won" a family discussion, code categories are applied to every statement in order to understand "how" the discussion proceded and "how" a member won.

Closely intertwined with this trend toward theoretically related measures is an increasing concern with the scientific adequacy of measuring instruments. There has been greater attention paid to objectivity of measurement; for example, investigation has moved from observer's ratings of "mother's warmth" to computer-counted measures of members' speeches (Haley, 1967a). Problems in the reliability of measurement have also received more attention (Waxler & Mishler, 1966). A number of these aspects of measurement have been discussed by M. Straus (1964).

The complexity of theoretical questions has been paralleled by an increased complexity of analytic methods. In a number of places in our discussion we have pointed to the utility of analysis of variance methods, or to other techniques that allow certain variables to be controlled and effects of others to be examined; movement beyond correlational analysis is required by the nature of current hypotheses. Further, there has been increasing interest in separating the effects of individual family members from the effect of the family as a whole. This has led to the development of multi-level data analysis techniques; both Reiss (1967) and Mishler and Waxler (1968c) have shown this to be a useful approach to the complexity of family structure. Finally, with increasing concern with family processes rather than simply with "before" and "after" measures of families, the development of statistical techniques for analyzing act sequences (Raush, 1965) may prove to be particularly fruitful.

While experimental studies of families have contributed to theoretical clarification and methodological rigor in family research, there has been continuing concern with the ethical issues. This is understandable in the light of increasing interest in ethical problems in all areas of human experimentation. Family experimenters are acutely aware that the same care must be exercised here as occurs in other small group experimentation; an additional problem, however, is the fact that family members continue their relationship far beyond their experience in an experiment. Is it harmful for them to participate in an experiment, particularly one in which the experimenter intervenes or controls some aspect of the family interaction?

Information about effects of the experimental experience on the family — positive or negative, present or absent — is notably absent from most research reports. Neither do many family researchers describe the measures taken to explain the research or to answer questions after it is over, a standard procedure in most small group experiments. Thus there is little objective information about the possible harmful effects of this experience. However, if one places a family's experimental experience in the context of that family's history, then the experimental hour becomes what it probably is for the family, a trivial though hopefully interesting experience. Our own experience indicates that where the usual care expected in responsible scientific work is exercised, a family's participation in an experiment is neither threatening nor harmful. There is no evidence that would suggest that these problems are different from those in other areas of research on human behavior.

REFERENCES

Bales, R. F. *Interaction process analysis*. Cambridge, Mass.: Addison-Wesley, 1951.

Bales, R. F. The equilibrium problem in small groups. In T. Parsons, R. F. Bales, & E. Shils (Eds.), *Working papers in the theory of action*. Glencoe, Ill.: Free Press, 1953. Pp. 111-161.

Bandura, A., Ross, D., & Ross, S. A comparative test of the status envy, social power and secondary reinforcement theories of identificatory learning. *Journal of Abnormal and Social Psychology*, 1963, **67**, 527-534.

Beaver, A. P. The initiation of social contacts by pre-school children. *Child Development Monographs*, 1932, No. 7.

Bell, N. W., & Vogel, E. F. *The family*. Glencoe, Ill.: Free Press, 1960.

Bell, R. A reinterpretation of the direction of effects of socialization. *Psychological Review*, 1968, **75**, 81-95.

Bell, R. Q. Retrospective and prospective views of early personality development. *Merrill Palmer Quarterly of Behavior and Development*, 1959-1960, **6**, 131-144.

Berkowitz, L. Personality and group position. *Sociometry*, 1956, **19**, 210-222.

Bishop, B. M. Mother-child interaction and the social behavior of children. *Psychological Monographs*, 1951, **65**, 11.

Bodin, A. Family interaction, coalition, disagreement, and compromise in problem, normal and synthetic family triads. Mimeo., Mental Research Institute, Palo Alto, Calif., 1965.

Borke, H. The communication of intent: A systematic approach to the observation of family interaction. *Human Relations*, 1967, **20**, 1.

Bronfenbrenner, U. Toward a theoretical model for the analysis of parent-child relationships in a social context. In J. C. Glidewell (Ed.), *Parental attitudes and child behavior*. Springfield, Ill.: Thomas, 1961. Pp. 90-109.

Burke, P. J. Role differentiation and the legitimation of task activity. *Sociometry*, 1968, **31**, 404-411.

Caputo, D. V. The parents of the schizophrenic. *Family Process*, 1963, **2**, 339-356.

Cheek, F. E. Family interaction patterns and convalescent adjustment of the schizophrenic. *Archives of General Psychiatry*, 1965, **13**, 138-147.

Farber, B. Perceptions of crisis and related variables in the impact of a retarded child on the mother. *Journal of Health and Human Behavior*, 1960, **1**, 108-118.

Farina, A. Patterns of role dominance and conflict in parents of schizophrenic patients. *Journal of Abnormal and Social Psychology*, 1960, **61**, 31-38.

Feldman, R. A. Interrelationships among three bases of group integration. *Sociometry*, 1968, **31**, 30-46.

Ferreira, A. Rejection and expectancy of rejection in families. *Family Process*, 1963, **2**, 235-244.

Ferreira, A., & Winter, W. Stability of interactional variables in family decision-making. *Archives of General Psychiatry*, 1966, **14**, 352-355.

Framo, J. L. Systematic research on family dynamics. In I. Boszormenyi-Nagy & J. L. Framo (Eds.), *Intensive family therapy: Theoretical and practical aspects.* New York: Harper & Row, 1965. Pp. 407-462.

Freilich, M. The natural triad in kinship and complex systems. *American Sociological Review*, 1964, **29**, 529-540.

Gates, G. S. The effect of an audience upon performance. *Journal of Abnormal and Social Psychology*, 1924, **18**, 334-342.

Greenberg, P. J. Competition in children: an experimental study. *American Journal of Psychology*, 1932, **44**, 221-248.

Haley, J. Research on family patterns: an instrument measurement. *Family Process*, 1964, **3**, 41-65.

Haley, J. Speech sequences of normal and abnormal families with two children present. *Family Process*, 1967, **6**, 81-97. (a)

Haley, J. Cross-cultural experimentation: an initial attempt. *Human Organization*, 1967, **26**, 110-117. (b)

Haley, J. Testing parental instructions to schizophrenic and normal children: a pilot study. *Journal of Abnormal Psychology*, 1968, **73**, 6, 559-565.

Haythorn, W., Couch, A., Haefner, D., Langham, P., & Carter, L. The behavior of authoritarian and equalitarian personalities in groups. *Human Relations*, 1956, **9**, 57-74.

Heinicke, C., & Bales, R. F. Developmental trends in the structure of small groups. *Sociometry*, 1953, **16**, 7-38.

Hetherington, E. M. A developmental study of the effects of the sex of the dominant parent on sex-role preference, identification, and imitation in children. *Journal of Personality and Social Psychology*, 1965, **2**, 188-194.

Hetherington, E. M., & Frankie, G. Effects of parental dominance, warmth, and conflict on imitation in children. *Journal of Personality and Social Psychology*, 1967, **6**, 119-125.

Hoffman, M. L. Power assertion by the parent and its impact on the child. *Child Development*, 1960, **31**, 129-143.

Hoffman, M. L. and L. W. Hoffman. *A review of child development research.* Vol. 1. New York: Russell-Sage Foundation, 1964.

Hopkins, T. K. *The exercise of influence in small groups.* Totowa, N. J.: Bedminster Press, 1964.

Hutchinson, J. G. Family interaction patterns and the emotionally disturbed child. Mimeo. Presented at the meeting of the Society for Research in Child Development, New York, March 1967.

Katz, I., Goldston, J., & Benjamin, L. Behavior and productivity in biracial work groups. *Human Relations*, 1958, **11**, 123-141.

Kenkel, W. F. Influence differentiation in family decision making. *Sociology and Social Research*, 1957, **42**, 18-25.

Kenkel, W. F. Dominance, persistence, self-confidence, and spousal roles in decision-making. *Journal of Social Psychology*, 1961, **54**, 349-358.

Leik, R. K. Instrumentality and emotionality in family interaction. *Sociometry*, 1963, **26**, 131-145.

Lennard, H. L., Beaulieu, M. R., & Embrey, N. G. Interaction in families with a schizophrenic child. *Archives of General Psychiatry*, 1965, **12**, 166-183.

Lerner, P. M. Resolution of intrafamilial role conflict in families of schizophrenic patients. I: Thought disturbance. *Journal of Nervous and Mental Disease*, 1965, **141**, 342-351.

Lidz, T., & Fleck, S. Family studies and a theory of schizophrenia. In American Psychiatric Association, *The American family in crisis*. Des Plaines, Ill.: Forest Hospital Publ., 1965.

Lidz, T., Fleck, S., & Cornelison, A. R. Family studies and a theory of schizophrenia. In T. Lidz *et al.* (Eds.), *Schizophrenia and the family*. New York: International Universities Press, 1965. Pp. 362-376.

Liu, W. T. Family interactions among local and refugee Chinese families in Hong Kong. *Journal of Marriage and Family*, 1966, August, 314-323.

March, J. Husband-wife interaction over political issues. *Public Opinion Quarterly*, 1954, **17**, 461-470.

Milgram, S. Group pressure and action against a person. *Journal of Abnormal and Social Psychology*, 1964, **69**, 137-143.

Mills, T. M. Power relations in three-person groups. *American Sociological Review*, 1953, **18**, 351-357.

Mishler, E. G., & Waxler, N. E. (Eds.) *Family processes and schizophrenia: Theory and selected experimental studies*. New York: Science House, 1968. (a)

Mishler, E. G., & Waxler, N. E. *Interaction in families: An experimental study of family processes and schizophrenia*. New York: Wiley, 1968. (b)

Mishler, E. G., & Waxler, N. E. Family interaction patterns and schizophrenia: a multilevel analysis. In J. Romano (Ed.), *The origins of schizophrenia*. Amsterdam: Excerpta Medica Found., 1968. (c)

Mishler, E. G., & Waxler, N. E. Interaction sequences in normal and schizophrenic family triads: applications of multivariate informational analysis. Unpublished manuscript, Boston: Massachusetts Mental Health Center, 1969.

Moore, J. C. Status influence in small group interactions. *Sociometry*, 1968, **31**, 47-63.

Moore, M. Consistency of interaction in normal and clinic families. *Dissertation Abstracts, Section A*, 1967, 12, **1**, 4564-4565.

Mussen, P., & Parker, A. Mother nuturance and girls' incidental imitative learning. *Journal of Personality and Social Psychology*, 1965, **2**, 94-97.

O'Connor, W. A. Patterns of interaction in families with high adjusted, low adjusted, and mentally retarded members. Unpublished doctoral dissertation, University of Kansas, 1967.

O'Rourke, J. Field and laboratory: The decision making behaviors of family groups in two experimental conditions. *Sociometry*, 1963, **26**, 422-435.

Parsons, T., & Bales, R. F. *Family socialization and interaction process*. Glencoe, Ill.: Free Press, 1955.

Patterson, G. R. Parents as dispensers of aversive stimuli. *Journal of Personality and Social Psychology*, 1965, **2**, 844-851.

Rapoport, R., & Rapoport, R. New light on the honeymoon. *Human Relations,* 1964, **17,** 33-56.

Raush, H. Interaction sequences. *Journal of Personality and Social Psychology,* 1965, **2,** 487-499.

Reiss, D. Individual thinking and family interaction. *Archives of General Psychiatry,* 1967, **16,** 80-93.

Riley, M. W. *Sociological research.* Vol. 1. *A case approach.* New York: Harcourt, Brace & World, 1963. Pp. 700-739.

Riskin, J. Family interaction scales. *Archives of General Psychiatry,* 1964, **11,** 484-494.

Ryder, R. Husband-wife dyads versus married strangers. *Family Process,* 1968, **7,** 233-238.

Sampson, E., & Brandon, A. The effects of role and opinion deviation on small group behavior. *Sociometry,* 1964, **27,** 261-281.

Schachter, S. Deviation, rejection, and communication. *Journal of Abnormal and Social Psychology,* 1951, **46,** 190-207.

Schutz, W. C. *FIRO: A three-dimensional theory of interpersonal behavior.* New York: Rinehart, 1958.

Scott, F. G. Family group structure and patterns of social interaction. *American Journal of Sociology,* 1962, **68,** 214-228.

Sharan (Singer), S. N. Family interaction with schizophrenics and their siblings. *Journal of Abnormal Psychology,* 1966, **71,** 345-353.

Siegel, G. M., & Harkins, J. P. Verbal behavior of adults in two conditions with institutionalized retarded children, *J. of Speech and Hearing Disorders Monographs,* 1963, **10,** 39-47.

Slater, P. Role differentiation in small groups. *American Sociological Review,* 1955, **20,** 300-310.

Slater, P. Parental role differentiation. *American Journal of Sociology,* 1961, **67,** 296-311.

Stabenau, J. R., Tupin, J., Werner, M., & Pollin, W. A comparative study of families of schizophrenics, delinquents, and normals. *Psychiatry,* 1965, **28,** 45-59.

Stevenson, H. W., Keen, R., & Knights, R. M. Parents and strangers as reinforcing agents for children's performance. *Journal of Abnormal and Social Psychology,* 1963, **67,** 183-186.

Stone, P. J., Dunphy, D. C., Smith, M. S., & Ogilvie, D. M. *The General Inquirer: A computer approach to content analysis.* Cambridge, Mass.: M.I.T. Press, 1966.

Straus, J., & Straus, M. A. Family roles and sex differences in creativity of children in Bombay and Minneapolis, *Journal of Marriage and Family,* 1968, February, 46-53.

Straus, M. A. Measuring families. In H. T. Christensen (Ed.) *Handbook of marriage and the family.* Chicago: Rand McNally, 1964. Pp. 335-400.

Straus, M. A. The influence of sex of child and social class on instrumental and expressive family roles in a laboratory setting. *Sociology and Social Research,* 1967, **52,** 7-21.

Straus, M. A. Communication, creativity, and problem-solving ability of middle- and working-class families in three societies. *American Journal of Sociology,* 1968, **73,** 417-430.

Strodtbeck, F. L. Husband-wife interaction over revealed differences. *American Sociological Review,* 1951, **16,** 468-473.

Strodtbeck, F. L. Family interaction, values and achievement. *In* D. McClelland (Ed.), *Talent and society.* Princeton, N.J.: Van Nostrand, 1958.

Strodtbeck, F. L., & Mann, R. D. Sex role differentiation in jury deliberations. *Sociometry,* 1956, **19,** 3-11.

Turk, H. Instrumental values and the popularity of instrumental leaders. *Social Forces*, 1961, **39**, 252-260.

Waxler, N. E. Families and schizophrenia: studies in deviance. Mimeo., Boston: Massachusetts Mental Health Center, 1967.

Waxler, N. E., Families and schizophrenia: alternatives to longitudinal studies. *In* M. Levitt (Ed.), *The mental health field: A critical appraisal*. Forthcoming publication, 1970.

Waxler, N. E., & Mishler, E. G. Scoring and reliability problems in interaction process analysis: a methodological note. *Sociometry*, 1966, **29**, 28-40.

Waxler, N. E., & Mishler, E. G. Sequential patterning in family interaction. *Family Process*, 1970, **9**, 211-220.

Wiggins, J., Dill, F., & Schwartz, R. On status liability. *Sociometry*, 1965, **28**, 197-209.

Winch, R. *Mate selection*. New York: Harper, 1958.

Wynne, L. C., Ryckoff, I., Day, J., & Hirsch, S. Pseudomutuality in the family relations of schizophrenics. *Psychiatry*, 1958, **21**, 205-220.

Wynne, L. C., & Singer, M. T. Thought disorder and family relations of schizophrenics. I. A research strategy. *Archives of General Psychiatry*, 1963, **9**, 191-198.

Ziller, R. C., & Exline, R. V. Some consequences of age heterogeneity in decision-making groups. *Sociometry*, 1958, **21**, 198-211.

WHY DO GROUPS MAKE RISKIER DECISIONS THAN INDIVIDUALS?[1]

Kenneth L. Dion,[2] Robert S. Baron,[3] and Norman Miller[4]
UNIVERSITY OF MINNESOTA

[1]Preparation of this paper was supported in part by National Institutes of Health Predoctoral Research Fellowships to Kenneth L. Dion and Robert S. Baron and both a Sabbatical Leave Fellowship from the University of Minnesota and a National Institutes of Health Special Research Fellowship to Norman Miller. We would like to thank our many colleagues who provided us with prepublication drafts of their recent research and/or comments on an early draft of this paper. In particular we wish to thank Penny Baron, Tom Bouchard, Roger Brown, Eugene Burnstein, Russell Clark III, Karen K. Dion, Calvin Hoyt, James P. Flanders, Jerald Jellison, Nathan Kogan, Helmut Lamm, George Levinger, David Myers, Serge Moscovici, P. Pilkonis, Dean Pruitt, Ivan Steiner, Allan I. Teger, Donald L. Thistlethwaite, Neil Vidmar, Michael A. Wallach, Robert Wolosin, Robert Zajonc, and Mark Zanna. We feel that this review has benefited substantially from their help. Of course, responsibility for its present content is our own and it should not be assumed that any completely agree with our own evaluations.

[2]Now at University of Toronto.
[3]Now at University of Iowa.
[4]Now at University of Southern California.

I. Introduction

In recent years the biggest surge of research on group processes focuses on group decision-making and risk-taking. The typical finding is that a person's willingness to take risks increases after participating in a group discussion of the problem. This change is usually referred to as the "risky-shift" and was first demonstrated by Stoner (1961).

The research impetus that followed Stoner's initial experiment sprang largely from the counterintuitive nature of the findings. At that time, most of the relevant evidence suggested that group interaction and group decision-making would reduce risk-taking. For example, the research on conformity indicated that pressure to reach a compromise or a consensus induces groups to direct influence attempts at "deviates" (e.g., Schachter, 1951). This suggests that group interaction should reduce the variability among individuals' tendencies to take risks and produce an averaging effect among group members. On the face of it, these effects seem incompatible with an overall increase in riskiness. In addition, Whyte (1956) contended that group discussion produces more conservative decisions. Supporting this view, Barnlund (1959) demonstrated that in a logic task, groups are more careful than isolated individuals. Why then did Stoner find a shift to greater risk-taking following group interaction? This chapter reviews the research that has sought to analyze why groups make riskier decisions than individuals. In doing so, it builds on an earlier and more general chapter on risk-taking by Kogan and Wallach (1967c).

A. THE BASIC RESEARCH PARADIGM

Paralleling the Stoner experiment, investigations of group risk-taking typically use a repeated measures design. Private, pretest measures of risk-taking are obtained first. Subjects are then exposed to an experimental situation. A typical treatment, for example, may assemble individuals into a discussion group and have them arrive at consensus decisions on each of the items (hypothetical situations) comprising the initial risk-taking measure. These decisions constitute a second measure of risk-taking (the treatment test). A difference between the mean pretest score and mean group (treatment) score in the direction of increased risk-taking typically defines the magnitude of the risky-shift.[5] After the group is dissolved, the posttest measures of individual risk-taking are often again obtained. While the comparison of this third measure to the other previous measures is interesting, differences between it and other measures generally are not what researchers are speaking of when they use the phrase "risky-shift."

When the treatment requires participation in group interaction, the several "shift" measures derived from the three-staged, repeated measures design may reflect different compliance processes. Wallach, Kogan, and Bem (1962) recognized that differences between the pretest and treatment may be due to the operation of external social pressures. That is, it is possible that such differences might at least in part reflect overt compliance processes. Maintenance of group-induced changes on private, posttest measures of risk-taking (taken after the group is dissolved) is interpreted as covert compliance; it reflects the effect of group exposure on the realignment of individual risk-taking preferences. In a more specific classification scheme, Mackenzie and Bernhardt (1968) proposed that the amount of recidivism observed in treatment-posttest comparisons defines the degree of overt compliance, and that pretest-posttest comparisons provide a measure of covert compliance. The important difference between these two classification systems is that the Mackenzie and Bernhardt scheme specifies the means for assessing the degree of overt compliance in the decision process. While Wallach et al. emphasize the role of covert changes, Mackenzie and Bernhardt regard the risky-shift as a mixture of both overt and covert compliance. It is important to note that the repeated-measures format typically used in the risky-shift research is minimally effective in detecting "overt-covert" differences. The Solomon Four-Group design (Campbell & Stanley, 1963)

---

[5]There are a few isolated exceptions to this rule. For example, Flanders and Thistlethwaite (1967) used the difference between pretest and posttest measures of private risk-taking as their index of the risky-shift.

offers a more effective procedure for determining overt and covert compliance effects.

B. Tasks

The paper-and-pencil Choice-Dilemmas questionnaire (Kogan & Wallach, 1964, Appendix E) has served as the primary instrument for assessing risk-taking preferences in risky-shift investigations. It consists of twelve hypothetical, "real life" situations in which a fictitious person must choose between a risky or a conservative course of action. Of these two alternatives, the risky option was constructed to be more desirable, but, of course, also had less chance of succeeding. For example, a sample item describes an electrical engineer who has a choice between: (*a*) remaining at his present, secure job — one with a modest salary but little hope of improvement or (*b*) joining a new firm which has a highly uncertain future but offers the possibility of sharing in the ownership. The respondent's task is to indicate what the odds for success would have to be before he would advise the fictitious person to attempt the risky alternative. On this task the respondent can choose among 1, 3, 5, 7, or 9 chances in 10 that the risky alternative will be successful. There is an additional category for each item which allows respondents to indicate whether they feel that the risky course of action should not be attempted no matter what the odds.

Authors of the Choice-Dilemma instrument have reported corrected split-half reliabilities ranging from .53 to .80 for various samples (Kogan & Wallach, 1964; Wallach & Kogan, 1961) and test-retest reliabilities (1 week) of .78 and .82 (Wallach *et al.,* 1962). In terms of validity, relationships with other risk-taking behaviors (Kogan and Wallach, 1964) and other types of risk-related phenomena (Kogan & Wallach, 1961; Wallach & Kogan, 1961) have been demonstrated. Pruitt and Teger (1967) pooled data from group risk-taking studies conducted in various locations throughout the country. They found that 10 of the 12 items exhibit consistent risky-shift effects across investigations.

A second type of group risk-taking task requires subjects to choose the level of difficulty they wish to attempt on various categories (e.g., antonyms, analogies, and mathematics) of old College-Board examination items (Wallach, Kogan, & Bem, 1964). These questions reflect nine levels of difficulty ranging from 10 to 90% failure in a national sample. The higher the difficulty level chosen, the greater the risk-taking.

Experimental gambling situations constitute the third type of risk-taking task. Zajonc and his associates used a simple light guessing situation in which one light has a high probability of occurrence with a small reward, while the other has a lower frequency but a somewhat larger reward. On a given trial, the aim is to guess which of these two lights will be illuminated. One of the important features of this task is that subjects immediately experience the outcomes of their decisions from trial to trial. A second gambling task (Pruitt & Teger, 1969) differs from the one used by Zajonc and his associates in that it manipulates stake as well as probability preferences.[6] In addition, it uses a wager format that provides no feedback from trial to trial.

In terms of frequency, the Choice-Dilemmas task accounts for approximately 80% of group risk-taking studies. The problem-solving and gambling tasks constitute a much smaller share—approximately 14% and 6%, respectively.

C. GENERALITY OF THE RISKY-SHIFT[7]

Risky-shifts are not characteristic of any one age or occupational category. They have been found with established professional groups (Siegel & Zajonc, 1967), industrial supervisors (Rim, 1965a), senior executives (D. G. Marquis, 1962), management trainees (Stoner, 1961), male and female undergraduates (Wallach *et al.*, 1962) as well as grade-school boys and girls (Kogan & Carlson, 1969). However, it is apparent that all of these groups (with the exception of the last) probably fall in the upper portion of the intelligence distribution. Although the bulk of research used American subjects, risky-shifts have also been found with other nationalities, including English (Bateson, 1966), Israeli (e.g., Rim, 1963), Canadian (Vidmar, 1970), French (Kogan & Doise, 1969), and German subjects (Lamm & Kogan, 1970).

Most of the aforementioned studies demonstrated risky-shifts under conditions in which group discussion continued until consensus was reached. However, increased risk-taking has also been obtained under

[6]A stake preference refers to the *amount* one will risk (for any given likelihood of a successful outcome). A probability preference refers to the *likelihood of success* (irrespective of the amount waged).

[7]A semantic problem arises in that careful consideration of the problems or tasks suggests that they tell us little about actual risk-taking (cf. Flanders, 1970). Rather, they provide a means of studying group processes—largely within the setting of a single type of experimental design. These issues are discussed more fully in the concluding section. But meanwhile, for the bulk of this paper we use the term used by those performing the research, *viz.*, "risky-shift." In the interests of a more proper conceptualization, the reader might profitably substitute a term like "polarization" or simply think of the term "risky-shift" as a nominal label for the process evoked by the various experimental designs. In other words, we postpone our discussion of the extent to which the results of the various experiments bear on the question of how groups behave when confronted with truly high risk alternatives that portend direct consequences for themselves.

discussion without consensus (Wallach & Kogan, 1965) and under conditions that minimize the impact of group discussion by preventing visual contact (Kogan & Wallach, 1967a) or face-to-face communication (Lamm, 1967; Kogan & Wallach, 1967d). In addition, risky-shifts have also been produced in two situations that completely eliminate any exposure to group discussion: (1) when subjects do not interact verbally but are aware of each others' risk preferences (Blank, 1968; Teger & Pruitt, 1967) and (2) when individual subjects are given a chance to restudy the Choice-Dilemma items and respond to them a second time (Bateson, 1966; Flanders & Thistlethwaite, 1967).

While most studies have used the Choice-Dilemmas task, risky-shifts have also been demonstrated with more realistic tasks involving monetary rewards for successful problem-solving performance (Wallach et al., 1964), and monetary rewards under threat of aversive consequences for failure on a problem-solving task (Bem, Wallach, & Kogan, 1965). On the other hand, the group risk-taking experiments that use gambling or betting tasks yield an equivocal pattern of outcomes. Several studies (Atthowe, 1960; Hinds, 1962; Hunt & Rowe, 1960; Lonergran & McClintock, 1961; Zajonc, Wolosin, Wolosin, & Sherman, 1968) report either no shift or a shift toward caution in group situations; others (Blank, 1968; Pruitt & Teger, 1969; Zajonc, Wolosin, Wolosin, & Sherman, 1969; Zajonc, Wolosin, Wolosin, & Loh, 1970) show shifts toward risk. Nevertheless, it is obvious that all told, the effect generalizes across subjects, situations, and tasks. The one reservation that must be reiterated is the extent to which the tasks lack any (much less severe) consequences for the group members.

D. Plan of the Paper

This chapter will review the literature manifestly concerned with group risk-taking comprehensively, and examine in detail the major alternative interpretations offered to explain the risky-shift. Four explanations receive particular consideration: (1) diffusion of responsibility, (2) persuasion, (3) familiarization, and (4) cultural values. Later sections spell out these explanations. They were chosen because they are the most frequently cited explanations in the literature and have generated the bulk of empirical research on group risk-taking. Other more specific hypotheses concerning the risky-shift effect have been considered elsewhere (Pruitt & Teger, 1967) and are not dealt with in detail here.[8]

[8] Likewise, this review does not consider recent experiments dealing with risk-taking in *intergroup* negotiation situations (Hermann and Kogan, 1968; Lamm and Kogan, 1970) or ethical risk-taking in social situations (e.g., Rettig, 1966).

The sections to follow use a standard format in considering each of the four selected interpretations. In each case, derivative hypotheses are specified and underlying mechanisms presumed responsible for the risky-shift effect are examined in detail. Relevant research is brought to bear upon these elements and serves as the basis for a judgment of the adequacy and validity of each of the four hypothesized explanations.

II. The Diffusion of Responsibility Explanation

According to the responsibility-diffusion explanation, the risky-shift represents a *true* group effect, namely, one that cannot occur with isolated individuals (Pruitt & Teger, 1967; Secord & Backman, 1964). It assumes that fear of failure primarily deters an individual's tendency to take risks. Group decision-making, in contrast to individual decision-making, presumably diffuses responsibility among the group members. This diffusion of responsibility reduces fear of failure and thereby enables people to make riskier decisions.[9]

The relationship between fear of failure and responsibility-diffusion has not been given a great deal of emphasis by those who advocate the responsibility-diffusion interpretation. However, they do imply that diffusion of responsibility reduces or eliminates fear of failure and thereby increases risk-taking. For example, consider the following excerpts from Kogan and Wallach (1967b):

> . . . failure of a risky course is *easier to bear* when others are implicated in a decision; . . . consider a homogeneous group composed of test anxious individuals, that is, individuals uniformly fearful of failure . . . [such people] might be especially willing to diffuse responsibility in an effort to *relieve the burden* of possible fear of failure. (p. 51).

> The burden of *fear* [carried by high test anxious subjects] will show *a sharp decline* when one does not have to bear all alone, the responsibility for failure of a risky course. [p. 56, all italics ours].

The major proponents of the responsibility-diffusion interpretation — Kogan, Wallach, and their associates — have consistently viewed responsibility-diffusion primarily as an "anxiety melioration" process. On the other hand, their view of the necessary and sufficient conditions for the occurrence of responsibility-diffusion has undergone substantial change. Their original formulation (Wallach *et al.*, 1964) stressed that

---

[9] Fear of failure has been characterized as "a capacity for reacting with shame and embarrassment when the outcome of performance is failure . . ." and is thought to be aroused "whenever it is clear to a person that his performance will be evaluated and failure is a distinct possibility" (Atkinson, 1964, p. 244).

the process of reaching a unanimous group decision diffuses feelings of personal responsibility for failure among group members and, therefore, leads to increased risk-taking. With the subsequent discovery that group consensus and joint decision had no additional impact over and above mere group discussion in producing a risky-shift (Wallach & Kogan, 1965), the emphasis upon group decision was obviously no longer tenable. As a result, they pointed to other consequences of group discussion or membership that might produce a feeling of shared responsibility for a risky decision and thereby lead to a risky-shift. They suggested that stronger affective bonds between group members was one consequence of group discussion that could increase feelings of shared responsibility. This notion will be referred to as the "affective bonds" hypothesis.

In summary, the diffusion of responsibility interpretation of group risk-taking now suggests the following causal chain: (1) group discussion creates affective bonds; (2) affective bonds permit diffusion of responsibility; (3) diffusion of responsibility reduces fear of failure; (4) reduced fear of failure produces the risky-shift. Those who advocate the responsibility-diffusion interpretation focus upon three basic derivations from this causal chain. (a) Group discussion is the necessary and sufficient condition to produce the risky-shift (from statements 1-4). (b) The affective bonds produced by group discussion permit diffusion of responsibility (from statements 2-4). (c) Responsibility-diffusion is the essential reason for the risky-shift (from statements 3 and 4).

These derivations are not necessarily basic or central points for a responsibility-diffusion explanation. For instance, one can easily argue that both hypothesis (a) and (c) are stated too strongly, and that neither (a) nor (b) need be true for (c) to remain valid. Nevertheless, these propositions are listed here because they have been most frequently espoused by those who favor the responsibility-diffusion explanation. Although most of the research on responsibility-diffusion explores or examines these hypotheses, other closely related hypotheses can be derived (and tested). For example, if as Wallach and Kogan (1965) maintain, the affective bonds formed in discussion enable the individual to feel less blame when he entertains the possible failure of a risky decision, then the magnitude of risky-shift should be directly proportional to the strength of these bonds. Although not considered by responsibility-diffusion theorists, another derivation is that the magnitude of risky-shift monotonically increases as a function of group size (e.g., Mackenzie & Bernhardt, 1968). When a large group of people share in a decision, each individual member should feel little responsibility for the outcome and further should feel relatively protected from retaliation or punishment since his own individual behavior is not apt to be a point of focus. The proposition that large groups are riskier than smaller ones suggests still another derivation — that anonymity might contribute to the risky-shift. This notion will be referred to as the anonymity hypothesis. Note that in contrast to the affective bonds hypothesis, the anonymity hypothesis seems to focus attention on fear of punishment as well as on guilt and fear of failure as inhibitors of risk-taking. Anonymity should increase risk-taking by facilitating deindividuation and lowering fear of punishment.

The following sections separately consider hypotheses (a), (b), and (c) (above) in terms of relevant empirical evidence. In addition, they discuss the evidence relevant to fear of failure and the anonymity hypothesis.

A. THE RESPONSIBILITY-DIFFUSION HYPOTHESIS

Wallach *et al.* (1964) tested the responsibility-diffusion mechanism by systematically manipulating features of individually shared and group shared responsibility within the basic discussion-to-consensus paradigm. The experimental task was a problem-solving situation in which rewards for correct solutions were commensurate with the difficulty of the problem. Feelings of responsibility for others were experimentally manipulated by varying whether or not individuals felt that either their own problem-solving performance or choice of difficulty level might determine the group outcome. Thus, the experimental conditions outlined in Table I can be viewed as varying along a continuum of responsibility.

For example, subjects in the "group-group" condition should feel least responsible in that no single individual is liable for the level of difficulty chosen, and, if a subject is chosen as group representative, it is the responsibility of those others in the group who chose him. In the "group-lot" condition, a given subject should feel slightly more responsible, for, although he is not responsible for the level of difficulty chosen, he cannot blame other members of the group if he is chosen as group representative. The results provide several sources of direct support for the responsibility-diffusion interpretation. First, a risky-shift only occured in those conditions in which there was a group decision. Second, when responsibility for others was experimentally created, a cautious shift occurred. Finally, the monotonic cell orderings array themselves in precisely the pattern that would be predicted from the responsibility-diffusion hypothesis.

On the other hand, several studies seem to challenge the responsibility-diffusion interpretation. D. G. Marquis (1962) designated as group leader the person whose initial risk-taking score on a set of hypothetical items was closest to the average for that group. This appointed leader was then given authority for conduct of the group discussion as well as sole responsibility for the final decision. Significant increases in risk-taking were found for both leaders and other group members after group discus-

TABLE I
DESCRIPTIONS AND RESULTS OF WALLACH et al. (1964)[a]

	Low Responsibility (Experimental Condition)			High Responsibility	
	Grp – Grp[b]	Grp – Lot[c]	Grp – Indiv[d]	Indiv – Indiv[e] (control)	Indiv – Grp[f]
Mean Change in	N.S.	N.S.			
Risk-Taking	12.5	9.4	5.6	2.4	−1.6
(over all items)		Sig.		Sig.	Sig.

[a]Scores are differences between mean initial risk level and mean risk level chosen for posttest stage. Higher scores denote a greater risky-shift.

[b]Group-group: After completing pretest, Ss reach unanimous consensus about the degree of difficulty that a representative of the group will attempt (on College Board items) where that representative is to be subsequently chosen by the group and where his performance determines the group outcome (monetary reward).

[c]Group-lot: Same as group-group condition except that group representative is chosen by lot.

[d]Group-individual: After completing pretest, Ss required to reach unanimous consensus about what level of difficulty they, as *individuals*, would attempt on College Board items where each individual's performance determines his outcome (monetary reward).

[e]Individual-individual: After completing pretest, Ss required to individually choose the difficulty level that they as *individuals* would attempt on College Board items.

[f]Individual-group: After completing pretest, Ss required to individually choose difficulty level and were told that they might be chosen to represent a group at whatever level they, as individuals, chose.

sion, with no significant difference between them. Because leaders were charged with sole responsibility for the group decision, Marquis argued that diffusion of responsibility could not operate for them. However, since group discussion preceded the leader's decision, there nevertheless was an opportunity for responsibility to be diffused. In other words, even though the leader had formal responsibility for all decisions, he may not have felt personally or psychologically responsible. He may have still viewed the decision as a group product.

More recently, Pruitt and Teger (1969) failed to find a risky-shift in a situation in which responsibility for the group decision was objectively shared by the entire group. After making individual private decisions, groups (of individuals) then discussed risk-irrelevant filler items. Before making their final decisions on Choice-Dilemma items, subjects were instructed that their preferred risk levels would be averaged with those of other group members to determine the group decision. Since everyone in the group objectively participated in the group decisions as to what risk to take, responsibility should have diffused and allowed riskier decisions. Instead a nonsignificant shift toward caution was observed. These data indicate that an objective sharing of responsibility does not necessarily lead to increased risk-taking. Although the data certainly seem incompatible with the Kogan and Wallach contention that diffusion of responsibility leads to increased risk-taking, the study is vulnerable to a criticism that applies in general to the research investigating the relationship between responsibility and risk-taking. Specifically, an apparently direct manipulation of responsibility may not result in a psychological state that corresponds to the intended manipulation. For example, although averaging individual decisions to form a group discussion may objectively diffuse responsibility, it does not necessarily follow that corresponding feelings of subjectively shared responsibility accompany this operationalization. The use of indirect situational manipulations of responsibility and the virtual absence of manipulation checks undermine our confidence that the specific operations do, in fact, result in actual variations of the desired psychological states. This criticism seems particularly important when the experimental tasks have no implication or consequence for the group.[10] Thus, whether or not a sharing of responsibility leads to increased risk-taking remains an empirical question.

B.   THE ROLE OF GROUP DISCUSSION

Stoner's (1961) original experiment was criticized for using managerial trainees as subjects—a sample that may have been more prone than average persons to make risky decisions. As indicated, Wallach and co-workers' (1962) subsequent replication with male and female undergraduates suggested to them that processes of group interaction and interpersonal confrontation (rather than the proclivities of business students) produced the preference for riskier decisions. To demonstrate further the importance of actual group discussion as the antecedent condition for the risky-shift, Bem et al. (1965) compared a discussion-to-consensus condition to several other treatments which led subjects to anticipate a discussion that never actually materialized. Only the actual discussion situation yielded a significant risky-shift. While these results support the idea that some form of group interaction increases risk-taking, they fail to pinpoint the specific aspect of interaction necessary and/or sufficient for the effect.

In a more analytical experiment, Wallach and Kogan (1965) contrasted two discussion situations (with and without consensus) to a consensus-without-discussion situation in which subjects communicated their risk preferences by written messages. Significant risky-shifts occurred in both discussion conditions but not in the consensus-only treat-

---

[10]This is not to argue that manipulation checks are a panacea. They are often particularly susceptible to the image-making or face-saving whim of the subject. When administered before the treatment they may have either a sensitizing effect or a commitment effect; when administered afterward, they may no longer reflect the psychological state that existed at the time of the treatment.

ment. On this basis, Wallach and Kogan concluded that group discussion is the minimal, necessary, and sufficient condition for the risky-shift effect.

However, as we noted earlier, subsequent research has not confirmed their contention that participation in group discussion is the only sufficient condition for producing the risky-shift. For example, Teger and Pruitt (1967) criticized the methodology of the consensus-without-discussion in the Wallach-Kogan study for appearing to "... encourage group convergence on the mean of initial decisions. . . ." Teger and Pruitt required groups to reach consensus by successive balloting and found a small but significant risky-shift in a nondiscussion "information exchange" condition in which subjects merely revealed their risk preferences publicly without verbal communication. Blank (1968) also obtained a risky-shift in an information exchange condition. He used a gambling task that made subjects aware of each other's risk choices but prevented them from interacting verbally.

In another related research procedure, subjects observed actual discussion situations but did not participate themselves. Kogan and Wallach (1967a) compared interacting discussion groups with groups that only listened to a tape recording of another interacting group. Although the magnitude of shift was greater for interacting groups, significant risky-shift effects were found for the listening as well as the interacting conditions. In addition, Lamm (1967) compared two vicarious discussion conditions: (1) observation of an interacting group through a one-way mirror, and (2) listening to group discussion over a loudspeaker. Significant increases in risk-taking were found under both conditions. Observation produced a numerically but not significantly greater increment in risk-taking than mere listening.

To explain these various results, Kogan and Wallach (1967c,d) suggested that vicariously experienced emotional interchange as well as the modeling and social facilitation effects that arise from exposure to actual group interactions may increase risk-taking in situations that only permit the observation of a discussion. The fact that a more complete exposure to actual interaction results in a greater risky-shift supports their argument. For example, it has been demonstrated that purely vocal content provides emotional cues as well as objective information (Levy, 1964). Apparently, however, emotional communications are judged more accurately with vocal, visual, facial information than with mere vocal cues (Levitt, 1964). The relative magnitude of risky-shifts in the experimental conditions of the Lamm study supports this interpretation (cf. Mackenzie & Bernhardt, 1968). However, in order to assess the importance of vicariously experienced affective interchanges fully, it would be necessary to control for modeling and information effects. If risky-shifts in vicarious exposure to discussion situations can be shown to be largely attributable to vicariously experienced emotional exchanges, the findings from this research paradigm could be accommodated by the responsibility-diffusion notion. Nevertheless, these results as well as Kogan and Wallach's account of them clearly contradict their earlier emphasis on the necessity and sufficiency of group discussion for producing riskier decisions.

Although Kogan and Wallach (1967d, p. 82) currently admit that information exchange and vicarious experience acquired through exposure to actual interaction may contribute to a risky-shift, they contend that: ". . . group interaction . . . introduce(s) still another determinant . . ., the effect of which is a further enhancement in risk-taking shifts." This generalization has been substantiated in two investigations (Kogan & Wallach, 1967d; Teger & Pruitt, 1967). Lamm, however, has found observation to produce as robust a risky-shift as participation in actual group discussion.

Studies investigating the familiarization interpretation are also relevant to the issue of the importance of group discussion as a necessary condition for the risky-shift. Although the familiarization explanation is discussed later in more detail, a brief mention of the relevant findings is appropriate here.

By having isolated individuals reconsider their initial decisions on Choice-Dilemma items, several investigators (Bateson, 1966; Flanders and Thistlethwaite, 1967) were able to produce significant increases in risk-taking in the complete absence of group discussion. However, a number of subsequent attempts to replicate reliable risky-shifts with familiarization procedures for individuals (Miller & Dion, 1970; Pruitt & Teger, 1967; Teger, Pruitt, St. Jean, & Haaland, 1970; Ferguson & Vidmar, 1970) have failed. Anticipating our conclusion in the familiarization section, we believe that it remains to be demonstrated that familiarization per se produces a risky-shift with *isolated* individuals.[11] Furthermore, it now seems unlikely that familiarization is the critical factor in risky-shifts produced by group discussion.

In sum, the available research indicates that participation in group discussion is not a necessary prerequisite for the risky-shift. Nonverbal information exchange and exposure to discussion by other persons constitute sufficient conditions for producing the effect. However, it appears that group discussion is still capable of producing increments in risk-taking over and above these sufficient conditions. Given the uncertain reliability of familiarization treatments and the lack of research on other variables that might increase risk-taking in isolated individuals, the answer to whether the risky-shift effect can occur in the complete absence of interaction or exposure to it awaits further research. Yet, as already indicated, it should surprise us if it cannot, and the demonstration that it can would not by itself strike us as particularly interesting.

[11]Of course, there are other variables besides familiarization that might increase risk-taking in socially isolated individuals. For instance, it seems quite feasible to apply procedures or instructions to isolated persons that directly reduce responsibility or fear of failure.

C. THE AFFECTIVE BONDS HYPOTHESIS

According to Kogan and Wallach (1967c,d; Wallach and Kogan, 1965), the development of affective bonds between individuals during group discussion forms an essential basis for the operation of the responsibility-diffusion mechanism which, in turn, presumably mediates any risky-shift. Two recent studies of personality factors present evidence for this assumption.

In one study, Kogan and Wallach (1967b) composed discussion groups of subjects who scored either high or low on the personality variables of defensiveness and test anxiety. Defensiveness is the personality variable of primary relevance to the present discussion. According to several theorists (Rogers, 1959; White, 1964), highly defensive persons approach others with a careful, guarded manner because they fear exposing personal weakness. Conceptualized in this manner, defensiveness should interfere with the formation of the affective bonds that are presumably essential for the diffusion of responsibility. Therefore, defensiveness should inhibit the shift toward risk normally produced by group discussion. Consistent with this expectation, groups of persons low in defensiveness showed greater risky-shifts on consensus decisions than groups of persons high in defensiveness.

In the second investigation, Wallach, Kogan, and Burt (1967) used scores from the Embedded Figures Test to compare discussion groups with either field-dependent or field-independent persons. Prior research indicates that the field independence-dependence distinction closely parallels a contrast between cognitive versus affective styles. While field-independent persons supposedly display interpersonal aloofness and a predominantly cognitive orientation, field-dependent individuals emphasize affective features in their self-descriptions and react more responsively to social stimuli (Witkin, Dyk, Faterson, Goodenough & Karp, 1962; Messick & Damarin, 1964). Therefore, the affective bonds hypothesis suggests that groups of field-independent persons will exhibit greater shifts toward risk than groups of field-independent persons. Contrary to predictions, field-dependent and field-independent groups produced risky-shifts of equal magnitude. An internal analysis revealed that considerably different outcomes emerged under conditions of high involvement—as inferred from the length of discussion time. Longer discussion times were associated with stronger risky-shifts for field-dependent groups and conservative-shifts for field-dependent groups. Since differences emerged only in an internal analysis, these data are less compelling; nevertheless, they are consistent with the affective bonds hypothesis.[12]

A further derivation from the affective bonds hypothesis is the prediction of a positive relationship between group cohesiveness and magnitude of the risky-shift. In the context of an experimental gambling situation requiring subjects to discuss actual bets, Pruitt and Teger (1969) included sociometric items on a postquestionnaire to derive an index of cohesiveness. Correlations between cohesiveness and risky-shift were all positive and, in one case, reached an acceptable level of significance. Albeit the evidence is weak, the results suggest that ". . . more cohesive groups shift more toward risk . . .," as would be expected from the affective bonds hypothesis. In a subsequent experiment, Pruitt and Teger (1969) established a similar level of cohesiveness by having groups of individuals discuss risk-irrelevant items. When individuals subsequently made private decisions, nonsignificant shifts toward caution resulted. If nothing else, these results suggest that the mere presence of affective bonds is not a sufficient condition for the risky-shift.

Unfortunately, none of the above studies provides an *experimental* test of the affective bonds hypothesis: *viz.*, that the affective bonds formed or present during discussion of risk-relevant items produce a risky-shift. Specifically, none of the previous investigations directly manipulated the strength of "affective bonds" among members of discussion groups. In the two personality investigations, independent variables were established by selecting subjects on the basis of scores on personality factors. Such a selection procedure precludes the possibility of randomly assigning subjects to experimental conditions. As a consequence of nonrandom assignment, extraneous variables may be systematically confounded with the independent variable. Thus, any observed effects on the dependent measure could be potentially attributable to a third, uncontrolled variable associated with the treatment. The positive correlations between cohesiveness may be either a cause or a consequence of the risky-shift. Finally, Pruitt and Teger's (1969) subsequent study primarily indicates that, in the absence of discussion, the formation of affective ties between persons is insufficient to increase risk-taking. However, it provides no information about the role of "affective bonds" in the paradigmatic situation in which group members discuss risk-relevant problems.

To remedy these difficulties, Dion *et al.* (1970) experimentally induced high and low levels of group cohesiveness. Contrary to the affec-

---

[12]It is important to note that any explanation that stresses the role of influence processes during group interaction would not find these results incompatible. In other words, this type of finding should not be thought of as providing exclusive support for a diffusion of responsibility explanation. They could easily be incorporated into leadership or cultural value explanations.

tive bonds hypothesis, however, the less cohesive groups exhibited greater risky-shifts than high-cohesive groups on both consensus and post consensus shift measures. Although the risky-shift is a robust phenomenon, high cohesiveness actually inhibited the shift toward risk in discussion groups. To account for these results, Dion, Miller, and Magnan suggest the intuitively plausible explanation that, as group members become more attracted to one another, they also become more loathe to minimize *personal* responsibility or displace responsibility for failure onto their fellow group members. Although the results diametrically oppose the predictions from the affective bonds hypothesis, this interpretation has the virtue of being consistent with the responsibility-diffusion notion. Nevertheless, this outcome and interpretation is paradoxical in the sense that the affective bonds hypothesis was initally proposed as a means of salvaging the responsibility-diffusion explanation from empirical disconfirmation. And in this respect, it is important to note that the affective bonds hypothesis was originally proposed without a careful examination or explanation of its relationship to the responsibility-diffusion notion (Pruitt & Teger, 1969).

D.   THE ANONYMITY HYPOTHESIS

As previously indicated, several investigators (Burnstein, 1967; Mackenzie & Bernhardt, 1968) suggest that the responsibility-diffusion explanation implies a positive relationship between the number of group members and the magnitude of the risky-shift. A larger group presumably permits greater diffusion of responsibility. Present evidence on this point is scanty. Teger and Pruitt (1967) found a strong positive relationship between group size and magnitude of risky-shift. Triads exhibited a nonsignificant shift toward risk, but a moderately strong significant risky-shift occurred in four-man groups, and the most robust risky-shift occurred in five-person groups.[13] Both four-person and five-person groups exhibited greater risky-shifts than three-person groups. although they did not differ from each other.[14]

Although the Teger and Pruitt results indirectly support the notion that anonymity increases risk-taking, the anonymity hypothesis itself

---

[13]Unfortunately, no differences between larger and smaller groups were found on postdiscussion, self-ratings of perceived responsibility. However, without information on the validity of this responsibility measure and with the possibility of floor or ceiling effects due to social desirability factors, the failure to find differences in responsibility does not clearly contradict the present line of thought.

[14]In an unpublished study, Marquis and Forward (cited in Burnstein, 1967) found no relationship between the risky-shift and group size with two, three, and five-person groups.

raises several conceptual issues. One of the inherent theoretical problems with any structural variable such as group size is that many other functional variables inevitably are associated with it (Kelley & Thibaut, 1954). In other words, it is likely that there is an underlying social psychological process responsible for any obtained group-size effect, and it is difficult to discover exactly what this is. Second, other explanations of the risky-shift (e.g., the leadership and cultural value interpretations) make essentially the same prediction regarding the effect of group size on the risky-shift. For that matter, it is not even clear that the responsibility-diffusion explanation necessarily predicts increased risk-taking as a result of increments in group size. Several investigators (e.g., Carter, Haythorn, Meirowitz, & Lanzetta, 1951; Gibb, 1951) report increased feelings of threat and increased inhibition to participate when groups are enlarged. Since these factors would undermine any sense of shared common fate, they should likewise inhibit the process of responsibility-diffusion and curtail risk-taking.

In sum, though plausible in principle, the anonymity hypothesis appears to be a theoretical blind alley when tied specifically to group size. However, anonymity can be directly manipulated in a variety of other ways that would avoid this theoretical ambiguity. To determine an effective experimental procedure, it is necessary to consider the characteristic qualities of anonymous social situations. Similar to a state of deindividuation (Festinger, Pepitone, & Newcomb, 1952; Singer, Brush, & Lublin, 1965), anonymity is basically an individual's subjective feeling of minimal self-consciousness and lowered identifiability. A feeling of anonymity can be created by allowing persons to communicate by means of written messages or intercoms. In addition, the relatively simple procedure of altering the seating pattern in discussion so that subjects do not directly face one another should lower identifiability. These manipulations of anonymity, however, may impair the interaction process somewhat (i.e., interfere with communication) in addition to reducing the salience of individual identity.

Other alterations of the experimental situation however, might lower individual feelings of self-consciousness while retaining the essential features of unrestricted interaction among group members. (a) For example, with the Choice-Dilemma task, one could heighten the feeling of anonymity by instructing subjects that their decisions are to be anonymous and forbid placing names on booklets. (b) Instead of the standard procedure in which each individual is given another blank copy of the Choice-Dilemma booklet on which to inscribe the consensus decisions in the group discussion situation, the experimenter might provide only a single booklet to the discussion group to increase the feeling of group participation and de-emphasize individuality. (c) In many group risk-taking situations, subjects are made to feel that their discussions are being monitored. A standard procedure, for example, is to have the experimenter remain present, but not participate, during discussion (e.g., Wallach & Kogan, 1965). Although the experimenter was not physically present, Teger and Pruitt (1967) told subjects that their discussions were being monitored by hidden microphones. Removing the experimenter's surveillance and minimizing other situational cues associated with monitoring (microphones, one-way mirrors, etc.) should enhance anonymity. (d) On the other hand, feelings of self-consciousness could be increased by having subjects wear name tags and/or telling them that their discussions are being monitored by a panel of experts who are rating members individually on their contribution to group problem-solving.

E. FEAR OF FAILURE

As noted earlier, one of the core ideas in the responsibility-diffusion explanation of the risky-shift asserts that an individual's fear of failure inhibits his willingness to take chances. Related to this proposition is the further assumption that responsibility-diffusion decreases fear of failure and, as a consequence, increases risk-taking. Some evidence substantiates the claims of the responsibility-diffusion interpretation concerning fear of failure. In one study, Kogan and Wallach (1967b reviewed above) systematically composed discussion groups with persons either homogeneously high or low on the traits of test anxiety and defensiveness. According to Atkinson (1964), the test-anxiety variable reflects an individual's predisposition or tendency to avoid failure and high test anxiety should therefore indicate a high fear of failure. Since group discussion presumably allays subjective fears of failure, Kogan and Wallach predicted that groups of individuals with high test anxiety would exhibit greater shifts toward risk than groups of persons low on test anxiety. These expectations were borne out. Furthermore, in an experiment discussed earlier, Bem et al. (1965) found that individuals who expected to suffer the aversive consequences of their decisions with others experiencing the same fate shifted to more conservative positions. When decisions with possible aversive consequences were made by the group, however, risky-shifts were obtained.

Although the above evidence is consistent with the responsibility-diffusion interpretation, there are some notable sources of uncertainty concerning the role of fear of failure in producing the risky-shift. In the first place, no study directly demonstrates that either the hypothetical or more realistic tasks used in the present research actually elicit fear of failure. Second, neither of the studies discussed above provides any *indepen-*

dent evidence that group discussion mitigates this fear. Even if fear of failure were found to be markedly lower in the group discussion setting than in the initial individual phase, this result might be due merely to the fact that group discussion follows individual decision-making in the usual risky-shift experimental paradigm. That is, a decline in fear of failure after (or during) group discussion might simply be attributable to an habituation process; individuals might become less responsive to the fear-evoking potential of the risk-taking situation after additional exposure or familiarity. To discount the possibility of habituation, one would have to examine either (*a*) the fear-reducing potential of group discussion without prior, individual exposure or (*b*) the comparative reduction in fear produced through group discussion versus individual reconsideration of initial decisions.

Further, in some instances, derivations from the responsibility-diffusion interpretation that deal with fear-of-failure are not supported by the available evidence. For example, one might predict that Choice-Dilemma items having the most serious consequences in the event of failure would exhibit the strongest risky-shifts. Yet the exact opposite occurs. Clark and Willems (personal communication) had subjects imagine that the hypothetical person had chosen the risky option and that it had failed. High negative correlations were found between mean ratings of the gravity of consequences and the Pruitt and Teger (1967) national risky-shift norms for Choice-Dilemma items. That is, stronger risky-shifts tend to be associated with items having the least serious repercussions in the event of failure.[15]

Finally, the unidirectional prediction between fear of failure and increased risk-taking is empirically disconfirmed in certain instances. For example, two of the twelve Choice-Dilemma items exhibit relatively consistent shifts toward caution with group discussion (Pruitt & Teger, 1967). With its present formulation, the responsibility-diffusion interpretation is totally inadequate to explain these instances of conservative shifts with group discussion. In this respect, the responsibility-diffusion interpretation is analogous to a one-tailed statistical test with all of its explanatory power focused on increased risk-taking. Consequently, instances of conservative shifts following group discussion strongly disconfirm the responsibility-diffusion thesis. However, since most of the Choice-Dilemma items are "risk-oriented," the responsibility-diffusion interpretation can generally predict main effects with some accuracy across Choice-Dilemma items.

In addition to this empirical problem, the responsibility-diffusion hypothesis concerning fear of failure stands in opposition to two alternative

---

[15]In fairness, one could argue that the success of any given discussion in reducing fear will be inversely related to the amount of fear aroused.

and opposite theoretical hypotheses about fear of failure. One is Atkinson's (1964) theory of risk-taking behavior, and the other can be called the Constriction Hypothesis.

According to predictions from Atkinson's theory, persons who exhibit little fear of failure should prefer intermediate risks. On the other hand, persons highly motivated to avoid failure should prefer either extremely conservative or extremely risky options. The choice of high or low odds presumably represents different strategies for coping with the aversive possibility of failure. By selecting particularly low odds, an anxious individual shields himself from the onus of failure by seemingly attempting the impossible. Blame for the failure on these very difficult tasks can be attributed to the relatively low likelihood of success. On the other hand, extremely favorable odds virtually guarantee the probability of success. Several experiments on individual risk-taking (e.g., Atkinson & Litwin, 1960; Edwards, 1953) confirm the prediction that persons with little fear of failure do, indeed, prefer intermediate risks. According to Atkinson's conception of the relation between fear of failure and risk-taking, reduction of fear—whether a consequence of group discussion or any other variable—should tend to reduce the *variance* among individual level of risk-taking *without* necessarily altering the mean level of risk. In other words, on the initial (individual) measure of risk-taking, fear of failure is presumably high and subjects select more extreme levels of risk or caution. The fear-reducing effect of group discussion should elicit more moderate or intermediate levels of risk among those at formerly extreme levels, thereby reducing the variance among individual decisions.[16] Yet the essential characteristic of the risky-shift is that groups of individuals become more extreme in their risk-taking. Of course, the predictions of achievement theory to risk-taking do not apply unless people view the possible outcomes largely as a function of their own skill. Perhaps they believe that the outcomes of (both hypothetical and real) tasks in risky-shift research are primarily under the control of chance factors.

A second and opposing hypothesis concerning fear of failure emphasizes the constricting functions of anxiety—the extent to which it pushes people to (a) look for social support (Schachter, 1959) and (b) behave in socially approved ways (Crowne & Marlowe, 1964). That is, high fear of failure might inhibit creative, atypical, or complex thinking and learning. This hypothesis argues that high fear of failure should lead people to

---

[16]Atkinson's theory doesn't state the relative frequencies with which persons fearing failure choose conservative versus high risk alternatives. If conservative or low risk choices were more normative, then of course mean shifts following a reduction in fear of failure would support the Kogan and Wallach predictions. At the same time however, the predictions regarding decreased variability following group discussion should still be confirmed. Yet needless to say, there are numerous other theoretical considerations that also predict reductions in variability following group discussion.

choose a level of risk-taking that is normative, intermediate, and not extreme in one direction or the other — one that inhibits or masks individualistic whims or idiosyncracies. When fear of failure is subsequently reduced by group discussion, such constricting tendencies no longer suppress individual, non-normative responses. Subjects should feel free to take risks that deviate more drastically from the level of risk ordinarily perceived as normative. Consequently, while the mean level of risk might show no change, the variability of risk-taking among individuals should be greater after group discussion.[17]

The preceding paragraphs demonstrate that at present there are no compelling theoretical or empirical reasons to support Kogan and Wallach's arguments about the role of fear of failure in group risk-taking. That is, when considered alone, neither Atkinson's theoretical approach nor the one outlined directly above predicts an increase in risk-taking as a consequence of reduced fear of failure.

F. CONCLUSION

The diffusion of responsibility explanation has not fared well. In the light of accumulating, contradictory evidence, its proponents have continually had to modify its central, underlying assumptions concerning the roles of group discussion and affective bonds as well as the necessary conditions for the occurrence of responsibility-diffusion. In another sense, however, this continual modification of the theory merits praise rather than reproval. Persistent theoretical modification is the preeminent symptom of the working scientist. It reflects the proper marriage of theory and experiment.

Nevertheless, many of the theoretical details proposed at one time or another have faltered under experimental scrutiny. For example, it is now clear that an actual group discussion experience is not the sole necessary precondition for the risky-shift — although some evidence suggests that group discussion produces an increment in risk-taking over and above that produced by information exchange or mere exposure to discussion. Similarly the fact that the risky-shift fails to occur when subjects (a) engage in risk-irrelevant discussion (Pruitt & Teger, 1969; Clark & Willems, personal communication) or (b) are part of a highly cohesive group (Dion et al., 1970) seriously detracts from the Wallach and Kogan contention that affective bonds per se underlie diffusion of responsibility. While the positive relationship observed between group size and the magnitude of the risky-shift (Teger & Pruitt, 1967) supports some of the an-

---

[17]When combined with the data indicating that individuals perceive themselves as riskier than they actually are relative to others, the Constriction Hypothesis does predict a risky shift as well as increased variance.

cillary theorizing by proponents of the responsibility-diffusion notion, it can also be derived from several other explanations of the risky-shift (e.g., cultural values). Moreover, methodological and conceptual considerations suggest that manipulation of group size is not in itself a very fruitful or efficient means for investigating the mechanisms that underlie the risky-shift.

We must recognize, however, that most of the reported data contradicting the responsibility-diffusion interpretation focus on the roles of group discussion and affective bonds. Despite the problems with these two variables, nevertheless, the hypothesized relation between responsibility-diffusion and risk-taking may be basically sound. That is, although neither group discussion nor affective bonds may effectively diffuse responsibility, successful diffusion of responsibility might nevertheless increase risk-taking. The recent disaffection of researchers with the responsibility-diffusion interpretation seems to stem in part from confusion about this point. In other words, confidence in the responsibility-diffusion explanation has waned primarily because some of the derivative and supporting hypotheses appear to be invalid. Notably absent, however, is evidence on the terminal process in the causal sequence outlined at the beginning of Section II (viz. responsibility-diffusion and fear of failure).

In fairness, certain aspects of this confusion are due to the Wallach and Kogan failure to specify clearly just what this causal sequence is. For example, as previously indicated, they have maintained that group discussion is the necessary and sufficient condition to produce the risky-shift, a statement that appears to be empirically false. Yet a broader view of their interpretation would emphasize instead that the risky-shift is mediated by a reduction in *individuals'* fear of failure. Since it should be possible to decrease fear of failure in the total absence of group interaction (e.g., via a manipulation of confidence in task ability), a reduction in fear of failure — not the occurrence of group discussion — should be considered the necessary and sufficient condition for the risky-shift.

Of course, even this emphasis on fear of failure leaves the responsibility-diffusion notion open to serious criticism for, as indicated, it is not at all clear from theoretical considerations that reducing fear of failure will enhance the mean extremity of group decision-making. It is possible, however, that diffusion of responsibility enhances risk-taking without reducing fear of failure. Perhaps group participation increases one's willingness (or ability) to engage in impulsive or irresponsible behavior and this — not a reduced fear of failure — increases risk-taking. In accord with this conjecture, a risky-shift has been found even when the risky alternatives had a lower expected value than the cautious alternatives

(Bem *et al.* 1965). Thus, in this sense the risky-shift can be viewed as an irrational phenomenon. In addition, some evidence implies that people behave more irresponsibly in groups than as individuals. For example, Darley and Latané (1968) demonstrated that in emergency situations subjects are less likely to offer help to people in need if they (the subjects) are in the presence of others rather than alone. Furthermore, Zimbardo (1969) recently reported that when anonymity is enhanced in a group setting, subjects engage in more impulsive aggression than non-anonymous subjects. This effect, however, appears to obtain only when anonymity is created within a group. At any rate it appears that at least under some circumstances irresponsible, impulsive behavior occurs more readily in groups than in individual settings.

The discussion above emphasizes that despite conceptual problems with the fear of failure concept and despite the contradicting evidence relating to group discussion and the role of affective-bonds, there is still reason to suspect that responsibility-diffusion may create increases in risk-taking behavior. Thus, it is unfortunate that most of the research relevant to the responsibility-diffusion interpretation only indirectly tests the basic premise of the explanation.

III. The Persuasion Explanation

A. The Leadership Hypothesis

According to the leadership hypothesis, the risky-shift is basically due to personality differences among the group members. Those people who initially make riskier decisions than others in the group presumably exert more influence in the subsequent discussion (Collins & Guetzkow, 1964; D. G. Marquis, 1962). In other words, the leadership explanation hypothesizes a relation between two dimensions of individual difference — viz., riskiness and persuasiveness. By virtue of their greater persuasiveness and initiative in social situations, high risk-takers lead other group members toward a riskier decision. Thus, a unique feature of the leadership interpretation is its stress upon personality factors as determinants of the risky-shift effect.

In order to establish the leadership hypothesis as viable, we must consider two types of related evidence: (1) that influence processes operate during group risk-taking, and (2) that those individuals favoring risk are the primary initiators of influence attempts and/or are more persuasive when they speak. Obviously, if the second proposition is true, so too is the first.

With respect to the first point, there is evidence that social influence processes do occur during group risk-taking. Several investigators report significant reductions in variability following either group decision (Flanders & Thistlethwaite, 1967; Teger & Pruitt, 1967; Wallach & Kogan, 1965) or group discussion (Wallach & Kogan, 1965). Since decreased variability is typically interpreted as a reflection of social influence, these findings imply that influence processes do operate in risky-shift situations. On the other hand, closer inspection of actual experimental procedures suggest that increased uniformity produced in group decision situations is often merely artifactual; the experimental procedures used in the risky-shift research typically instruct groups to reach consensus. However, Wallach & Kogan (1965) found equal amounts of convergence following a group decision procedure that required consensus and one that did not explicitly require consensus but instead encouraged "diversity of opinion." While this parallel outcome superficially suggests that all variability reduction is not artifact, closer inspection of the Wallach and Kogan procedure reveals further difficulty. The reduced variability produced by group discussion is easily attributable to "demand characteristics" — implicit suggestions to group members that they really should end up agreeing with one another. While there is an implicit demand for either exaggerated change or consistency in any multiple measurement design, the implication for change seems to be particularly evident in the Wallach and Kogan procedure. The instructions were given after group discussion and required subjects to reconsider their initial decisions *in light of the opinion diversity* that had been generated. As is obvious from this succession of arguments and counterarguments, the question of whether or not influence processes (separate from artifact and demand) do operate in group risk-taking is an extremely complex one. However, since the effect of demand characteristics in this particular situation is likely to be an accentuation of influence processes already present, we find it hard to imagine that no true influence occurs in group discussion situations (in spite of the problems mentioned above).

But granting that influence does occur, a more critical question is whether or not group pressures toward uniformity are related to the risky-shift. Teger and Pruitt (1967) reported significant positive correlations between magnitude of risky-shift and the decrease in variability produced by group decision — the more the decrease, the greater the shift toward risk. Although correlations were not computed, Wallach and Kogan (1965) also noted the relation between marked convergence in decisions and large risky-shift for both group decision and group discussion. In light of this evidence, they suggested that influence processes are directed primarily toward conservative members and that these persons exhibit more change during group interaction than initially risky individuals. Obviously, however, a causal interpretation of correlational data always invites suspicion. The demonstration of an intrinsic connection between influence processes and the risky-shift requires experimental manipulation of the strength of influence processes and an independent assessment of the magnitude of risky-shift.

Consistent with the leadership hypothesis, several studies (Flanders & Thistlethwaite, 1967; Wallach et al., 1962; Wallach, Kogan, & Burt, 1965) report significant, positive correlations between individuals' initial riskiness and postsession ratings of perceived influence by group members. This latter evidence, however, is still indirect. A more satisfactory procedure for demonstrating the relation between influence processes and the persuasiveness of the high risk-taker would use external observers who independently rate the amount and source of influence during the process of group discussion.

To test the hypothesis that initially risky persons exert more influence toward a risky decision than other group members, a number of studies attempt to isolate individual difference factors that might contribute to this relationship. Rim found that those high in extraversion (Rim, 1964c), high in need achievement (Rim, 1963), and more tolerant of ambiguity (Rim, 1964b) take higher risks on initial measures of risk-taking.[18] Since group decisions shifted in their direction, Rim *inferred* that the high initial risk-takers exerted influence over the decisions of other group members. The truth of this conjecture obviously remains untested, however. Rim also extended his program of research to interpersonal attitudes. Those who tended to take greater initial risks valued leadership and recognition (Rim, 1964a). In addition, they scored higher on personality tests measuring adeptness at manipulating interpersonal relations (Rim, 1966) and affective expressiveness (Rim, 1965b). On the other hand, Stoner (1961) correlated level of participation—a dimension of leadership related to task ability—with initial riskiness and found no relationship.

In a somewhat different vein, Burnstein (1967) suggested that persons initially prone toward risk may achieve greater influence in group discussion due to their greater commitment to, and confidence in, their prior decisions. Using a problem-solving task that required subjects to bid for problems of varying difficulty, Clausen (1965) reported a few significant, positive correlations between initial riskiness and confidence

---

[18]With respect to extraversion, however, Flanders and Thistlethwaite (1967) reported nonsignificant correlations between extraversion and initial riskiness as well as between extraversion and perceived influence ratings from group members.

in their decisions on the initial measure of risk.[19] In a later phase of the experiment, Clausen systematically varied the structural composition of groups to manipulate confidence and initial risk-taking. All groups were constructed to contain a risky person and two conservative members. In high-confidence risky groups (HCR), the risky member expressed high confidence in his initial decision; in low-confidence risky groups (LCR), the risky person expressed little confidence in his initial choice. Similarly, half the groups contained highly confident conservative members and, the other half contained conservative members with little confidence in their initial decisions. In addition, the design included two other conditions: groups homogeneously confident and groups homogeneously unconfident. Strongest risky-shifts were predicted for HCR groups and conservative shifts for LCR groups. No shift was expected for groups homogeneous in confidence. As predicted, HCR groups did exhibit greater increases in risk-taking than LCR groups. However, confidence level of conservative members did not mediate shifts toward either risk or caution. These latter two instances in which Burnstein's predictions were not borne out may be attributable to a "natural" correlation between risk and confidence. As discussed earlier, there is some evidence for a positive relationship between initial riskiness and reported confidence. If so, it would not be possible to compose equivalent groups. At any rate, the overall results of the Clausen study give some support to a direct relationship between confidence in initial risk-taking and risky-shift.

Further research on the leadership hypothesis might profitably explore other aspects of confidence. For example, the importance of differential confidence in initial decisions might well be more pronounced in larger groups in which participation in discussion is less evenly distributed (Allen, 1965). The amount of confidence exhibited during actual group discussion might be a key variable. In a recent study of persuasion, London, Meldman, and Lanckton (1970) assembled dyads to discuss issues and attempt to reach agreement. They found no relation between persuasion and either initial position or initial conviction; but expression of confidence *during* discussion did predict influence.[20]

Detractors of the leadership hypothesis propose that the relation between initial riskiness and attributed influence is more apparent than

---

[19]These findings may simply be variations of the oft-reported relation between extremity of position and certainty of belief (Suchman, 1950). However, both Stoner (1961) and Teger and Pruitt (1967) found no evidence between confidence and risk-taking with Choice-Dilemma items.

[20]Instead of self-reports, they derived objective measures based upon judge's ratings of the transcribed discussions in terms of pre-established categories of confidence and doubt.

real. For example, Kelley and Thibaut (1968, p. 81) suggest that: "The correlations between initial riskiness and influence may simply reflect what has happened: subjects observe the shift to occur and infer from it that the initially risky persons must have been more influential." Enhancing the credibility of this interpretation, Wallach *et al.* (1965) demonstrated that subjects are aware of a shift toward greater risk-taking during discussion but inaccurately estimate its magnitude. Moreover, in studies that report conservative shifts (Nordhøy, 1962; Rabow, Fowler, Bradford, Hofeller & Shibuya, 1966), initially conservative persons are rated as more influential. Although these results suggest that retrospective perceptions of influence may merely reflect the direction of shift, they do not by themselves discredit the notion that high risk-takers exert greater influence over group discussion.

On the other hand, direct experimental tests of the leadership hypothesis generally yield negative results. In order to provide an opportunity for social influence processes to occur, Wallach *et al.* (1968) systematically formed groups of individuals who represented a wide variability in risk-taking propensities. They used items that did not involve risk assuming that if initially high risk-takers generally exert more influence, they should do so regardless of the specific content of the discussion. A weak significant tendency to perceive high risk-takers as more influential was found for groups of females; however, no such relation obtained for groups of males. A second study (discussed earlier in this chapter) examined groups uniformly composed of either field-dependent or field-independent persons (Wallach *et al.*, 1967). Presumably, the perceptual dependence of field-dependent persons also reflects a greater susceptibility to social influence (Witkin, Lewis, Hertzman, Machover, Meissner, & Wapner, 1954; Witkin *et al.*, 1962). Therefore, the leadership hypothesis predicts a stronger impact of persuasion attempts and influence processes on risk-taking in groups of field-dependent than field-independent persons. However, both types of groups exhibited similar levels of initial and subsequent risk-taking. Contrary to the leadership hypothesis, high initial risk-takers were perceived as more influential only in field-independent groups. Although a similar relationship failed to obtain for field-dependent groups, group members did agree on who was the most influential. Therefore, field-dependent groups apparently made systematic distinctions among themselves but not in the direction predicted by the leadership hypothesis.

In a recent study, Hoyt and Stoner (1968) attempted to devise a crucial test of the leadership hypothesis. To control for any initial leadership differences among group members, they assembled discussion groups composed of individuals with highly similar, initial risk-taking scores. Under these conditions, the leadership hypothesis predicts little or no shift. However, significant risky-shifts occurred on the majority of Choice-Dilemma items. In addition, comparisons with two previous studies (Stoner, 1961; Wallach et al., 1962) that used groups heterogeneous in initial risk-taking revealed no appreciable differences in magnitude of obtained risky-shifts. Although the investigators interpret these results as failing to confirm the leadership hypothesis, inadequacies in their homogeneity manipulation may impugn their conclusion. Individual levels of initial risk-taking were determined on the basis of total scores across items. Consequently, the supposedly homogeneous, groups retained a considerable amount of within-group heterogeneity on each item. As the authors note, although their homogenization procedure reduced the range of *total* individual scores, it decreased the range on individual items by only one-seventh.

B. The Rhetoric-of-Risk Hypothesis

A recent variant of persuasion theory does not consider riskiness as an individual difference factor and avoids the leadership issue entirely. Essentially, it views persuasiveness as intrinsic to a *position* rather than a person. This explanation — the rhetoric of risk hypothesis — is more inclusive than the original leadership hypothesis; it presumably explains *both* the positive correlations between initial riskiness and perceived influence as well as the risky-shift itself (Kelley & Thibaut, 1968). As outlined by its major proponents, the rhetoric of risk position maintains that:

> There are two related aspects of the risky position that may give the proponent of such a position a disproportionate weight in open discussion: (1) the "rhetoric of risk" is more dramatic, and (2) the conflicts and uncertainties entailed in accepting the riskier alternative might lead the proponent of such alternatives to state his arguments with a heightened intensity and amplitude. In short, he may have the advantage of a more potent language, more intensively produced (Kelley & Thibaut, 1968, p. 82).[21]

Evidence for the rhetoric of risk interpretation is meager, although suggestive. For example, Rettig (1966) observed that the group discussions that led toward greater risk-taking also enhanced the reinforc-

---

[21]In some respects the rhetoric of risk hypothesis is similar to the cultural-value explanation which is discussed later. The major point of departure is one of emphasis. It stresses the intensity of the influence attempts by the riskier group members. While the cultural-value explanation also implies a greater influence of risk-oriented statements, it does not specifically attribute the effect to the forcefulness of particular group members. Values are seen as censoring the flow and quantity of information, and not as determining the intensity of forcefulness with which different positions are presented.

ing value of the desirable features of a risky decision. Presumably, "rhetorical advantage" would operate in a similar manner and increase the group's valuation of the gains arising from increased riskiness. Kelley and Thibaut also cite the Lonergran and McClintock (1961) study that failed to find a risky-shift in a betting situation as indirect support. Supposedly, the simplicity of the experimental situation and its sparse potential for discussion allowed little room for the rhetorical advantage of risk to manifest itself.

As argued in the case of the leadership explanation, ratings or evaluations of segments of the group interaction and decision-making process offer the most direct means of assessing the validity of the rhetoric of risk hypothesis. Judges listening to segments of the interaction should judge statements uttered in support of risky positions as more forceful or confident in the absence of knowledge about the level of riskiness being advocated. They should also (or alternatively) judge statements specifically advocating a risky decision as more powerful or persuasive. Alternatively, when subjects are asked to role-play different positions, judges should be able to detect these same differences as a function of the riskiness of the position that is role-played.

C. Conclusion

The proposition that high initial risk-takers more persuasively argue their own position during group discussions receives little support from existing research. The demonstrated relationship between initial risk-taking and attributed influence constitutes the major support for the leadership hypothesis and counter-evidence (Nordhøy, 1962; Rabow *et al.*, 1966) suggests that this relationship may be a consequence, rather than a cause, of the risky-shift. Furthermore, since correlations between initial riskiness and perceived influence are generally low, and since risky-shifts occur even when subjects have had no exposure to group discussion (e.g., Teger & Pruitt, 1967), investigators have been prompted to relegate the leadership position to the role of a limited, partial explanation of the risky-shift effect (Jones & Gerard, 1967; Kelley & Thibaut, 1968; Kogan & Wallach, 1967c; Mackenzie & Bernhardt, 1968). On the other hand, low correlations may merely reflect lack of reliability or validity of the relevant measures. The type of evidence that could most directly speak on the leadership hypothesis is some type of interaction process analysis of the group decision. With independent raters evaluating who contributes most persuasively to the group discussion, one could directly assess whether it is indeed those whose prior initial decisions are the riskiest. At present, such evidence is simply not available.

The rhetoric of risk hypothesis, although interesting, awaits empirical support. Evidently, direct tests of this view would be difficult to devise (Jones & Gerard, 1967; Kelley & Thibaut, 1968). Furthermore, even if direct tests were feasible and proved satisfactory, Kelley and Thibaut feel that an explanation based on "rhetorical advantage" would nevertheless require supplementation from additional explanations such as responsibility-diffusion. But, more importantly, in their present form, both the leadership and rhetoric of risk hypotheses suffer the defect of considering only unidirectional tendencies toward risk and not accounting for conservative shifts.[22]

Although social influence processes do seem to occur in the group discussions that induce risky-shifts, little systematic effort has been devoted toward directly assessing these persuasion and/or influence processes. Although greater use could be made of the research strategy of assembling groups that systematically vary in terms of personality factors thought to be related to social influence, the inconsistent outcomes of research relating personality differences to persuasion (McGuire, 1968) as well as the evidence that personality factors play a minor role in determining persuasibility (Cohen, 1964; Hovland & Janis, 1959) argue against this approach. Instead, as suggested above, observational analysis of interactions in group risk-taking situations seems a better alternative. It might reveal the importance of such unexplored factors as talkativeness, expressed confidence, and volume of arguments as persuasive elements that induce greater risk-taking.[23] Other sources of personal influence such as status and authority have similarly been neglected in risky-shift investigations. Norms may also be a potent source of influence in risk-taking situations, either enhancing or substituting for the expression of personal influence. Whereas Rabow *et al.* (1966) suggest that an individual's effectiveness at interpersonal persuasion in a risk-taking situation is contingent upon eliciting normative support for his advocated position, Thibaut and Kelley (1959) propose that norms may serve as surrogates for personal influence. In short, an investigation of normative processes in group risk-taking might well reveal the operation of personal and/or impersonal sources of social influence related to the risky-shift.

---

[22]Of course, the major premise of persuasion theory can be altered so that it can account for conservative as well as risky-shifts. For instance, if the hypothesis is altered to state that the most extreme person in the group is most influential, regardless of his direction of extremity, both risky and conservative outcomes can be expected with frequencies that depend on the relative natural occurrence of these two types in the population (see Burns, 1967).

[23]Kogan and Doise (1969) attempt to grapple with some of these issues.

IV. The Familiarization Explanation

Contrary to other explanations of the risky-shift, Bateson's (1966) familiarization hypothesis implies that the risky-shift is a pseudo group effect—explainable in terms of individual processes and not restricted to group situations. The familiarization hypothesis argues that enhanced risk-taking results from increased familiarity with risk-related items. In other words, any procedure that increases familiarity with the elements relevant to a decision will increase the riskiness of the decision; it matters little whether increased familiarity occurs with isolated individuals or among members of a discussion group. Presumably when individuals consider novel or ambiguous problems, their initial uncertainty produces caution. With increased familiarization, either through further private study or group discussion of the problem, uncertainty (and caution) subsides, thereby freeing individuals to make riskier decisions (Bateson, 1966). In a similar formulation, Flanders and Thistlethwaite (1967) propose a comprehension interpretation of the risky-shift, in which private study produces greater comprehension of risk related problems. This, in turn, increases risk-taking by reducing uncertainty.

Whereas Bateson's interpretation seems simply to emphasize the effect of increased familiarity or experience without mentioning intellectual comprehension of the problem, Flanders and Thistlethwaite place emphasis primarily on the effect of greater comprehension. Although Flanders and Thistlethwaite consider their formulation primarily as a restatement of Bateson's position, the difference in emphasis suggests two distinct interpretations. One can conceptualize the familiarization hypothesis as essentially focusing on the emotional process of uncertainty reduction as the explicit mediator of risk-taking or, alternatively, one might conceptualize enhancement of risk-taking as the consequence of a cognitive process that has little relation to emotional states. For example, it is possible that familiarization leads to a fuller understanding of the relative merits and drawbacks of the various choice alternatives and that risk-taking increases only when risky choices become more attractive for rational reasons (e.g., the risky choices might have greater expected value than conservative choices).

Nevertheless, the formulations considered above imply that familiarization with the task necessarily precedes risky-shifts; that is, increased familiarity is a critical mechanism underlying instances of heightened risk-taking—whether in group situations or with socially isolated individuals.[24]

[24]An alternative and more limited position is that familiarization is a sufficient condition for increased risk-taking only under certain specified conditions such as with isolated

There are two separate issues raised by a familiarization interpretation of the risky-shift. The first is whether the risky-shift is a true or pseudo group-effect. A second separate consideration is whether the explanatory mechanisms postulated by advocates of the familiarization hypothesis adequately account for shifts in risk-taking. The following sections consider each of these issues separately.

A. THE RISKY-SHIFT: TRUE OR PSEUDO GROUP EFFECT?

In terms of empirical support, two studies found an increase in risk-taking after exposing individuals to a familiarization procedure. In both, the increase approximately equalled that produced by group discussion. Bateson (1966) instructed individuals to restudy their initial decisions carefully on Choice-Dilemma items and generate arguments for and against the risky course of action. He compared this familiarization procedure to group discussion and control conditions. Postsession recollection tests were administered to determine how much specific information subjects remembered from the hypothetical problem. As indicated in earlier sections of this chapter, risky-shifts occurred for familiarization and group discussion with no significant differences between them. But, further, these two conditions did not differ on the measure of recollection. Bateson views the similar outcomes on both measures as support for the familiarization hypothesis. Since the two procedures—individual familiarization and group discussion—produced equal familiarity as measured by recall, he expected equal shifts toward risky decisions.

In a more sensitive study, Flanders and Thistlethwaite (1967) systematically varied familiarization and group discussion in a 2×2 factorial design to examine interactions or additive effects. The familiarization manipulation required subjects to reconsider their original decisions on Choice-Dilemma items and improvise "pro" and "con" arguments for the risky alternative as preparation for a subsequent discussion in which they would argue forcefully for their own decisions. The four conditions of the design were: neither familiarization nor discussion; familiarization without discussion; discussion without familiarization; and familiarization followed by discussion. A significant risky-shift occurred in the three conditions containing discussion and/or familiar-

---

individuals. This less inclusive view depicts familiarization as one among several mechanisms necessary to account for the risky-shift under different conditions. These different perspectives should be kept in mind while the relevant data are considered.

ization. However, these three conditions did not differ from each other. Since the joint presence of familiarization and discussion did not enhance the magnitude of risky-shift, Flanders and Thistlethwaite concluded that not only was familiarization sufficient to produce the risky-shift but they also seem to imply that it was the sole mediator of the effect. That is, they interpret the finding of "no difference" between familiarization alone, and either group discussion or familiarization plus group discussion as discrediting the possibility that familiarization and responsibility-diffusion are either independent or complementary processes, both capable of producing a risky-shift.[25]

The "strong interpretation" of the Bateson (1966) and Flanders and Thistlethwaite (1967) studies—that familiarization is the source of risky-shifts—seems unjustified. Both studies use a design in which partial support for the hypothesis requires an outcome of no difference (between cells). Although the observed, within-cell differences lend some support to the familiarization interpretation (i.e., familiarization did produce a risky-shift), the unknown likelihood of a Type II error makes the "no difference" outcome a weak basis for making inferences about the relative effects of the two separate treatments.

A more serious problem for any form of the familiarization interpretation is the fact that some later investigations fail to confirm its initial support. (1) In a series of five replications using both the Bateson and Flanders and Thistlethwaite manipulations of familiarization, Pruitt and Teger (1967) found either weak conservative or weak risky-shifts, none of which reached significance.[26] (2) Miller and Dion (1970) tried to analyze the separate components of the familiarization procedure. They suggested that the typical familiarization procedure might contain three separate processes: improvisation, comprehension, and serious reconsideration. Although the process of comprehension and serious reconsideration have received attention in prior interpretations of familiarization (Flanders and Thistlethwaite, 1967), the possible role of improvisation merits some discussion. In both Bateson and Flanders and Thistlethwaite's studies, subjects actively engaged in listing relevant points for and against the risky alternative. In the latter study, subjects also antici-

[25]Although we initially interpreted them as advocating this strong stand of "necessary and sufficient," both Flanders and Thistlethwaite (personal communication) have recently made it clear that they meant to interpret their results as simply indicating that familiarization is a sufficient condition for producing a risky-shift.

[26]However, these studies used few subjects and with one exception were performed with intact classes. As a consequence, involvement in the task might have been reduced.

pated using the list of points in a subsequent discussion. Such activity closely resembles the active improvisation procedures used in studies of self-persuasion (e.g., King & Janis, 1956). Thus, it seemed possible that increased risk-taking following familiarization might simply be an instance of self-persuasion arising from improvisation.[27] None of the comparisons between conditions supported a familiarization effect. Second, the relative effects of familiarization and group discussion upon risk-taking were investigated in the two different sequences in which these two treatments can be combined. Contrary to Flanders and Thistlethwaite (1967), group discussion produced a significant risky-shift following familiarization. However, familiarization failed to increase risk-taking over and above that produced by prior discussion. (3) Using a familiarization procedure designed to parallel that of Flanders and Thistlethwaite (1967), Myers (1967) obtained a within subject shift toward increased risk on risk-oriented items. However, (a) a between group comparison of the familiarization condition and a control group that worked on irrelevant problems before a readministration of the risk-taking measure showed no difference; (b) between group comparisons of both the familiarization condition and control condition to a group discussion yields stronger risky shifts than familiarization; and (c) a familiarization condition requiring overt individual rereading and discussion in front of an observer failed to show even a within-subject shift. This last lack of effect points away from comprehension or intellectual understanding as critical and points instead toward the inhibiting effects of emotional factors such as anxiety or evaluation apprehension. (4) In several attempts at exact replications of Bateson's and Flanders and Thistlethwaite's familiarization procedures, Ferguson and Vidmar (1970) also failed to obtain risky-shifts when subjects familiarized themselves with risk-oriented items. Thus, there is certainly no clear support for the hypothesis that increasing familiarity with the task is a *sufficient* condition to enhance risk-taking. But additionally, a number of studies fail to replicate the original familiarization results.

[27]To isolate the effects of these processes, Miller and Dion created three experimental conditions: (1) a replication of Flanders and Thistlethwaite's familiarization manipulation that presumably engaged all three mechanisms; (2) a private-study condition that required subjects to engage passively in further study of each risk problem without improvising arguments. This treatment presumably elicited the processes of comprehension and serious reconsideration (Flanders & Thistlethwaite, 1967) and (3) a reconsideration procedure that required subjects to reconsider their decisions in considerably less time than that provided in the familiarization and private-study conditions. For purposes of comparison, a group discussion condition was also included. Miller and Dion found that only group discussion produced a significant risky-shift.

B. Explanatory Mechanisms: Uncertainty-Reduction
   and Comprehension

Not only is the present evidence currently weighted against the validity of the familiarization interpretation, but there are conceptual and empirical difficulties with the underlying processes posited to explain the risky-shift.

1. Uncertainty-Reduction

Bateson (1966) postulates that decreasing uncertainty produces the risky-shift. Akin to our arguments in the responsibility-diffusion section about reducing fear of failure, there does not appear to be any logical reason why there should be a necessary relationship between uncertainty-reduction and shifts toward risk unless one includes additional assumptions or propositions. One expectation about uncertainty-reduction is that it might encourage individuals to behave non-normatively. That is, a reduction of uncertainty might liberate subjects from choosing a middling or normative response; consequently, in comparison to another condition in which uncertainty is not lowered, they would exhibit greater variability in risk-taking. However, as argued before, such an increase in variability would not necessarily create differences in *average* risk-taking between conditions in which the amount of uncertainty-reduction varies. Thus, predictions of differences in mean risk-taking on the basis of the uncertainty-reduction explanation seem unwarranted.[28]

Setting aside our arguments above for the moment, let us grant for argument's sake that reducing uncertainty does promote risky decisions. If so, the uncertainty-reduction explanation encounters further difficulty in that it fails to account for conservative shifts. That is, if study or comprehension only affects risk-taking by reducing uncertainty, presumably what is studied or what is comprehended is irrelevant. Thus, increasing familiarity with Choice-Dilemma items that typically show a conservative shift (following discussion) should reduce initial uncertainty and produce a risky-shift. D. G. Marquis (1968) provided some suggestive evidence against this latter point in a recent experiment in which individuals familiarized themselves with several of the "caution-oriented" items developed by Stoner (1968). Individuals shifted in a cautious rather than a

---

[28]If Bateson's conceptualization of uncertainty is similar to "fear of failure" then our previous discussion of the Atkinson model (in the section on responsibility-diffusion) would also apply here. But, as previously indicated, that model does not predict main effects for the direction of shift.

risky direction on caution-oriented items. Myers (1967) and Ferguson and Vidmar (1970) provide additional contrary data.

2. Comprehension

According to the comprehension interpretation, familiarization clarifies the relative merits and drawbacks of the various choice-alternatives. Presumably, this is a cognitive nonemotional process. Thus, we interpret Flanders and Thistlethwaite's emphasis upon comprehension as stressing the notion of rationality. With its underlying assumption of rationality, the comprehension interpretation — in contrast to an explanation such as uncertainty-reduction that seems to include some emotional components — appears better equipped to predict both risky- and conservative-shifts. If the rationality of a decision favors conservatism, one would expect a cautious shift after additional familiarization. On the other hand, if the rationality is weighted toward riskiness, increased familiarity should produce a risky-shift.

Unfortunately, some evidence contradicts the expectation that group discussion leads to a more rational decision. Two experiments examined the "rationality" of risky decisions achieved through group discussion by manipulating the payoffs and probabilities on the problem-solving task so as to discourage riskiness. In one study (Wallach et al., 1964) there were positive, monetary incentives for all choices among the decision alternatives but all alternatives had a constant expected value (i.e., probability value multiplied by reward value). Thus, failure on the problem-solving tasks meant forfeiting the prize but did not incur any further loss from prior winnings. However, since the expected values were the same for the various decision alternatives, there was no rational reason, in terms of objective value, to prefer the riskier alternative. Nevertheless, a significant risky-shift occurred following discussion. In another experiment, Bem et al. (1965) arranged expected values to favor the conservative decision. That is, greater risk-taking was associated with increased aversive consequences in the event of failure. Yet, here too, group discussion enhanced risk-taking.

On the other hand, Flanders (1970) argues that in the absence of independent empirical information we cannot know whether lower probability (or for that matter, higher probability) outcomes are riskier in equal expected outcome tasks. In other words, without independent evidence on the meaning of "rationality" for these situations, we cannot look at these studies as disconfirming the notion that either group discussion or increased comprehension increases the rationality of a decision. It is also possible that expected value is not considered by subjects when they contemplate the efficacy of a course of action. Indeed, Kogan and Wallach (1967) stress this point themselves. If so, this too argues that the studies presented directly above are not necessarily inconsistent with a familiarization position that emphasizes increased comprehension.

C. Conclusion

In sum, neither of the explanations underlying the familiarization interpretation fare very well. The uncertainty-reduction explanation does not appear to have an unambiguous logical or psychological basis, and it is also disconfirmed by instances of conservative shifts. The studies on expected values can be interpreted as contradicting Flanders and Thistlethwaite's hypothesis that increased comprehension mediates risk-taking by emphasizing the rationality of various choice alternatives. But more importantly, there is no powerful direct evidence supporting the comprehension explanation. Recall data on Choice Dilemma items probably cannot persuasively speak on it because their contents are too brief and simple. Lastly, the fact that various investigators fail to replicate the early familiarization results adds to our conclusion that the familiarization hypothesis does not adequately explain the risky-shift.

Of course, it is possible that as an independent mechanism operating out of the context of group discussion, some characteristic of familiarization procedures will increase risk-taking in individuals. If so, this would not, of course, explain the risky-shift literature, but it would have to be integrated into a larger theory of risk-taking. Evidence that familiarization produces a pattern of risky-shift across Choice-Dilemma items that differs markedly from the standard pattern produced by group discussion supports this point. Teger et al. (1970) found significant positive correlations for the mean risky-shift across items for the group discussion conditions in several investigations (Teger & Pruitt, 1967; Wallach et al., 1962; Flanders & Thistlethwaite, 1967). However, in the Flanders and Thistlethwaite study, correlations between the familiarization-induced pattern of risky-shift and the group-induced patterns of risky-shifts were low, positive, and nonsignificant. Assuming that the pattern of risky-shift across items reflects the underlying mechanism, Teger et al. concluded that different mechanisms must increase risk in the individual familiarization and the group discussion procedures. However, the kind of familiarization mechanism that might increase risk-taking in isolated individuals remains unknown.

While failures to produce risky-shifts with familiarization procedures cast doubt upon familiarization as a sufficient condition for increased risk-taking, they do not at the same time establish the risky-shift as solely a group effect. To a large extent, theoretically oriented research on the risky-shift has been misguided by a simplistic belief that there exists a single unique antecedent condition which when discovered will explain the phenomenon completely (Zajonc *et al.*, 1970). In contrast, the existing literature suggests that numerous social (e.g., group decision, group discussion) and quasisocial (e.g., information exchange, vicarious exposure to discussion) conditions may enhance risk-taking. Likewise, other untested variables may increase the risk-taking of socially isolated individuals.

V. The Culture-Value Explanation

A fourth interpretation of the risky-shift proposed by Brown (1965)[29] is the cultural-value explanation. This explanation invokes two separate propositions to account for the risky-shift. These will be referred to as the *value hypothesis* and the *relevant information hypothesis*.

According to the value hypothesis, when an individual confronts a decision problem that contains an element of risk, the problem elicits one of two cultural values: risk or caution. Although Brown originally maintained that the American value system primarily encourages risk and daring, he later recognized the existence of cultural values for caution in response to Nordhøy's (1962) finding that group discussion of certain hypothetical decision items generally yielded conservative shifts. Accordingly, the value hypothesis assumes that in certain situations the culture condones or values risky behavior while in others it values cautious behavior. Presumably, a risky-shift only occurs in those situations that elicit values favoring risk.

Once a cultural value becomes salient, two mechanisms postulated by the relevant information hypothesis presumably lead group members to shift their final decisions in a direction consistent with the value. First, the value censors the flow of information during discussion so that more verbal statements support the value than oppose it. Since no single group member possesses all the relevant information, the value-oriented discussion provides each individual with additional reasons for agreeing with the underlying cultural value. Second, group discussion informs each group member of the level of risk other group members are willing to take. By revealing the distribution of risk preferences, group discussion establishes a social reality against which individuals can concretely define "riskiness." By providing an opportunity for

---

[29]Nordhøy (1962) also presented this view at approximately the same time. Our presentations will focus on Brown's analysis.

social comparison, group discussion enables an individual to determine the level of risk-taking he must choose in order to appear or act risky or cautious in respect to others. For example, if a decision situation elicits a cultural value of risk, individuals will initially make decisions they privately believe are risky. In a subsequent discussion, however, an individual may discover that he is not as risky as (or not substantially more risky than) others. Consequently, he will tend to adjust his level of risk-taking in a more risky direction in order to be consistent with the underlying cultural value. Presumably, these adjustments in risk-taking are motivated both by the desire to feel that one is adhering to the elicited value and also because the group enhances the salience of the value.

A.   THE VALUE HYPOTHESIS

To confirm the value hypothesis, one must establish: (1) that situations typically found to provoke a risky-shift elicit values that favor risk and (2) that situations which typically provoke conservative shifts elicit values that favor caution. The present section reviews, in sequence, the data relevant to each of these two points. Following this, we discuss two studies that investigate a more general question concerning the importance of value considerations in group risk-taking.

To test either of these two points, one must develop operations for assessing values that are distinct from simply observing the direction of shift. The fact that a given item consistently shifts in either a risky or cautious direction does not by itself constitute particularly compelling evidence that cultural values are at work. One would prefer some independent data that more directly reflect what we commonly conceptualize as a value. Moreover, such data would permit an *a priori* specification of what value a given item (or situation) will elicit. For instance, since values can be conceptualized as referring to ideal behavior, one operation for assessing the value elicited by an item is to ask the subject for the "best" or "ideal" level of risk on a given item (as well as that which he would personally choose). Items for which the "ideal" is riskier than "own" can then be defined as eliciting risk, whereas the opposite direction of difference suggests that caution is the elicited value. This procedure would enable one to predict the direction of the effect of group discussion—a risky-shift or a cautious-shift—on any single Choice-Dilemma item.

Using this type of procedure, several investigators (Levinger & Schneider, 1969; Pilkonis & Zanna, 1969) find that individuals typically select odds riskier than their own when asked to indicate that level of risk-taking which they most admire. Consistent with the value hypothesis, this outcome occurred only on items that typically exhibit a risky-shift following group discussion. By means of a somewhat different procedure, Madaras and Bem (1968) demonstrated greater preference for risk than for caution on Choice-Dilemma items that previously produced risky-shifts (e.g., Wallach *et al.*, 1962). They used a series of semantic differential scales to obtain evaluations of a fictitious person who had supposedly accepted or rejected a risky decision at various levels. Fictitious persons who were "risk-takers" were rated more favorably than those depicted as "risk-rejectors."

These data are in accord with the value hypothesis. The value hypothesis holds that in certain settings, risky behavior is encouraged by the value structure of a culture. That is, supposedly risk-taking in certain settings implies that the risk-taker possesses certain personal characteristics that are valued in the culture. If one assumes that people like to view (and present) themselves favorably, this explains why riskiness relative to others becomes desirable. In short, the cultural-value explanation emphasizes, not that people like to take risks per se but instead that they like to view themselves as daring, adventurous, etc. Further, taking risks allows them to attribute such qualities to themselves. It is important to note that the personal quality of daring or riskiness is not the only valued personal characteristic that risk-taking denotes (Brown, personal communication). Indeed, daring or riskiness probably is just one of the qualities typically implied by risk-taking behavior. Moreover, to the extent that risk-taking implies *any* valued trait (e.g., selflessness, strength, confidence, and intelligence), the *behavior* of risk-taking would be culturally valued. Indeed, this is true even if the behavior does not denote daring at all. Accordingly, one would expect that in situations provoking the risky-shift, risk-takers would generally be evaluated more positively than risk-rejectors. One would expect this effect to be particularly pronounced on those traits that seem directly related to the behavior in question, but quite conceivably a halo effect would cause this difference in rated favorability even on relatively unrelated traits.[30]

---

[30]The results of Madaras and Bem (1968) have recently been corroborated by Jellison and Riskind (1970). In one experiment the favorability of subjects' ratings of others were positively related to the latters' riskiness on Choice-Dilemma items, although this pattern was reversed for traits related to responsibility. In a second study, others who presumably were high in academic ability were expected to take higher risks than persons low in ability. These results also support the value hypothesis. If risky behavior implies certain valued characteristics (see text above), it is reasonable that valued characteristics in turn should imply risky behavior.

Another means for determining the value elicited by a given item is to gauge how people view themselves relative to others. People generally try to present themselves favorably. Therefore if risk or caution is particularly valued, one would expect people to make decisions which deviate from those of others in the valued direction. In accord with the value hypothesis, individuals perceive themselves as riskier than their peers in initial decisions on those Choice-Dilemma items that consistently produce risky-shifts (Baron, Dion, Baron, & Miller, 1970; Hinds, 1962; Levinger & Schneider, 1969; Pruitt & Teger, 1967; Wallach & Wing, 1968). A similar outcome occurs on risk-oriented life situation items[31] (Stoner, 1968). This evidence on *relative perceived riskiness* supports Brown's notion that for certain Choice-Dilemma situations, our culture values risk. That is, we would hardly expect people to exaggerate the extent to which they are risky relative to others, unless they think that riskiness is a desirable trait.

There is one instance, however, in which individuals did not consider themselves to be riskier or more conservative than others. Zajonc *et al.* (1970) found that in a gambling situation, individuals' estimates of their own and a typical peer's level of risk-taking did not differ. Ordinarily there is little point trying to account for no effect when one is expected. However, one possible explanation for this discrepant finding is that experimental gambling situations may severely limit the opportunity for the elicitation of cultural values. That is, with trivial stakes and payoffs, cultural values may not indicate a particular course of action (Stoner, 1968). On the other hand, cultural values may be more salient in hypothetical situations than under more realistic conditions in which riskier decisions may actually incur negative outcomes.

There have also been efforts to demonstrate that caution is culturally valued in certain situations. As indicated, Nordhøy (1962) found that some of the items used by Stoner (1961) and Wallach *et al.* (1962) elicited cautious shifts following group discussion. Consistent with the notion that caution is positively valued under some circumstances, individuals perceive themselves as more cautious than peers on the two Choice-Dilemma items that typically show conservative shifts (Levinger & Schneider, 1969; Pruitt & Teger, 1967). In addition, Levinger and Schneider (1969) find that on these same two items, subjects are less likely to admire a decision riskier than their own.

---

[31]Life-situation items are similar to Choice-Dilemma items in that they describe a series of hypothetical, risk-taking situations. In addition, however, Stoner specifically attempted to design these items so that they would engage "widely held" values of either risk or caution.

Unfortunately these data on relative perceived caution and admiration constitute the only evidence that conservative shifts are due to the
elicitation of values favoring caution. One's confidence in this relationship would be considerably strengthened if compatible data resulted
from the application of other independent methods such as the semantic
differential technique described above.

Another possible procedure for demonstrating cultural values of
risk and caution with hypothetical decision-items would be to factor
analyze the item-by-item correlation matrix of risk-scores for large samples of subjects. The value hypothesis predicts that a single bipolar
factor (with risk and caution as the opposite poles) accounts for substantial variance among the variables. If Stoner (1968) succeeded in devising
items that engage either the value of risk or caution, unifactor solutions
(with all positive loadings) should be found for his risk-oriented and
caution-oriented items respectively. In addition, factor scores derived
from a factor analysis of initial decisions should predict the magnitude
of shift with discussion. Moreover, the relative magnitude of factor
loadings for initial risk-taking scores on Choice-Dilemma items should
correspond closely to Pruitt and Teger's (1967) national risky-shift norms
for each item. Finally, factor analysis would provide a reasonably precise
determination of the amount of variance in risk-taking accounted for by a
factor for cultural values – if such a factor indeed appears in the analysis.

So far, the discussion in this section has focused on whether the
Choice-Dilemma items elicit values that coincide with the direction of
shift. A broader issue concerns the importance of value considerations
in the group risk-taking situation. In several instances, advocates of the
responsibility-diffusion explanation tried to discredit experimentally the
notion that cultural values influence group risk-taking. These studies
approach the problem by varying the salience or importance of value
considerations. Presumably, if values influence group risk-taking, one
would expect particularly strong shifts in those situations in which value
considerations are highly salient. In an "anticipated disclosure" condition, Bem *et al.* (1965) told subjects that each person's private decisions
would be made public. If group discussion enhances risk-taking because
subjects desire to adhere to cultural values in the presence of others, one
might expect this condition to produce a risky-shift. Bem *et al.* found a
weak nonsignificant risky-shift. Unfortunately, little can be made of
negative results, and, furthermore, this experimental condition does not
adequately test the cultural-value explanation subsequently proposed by
Brown (1965). Since it omits any actual group discussion, subjects remain
unaware of other group members' risk levels. As a result, subjects lack
a reference point and consequently cannot know what odds to choose in

order to maintain a cultural value of risk (relative to other group members). In other words, without discussion or information exchange, the cultural-value interpretation predicts no shift. A further criticism of the Bem *et al.* study concerns the subjective meaning of "anticipated disclosure." One effect might be that of increasing feelings of anxiety or fear of failure—the very state that responsibility-diffusion protagonists proclaim as the factor that inhibits risk-taking.

In another case, Kogan and Carlson (1969) compared group risk-taking under noncompetitive and competitive conditions. They used a problem-solving format that required subjects to choose problems varying in difficulty and payoff. Most investigations of group risk-taking consist of cooperative situations, e.g., generating a unanimous consensus concerning the level of risk-taking on Choice-Dilemma items. In the competitive situation, risk may become a more salient cultural value. Kogan and Carlson told subjects that only one group member would receive the monetary reward for a given trial. That person choosing the most difficult problem (i.e., the riskiest alternative) attempted the task first. If he failed, the individual with the next riskiest choice made his attempt to solve his chosen problem, and so on. In the noncompetitive situation, group consensus determined the difficulty level of the problem attempted by either a member delegated by the group or by the group as a whole. The responsibility-diffusion explanation predicts risky-shifts only in noncompetitive situations in that only in these situations do individuals share a sense of common fate. However, if risk is positively valued, individuals in a competitive situation might also exhibit increased risk-taking. Among undergraduates, the noncompetitive group risk-taking task produced significant risky-shifts; whereas competitive situations did not differ from a control condition. However, the unusual, sequential nature of the competitive situations of the experiment probably encouraged individuals to avoid being too risky. Given the plausible assumption that an individual choosing a very difficult problem would fail, a rational strategy dictates moderate risk-taking. By choosing a moderately difficult problem, an individual would maintain an advantageous position in terms of the sequencing of attempts yet more realistically expect to achieve a correct solution. As Kogan and Carlson noted, greater risk-taking might well be found in a competitive situation in which *only* that person choosing the most difficult problem is given an opportunity to try for the monetary prize. In addition, the average expected value across problems of different difficulty levels was negative, i.e., weighted to favor caution. Since the payoff structure is probably a more salient determinant of risk-taking in a competitive than in a cooperative group condition, this negative expected value might have inhibited risk-taking in the competitive cells. Although the results of the above experiment remain inconclusive with respect to the value hypothesis, we do agree that competitive group situations would be a fruitful site to test implications of the cultural-value explanation.

In short, the accumulated evidence provides impressive support for the basic assumption that the content of Choice-Dilemma items elicits values favoring either risk (primarily) or caution (occasionally). Prior to group discussion, subjects act in a manner consistent with expectations derived from a cultural-value explanation of group risk-taking. Whether one examines semantic differential scale data, subject perceptions concerning their own relative risk or caution, or subject expressions of admiration, the data are consistent. Each of the items typically used in studies of group risk-taking consistently elicits values of either risk or caution that coincide with the direction of shift. Moreover, studies suggesting that cultural values do not influence risk-taking (Bem *et al.*, 1965; Kogan & Carlson, 1969) are vulnerable to either conceptual or methodological criticism.

Unfortunately, the validity of the value hypothesis cannot by itself explain the risky-shift; nor does its validity necessarily threaten alternative explanations of the risky-shift.[32] The cultural-value explanation rests primarily upon the second proposition—the relevant information hypothesis. Do elicited values of risk or caution determine the direction and outcome of the subsequent group discussion?

B. THE RELEVANT-INFORMATION HYPOTHESIS

According to Brown's relevant-information hypothesis, group discussion increases the salience of the values elicited in initial decision-making. Two mechanisms presumably produce this effect: (1) discussion provides an opportunity for group members to exchange information concerning the distribution of risk-preferences among them and (2) elicited values bias and sensitize the ensuing discussion so that the greater proportion of arguments favor the salient value. To date, most of the available research focuses on the information-exchange mechanism and the general proposition that discussion increases the strength of elicited values.

Considerable evidence supports the notion that group discussion

---

[32]Indeed Kogan (personal communication) would anticipate these results and would concur with our conclusions in that he claims that the Choice-Dilemma items were specifically constructed so that for each item the risky (or uncertain) alternative was more valued than the conservative (or certain) alternative.

increases the salience of elicited values. According to Pruitt and Teger (1967), levels of initial risk indicate the extent to which a given item elicits a value of risk. In these terms, a positive correlation between initial risk-taking and risky-shift supports the notion that group discussion enhances the initial directional tendencies arising from the content of the decision items. Stating it another way, items that initially elicit tendencies toward risk produce even riskier decisions following discussion; those that initially produce cautious tendencies produce even more conservative decisions after discussion.

Stoner (1968) provides perhaps the strongest support for the notion that values affect the direction of a group decision. Under the guise of a different experiment, subjects initially ranked the importance of a series of value statements. They then completed a set of risk-oriented and caution-oriented "life-situation" items. As mentioned previously, these life situation items presumably engage "widely held" values so that either risky or cautious considerations predominate. The value statements described the alternative outcomes implicit in each of the life situation items. That is, for each item, the risky and conservative outcome corresponded to a given value statement. On "risk-oriented" items, subjects ranked value statements corresponding to the risky alternative as more important than value statements associated with the cautious alternative. On the other hand, for "caution-oriented" items, subjects ranked value statements associated with the conservative alternative as significantly more important than those relating to the risky alternative. As previously indicated, all items engaging values favoring the risky alternative elicited initial tendencies toward risk. But more importantly, group discussion significantly increased these tendencies. Although trends were not as strong or consistent, opposite patterns were observed for caution-oriented items.

In a recent series of investigations, Pruitt (1969) suggests an important conceptual link for understanding the way in which group discussion enhances values elicited by initial individual decisions. When making their initial decisions on Choice-Dilemma items, subjects in risky-shift investigations must not only decide whether a given hypothetical situation warrants a risky or cautious approach; they must also determine acceptable odds for the risky alternative if chosen. In the initial experiment, Pruitt separated these steps by first requiring subjects to label each of the probability alternatives on every Choice-Dilemma item as either risky or cautious. In a *second* administration of the Choice-Dilemma situations, they advised the fictitious person confronting the decision what level of risk-taking they felt was appropriate. On all items, subjects responded with a level of risk-taking they previously labeled as cautious.

On the face of it, these results contradict the prediction from the cultural-value interpretation which suggests that individuals view their initial decisions as risky on "risk-oriented" Choice-Dilemma items and conservative on "caution-oriented" items. In subsequent studies, Pruitt replicated this initial finding and investigated further conditions in which subjects: (1) *simultaneously* make judgments of risk and caution on alternatives of Choice-Dilemma items and choose an appropriate level of risk-taking or (2) make judgments of riskiness or caution *after* making their initial decisions. Under these two conditions, Pruitt did confirm the prediction of the cultural-value interpretation. That is, subjects generally considered their decisions on risk-oriented items to be subjectively risky and those on caution-oriented items, subjectively conservative. In sum, when the labeling operation preceded decision-making, individuals subsequently selected answers that they had previously considered cautious. However, when the decision occurred simultaneously with (or prior to) labeling, subjects subsequently labeled their answers risky.

Pruitt interpreted these results as depicting a "Walter Mitty" effect. Prior to discussion, the value of risk compels subjects to be risky. On the other hand, a fear of "putting themselves out on a limb" restrains them.[33] As a result, initial risk-taking represents a compromise between these opposing forces. Similar to Walter Mitty, subjects resolve their conflict by imagining and representing themselves as "risky" while making decisions that they themselves judge to be truly cautious. In Pruitt's initial study, however, subjects labeled the various alternatives before making a decision. As a result, these subjects had little need to bias their labeling in any way. That is, they had no decisions to misrepresent at that time. Pruitt's analysis provides insights into the particular manner in which group discussion may strengthen initial tendencies toward risk elicited by values, *viz.*, by demonstrating that others are equally or more risky and thereby providing social support for riskiness.

One of the theoretical notions underlying the relevant-information hypothesis is that group discussion primarily provides an occasion for members to exchange information about their levels of risk-taking. Presumably, information-exchange alone (i.e., the knowledge of the pattern of risk-taking among group members) is sufficient to produce a risky-shift (Brown, 1965). As discussed earlier in the context of responsibility-diffusion theory, several experiments using Choice-Dilemma items

---

[33]Pruitt's speculation that a fear of putting one's self out on a limb inhibits risk-taking prior to discussion seems similar to the diffusion of responsibility notion that fear of failure restricts risk-taking.

(Kogan & Wallach, 1967; Teger & Pruitt, 1967) find that mere information-exchange produces increased risk-taking. Also, recent experiments (Clark & Willems, personal communication; Pruitt & Teger, 1969), which contrast the responsibility-diffusion and cultural-value explanations, demonstrate that group discussion primarily produces a risky-shift by allowing an exchange of information about each member's level of risk. Thus, at least with decisions involving Choice-Dilemma items, information exchange appears to be sufficient to produce the risky-shift. A related question is whether this effect holds for situations involving something other than Choice-Dilemma items.

Blank (1968) reported a significant risky-shift in a gambling situation that made subjects aware of others' risk preferences but did not allow them to interact verbally. In contrast, Zajonc *et al.* (1970) present evidence that information concerning others' risk preferences in a gambling situation is not sufficient to account for risky-shifts induced by group discussion. Kogan and Carlson (1969) found that in a problem-solving situation, overt competition (subjects made public bids for problems that varied in difficulty) did not produce greater risky-shifts than covert competition (private bids). In both instances, they found only weak nonsignificant trends toward increased risk-taking. Therefore, the information exchange occurring in the overt competition situation was apparently insufficient to produce a risky-shift. However, unusual features of the competitive situations, discussed earlier, were probably responsible for the failure to find any difference between overt and covert competition conditions as well as for the attenuation of the risky-shift in these situations.

In summary, it is an open issue whether information-exchange is sufficient to produce the risky-shift in either gambling situations or under competitive conditions. On the other hand, the results of those studies that use Choice-Dilemma or hypothetical items do substantiate the relevant information hypothesis. There is evidence (Stoner, 1968) that the direction of the shift observed after group discussion is a function of the dominant value in the situation. Moreover, the positive correlation observed between initial decisions and subsequent risky-shifts indicates that the more salient or important the value, the greater the risky-shift. That information exchange per se is sufficient to produce the risky-shift (Kogan & Wallach, 1967d; Teger & Pruitt, 1967) is quite in accord with the relevant information hypothesis — as is the finding that group discussion elevates risk-taking even more than mere information exchange. Finally, Pruitt's recent "Walter Mitty" explanation is consistent with an interpretation emphasizing the role of cultural values in decision-making.

On the other hand, this type of datum sheds little light on the mechanism presumably causing the risky-shift — the unidirectional social comparison process. The following section examines the data relevant to this process in detail.

C. The Social Comparison Mechanism

One of the more important, implicit features of the cultural value explanation is the idea that information exchange induces social comparison processes. Essentially, this interpretation assumes that social comparison pressures operate in conjunction with elicited values. Presumably, prior to discussion, individuals privately believe that compared to others they are more consistent with the implicit norms elicited by different types of decision items. For example, with risk-oriented items, individuals initially consider themselves to be riskier than their peers. Upon entering into discussion, an individual may discover that he is, in fact, not as risky as others present. To maintain consistency with his self-perception as a high risk-taker, he must then shift to a riskier position. Thus, the value explanation presumes that social comparison pressures operate selectively in the direction of the value made salient by the type of item or situation; i.e., it hypothesizes a "unidirectional push" toward maximal endorsement of the elicited value. In short, subjects who deviate in the valued direction should not shift. Thus, the cultural value explanation considers only a relatively specific instance of the operation of social comparison factors in risk-taking.[34]

One could ignore the possible effects of elicited values and still apply social comparison theory (Festinger, 1954) to group decision-making. Even though no one attempts to do so, the intellectual exercise highlights some interesting points. First, if decisions about appropriate levels of risk are matters of opinion, and if a value is not normatively elicited by

[34]Recently Jellison and Riskind (1970) apply Festinger's notions about the social comparison of *abilities* to the risky shift literature. In this case the predictions coincide with those of the cultural-value explanation. To support their application of Festinger's theorizing on the social comparison of ability, Jellison and Riskind attempt to show that people infer that those who take higher risks possess greater ability. Their efforts support Brown's position that risk is a positive value. Whether increased risk-taking occurs because risk-taking implies ability remains moot. That is, the unidirectional social comparison effect that Festinger postulates for abilities need not be restricted to ability. Instead, as Brown implies, it may apply to any trait that can normatively be placed or located on the good-bad evaluative dimension. As previously indicated, Brown's position implies that when a group discusses a decision problem that elicits any positive value — e.g., generosity — polarization toward the value will ensue. Need this be true only if generosity implies ability? It seems unlikely. If so, Jellison and Riskind may only add unnecessary baggage to the cultural-value explanation (see the discussion and footnote on page 344).

a given decision problem, social comparison theory cannot adequately explain the risky-shift. If group risk-taking solely reflects a social comparison process that permits assessment of others opinions, individuals would accommodate their level of risk-taking to those most similar to them. Considered over the entire group, an averaging effect with little or no shift would result. Second, if one assumes that the decision problem does not normatively elicit a value, social comparison theory generates predictions that compete with those of cultural value theory. For example, considering the range of initial risk-taking on risk-oriented Choice-Dilemma items, the cultural-value position predicts shifts toward risk for all individuals in a group except for the high initial risk-taker. This person should show no shift as a consequence of discussion since the revealed pattern of risk-taking among group members confirms his initial self-perceptions as a high risk-taker. In contrast, Festinger's theorizing about the social comparison of opinions predicts regression-like shifts toward the mean for both initially high and low risk-takers with little or no change on the part of the medium risk-takers. The purpose of this discussion is to demonstrate that social comparison and value considerations are not necessarily always congruent. It is possible to imagine situations in which they might be made to conflict, and in which the issues raised above are relevant.

The bulk of recent research on the cultural value explanation focuses upon identifying the nature and impact of social-comparison factors as determinants of individual and group shifts in risk-taking. With respect to individual shifts, one factor receiving attention is perceived relative initial riskiness. Given that individuals perceive themselves to be riskier than their typical peers in their initial decisions, Pruitt and Teger (1967) reasoned that the *difference* between one's initial risk preferences and those risk preferences attributed to others should predict the amount of risky-shift. Their logic rests on the unidirectional social comparison process implicit in the cultural-value explanation. They assumed that: "The farther ahead of the pack one initially thinks he is, the more catching up he has to do when he finds that he is performing in an average fashion" (Pruitt & Teger, 1967, p. 16). However, only weak nonsignificant correlations were found between relative perceived riskiness and risky-shift. Partialing out the common factor of initial risk further reduced the weak correlations between these two variables. In sum, these results suggest that elicited values are irrelevant to subsequent individual shifts in risk-taking following discussion.

The independent variable of *true relative initial riskiness* provides more favorable results for Brown's social comparison mechanism. While *perceived relative riskiness* refers to subjects' subjective opinions concerning how risky they are relative to others, *true relative initial risk* is the subjects' actual, relative position in the distribution of initial risk decisions in the group. On this measure, regardless of the within-group range of scores, Vidmar (1970) found an inverse relation between the extent to which an individual shifts toward risk and his true initial risk-iness relative to others in the group. In other words, the greater the level of risk-taking, the less the subsequent increase in risk-taking following discussion. Furthermore, persons with the highest initial risk scores also exhibited a risky-shift after discussion. Considered by itself, the social comparison process implied by the cultural value explanation predicts no change for the initially riskiest group member. However, the cultural-value explanation also hypothesizes that group discussion will increase the salience of the elicited value. While increased salience may account for this latter result, it is more probably an artifact of the procedure of summing risk scores across items to obtain an overall index of initial risk for individuals. That is, the risky-shift for high initial risk-takers is attributable to specific items on which they were not the riskiest member of the group. An internal analysis of individual items showed that the riskiest person on any given item exhibited no shift or a cautious shift. These findings on relative initial risk provide some support for the impor-tance of social comparison factors as determinants of individual shifts. On the basis of social comparison theory's predictions about the compar-ison of opinions, the initially riskiest person should exhibit a cautious shift during discussion. On the other hand, if value considerations interact with social comparison processes as Brown suggests, the high risk-taker should show no shift (or considering the salience-increasing effect of group discussion, a risky-shift). Vidmar's evidence favors the first of these two predictions. On the internal analysis, some of the initially high risk-takers exhibited a cautious-shift. However, since regression effects also predict these cautious-shifts, their meaning remains ambiguous.

    In an attempt to assess the validity of Brown's social comparison mechanism, Madaras and Bem (1968) had groups discuss only half of a set of hypothetical risk items after individuals indicated initial risk preferences on the entire set. They assumed that knowledge of members' risk preferences on the discussed items would generalize to undiscussed items (thus allowing social comparison on all items). Brown (1965) originally stated that, beyond providing information concerning the level of risk-taking of other group members, the content of discussion is "irrelevant." That is, he placed greater emphasis upon the (unidirectional) social comparison function of group interaction than upon persuasion resulting from the biased group discussion favoring the elicited value. If, however, the content of discussion transmits item-specific information in addition to each group member's typical tendency to be risky, and, if such item-specific information facilitates the risky-shift (say through persuasion), risk tendencies on undiscussed items should be weaker.

Madaras and Bem found risky-shifts only on discussed items. They interpreted this outcome as disconfirming Brown's unidirectional, social comparison mechanism. To account for their results, they suggested instead that the risky-shift occurs because "... individuals are culturally disposed to generate and favor risk arguments when considering risky dilemmas in detail" (Madaras & Bem, 1968, p. 360). Unfortunately, this conclusion assumes that subjects use discussed items to infer the distribution of risk preferences on undiscussed items. If they do not, the obtained outcome may simply reflect subjects' inability to engage in social comparison on the undiscussed items. To test the two hypotheses in question critically, subjects who discuss only half of the items should receive information about the pattern of risk-taking among group members on the undiscussed items. Comparison of shifts on discussed and undiscussed items would reveal whether the biased flow of arguments during group discussion provides additional impetus for increased risk-taking over and above the risky-shift produced by mere information exchange. In sum, it is difficult to conclude that the Madaras and Bem study invalidates Brown's social comparison mechanism.

Other attempts to assess the effects of social comparison upon group shifts focus upon the extent to which the discussion group contains members with homogeneous or heterogeneous initial risk scores. The greater the initial dispersion in levels of risk-taking, the more likely it is that most group members will note that *someone* is more risky. As a consequence, since individuals initially consider themselves riskier than others, group discussion should provide greater disconfirmation of initial self-perceptions and a greater risky-shift when group members' initial risk scores are heterogeneous (i.e., when one group member is particularly risky). In other words, the cultural-value explanation predicts a positive correlation between initial range of risk scores and magnitude of risky-shift. Unfortunately, this prediction is not unique to the cultural value interpretation. Alternative explanations of the risky-shift, such as the leadership hypothesis, clearly suggest the same outcome (i.e., members homogeneous in riskiness should be equally persuasive and no shift should result). However, in the case of perfect homogeneity, differential prediction is possible. The leadership explanation predicts no shift in this situation, but the cultural-value explanation can be interpreted as implying increased risk-taking. In a homogeneous group, all individuals find that they are not riskier than anyone else. Since it is better to have more of a desired trait than others, each individual member must shift toward

risk in order to fulfill the desire to be riskier than other group members.[35]
Furthermore, as previously indicated, since the group discussion should
enhance the salience of the elicited value, this too should promote greater
risk-taking even in the case of homogeneous group composition.

There is considerable evidence for a positive relationship between
the range of initial risk scores among group members and the magnitude
or risky-shift produced by group discussion. Hermann and Kogan (1968)
note that shifts toward risk are generally stronger in groups with large
divergences among individuals. More concretely, Hoyt and Stoner (1968)
report a significant, positive correlation between within-group range of
risk scores and the magnitude of shift induced by the group. In a recent
experiment, Vidmar (1970) compared three types of homogeneous
groups — persons who were high, medium, or low on the initial measure
of risk-taking — to heterogeneous groups. The homogeneous groups
were not precisely identical, but their range of risk scores was small
relative to heterogeneous groups. Except for the homogeneous groups
of medium risk-takers (which inadvertently had the smallest range of
initial scores), all other types of groups produced a risky-shift following
discussion. In addition, heterogeneous groups shifted more toward risk
than any of the homogeneous groups (who did not differ from one
another). Brown's cultural-value interpretation cannot easily account
for the absence of a risky-shift in the most homogeneous groups. As
previously argued, not only does it imply that people who find that they
are only "average" in riskiness should increase their risk-taking so as
to conform to the elicited value of risk, but also the group discussion
should increase the salience of risk as a value and thereby promote riskiness. Yet, this does not occur. Moreover, these results have recently
been replicated. Using a more stringent criterion of homogeneity than
Vidmar (1970), Clark and Willems (personal communication) compared
homogeneous and heterogeneous groups under two different experimental conditions: information exchange and group discussion. Using
a set of three Choice-Dilemma items, individuals in homogeneous groups
could not differ by more than two scale points. Those in heterogeneous

---

[35]This interpretation states that it is a cultural value to be more risky than other
members. Brown appears to take a more modest position on this particular point: "each
individual answering the Stoner problems means to be at least as risky as people like
himself. . . . Each man, on his own, guesses the norm to be at or below his own selection. . . . Those who find themselves below the mean of the six members of the group discover they are failing to realize the ideal of riskiness that they thought they were realizing.
Consequently, they feel impelled to move in a risky direction both in accepting the decision
of the group and in changing their private opinions. Subjects at or above the group mean
feel no impulsion; they are relatively risky just as they meant to be."

groups exhibited risky-shifts under both experimental conditions. In contrast, homogeneous groups did not differ from a control condition.

Thus the data contradict the predictions made by Brown's social comparison mechanism for groups highly homogeneous in their initial risk preferences.[36] Furthermore, recent evidence suggests that social comparison pressures in group risk-taking situations need not always be biased toward the implicit values of the decision items. In a pilot investigation, Steiner (personal communication) initially required subjects to complete risk-oriented and caution-oriented items and also to indicate what they consider to be the average response of a self-selected, reference group (e.g., "20 to 30 persons like yourself"). In a subsequent phase of the experiment, he presented subjects false norms about the actual distribution of others' responses. This false feedback disconfirmed the subject's initial expectations concerning the responses of others. For one risky item, the norm was one scale position riskier; whereas for another, the norm was one scale position in a more conservative position. A similar procedure was used with caution-oriented items. The manipulated norms produced marked conformity with virtually no trace of an interaction between type of item and direction of deviation from the subject.

Baron et al. (1970) also conducted a study in which social-comparison pressures were pitted against value considerations. Subjects discussed either risk-oriented or caution-oriented items. Confederates created a majority consensus which was either two scale positions riskier or more conservative than the naive subject's initial decision. Similar to Steiner's findings, subjects exhibited marked conformity to the artificially established group consensus—regardless of whether the group norm coincided or conflicted with the underlying value elicited by the type of the item. Further, these shifts toward majority consensus largely remained intact on private, posttest measures of risk-taking.[37]

These preliminary results do not, on the face of it, argue well for the cultural value explanation of risk-taking as the only relevant theory. If risk and caution are indeed cultural values and if cultural-value theory

[36]Vidmar (personal communication) points out that although the above results do fall short of significance (i.e., show no effect) for homogeneous groups, these groups do exhibit shifts in the expected direction. He argues that the magnitude of effect will simply be smaller if group members are similar to begin with, and, consequently, it is more difficult to obtain significance. By implication, when these studies are replicated with large samples, this conclusion will require modification.

[37]Unfortunately, the possibility of regression effects might also account for these observed outcomes; analyses assessing this possibility have not yet been completed and, therefore, these results are not conclusive.

is the only theory relevant to this situation, individuals should *selectively* adjust their levels of risk-taking to coincide with the dominant values underlying risk-oriented and caution-oriented items, respectively. That is, on risky items, the riskiest subject should not conform to a more conservative group norm; conversely, on conservative items, the most cautious subjects should not conform to a riskier group norm. In both cases these subjects presumably deviate in a valued direction. Yet experimental results show that responsiveness to disconfirmation does not depend solely upon direction of deviation from the value orientation of the different types of decision items. Subjects conform dramatically to the majority consensus provided them. These results suggest that, when the effects of value are pitted against those of normative influence, the latter primarily determine risk-taking.

Another means of evaluating the importance of social comparison processes in group risk-taking is to examine the parameter of "certainty-uncertainty." Without any objective information for an appropriate course of action in a given situation, social comparison pressures should strongly influence risk-taking because "social reality" provides the only guidelines for behavior. The hypothetical situations depicted in Choice-Dilemma items are "uncertain" risk problems in that one cannot assign definite values to outcomes or provide objective specification of consequences for alternative outcomes. Under these circumstances, the pressures of normative influence should prevail. Stooges primed to exert influence (or merely display opinions) in a particular direction should produce dramatic influence effects. On the other hand, situations such as gambling tasks provide more concrete and objective cues for deciding an appropriate course of action. In these settings, the effect of others' opinions about the optimal level of risk should be diminished. Using a gambling task with an element of uncertainty (i.e., probabilities of events were unspecified), Zajonc *et al.* (1970) investigated the effect of information about other's risk preferences upon individuals choices in isolation and coaction situations. They conclude that information about others' level of risk-taking "had a numerically negligible" effect even on this gambling task—one that did have some element of uncertainty (Zajonc, *et al.*, 1970, p. 44). Extrapolating from these results, knowledge of others opinions should have little or no effect upon risk-taking in a "pure-risk" gambling situation (i.e., one in which outcomes, event probabilities, and stakes are all clearly specified). That is, the more minimal the uncertainty in a risk-taking situation, the less an individual must depend upon social reality as a means of validating a course of action.[38]

---

[38]These remarks suggesting that ambiguity or uncertainty increases the impact of group discussion—increases social influence effects, should not be interpreted as con-

D. SUMMARY

The research findings pertaining to cultural-value theory reveal a reasonably clear-cut pattern. The existing evidence strongly confirms the value hypothesis — more strongly for the value of risk than for the value of caution — and basically supports the general predictions from the relevant-information hypothesis. On the other hand, its implicit social-comparison mechanism does not fare so well. For example, the variable "relative perceived riskiness," a cornerstone of the cultural-value explanation, is sadly deficient as a predictor of individual shifts (Pruitt and Teger, 1967). Similarly, the absence of a risky-shift with groups composed of members homogeneous in their initial risk scores (Clark & Willems, personal communication; Vidmar, 1970) embarrasses the theory. Finally, some evidence (Baron et al., 1970; Steiner, personal communication) suggests that persons who initially deviate from others in a culturally valued direction will nevertheless subsequently conform to manipulated group norms that conflict with the initially elicited value. In fairness, however, many of these "contradictory" data are tentative; they stem from preliminary studies that investigate the role of social-comparison processes in group risk-taking. Also, there is no reason to suspect that the operation of other social psychological principles (e.g., normative influence) should be completely precluded by the group processes postulated by the cultural-value explanation. Instead, these studies in conjunction with other social comparison models (e.g., Levinger & Schneider, 1969) may well define the boundaries of the cultural-value explanation. Finally, a variety of other questions about the generality of the cultural-value explanation also await exploration. The possibility that the cultural-value explanation applies to decision problems that elicit any one of a variety of other values besides risk and caution awaits testing. Another consideration is the extent to which the explanation applies when one alters structural properties of the group (other than homogeneity of group members in respect to original propensity toward risk or caution). For instance, would status differences preclude the postulated effects concerning the flow of relevant information? Likewise, would groups comprised of individuals who know one another well and presumably have little to learn about one another's values show smaller risky shifts? Clearly, these are problems for future research.

---

tradicting our earlier comments about uncertainty and fear of failure in the sections on responsibility diffusion and familiarity. Here we make the point that to the extent that tasks differ in the extent to which they offer an unambiguous "right answer," individual decisions are more susceptible to normative influence.

VI. Recent Theoretical Trends

Most recent theoretical efforts conveniently fall into two categories: enhancement and social comparison models. Respectively, they attend to the polarization and the social comparison functions of group discussion. Enhancement models assert that group discussions enhances (or polarizes) whatever tendency was present on initial (individual) decisions. This position superficially resembles the cultural-value interpretation, i.e., that group discussion increases the salience of whatever cultural value a decision problem happens to elicit. Enhancement models, however, explain polarization by invoking explanatory mechanisms suggested by leadership, familiarization, and involvement interpretations of the risky-shift. In contrast to enhancement models, social comparison models more directly extend cultural-value theory. More specifically, they precisely examine, emphasize, and extend the social comparison processes implicit in the cultural-value explanation. Despite their differences, both enhancement and social comparison models exhibit a similar attention to variables only tacitly assumed important by previous explanations.

A. ENHANCEMENT MODELS

Burns (1967) proposes an extremity-variance model that assumes groups behave more decisively (i.e., more extremely) than individuals. This notion resembles the leadership explanation; it assumes that those who hold a more extreme view or position exert a greater influence in group decision-making. This broad assumption enables Burns to also take into account the possibility of cautious-shifts. Using this model, he accurately predicted the outcome of over half of 361 group decisions while using only two parameters: initial extremity of the most extreme group member and the within-group variance among group members' initial decisions.

Marquis and Reitz (1969) also stress the enhancing function of group discussion; however, their position has closer conceptual ties to the familiarization explanation. Specifically, they suggest that group discussion has two effects. First it enhances the prior expected value of various possible outcomes. This characterization of group discussion is similar to heightening the reinforcement value of the decision alternatives; a process Rettig (1966) postulates to be a function of group discussion. Second, they hypothesize that when there is initial uncertainty, subsequent discussion increases risk-taking. The two assumptions that underlie this second hypothesis also underlie the familiarization and responsibility diffusion interpretations: (1) uncertainty inhibits risk-taking and (2) group discussion reduces uncertainty. Finally, they assume that enhancement of expected value and uncertainty-reduction operate independently. For example, group discussion presumably increases the salience of the expected value regardless of whether the risk-taking situation is uncertain or not. Conversely, reducing uncertainty presumably heightens risk-taking regardless of whether the expected value is positive, zero, or negative. In sum, Marquis and Reitz's model explicitly specifies two independent parameters of group risk-taking, both of which require consideration before generating a prediction.

Marquis and Reitz tested various predictions and assumptions of their model by using gambling problems varying in expected value and uncertainty. They manipulated uncertainty in the following manner. For "pure risk" (i.e., certain) problems, they precisely specified for each problem the stake, the probability of winning, and the prize. For uncertain problems, they only indicated the value of those elements of the risk-taking situation with a range of possible values. In support of their model, they cited previous research (Hubbard, 1963; Reitz, no year indicated) in which individuals made larger bets on certain than on uncertain gambling items. These data, then, support the assumption that uncertainty reduces the willingness of individuals to take risks. Nevertheless, whether group discussion simultaneously reduces uncertainty *and* increases the salience of the expected value on gambling problems remained questionable. However, Marquis and Reitz confirmed the following predictions of the model: (1) With initial *certainty* in the risk-taking situation, the direction of shift after discussion will depend on the expected value of the risky outcome—a positive expected value will produce a risky-shift, a negative expected value will produce a conservative shift, and zero expected value will produce no shift, (2) When *uncertainty* exists, group discussion will produce shifts toward risk when the risky outcome has either positive or zero expected value. When the risky outcome has negative expected value, the direction of shift depends upon which force is stronger, the decrease of uncertainty or the increased salience of negative expected value.

Given this preliminary support, Marquis and Reitz's model appears promising. Its particular appeal is that it can also account for risky-shifts obtained on the Choice-Dilemma items since one can argue that such items are uncertain risk problems (i.e., they do not specify the exact value of success and failure cf., Hubbard, 1963).

In a recent paper, Moscovici and Zavalloni (1969) similarly take an enhancement position to account for risky-shifts. According to their analysis, the various treatments (e.g., familiarization, group discussion, ballotting) that have produced the risky-shift have one thing in common; they involve subjects in the situation in which they are embedded and increase the importance of the common judgmental object – the problem requiring a decision. It is this increase in involvement that presumably causes a polarization of initial risk-taking tendencies. Although the design of their own research does not (and cannot) experimentally confirm this view, there is a substantial literature in attitude change research that makes this position tenable (Miller, 1965; Sherif & Hovland, 1961; Sherif, Sherif, & Nebergall, 1967). The attitude change research shows that persons who are more involved with their position on an issue take a more extreme stand in reporting their position. In addition, when subjects' involvement with a position is experimentally increased, their stand becomes more extreme (Miller, 1965). Other research shows that those who are more certain about their position on an issue hold more extreme views (Suchman, 1950), Moscovici and Zavalloni also suggest that the degree of opinion polarization will be a function of the initial diversity in risk-taking levels. Diversity, they argue, produces interpersonal disagreement, tension, and anxiety. They further assume that anxiety is associated with taking extreme stands. While these suppositions seem reasonable, it remains to be seen if they will be substantiated with empirical data. Particularly important is whether the various treatments that produce the risky-shift do indeed increase subject involvement as Moscovici and Zavalloni contend.

B. SOCIAL COMPARISON MODELS

As indicated in the discussion of the cultural-value explanation, several investigators focus on social comparison processes in group risk-taking. Levinger and Schneider (1969) propose a "conflict-compromise" model to account for the risky-shift. Presumably, prior to discussion, individual choices on Choice-Dilemma items must compromise between two conflicting pressures: (1) personal idealistic considerations and (2) realistic considerations. Similar to the cultural-value interpretation, Levinger and Schneider view discussion as performing an information function. The group provides a reference function by defining a realistic choice. Prior to discussion, a realistic choice is governed by an individual's expectation concerning the choices of others. Upon entering discussion, individuals discover that others are actually riskier than expected. The effect of this discovery is to move the group's reference point to a position closer to the average, ideal level of risk-taking and to result in a risky-shift. Steiner (personal communication) proposes a similar model, which assumes that group discussion corrects the "pluralistic ignorance" of individuals' initial considerations. Group discussion alters initial decisions in the direction of disconfirmation.

Recent research provides instances of evidence consistent with the conflict-compromise model. Pruitt's (1969) interpretation of the "Walter Mitty" effect (*viz.*, that prior to discussion, subjects imagine and represent themselves as "risky" while making objectively cautious decisions) is essentially congruent with a conflict-compromise model. Similar to Levinger and Schneider's analysis, Pruitt explains the latter phenomenon as a compromise between two conflict forces: (1) the desire to be consistent with a cultural value favoring riskiness and (2) fear of putting one's self out on a limb. Pilkonis and Zanna (1969) also provide some evidence for the conflict-compromise explanation in an experiment specifically designed to test predictions derived from it.

In contrast to some researchers' recent focus on social comparison processes, Madaras and Bem (1968) present a version of cultural-value theory that differs from Brown's (1965) position primarily in that it denies the importance of the social comparison mechanism. Their position also resembles the rhetoric-of-risk interpretation in some respects. According to Madaras and Bem, the risky-shift is primarily due to persuasion resulting from individual's inclinations to "generate and favor risky arguments" when seriously considering decision situations that elicit values favoring risk. However, unlike the rhetoric-of-risk interpretation, if a situation elicited values favoring caution, individuals presumably should favor cautious arguments. This version of cultural-value theory possesses several advantages. It can accommodate the familiarization studies of Bateson and Flanders and Thistlethwaite, it explains evidence supporting the leadership hypothesis and finally, it does not rely on a selective (or undirectional) social comparison mechanism. However, since there are problems with their study, their explanation lacks strong empirical support.

VII. Retrospective Wisdom

In many respects a review of the literature on the risky-shift illustrates several of the poor methodological practices that characterize much social psychological research. While prescience is rare, retrospective wisdom is pedestrian. Nevertheless, it is instructive to review and reiterate some of these indiscretions. The major points of criticism can be organized under four headings: (1) theoretical chauvinism (or the folly of particularistic explanations), (2) single testing sites (or problems of generality and demand), (3) oblique experimentation (or indirect tests of hypotheses), and (4) myopic scholarship (or inattention to the work of others).

A. THEORETICAL CHAUVINISM

Much of the available research on the risky-shift (particularly the early studies) implies that a single process or explanation accounts for the observed effect. Discussions of results often seem to presume that if a given explanation receives support, no other competing explanation (even though untested by the design of the particular experiment) conceivably remains true or relevant. This view of social psychological processes is too simplistic and, consequently, naive. Little empirical precedent exists for assuming that any single hypothesis or social psychological process operates to the exclusion of all others in a given setting. There certainly is no *a priori* logical incompatibility between any of the four explanations treated in detail in this chapter. Indeed, the various explanations proposed seem to complement one another rather than imply mutual incompatibility. As previously reiterated, the explanations often make similar rather than competing predictions. In fact, it is not easy to construct critical experimental tests among them. To illustrate the point, there is no reason why the essential truth of the cultural-value explanation must preclude the possibility that the leadership explanation also has a core of truth. For instance, it may be the case that those whose initial decisions are riskier do in fact exert more influence in the group setting, but, further, that this greater influence is restricted to situations in which the value of risk is salient. Or considering things in a slightly different way, the critical proposition of the leadership explanation might require incorporation as a special subproposition or subhypothesis of cultural value theory. More specifically, it is conceivable that the greater influence of those whose initial decisions were most risky is restricted to group discussions of risk-relevant problems. In other spheres of life they may be no more influential than others. Likewise, if cultural-value theory is essentially true, this in no way precludes the additional possibility that group discussion also diffuses responsibility or that the diffusion of responsibility can by itself produce shifts toward risks. Similar arguments could be made for the familiarization explanation and its relation to other hypothesized explanations. Yet many authors unfortunately speak as if support for their own hypothesis disconfirms the other alternative hypotheses explaining shifts toward risks. Given that the various interpretations of the risky-shift seem to complement rather than contradict one another, this type of "disconfirmation" is clearly specious and misleading.

B. SINGLE TESTING SITES

The exclusive focus on a single experimental arena is a second problem with the risky-shift research. This problem has two facets: (*a*) most research on the risky-shift uses a particular type of risk-taking task (or measure), the Choice-Dilemma items and (b) material is generally employed within a single type of experimental design: the repeated measures design.[39] Although the hazards are probably well known, some of the issues associated with each of these methodological practices warrant continued airing.

While some researchers rightly argue that some advantages result from loyalty to a single set of materials (or a single apparatus), the long-run disadvantages are greater. The most obvious point is that standardization severely limits the generalizability of any obtained effects. Numerous, unknown subtle characteristics of the specific experimental materials may be essential for producing the observed effects. For example, one possible explanation for the high frequency of risky-shifts obtained with Choice-Dilemma items is that this task requires decisions about hypothetical situations with no personal consequences for the decision-maker. In this respect, one could effectively argue that the research on the risky-shift tells us very little indeed about group risk-taking, although it may provide substantial information about group processes.

Relatedly, the specific content of the Choice-Dilemma items may be responsible for producing the effects obtained with them. The authors of the Choice-Dilemma items defined risk in a particular way (Mackenzie & Bernhardt, 1968) and the items hardly constitute a random sample of all possible risk-taking situations. Consequently, it is impossible to ascertain the extent to which the results of the studies reviewed in this paper depend upon a specific narrow definition of "riskiness." The markedly lower frequency of risky-shift effects on gambling tasks as opposed to Choice-Dilemma items probably reflects a systematic difference in the components of risk-taking behavior being assessed by these two measuring procedures. A lack of correspondence among presumably similar measures of the same behavior or construct is hardly novel in psychology. Investigators of learning once believed that a diverse set of response measures (resistance to extinction, latency, number of trials to criterion) were equivalent. However, subsequent research showed that these measures often correlated poorly with one another. This same problem may exist for the risky-shift literature.

---

[39]The exclusive reliance on the pretest-posttest design in research on the risky-shift is rather curious. The question as to whether or not groups make riskier decisions than individuals in no way requires a design in which members of groups must be the same persons who previously made the same decisions as individuals. Nor is the pretest necessarily indispensable to experimental method (Campbell & Stanley, 1963). Indeed, the alternative "after-only" design offers the additional advantages that (1) the obtained results do not depend upon the sensitizing effect of a pretest and (2) greater generality of the outcome to a nonpretested population of people.

Of course, the specific content of the Choice-Dilemma items is not the only source of difficulty with this material. Clark and Willems (1969) recently illustrated that the instructions accompanying the Choice-Dilemma items can strongly influence group decisions. They noted that the standard instructions characteristically employed with Choice-Dilemma items require subjects to indicate the *lowest* probability or riskiest odds they consider reasonable for a hypothetical person if he were to choose the risky option. Clark and Willems compared the effect of these risk-oriented instructions to neutral instructions which omitted the word "lowest" across four conditions: (1) a test-retest control condition, (2) information-exchange, (3) group discussion, and (4) a listening condition in which subjects heard recorded tapes of an interacting group. The result was an interaction between types of instructions and particular treatments. Specifically, risky-shifts occurred in the information exchange and group discussion situations provided that risk-oriented instructions were employed. Since the subjects in both instruction conditions had equivalent initial pretest scores, the differential effects of the risk-oriented instructions apparently produced their effect in interaction with the treatments.

The outcome above illustrates the kind of interaction that particularly worries those concerned about demand characteristics (*viz.*, a circumstance in which a standard feature of the experiment or the instructions interacts with only certain treatments and thereby produces different outcomes across treatments). Similar problems characterize the within-subject repeated measures or multiple treatments design that dominates the risky-shift research. Perhaps most important, these designs, while sometimes recommended for their sensitivity, create more experimental demand (Orne, 1962) than other types of designs (A. L. Edwards, 1963; Rosenblatt and Miller, 1970). When such designs are used, the subject must inevitably ask himself: "Why am I being measured again?" or "What is the point of this part of the experiment?" The subject's answer to this type of question probably is some interpretation of the intervening experimental treatment. Specifically, subjects in a treatment condition may think: "I am supposed to be influenced." On the other hand, those in a control condition might reason: "Maybe it is my consistency from one measurement to the next that is being assessed. I can create a better image by responding as identically as possible to the way I did the first time and prevent the experimenter from thinking I am wishy-washy." Of course, demand characteristics are less problematic if they are uniformly present in all conditions. The problem becomes critical when different treatments elicit different kinds or amounts of demand. *Post hoc* analysis of the data can never reveal an interaction between demand characteristics and treatments. Instead, an accurate assessment of the role played by demand in any given experiment requires either additional comparison groups or another experiment. Of course, demand is never tied solely to one particular type of design or one set of experimental materials. Any of several facets of an experimental situation can produce demand. For this reason, methodologists generally recommend replication of experiments in a nonstandardized manner as a means of determining the generalizability of any experimental finding.

C. OBLIQUE EXPERIMENTATION

A third problem with the research on group risk-taking is that researchers tend to construct either indirect or weak tests of their hypotheses. The failure to confront predictions directly erodes much of the true power of experimentation. By far, the most glaring disappointment in this respect is the absence of direct experimental analysis of actual group decision-making. Each interpretation of the risky-shift postulates the occurrence of different processes during group discussion. They interpret the risky-shift as mediated by different psychological and/or social psychological changes during group interaction. The implication is obvious: directly observe groups in the process of decision-making and directly assess the presence or absence of these processes and changes. Unfortunately, researchers never directly examine these processes (i.e., characteristics of group interaction) or if they do, they do not present their analysis of them. Instead, they impose some restriction upon discussion and then *assume* that this "manipulation" distorts or alters the essential process(es) occurring during discussion. If subsequent differences coincide with the expected outcomes, they summarily *assume* a successful manipulation of the crucial process without making a direct assessment. As a specific example, the direct observation and recording of events during discussion is clearly the simplest and most straightforward technique for testing the central proposition of the leadership explanation—that the riskiest group member on the premeasure exerts more influence. All we need are judges to rate participants on influence.

Apart from the omission of direct analysis of group process, we frequently had the feeling that a better procedure could have been used to test the experimental hypothesis under consideration. Most researchers agree that if one has a hypothesis to test, one should devise the strongest test possible. Obviously this does not mean using a design or set of materials which, through artifactual means or other experimental blunder, may enable one to obtain one's preferred outcome. What it does mean is that one should use procedures or materials that are most likely to detect a difference when one does indeed exist (in statistical terms this is referred to as "power"). Unfortunately, such considerations have not been adequately emphasized in the risky-shift research. We will present some examples of this below. We do so not to embarrass particular researchers for we do indeed write from the vantage point of retrospective wisdom. Rather, we hope to make explicit for the future that which can be learned from our collective experience in the past.

1. If one takes the stand that the diffusion of responsibility is critical (or at least important) for producing shifts toward risk, it seems logical to use materials or situations in which the outcome of the decisions has real consequences in terms of felt or perceived gains and losses for the decision-makers. From this standpoint, the use of Choice-Dilemma items as the primary arena for testing the responsibility-diffusion explanation seems a poor choice. These materials may best allow other processes besides responsibility-diffusion to affect the outcome. What difference can it make to any one subject whether or not he alone or other group members are responsible for the decision of the group when, in fact, whatever their decision, it hardly matters to anybody?

2. A similar argument can be made about the use of Choice-Dilemma items in studies concerning the familiarization hypothesis. In tests of the familiarization explanation, researchers typically use private study of the Choice-Dilemma items to induce greater comprehension. Indeed, some forms of the familiarization explanation view comprehension as the critical ingredient. This being the case, it makes little sense to use the Choice-Dilemma items since it is not clear what comprehension could mean in terms of these items. What is there to comprehend? The hypothetical situations do not have such a vast array of ingredients that one is pressed to weigh things properly within a short period of time. If one thinks that comprehension is in fact a critical element, one would want to use materials that allow one to assess readily the level of comprehension postexperimentally. This does not seem particularly possible with Choice-Dilemma items, and may explain why researchers are forced to rely on a response measure that has little to do with comprehension, namely, recall of the content of the items.[40]

3. The manipulation of affective bonds provides another illustration of weak hypothesis testing. For example, affective bonds have been manipulated by varying whether or not subjects are allowed to engage in

___

[40]Of course, in fairness, some of the familiarization research was done to test whether previously stated effects with Choice-Dilemma items could be explained via familiarization.

discussion. This seems to be attacking the problem from the wrong direction since the level of affective bonding produced within the interaction period of a single experiment cannot be very great. As a result, such procedures are not optimal since they seem incapable of producing the strong differences in affective feelings that one would like to create between experimental conditions so as to test the effect of this variable. The better procedure might be to use enduring groups, cliques, or families. Here one knows in advance that strong affective feelings exist.

D. MYOPIC SCHOLARSHIP

In reviewing the literature on the risky-shift, one is struck by the frequency with which researchers fail to see or discuss the relevance of their findings to theoretical explanations other than their own. Relatedly, in many cases, researchers could have easily added other dependent measures to test predictions derived from alternative interpretations of the risky-shift. In still other instances, the investigators regrettably failed to note that their data pertained to the competing predictions stemming from a different theoretical explanation. Citing specific instances to document each type of omission needlessly embarrasses us all. Perhaps the mere mention of these problems will be sufficiently corrective.

E. SUMMARY

This paper reviewed the four major explanations of the risky-shift as well as more recent theoretical trends in this research area. At this point, we will recapitulate our overall conclusions. (1) Although the initial data made the diffusion of responsibility explanation appear promising, subsequent empirical disconfirmations led its proponents to revise its underlying assumptions and corollary hypotheses continually — many of which are not necessarily relevant to the basic truth or falsity of a responsibility-diffusion explanation. Furthermore, the relevant disconfirmations may stem from the use of inappropriate tasks (i.e., hypothetical risk-taking situations). In other words, although data suggest that many of the corollary hypotheses associated with the responsibility-diffusion explanation may indeed be false, responsibility-diffusion itself may effectively explain risky-shifts in situations in which persons experience (or are led to anticipate) actual consequences from their decisions. (2) There are few "firm" data to support the leadership interpretation. Most of the supporting evidence consists of correlations between initial riskiness and participant's ratings of one another's relative influence during discussion. Unfortunately, such data do not permit causal inference. For example, they may reflect rationalizations of the fact that the raters themselves did become more risky (for other reasons). That is, after group discussion, participants may say to themselves "Since I became riskier, I must have been influenced, and I was probably influenced most by the guy who was initially riskiest". Thus as we have stressed, the leadership explanation and its underlying assumptions still await critical or direct tests. (3) The familiarization explanation appears to be a theoretical "blind-alley." Unsuccessful attempts to produce a risky-shift with familiarization procedures naturally cast doubt upon its validity. But more importantly, it now seems likely that the risk-inducing features of group discussion do not solely depend on greater familiarity with the materials. (4) As a *single* explanation of the risky-shift, the cultural-value interpretation fares best. It has a solid core of supporting evidence behind some of its basic assumptions. Furthermore, it served as a direct stimulus for recent attempts to develop more precise models of the risky-shift. Lastly, when we reach a complete understanding of group decision-making and risk-taking, it should not surprise us if propositions from several of the competing theoretical positions turn out to be true.

The ultimate significance of risky-shift research rests not with the finding that group decisions are riskier than individual decisions. Indeed, as Flanders (1970) strongly argues, from the standpoint of the dictionary definition or the man in the streets' understanding of the term risk, we may have learned little thus far about group risk-taking. Rather, the constructive stance takes the research on group risk-taking as a window through which one can view the processes of group interaction.

To take one example and elaborate on it a bit, consider the basic question of the effect of the group on individual judgments. As mentioned at the outset of this chapter, the position that groups exert a moderating influence on individual judgments held sway since the time of Allport (1924). In contradiction to this view, the research on the risky-shift suggests a quite different conclusion concerning the impact of group discussion on individual judgments and decisions — namely, that, under some conditions, groups engender greater extremity or polarization in judgments and decisions. Supporting this generalization, recent studies find that groups adopt more extreme positions after they consider political (Moscovici and Zavalloni, 1969) or racial attitudes (Myers & Bishop, 1970). Related to the polarization principle, advocates of the cultural-value interpretation suggest that group discussion enhances any underlying dominant value, e.g., intellectualism, generosity, and altruism (Brown, personal communication; Levinger & Schneider, 1969). Second, some research on the risky-shift (Bem *et al.*, 1965; Wallach *et al.*,

1964) reinforces the conclusion also emerging from such other research areas as bystander intervention—that groups are less responsible than individuals. Finally, some research on the responsibility diffusion interpretation (e.g. Bem *et al.*, 1965) of the risky-shift suggests that group decisions are less rational than those of individuals. In these respects, risky-shift research serves as a general model of group effects and suggests several interesting contrasts between groups and individuals.

Although we have frequently made research suggestions throughout this chapter, most of them consist of alternate procedures for testing hypotheses related to the various explanations of the risky-shift. Before concluding this chapter, it seems important to note that there are other directions in which research might be profitably directed. In particular, more attention might be focused on the characteristics of "real" or "naturally existing" groups. Indeed, the research on group risk-taking attracts the interest of those concerned with organizational psychology in that it is thought to comment on the decision-making process in real ongoing organizations. Yet interestingly, few of the actual characteristics of the decision making groups that exist in organizations are paralleled in those studied in the laboratory. For instance, real groups typically contain status differentiations. Few of the laboratory experiments on group risk-taking experimentally introduce status differences between group members. When groups with status differentiation confront a decision problem we might expect the temporal sequence in which individuals present their initial propensities to be correlated with status. That is to say, group members with high status might be expected to present their initial inclinations about the decision problem at an earlier point in the discussion than those of lower status. If so, this implies the possibility of making predictions about group decisions in a particular organization by combining (1) what we know about the influence of primacy in persuasion with (2) knowledge about the correlation of status and advocacy of a particular position on the dimension in question. Also, if high status persons are more prone to speak early in a discussion, it may lead other group members to associate certain values (other than those implicit in the decision problem itself) with particular decision alternatives about the problem. Another problem that needs to be considered concerns the extent to which sanctions are tied with status differentiation. Surely real groups must differ in the extent to which the status differences among group members also reflect fate control or behavioral control over other group members.

Other questions that have not been systematically studied focus on who the decision affects. Does the decision primarily have consequences for: some large impersonal entity (like a corporation) with which the decision-makers are not directly tied but which must nevertheless be responsive to the decision outcome; an impersonal entity in which the decision makers hold administrative or executive positions; the individual group members making the decision; or lastly, one individual member in the group? While we have commented on the fact that most of the laboratory experimentation on group decision-making uses a task that has no important consequences for the decision-making group, the question above focuses on the comparison or potential difference in outcome depending upon the target of the decision. Additional interesting questions arise from a consideration of surveillance and anonymity. The extent to which the group decision is public or subject to the surveillance of others should enhance the impact of such values as social responsibility. Lastly, none of the research on group decision making has considered the question of whether the group discussion redefines the end points of the scale implicitly used by the decision-makers. In sum, many of the structural and psychological dimensions along which real groups in ongoing organizations vary have yet to be studied. Although the research on group risk-taking is one of the most voluminous of any concerned with group behavior, it is clear that our knowledge of group decision-making remains very modest at this point.

REFERENCES

Allen, V. L. Situational factors in conformity. In L. Berkowitz (Ed.), *Advances in experimental social psychology*. Vol. 2. New York: Academic Press, 1965. Pp. 133-170.

Allport, H. *Social Psychology*. Boston: Houghton Mifflin, 1924.

Atkinson, J. W. (Ed.) *Motives in fantasy, action and society*. Princeton, N. J.: Van Nostrand, 1958.

Atkinson, J. W. *An introduction to motivation*. Princeton, N. J.: Van Nostrand, 1964.

Atkinson, J. W., & Litwin, G. H. Achievement motive and test anxiety conceived as motive to approach success and motive to avoid failure. *Journal of Abnormal and Social Psychology*, 1960, **60**, 52-63.

Atthowe, J. M., Jr. Types of conflict and their resolution: A reinterpretation. *Journal of Experimental Psychology*, 1960, **59**, 1-9.

Barnlund, D. C. A comparative study of individual majority and group judgment. *Journal of Abnormal and Social Psychology*, 1959, **58**, 55-60.

Baron, R. S., Dion, K. L., & Baron, P. and Miller, N. Group norms, elicited values and risk-taking. Unpublished manuscript, University of Minnesota, 1970.

Bateson, N. Familiarization, group discussion, and risk taking. *Journal of Experimental Social Psychology*, 1966, **2**, 119-129.

Bem, D. J., Wallach, M. A., & Kogan, N. Group decision-making under risk of aversive consequences. *Journal of Personality and Social Psychology*, 1965, **1**, 453-460.

Blank, A. Effects of group and individual conditions on choice behavior. *Journal of Personality and Social Psychology*, 1968, 8, 294-298.

Brown, R. *Social psychology*. New York: Free Press, 1965.

Burns, J. F. An extremity-variance model of risk-taking. Unpublished doctoral dissertation, School of Industrial Management, Massachusetts Institute of Technology, 1967.

Burnstein, E. Decision-making and problem-solving in groups. Unpublished manuscript, University of Michigan, 1967.

Campbell, D. T., & Stanley, J. C. *Experimental and quasi-experimental designs for research*. Chicago: Rand McNally, 1963.

Carter, L., Haythorn, W., Meirowitz, B., & Lanzetta, J. The relation of categorizations and ratings in the observation of group behavior. *Human Relations*, 1951, 4, 239-254.

Clark, R., III, & Willems, E. P. Where is the risky shift? Dependence on instructions? *Journal of Personality and Social Psychology*, 1969, 13, 215-221.

Clausen, G. Risk taking in small groups. Unpublished doctoral dissertation, University of Michigan, 1965.

Cohen, A. R. *Attitude change and social influence*. New York: Basic Books, 1964.

Collins, B. E., & Guetzkow, H. *A social psychology of group processes for decision-making*. New York: Wiley, 1964.

Crowne, D. P. & Marlowe, D. *The approval motive: Studies in evaluative dependence*. New York: Wiley, 1964.

Darley, J. M., & Latané, B. Bystander intervention in emergencies: Diffusion of responsibility. *Journal of Personality and Social Psychology*, 1968, 9, 142-146.

Dion, K. L., Miller, N., & Magnan, M. A. Group cohesiveness and social responsibility as determinants of the risky-shift. Paper presented at the convention of the American Psychological Association, Miami, Florida, September, 1970.

Edwards, A. L. *Experimental design in psychological research*. New York: Holt, Rinehart & Winston, 1963.

Edwards, W. Probability preferences in gambling. *American Journal of Psychology*. 1953, 66, 349-364.

Ferguson, D. A. & Vidmar, N. Familiarization-induced risky and cautious shifts: A replication of sorts. Paper presented at the Midwestern Psychological Association Convention: Cincinnati, Ohio, 1970.

Festinger, L. A theory of social comparison processes. *Human Relations*, 1954, 7, 117-140.

Festinger, L., Pepitone, A., & Newcomb, T. M. Some consequences of deindividuation in a group. *Journal of Abnormal and Social Psychology*, 1952, 47, 382-389.

Flanders, J. P. Research on the risky-shift: Questions asked and unasked. Unpublished manuscript. Walter Reed Army Institute of Research, 1970.

Flanders, J. P. & Thistlethwaite, D. L. Effects of familiarization and group discussion upon risk-taking. *Journal of Personality and Social Psychology*, 1967, 5, 91-97.

Gibb, J. R. The effects of group size and of threat reduction upon creativity in a problem-solving situation. *American Psychologist*, 1951, 6, 324. (Abstract)

Hermann, M., & Kogan, N. Negotiation in leader and delegate groups. *Journal of Conflict Resolution*, 1968, 12, 332-344.

Hinds, W. C. Individual and group decisions in gambling situations. Unpublished master's thesis, School of Industrial Management, Massachusetts Institute of Technology, 1962.

Hovland, C. I., & Janis, I. L. (Eds.) *Personality and persuasibility*. New Haven: Yale University Press, 1959.

Hoyt, G. C., & Stoner, J. A. F. Leadership and group decisions involving risk. *Journal of Experimental Social Psychology*, 1968, 4, 275-285.

Hubbard, J. H. Effects of uncertainty on individual and group risk-taking. Unpublished master's thesis, School of Industrial Management, Massachusetts Institute of Technology, 1963.

Hunt, E. B., & Rowe, R. R. Group and individual economic decision making in risk conditions. In D. W. Taylor (Ed.), *Experiments on decision making and other studies*. Arlington, Va.: Armed Services Technical Information Agency, 1960. Pp. 21-26.

Jellison, J. M., & Riskind, J. A social comparison of abilities interpretation of risk taking behavior. *Journal of Personality and Social Psychology*, 1970, 15, 375-390.

Jones, E. E. & Gerard, H. B. *Foundations of social psychology*. New York: Wiley, 1967.

Kelley, H. H., & Thibaut, J. W. Experimental studies of group problem solving and process. In G. Lindzey (Ed.), *Handbook of social psychology*. Vol. 2. Reading, Mass.: Addison-Wesley, 1954. Pp. 735-785.

Kelley, H. H., & Thibaut, J. W. Group problem-solving. In G. Lindzey & E. Aronson (Eds.), *Handbook of social psychology*. (Rev. ed.) Vol. 4. Cambridge, Mass.: Addison-Wesley, 1968. Pp. 1-104.

King, B. T., & Janis, I. L. Comparison of the effectiveness of improvised versus non-improvised role-playing in producing opinion change. *Human Relations*, 1956, 9, 177-186.

Kogan, N., & Carlson, J. Group risk taking under competitive and noncompetitive conditions in adults and children. *Journal of Educational Psychology*, 1969, 60, 158-167.

Kogan, N., & Doise, W. Effects of anticipated delegate status on level of risk-taking in small decision-making groups. *Acta Psychologica*, 1969, 29, 228-243.

Kogan, N., & Wallach, M. A. The effect of anxiety on relations between subjective age and caution in an older sample. In P. Hoch & J. Zubin (Eds.), *Psychology of aging*. New York: Grune & Stratton, 1961. Pp. 123-135.

Kogan, N., & Wallach, M. A. *Risk-taking: A study in cognition and personality*. New York: Holt, 1964.

Kogan, N., & Wallach, M. A. Effects of physical separation of group members upon group risk taking. *Human Relations*, 1967, 20, 41-49. (a)

Kogan, N., & Wallach, M. A. Group risk taking as a function of members' anxiety and defensiveness levels. *Journal of Personality*, 1967, 35, 50-63. (b)

Kogan, N., & Wallach, M. A. Risk taking as a function of the situation, the person and the group. In G. Mandler, P. Mussen, N. Kogan & M. A. Wallach (Eds.), *New directions in psychology*. Vol. III, New York: Holt, Rinehart & Winston, 1967. Pp. 224-266. (c)

Kogan, N., & Wallach, M. A. The risky-shift phenomenon in small decision-making groups: A test of the information-exchange hypothesis. *Journal of Experimental Social Psychology*, 1967, 3, 75-85. (d)

Lamm, H. Will an observer advise high risk taking after hearing a discussion of the decision problem? *Journal of Personality and Social Psychology*, 1967, 6, 467-471.

Lamm, H., & Kogan, N. Risk-taking in the context of intergroup negotiation. *Journal of Experimental Social Psychology*, 1970, 6, 351-363.

Levinger, G., & Schneider, D. J. Test of the "Risk is a value" hypothesis. *Journal of Personality and Social Psychology*, 1969, 11, 165-170.

Levitt, E. A. The relationship between abilities to express emotional meanings vocally and facially. In J. R. Davitz (Ed.), *The communication of emotional meaning*. New York: McGraw-Hill, 1964. Pp. 87-100.

Levy, P. K. The ability to express and perceive vocal communication of feeling. In J. R. Davitz (Ed.), *The communication of emotional meaning*. New York: McGraw-Hill, 1964. Pp. 43-55.

London, H., Meldman, P. J. & Lanckton, A. Van C. The jury method: How the persuader persuades. *Public Opinion Quarterly*, 1970, 34, 171-183.

Lonergran, B. G. & McClintock, C. G. Effects of group membership on risk-taking behavior. *Psychological Reports*, 1961, 8, 447-455.

Mackenzie, K. D., & Bernhardt, I. The effect of status upon group risk taking. Unpublished manuscript, Wharton School of Finance and Commerce, University of Pennsylvania, 1968.

Madaras, G. R., & Bem, D. J. Risk and conservatism in group decision making. *Journal of Experimental Social Psychology*, 1968, **4**, 350-366.

Marquis, D. G. Individual responsibility and group decisions involving risk. *Industrial Management Review*, 1962, **3**, 8-23.

Marquis, D. G. Individual and group decisions involving risk. *Industrial Management Review*, 1968, **9**, 69-76.

Marquis, G., & Reitz, H. J. Uncertainty and risk taking in individual and group decisions. *Behavioral Science*, 1969, **14**, 281-288.

McGuire, W. J. Personality and susceptibility to social influence. In E. F. Borgatta & W. W. Lambert (Eds.), *Handbook of personality theory and research*. Chicago: Rand McNally, 1968. Pp. 1130-1187.

Messick, S., & Damarin, F. Cognitive styles and memory for faces. *Journal of Abnormal and Social Psychology*, 1964, **69**, 313-318.

Miller, N. Involvement and dogmatism as inhibitors of attitude change. *Journal of Experimental Social Psychology*, 1965, **1**, 121-132.

Miller, N. and Dion, K. L. An analysis of the familiarization explanation of the risky-shift. Paper presented at the convention of the American Psychological Association, Miami, Florida, September, 1970.

Moscovici, S., & Zavalloni, M. The group as a polarizer of attitudes. *Journal of Personality and Social Psychology*, 1969, **12**, 125-135.

Myers, D. G. Enhancement of initial risk-taking tendencies in social situations. Unpublished doctoral dissertation, University of Iowa, 1967.

Myers, D. G., & Bishop, G. Discussion effects on racial attitudes. Paper presented at the convention of Midwestern Psychological Association, Cincinnati, Ohio, 1970.

Nordhøy, F. Group interaction in decision-making under risk. Unpublished master's thesis, School of Industrial Management, Massachusetts Institute of Technology, 1962.

Orne, M. T. On the social psychology of the psychological experiment: With particular reference to demand characteristics and their implications. *American Psychologist*. 1962, **17**, 776-783.

Pilkonis, P. A., & Zanna, M. P. The choice-shift phenomenon in groups: Replication and extension. Unpublished manuscript, Yale University, 1969.

Pruitt, D. G. The "Walter Mitty' effect in individual and group risk-taking. Paper presented at the convention of the American Psychological Association, Washington, D. C., September 1969.

Pruitt, D. G., & Teger, A. I. Is there a shift toward risk in group discussion? If so, is it a group phenomenon? If so, what causes it? Paper presented at the convention of the American Psychological Association, Washington, D. C., September 1967.

Pruitt, D. G., & Teger, A. I. The risky shift in group betting. *Journal of Experimental Social Psychology*, 1969, **5** 115-126.

Rabow, J., Fowler, F. J., Jr., Bradford, D. L., Hofeller, M. A., & Shibuya, Y. The role of social norms and leadership in risk-taking. *Sociometry*, 1966, **29**, 16-27.

Rettig, S. Group discussion and predicted ethical risk taking. *Journal of Personality and Social Psychology*, 1966, **3**, 629-633.

Rim, Y. Risk-taking and need for achievement. *Acta Psychologica*, 1963, **21**, 108-115.

Rim, Y. Interpersonal values and risk-taking. Paper presented at the First International Congress of Psychiatry, London, 1964. (a)

Rim, Y. Intolerance of ambiguity and risk-taking. *Revue Suisse de Psychologie et de Psychologie Apliquée*, 1964, **23**, 253-259. (b)

Rim, Y. Personality and group decisions involving risk. *Psychological Record*, 1964, **14**, 37-45. (c)

Rim, Y. Leadership attitudes and decisions involving risk. *Personnel Psychology*, 1965, **18**, 423-430. (a)

Rim, Y. Dimensions of interpersonal behavior and risk-taking. *Revista de Psicologia General of Applicada*, 1965. (b)

Rim, Y. Machiavellianism and decisions involving risk. *British Journal of Social and Clinical Psychology*, 1966, **5**, 30-36.

Rogers, C. R. A theory of therapy, personality, and interpersonal relationships as developed in the client-centered framework. In S. Koch (Ed.), Vol. 3. *Psychology: A study of a science*. New York: McGraw-Hill, 1959. Pp. 184-256.

Rosenblatt, P. C. & Miller, N. Experimental methods. In C. G. McClintock (Ed.), *Experimental social psychology*. New York: Holt, Rinehart and Winston, 1970.

Schachter, S. Deviation, rejection and communication. *Journal of Abnormal and Social Psychology*, 1951, **46**, 190-207.

Schachter, S. *The psychology of affiliation: Experimental studies of the sources of gregariousness*. Stanford, California: Stanford University Press, 1959.

Secord, P. F., & Bachman, C. W. *Social psychology*. New York: McGraw-Hill, 1964.

Sherif, C. W., Sherif, M., & Nebergall, R. E. *Attitude and attitude change; the social judgment-involvement approach*. Philadelphia: Saunders, 1965.

Sherif, M., & Hovland, C. I. *Social judgment: Assimilation and contrast effects in communication and attitude change*. New Haven: Yale University Press, 1961.

Siegel, S., & Zajonc, R. B. Group risk-taking in professional decisions. *Sociometry, 1967*, **30**, 339-350.

Singer, J. E., Brush, C. A., & Lublin, S. C. Some aspects of deindividuation: Identification and conformity. *Journal of Experimental Social Psychology*, 1965, **1**, 356-378.

Stoner, J. A. F. A comparison of individual and group decisions involving risk. Unpublished master's thesis, School of Industrial Management, Massachusetts Institute of Technology, 1961.

Stoner, J. A. F. Risky and cautious shifts in group decisions: The influence of widely held values. *Journal of Experimental Social Psychology*, 1968, **4**, 442-459.

Suchman, E. A. The intensity component in attitude and opinion research. In S. A. Stouffer et al. (Eds.), *Studies in social psychology in World War II*. Vol. 4. *Measurement and prediction*. Princeton: Princeton University Press, 1950. Pp. 213-276.

Teger, A. I., & Pruitt, D. G. Components of group risk taking. *Journal of Experimental Social Psychology*, 1967, **3**, 189-205.

Teger, A. I., Pruitt, D. G., St. Jean, R., & Haaland, G. A re-examination of the familiarization hypothesis in group risk-taking. *Journal of Experimental Social Psychology*, 1970, **6**, 346-350.

Thibaut, J. W., & Kelley, H. H. *The social psychology of groups*. New York: Wiley, 1959.

Vidmar, N. Group composition and the risky-shift. *Journal of Experimental Social Psychology*, 1970, **6**, 153-166.

Wallach, M. A., & Kogan, N. Aspects of judgment and decision making: Interrelationships and changes with age. *Behavioral Science*, 1961, **6**, 23-36.

Wallach, M. A., & Kogan, N. The roles of information, discussion, and consensus in group risk taking. *Journal of Experimental Social Psychology*, 1965, **1**, 1-19.

Wallach, M. A., Kogan, N., & Bem, D. J. Group influence on individual risk taking. *Journal of Abnormal and Social Psychology*, 1962, **65**, 75-86.

Wallach, M. A., Kogan, N., & Bem, D. J. Diffusion of responsibility and level of risk taking in groups. *Journal of Abnormal and Social Psychology,* 1964, **68**, 263-274.

Wallach, M. A., Kogan, N., & Burt, R. Can group members recognize the effects of group discussion upon risk taking? *Journal of Experimental Social Psychology,* 1965, **1**, 379-395.

Wallach, M. A., Kogan, N., & Burt, R. Group risk taking and field dependence-independence of group members. *Sociometry,* 1967, **30**, 323-339.

Wallach, M. A., Kogan, N., & Burt, R. Are risk takers more persuasive than conservatives in group decisions? *Journal of Experimental Social Psychology,* 1968, **4**, 76-89.

Wallach, M. A., & Wing, C. W., Jr. Is risk a value? *Journal of Personality and Social Psychology,* 1968, **9**, 101-107.

White, R. W. *The abnormal personality.* New York: Ronald Press, 1964.

Whyte, W. H., Jr. *The organization man.* New York: Simon & Schuster, 1956.

Witkin, H. A., Dyk, R. B., Faterson, H. F., Goodenough, D. R., & Karp, L. A. *Psychological differentiation.* New York: Wiley, 1962.

Witkin, H. A., Lewis, H. B., Hertzman, M., Machover, K., Meissner, P. B., & Wapner, S. *Personality through perception.* New York: Harper & Row, 1954.

Zajonc, R. B., Wolosin, R. J., Wolosin, M. A., & Loh, W. D. Social facilitation and imitation in group risk taking. *Journal of Experimental Social Psychology,* 1970, **6**, 26-46

Zajonc, R. B., Wolosin, R. J., Wolosin, M. A., & Sherman, S. J. Individual and group risk taking in a two-choice situation. *Journal of Experimental Social Psychology,* 1968, **4**, 89-107.

Zajonc, R. B., Wolosin, R. J., Wolosin, M. A., & Sherman, S. J. Group risk taking in a two-choice situation: Replication, extension, and a model. *Journal of Experimental Social Psychology,* 1969, **5**, 127-140.

Zimbardo, P. G. The human choice: Individuation, reason, and order versus deindividuation, impulse, and chaos. In W. J. Arnold and D. Levine (Eds.), *Nebraska symposium on motivation.* Lincoln, Nebraska: University of Nebraska Press, 1969. Pp. 237-308.

AUTHOR INDEX

Numbers in italics refer to the pages on which the complete references are listed.

SUBJECT INDEX

A

Acquisition, of aggresive behavior, 6–7
Adaptation, cognitive control of, 169
Affective bonds, group decisions and,
 318–320
Aggression, see under Media violence
Ambiguity, Negro–white relationships
 and, 93–100
Ambivalence, Negro–white relationships
 and, 93–100
Anonymity, group decisions and,
 320–322
Arousal, facilitation of impulsive
 aggression and, 26–27
Attitude(s), as predictors of behavior,
 81–89
Attitude change,
 compliance and, 229–234
 interracial contact and, 76–81
Attribution, perceived fear and, 208–216
Authority, source of, leadership and,
 44–50, 53

B

Behavior,
 aggressive, see under Media violence
 attitudes as predictors of, 81–89
 in biracial work groups, 90–93
 consistency of, norms and, 277–279

C

Catharsis, symbolic aggression, see under
 Media violence
Causation, direction of, 291–296
Cognitive control, of adaptation, 169
Cognitive operations,
 nature of, 178–179
 sequences of, 175–178
Cognitive operator, 172–174
Communications, see also Fear
 communications; Media violence
 of leader, 63–64
Competence, leadership and, 44–50, 53

Compliance, attitude change and,
 229–234
Comprehension, familiarization and,
 in group decisions, 340–341
Control,
 cognitive, of adaptation, 169
 of danger and fear, 174–175
 perceived locus of, 205–208
 by stimulus, 171–172
Coping,
 failure of influence and, 143–151
 manipulations directed at mechanism
 for, 151–157
Cost, perceived, expected payoffs and,
 200–204
Cue, aggression-evoking, 24–26
Cultural background, family structure
 and, 259–262
Cultural values, see under Group
 decisions

D

Decision(s), see Group decisions
Decision freedom, 194–197
 attributed, consequences of, 232–233
 breadth of power and, 225–227
 ingratiation and, 223–225
 stress and, 227–229
Defense, fear communications and,
 139–143
Delay, fear communications and,
 139–143
Desensitization, emotional, 14–15
Deviation,
 from family norms, 280–281
 leadership and, 61–62
Discussion, role of in group decisions,
 315–317
Drive, see under Fear communications

E

Emotional responses, blunting of, 12–15,
 27

388